## CAVE ⊕ CARSON
### HAS A CYBERNETIC EYE

**VOL. 2: EVERY ME, EVERY YOU**

**JON RIVERA GERARD WAY** Writers
**MICHAEL AVON OEMING** Artist

**NICK FILARDI** Colorist

**CLEM ROBINS** Letterer

**MICHAEL AVON OEMING**
and **NICK FILARDI** Cover Art and Original Series Covers

**SUPERMAN CREATED BY JERRY SIEGEL AND JOE SHUSTER**
**BY SPECIAL ARRANGEMENT WITH THE JERRY SIEGEL FAMILY**

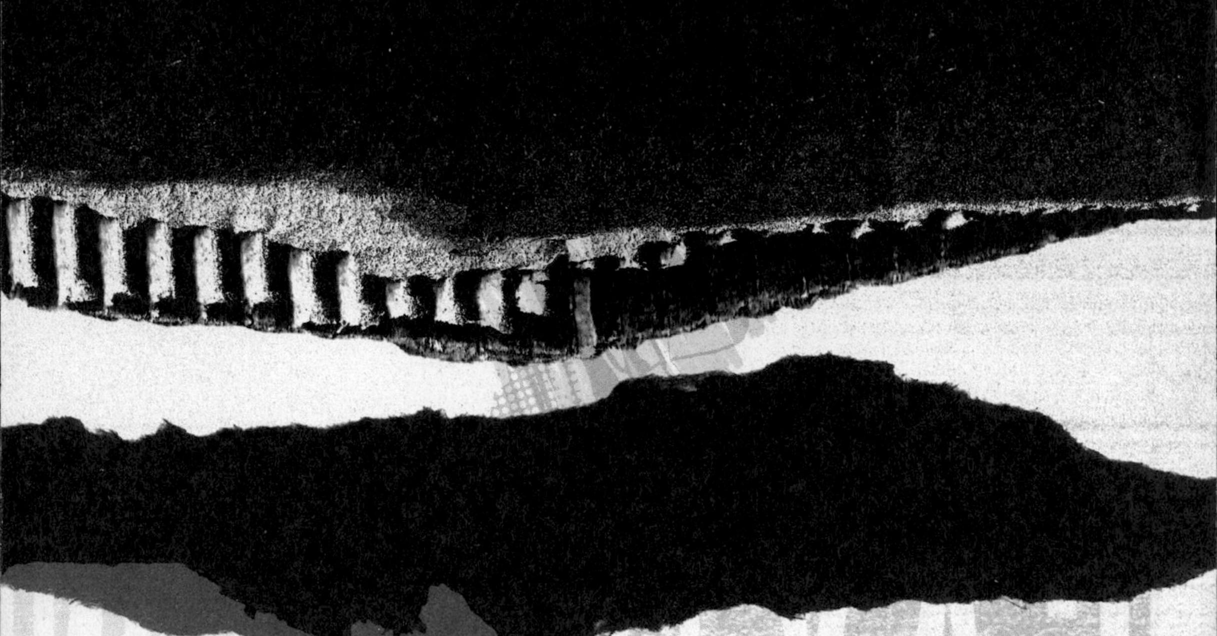

Molly Mahan Editor – Original Series
Jeb Woodard Group Editor – Collected Editions
Scott Nybakken Editor – Collected Edition
Steve Cook Design Director – Books
Louis Prandi Publication Design

Bob Harras Senior VP – Editor-in-Chief, DC Comics
Mark Doyle Executive Editor, Vertigo

Diane Nelson President
Dan DiDio Publisher
Jim Lee Publisher
Geoff Johns President & Chief Creative Officer
Amit Desai Executive VP – Business & Marketing Strategy, Direct to Consumer & Global Franchise Management
Sam Ades Senior VP & General Manager, Digital Services
Bobbie Chase VP & Executive Editor, Young Reader & Talent Development
Mark Chiarello Senior VP – Art, Design & Collected Editions
John Cunningham Senior VP – Sales & Trade Marketing
Anne DePies Senior VP – Business Strategy, Finance & Administration
Don Falletti VP – Manufacturing Operations
Lawrence Ganem VP – Editorial Administration & Talent Relations
Alison Gill Senior VP – Manufacturing & Operations
Hank Kanalz Senior VP – Editorial Strategy & Administration
Jay Kogan VP – Legal Affairs
Jack Mahan VP – Business Affairs
Nick J. Napolitano VP – Manufacturing Administration
Eddie Scannell VP – Consumer Marketing
Courtney Simmons Senior VP – Publicity & Communications
Jim (Ski) Sokolowski VP – Comic Book Specialty Sales & Trade Marketing
Nancy Spears VP – Mass, Book, Digital Sales & Trade Marketing
Michele R. Wells VP – Content Strategy

**CAVE CARSON HAS A CYBERNETIC EYE
VOL. 2: EVERY ME, EVERY YOU**

DC Comics
2900 West Alameda Avenue
Burbank, CA 91505
Printed by LSC Communications, Owensville, MO, USA. 1/5/18. First Printing.
ISBN: 978-1-4012-7747-5

Library of Congress Cataloging-in-Publication Data is available.

MIX
Paper from responsible sources
FSC® C132124

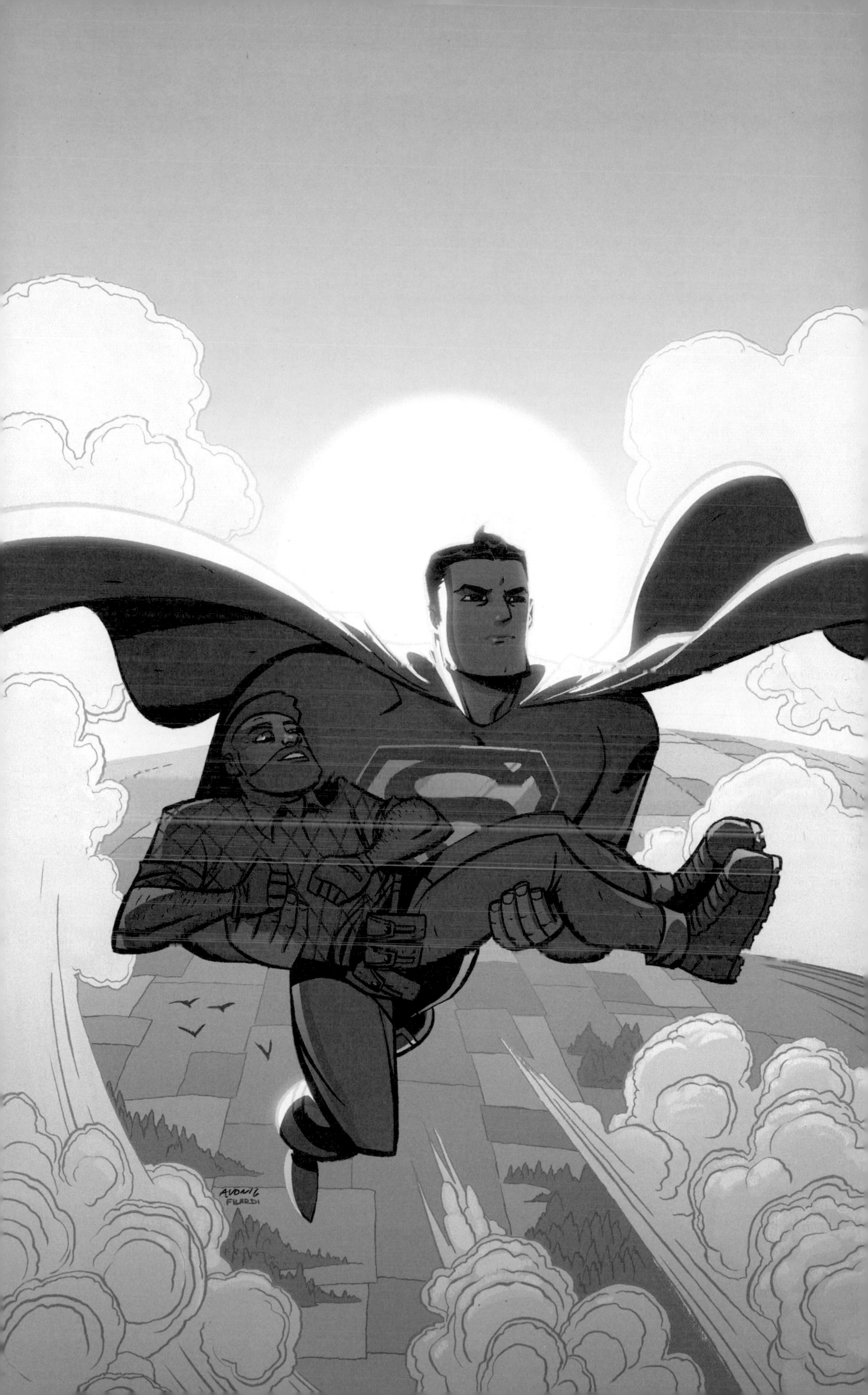

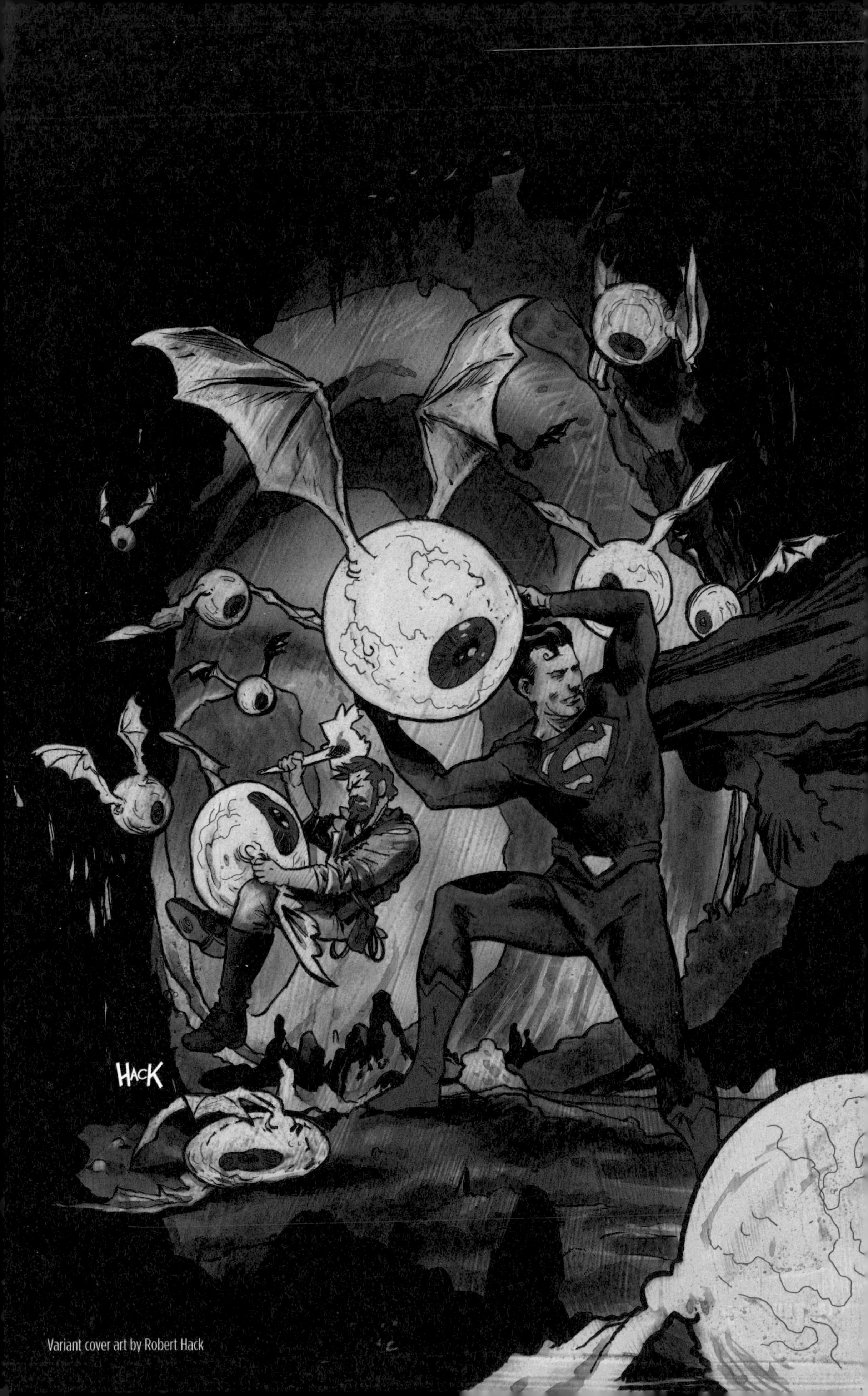
HACK

Variant cover art by Robert Hack

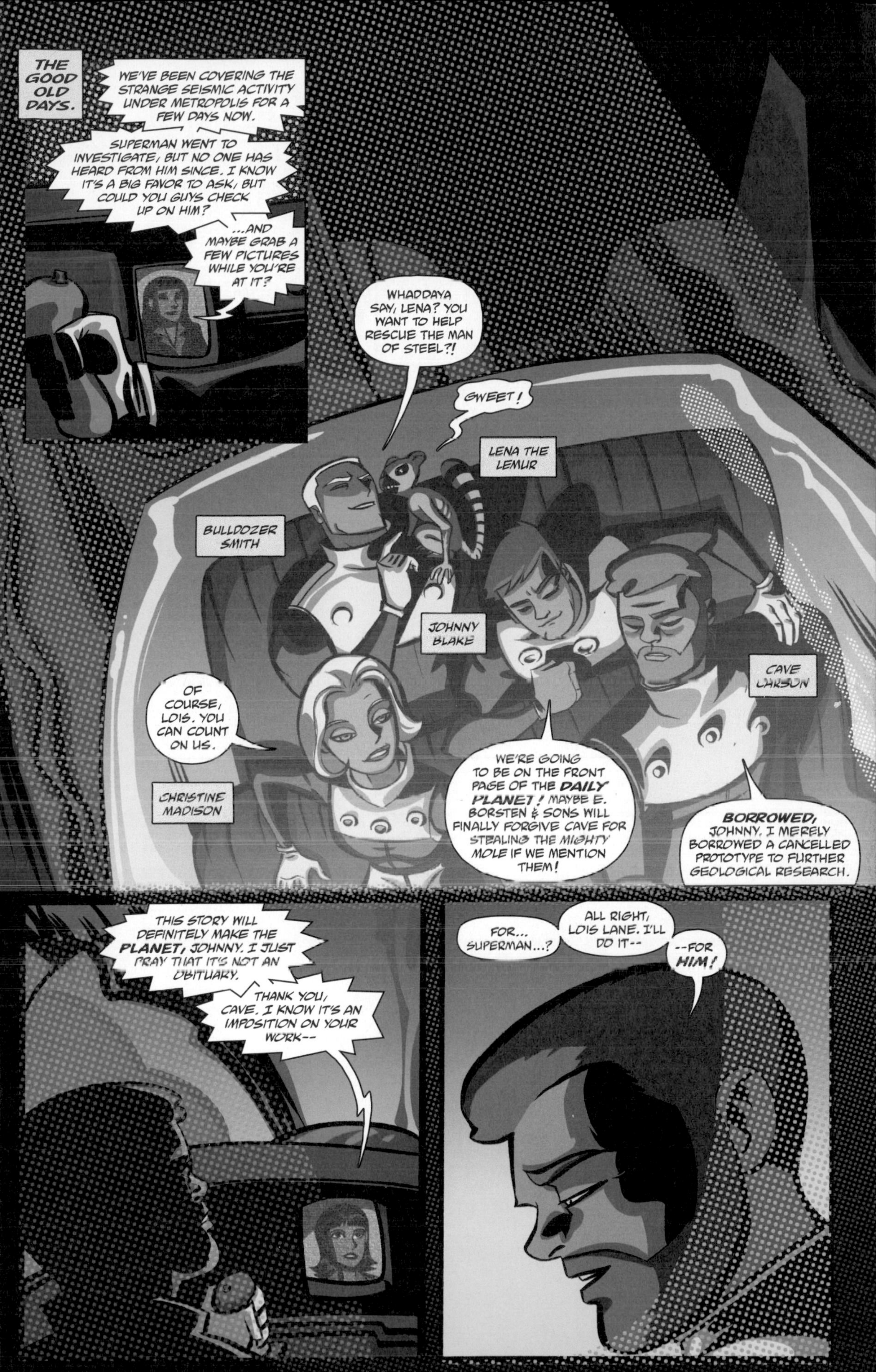

THE GOOD OLD DAYS.
WE'VE BEEN COVERING THE STRANGE SEISMIC ACTIVITY UNDER METROPOLIS FOR A FEW DAYS NOW.
SUPERMAN WENT TO INVESTIGATE, BUT NO ONE HAS HEARD FROM HIM SINCE. I KNOW IT'S A BIG FAVOR TO ASK, BUT COULD YOU GUYS CHECK UP ON HIM?
...AND MAYBE GRAB A FEW PICTURES WHILE YOU'RE AT IT?
WHADDAYA SAY, LENA? YOU WANT TO HELP RESCUE THE MAN OF STEEL?!
GWEET!
LENA THE LEMUR
BULLDOZER SMITH
JOHNNY BLAKE
CAVE CARSON
OF COURSE, LOIS. YOU CAN COUNT ON US.
CHRISTINE MADISON
WE'RE GOING TO BE ON THE FRONT PAGE OF THE DAILY PLANET! MAYBE E. BORSTEN & SONS WILL FINALLY FORGIVE CAVE FOR STEALING THE MIGHTY MOLE IF WE MENTION THEM!
BORROWED, JOHNNY. I MERELY BORROWED A CANCELLED PROTOTYPE TO FURTHER GEOLOGICAL RESEARCH.
THIS STORY WILL DEFINITELY MAKE THE PLANET, JOHNNY. I JUST PRAY THAT IT'S NOT AN OBITUARY.
THANK YOU, CAVE. I KNOW IT'S AN IMPOSITION ON YOUR WORK--
FOR... SUPERMAN...?
ALL RIGHT, LOIS LANE. I'LL DO IT--
--FOR HIM!

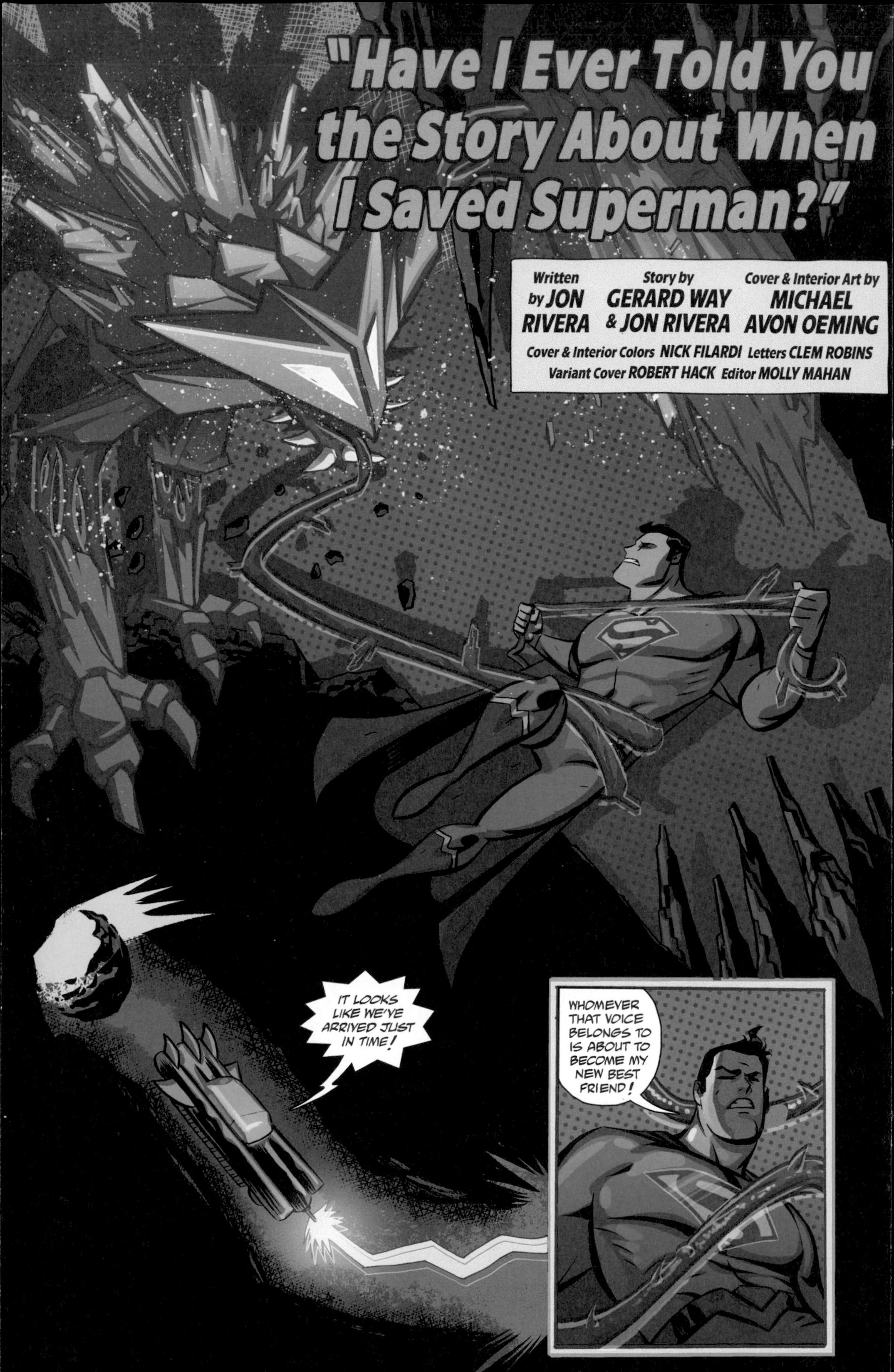
"Have I Ever Told You the Story About When I Saved Superman?"
Written by JON RIVERA Story by GERARD WAY & JON RIVERA Cover & Interior Art by MICHAEL AVON OEMING
Cover & Interior Colors NICK FILARDI Letters CLEM ROBINS
Variant Cover ROBERT HACK Editor MOLLY MAHAN
IT LOOKS LIKE WE'VE ARRIVED JUST IN TIME!
WHOMEVER THAT VOICE BELONGS TO IS ABOUT TO BECOME MY NEW BEST FRIEND!

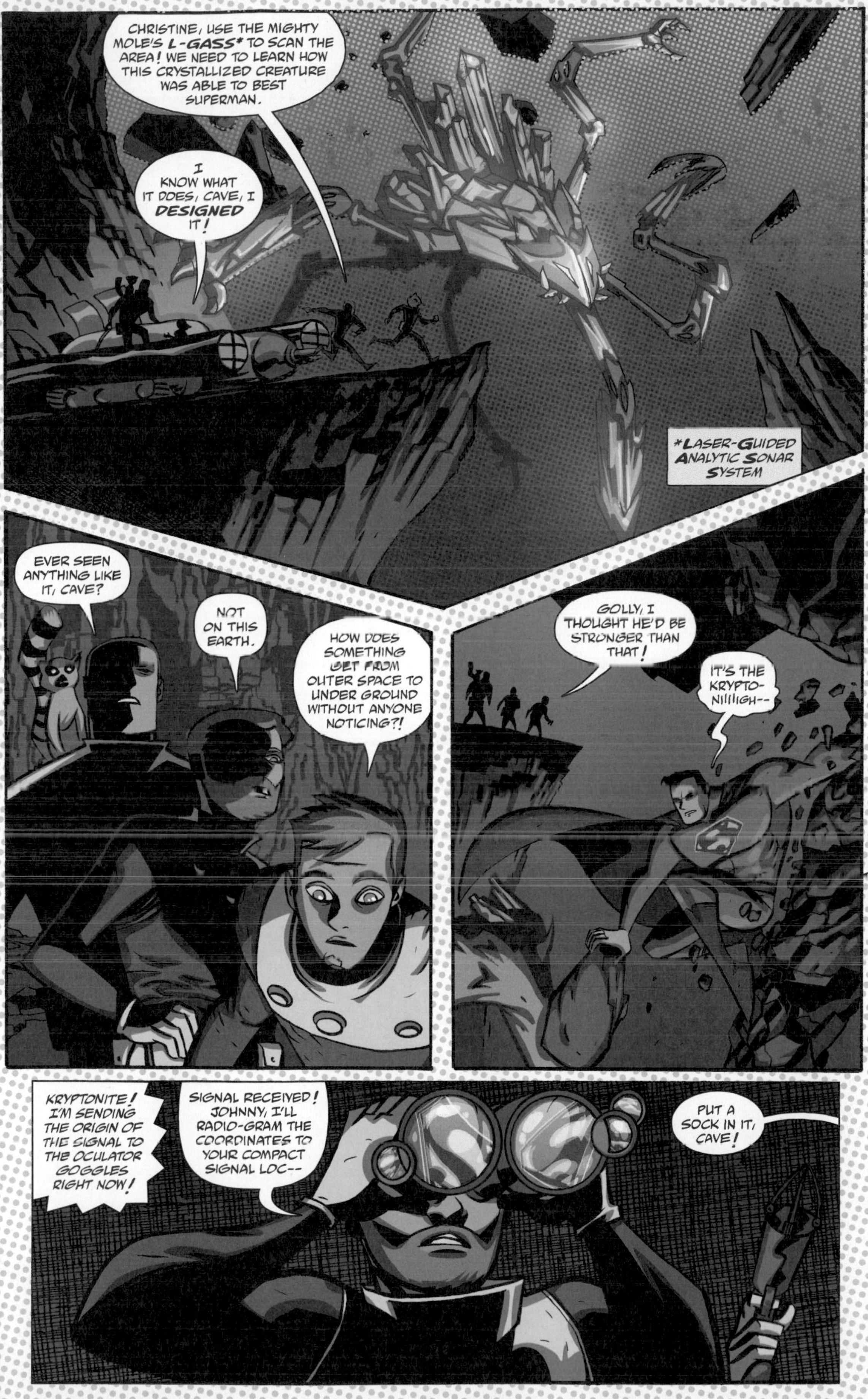

CHRISTINE, USE THE MIGHTY MOLE'S L-GASS* TO SCAN THE AREA! WE NEED TO LEARN HOW THIS CRYSTALLIZED CREATURE WAS ABLE TO BEST SUPERMAN.
I KNOW WHAT IT DOES, CAVE, I DESIGNED IT!
*LASER-GUIDED ANALYTIC SONAR SYSTEM
EVER SEEN ANYTHING LIKE IT, CAVE?
NOT ON THIS EARTH.
HOW DOES SOMETHING GET FROM OUTER SPACE TO UNDER GROUND WITHOUT ANYONE NOTICING?!
GOLLY, I THOUGHT HE'D BE STRONGER THAN THAT!
IT'S THE KRYPTO-NIIIIGH--
KRYPTONITE! I'M SENDING THE ORIGIN OF THE SIGNAL TO THE OCULATOR GOGGLES RIGHT NOW!
SIGNAL RECEIVED! JOHNNY, I'LL RADIO-GRAM THE COORDINATES TO YOUR COMPACT SIGNAL LOC--
PUT A SOCK IN IT, CAVE!

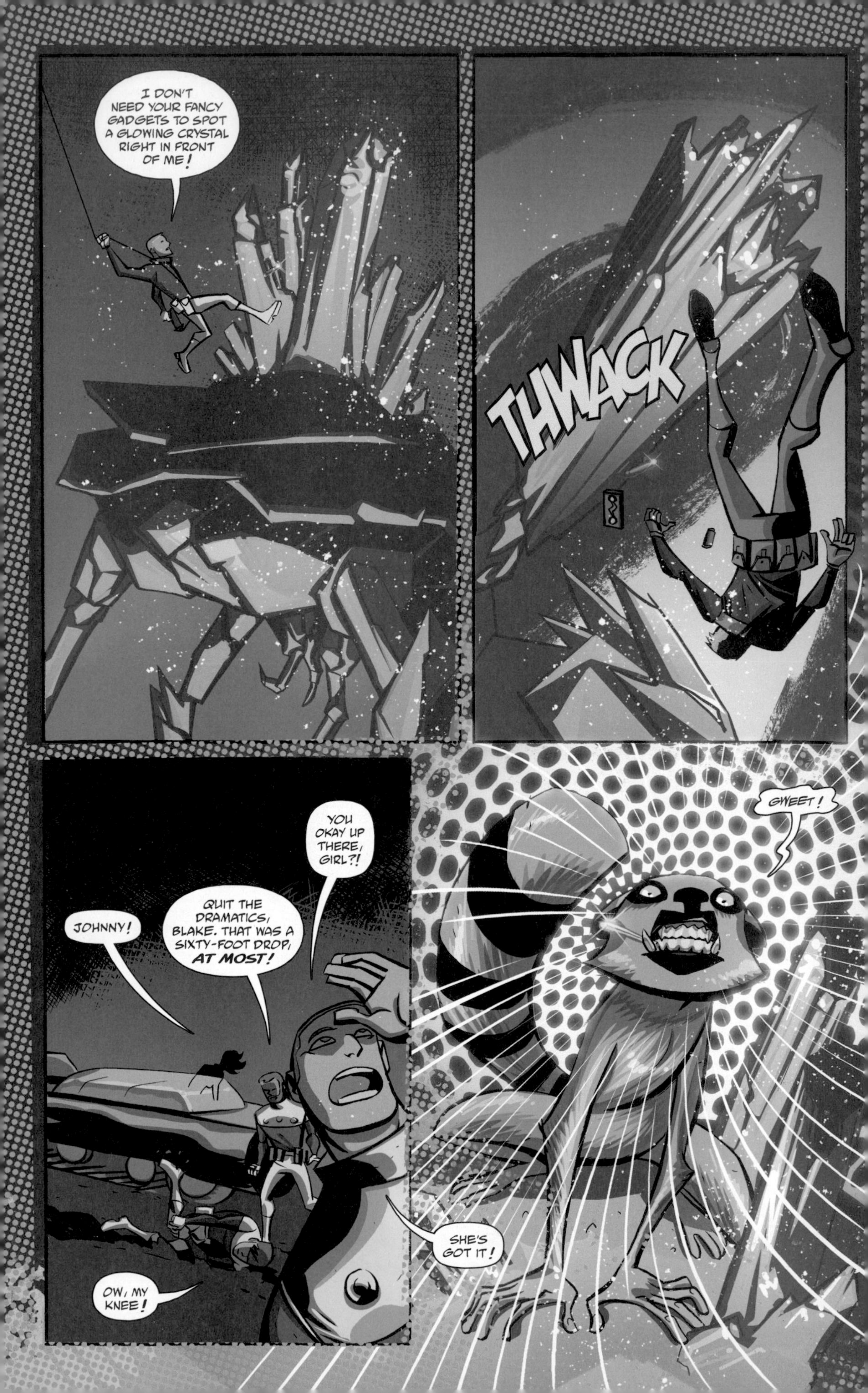
I DON'T NEED YOUR FANCY GADGETS TO SPOT A GLOWING CRYSTAL RIGHT IN FRONT OF ME!
THWACK
JOHNNY!
QUIT THE DRAMATICS, BLAKE. THAT WAS A SIXTY-FOOT DROP, AT MOST!
YOU OKAY UP THERE, GIRL?!
OW, MY KNEE!
SHE'S GOT IT!
GWEET!

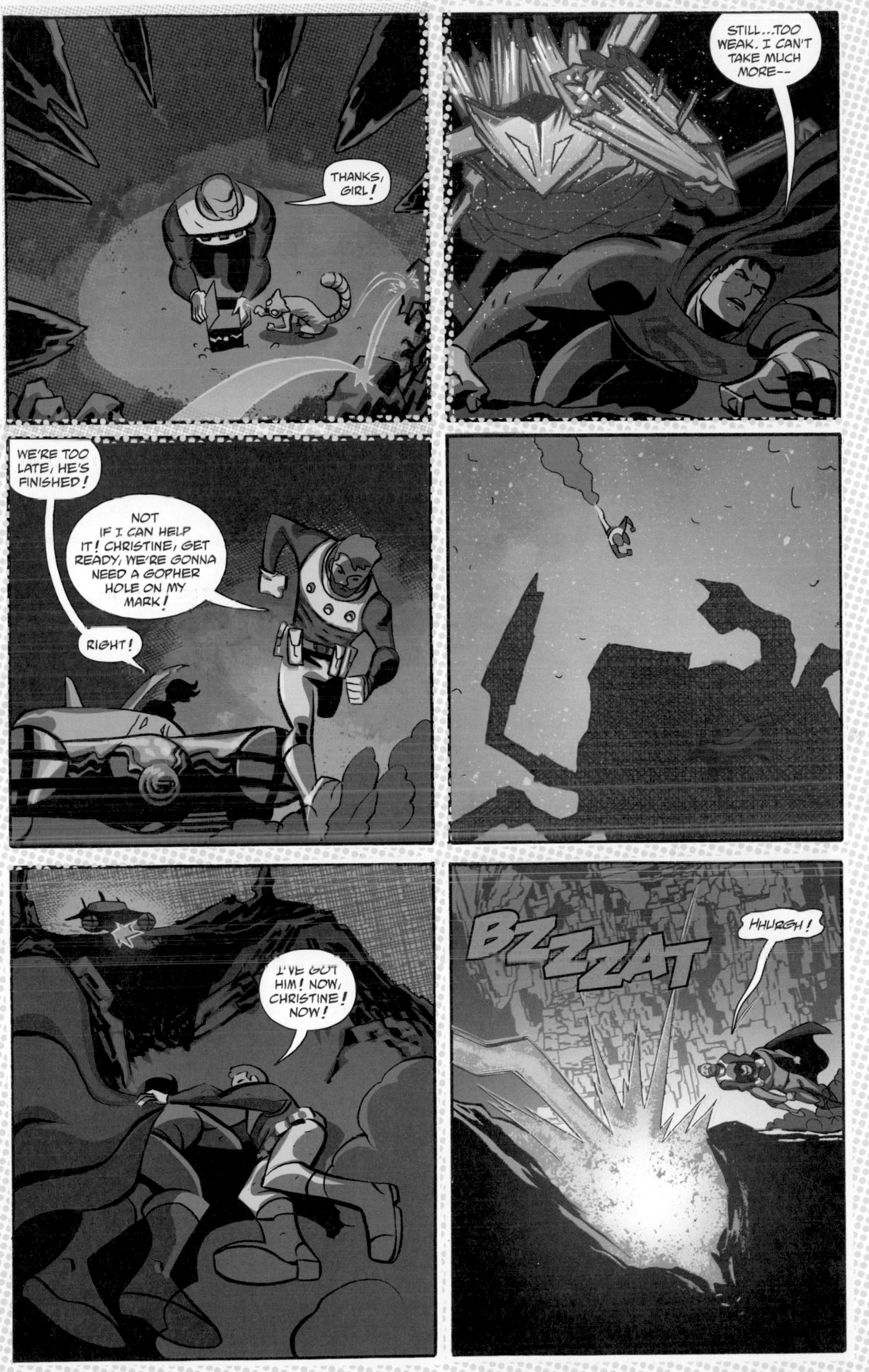
THANKS, GIRL!
STILL...TOO WEAK. I CAN'T TAKE MUCH MORE--
WE'RE TOO LATE, HE'S FINISHED!
NOT IF I CAN HELP IT! CHRISTINE, GET READY, WE'RE GONNA NEED A GOPHER HOLE ON MY MARK!
RIGHT!
I'VE GOT HIM! NOW, CHRISTINE! NOW!
BZZZAT
HHURGH!

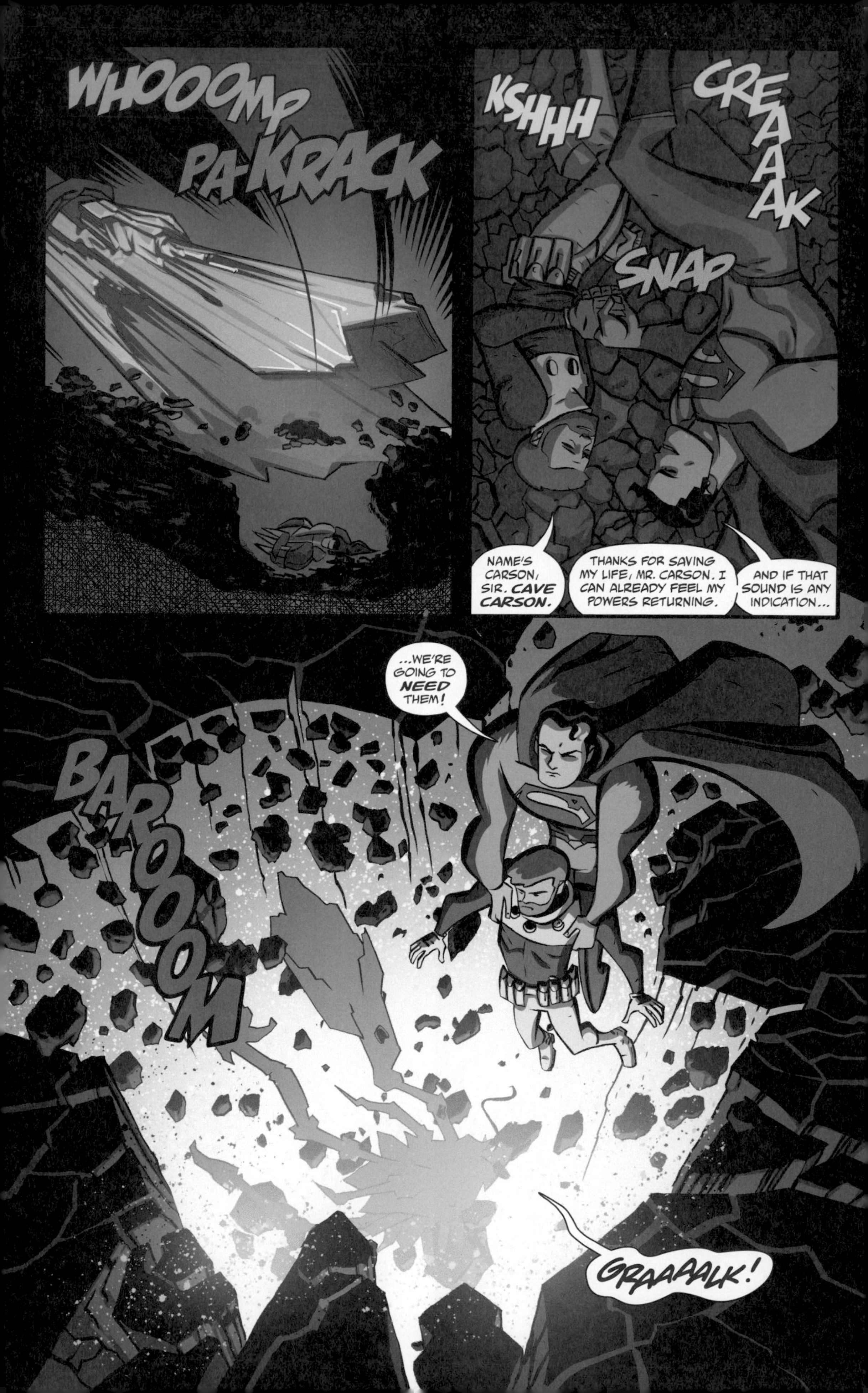
WHOOOMP
PA-KRACK
KSHHH
CREAAAK
SNAP
NAME'S CARSON, SIR. CAVE CARSON.
THANKS FOR SAVING MY LIFE, MR. CARSON. I CAN ALREADY FEEL MY POWERS RETURNING.
AND IF THAT SOUND IS ANY INDICATION...
...WE'RE GOING TO NEED THEM!
BAROOOOM
GRAAAALK!

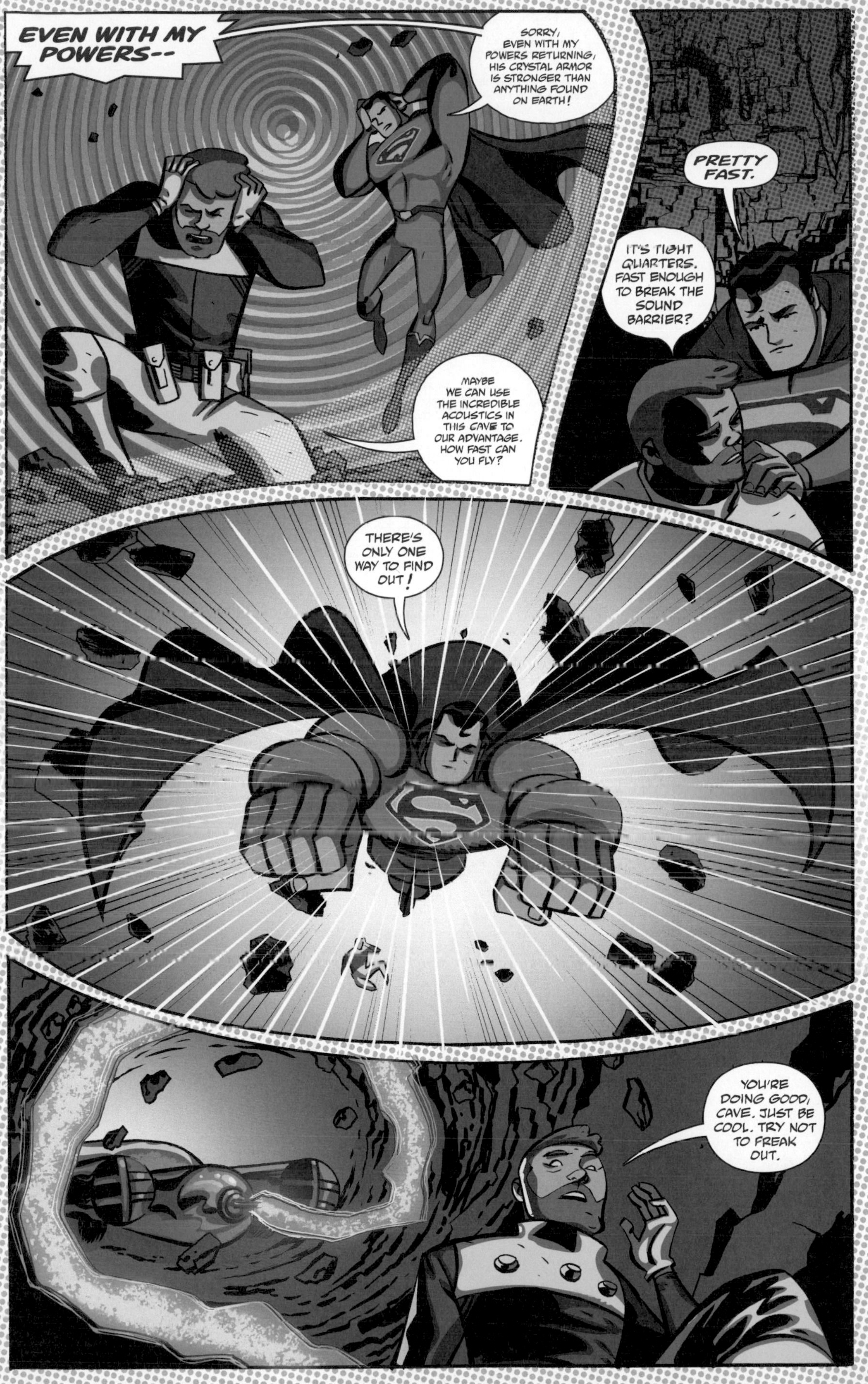
EVEN WITH MY POWERS--
SORRY, EVEN WITH MY POWERS RETURNING, HIS CRYSTAL ARMOR IS STRONGER THAN ANYTHING FOUND ON EARTH!
MAYBE WE CAN USE THE INCREDIBLE ACOUSTICS IN THIS CAVE TO OUR ADVANTAGE. HOW FAST CAN YOU FLY?
PRETTY FAST.
IT'S TIGHT QUARTERS. FAST ENOUGH TO BREAK THE SOUND BARRIER?
THERE'S ONLY ONE WAY TO FIND OUT!
YOU'RE DOING GOOD, CAVE. JUST BE COOL. TRY NOT TO FREAK OUT.

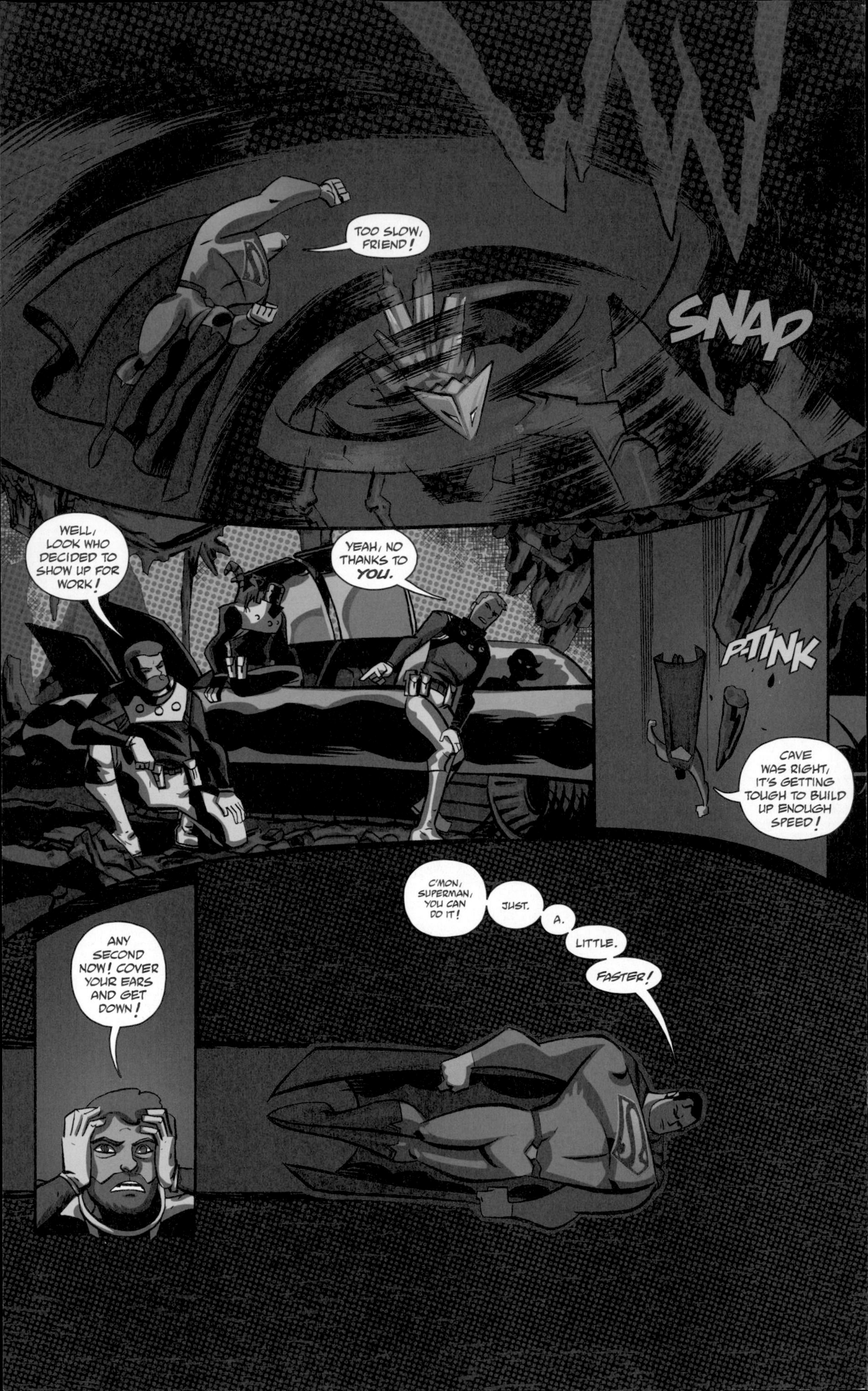
TOO SLOW, FRIEND!
SNAP
WELL, LOOK WHO DECIDED TO SHOW UP FOR WORK!
YEAH, NO THANKS TO YOU.
P-TINK
CAVE WAS RIGHT, IT'S GETTING TOUGH TO BUILD UP ENOUGH SPEED!
C'MON, SUPERMAN, YOU CAN DO IT!
JUST.
A.
LITTLE.
FASTER!
ANY SECOND NOW! COVER YOUR EARS AND GET DOWN!

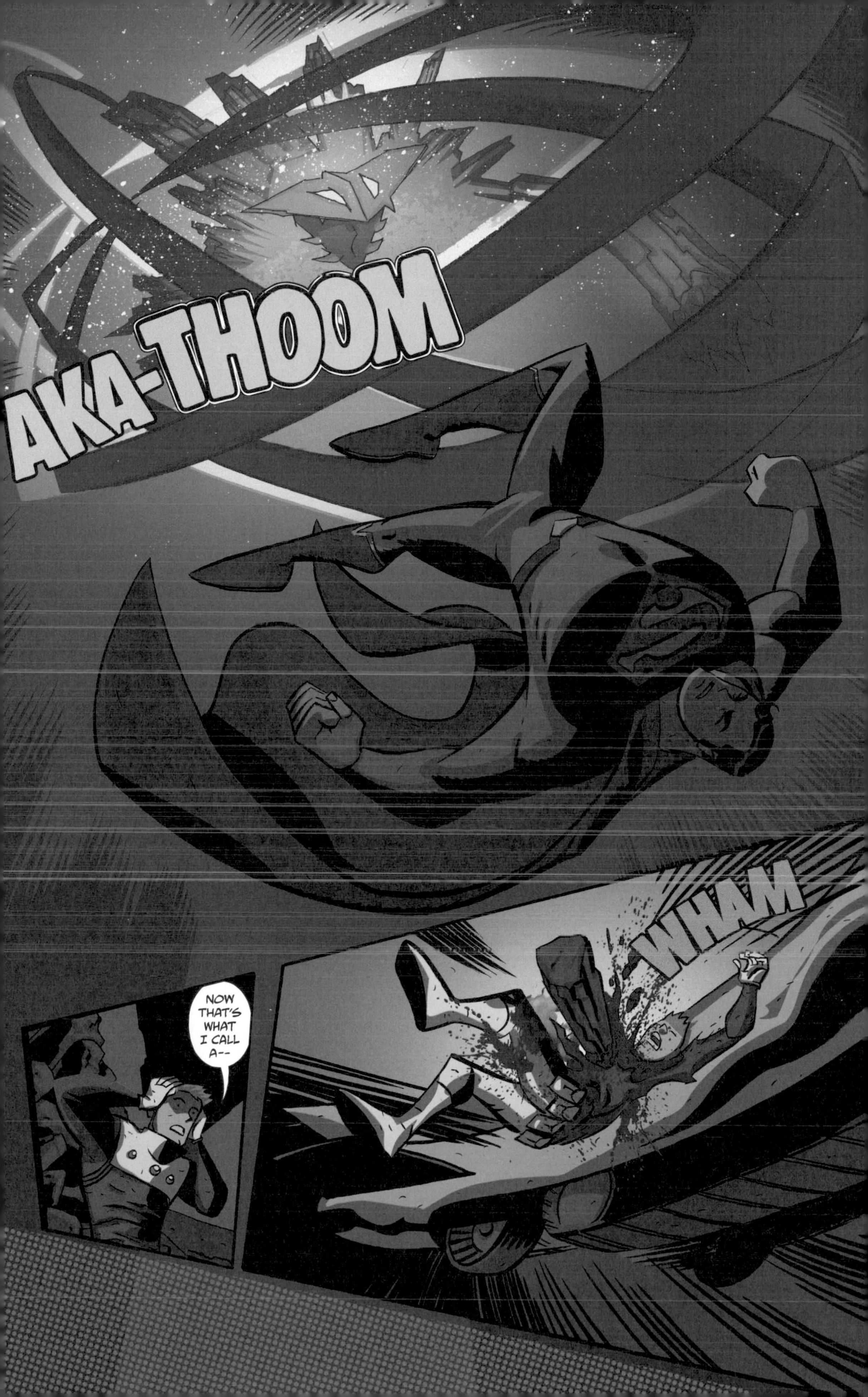
AKA-THOOM
WHAM
NOW THAT'S WHAT I CALL A--

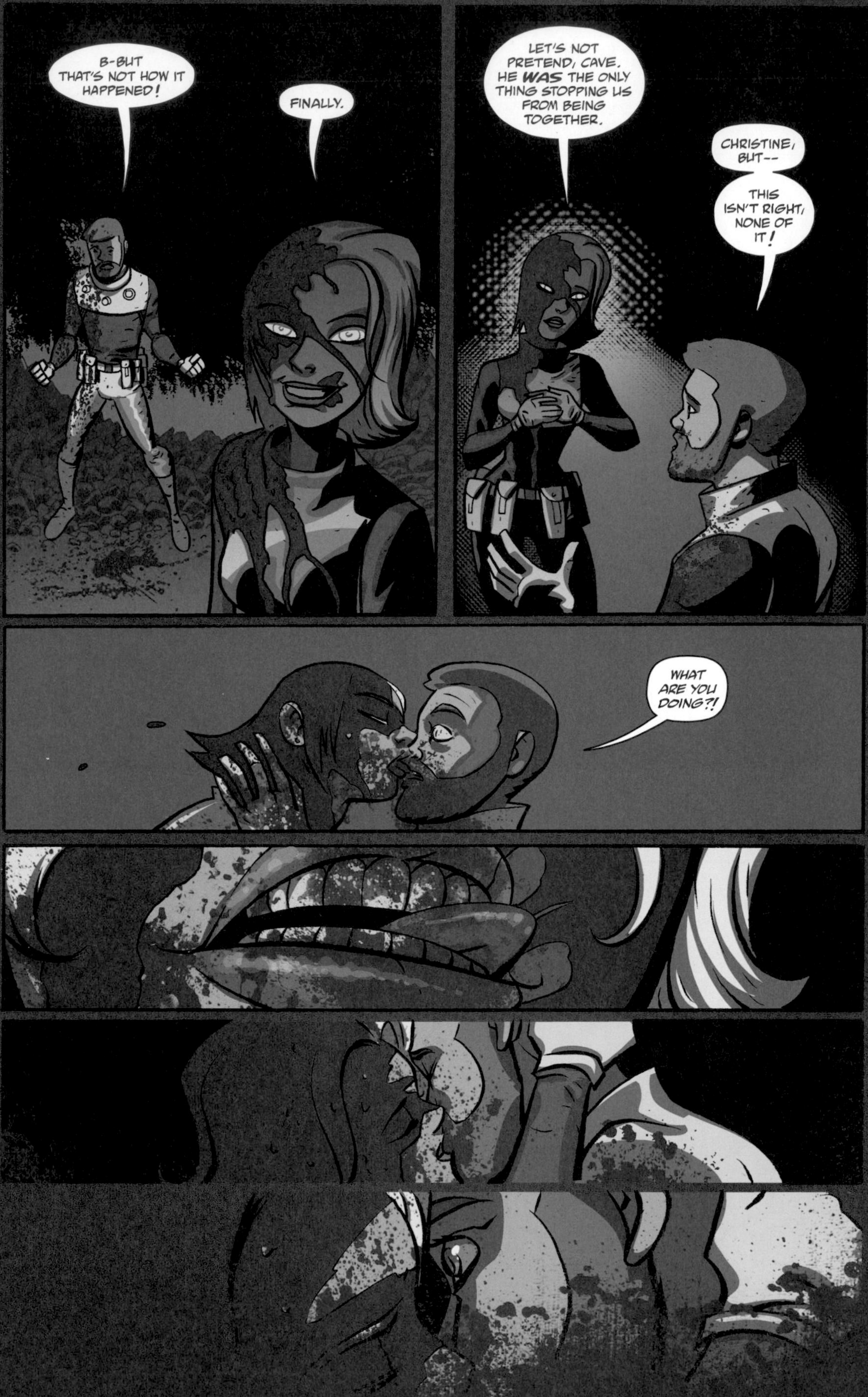
B-BUT THAT'S NOT HOW IT HAPPENED!
FINALLY.
LET'S NOT PRETEND, CAVE. HE WAS THE ONLY THING STOPPING US FROM BEING TOGETHER.
CHRISTINE, BUT--
THIS ISN'T RIGHT, NONE OF IT!
WHAT ARE YOU DOING?!

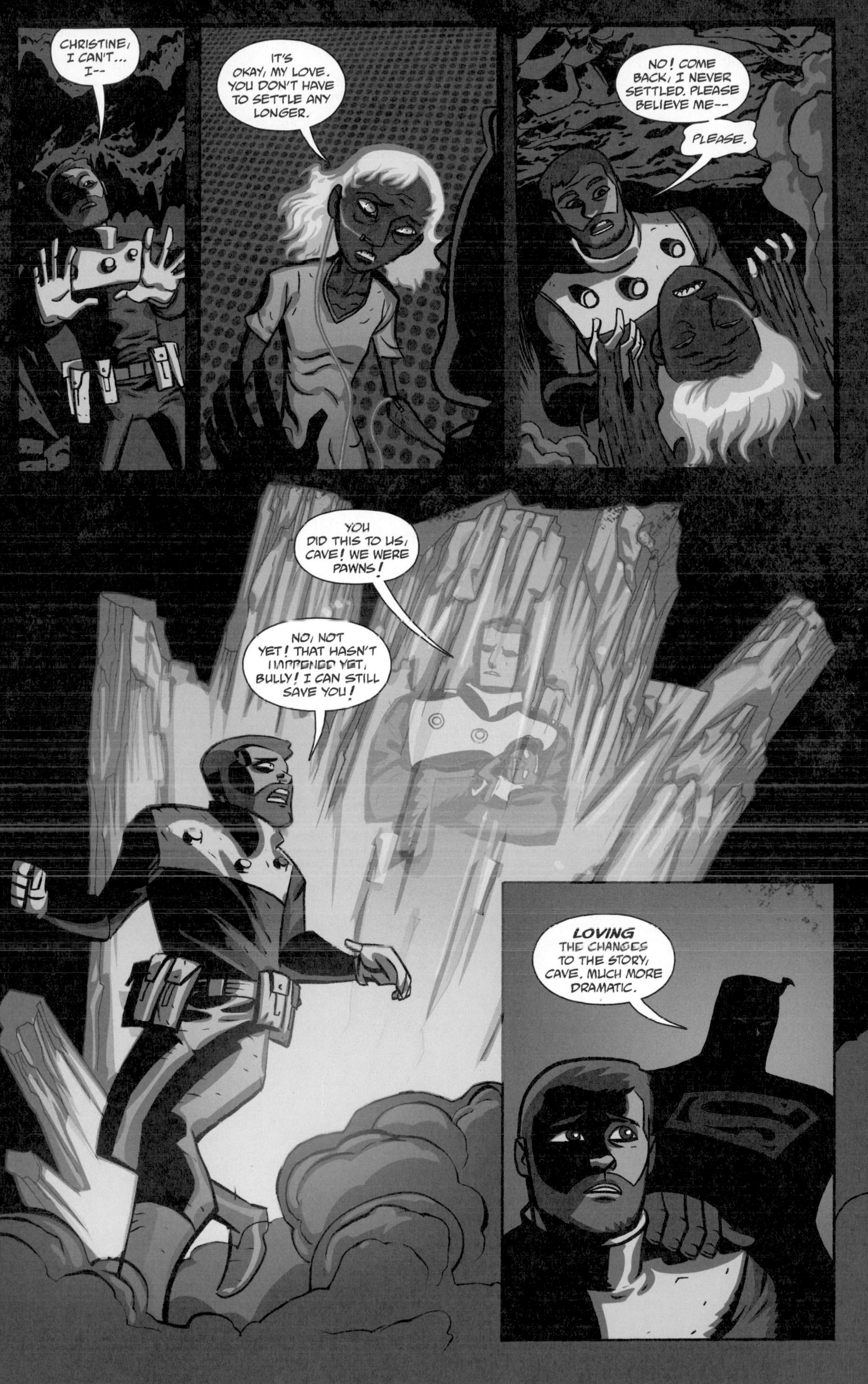
CHRISTINE, I CAN'T... I--
IT'S OKAY, MY LOVE. YOU DON'T HAVE TO SETTLE ANY LONGER.
NO! COME BACK, I NEVER SETTLED. PLEASE BELIEVE ME--
PLEASE.
YOU DID THIS TO US, CAVE! WE WERE PAWNS!
NO, NOT YET! THAT HASN'T HAPPENED YET, BULLY! I CAN STILL SAVE YOU!
LOVING THE CHANGES TO THE STORY, CAVE. MUCH MORE DRAMATIC.

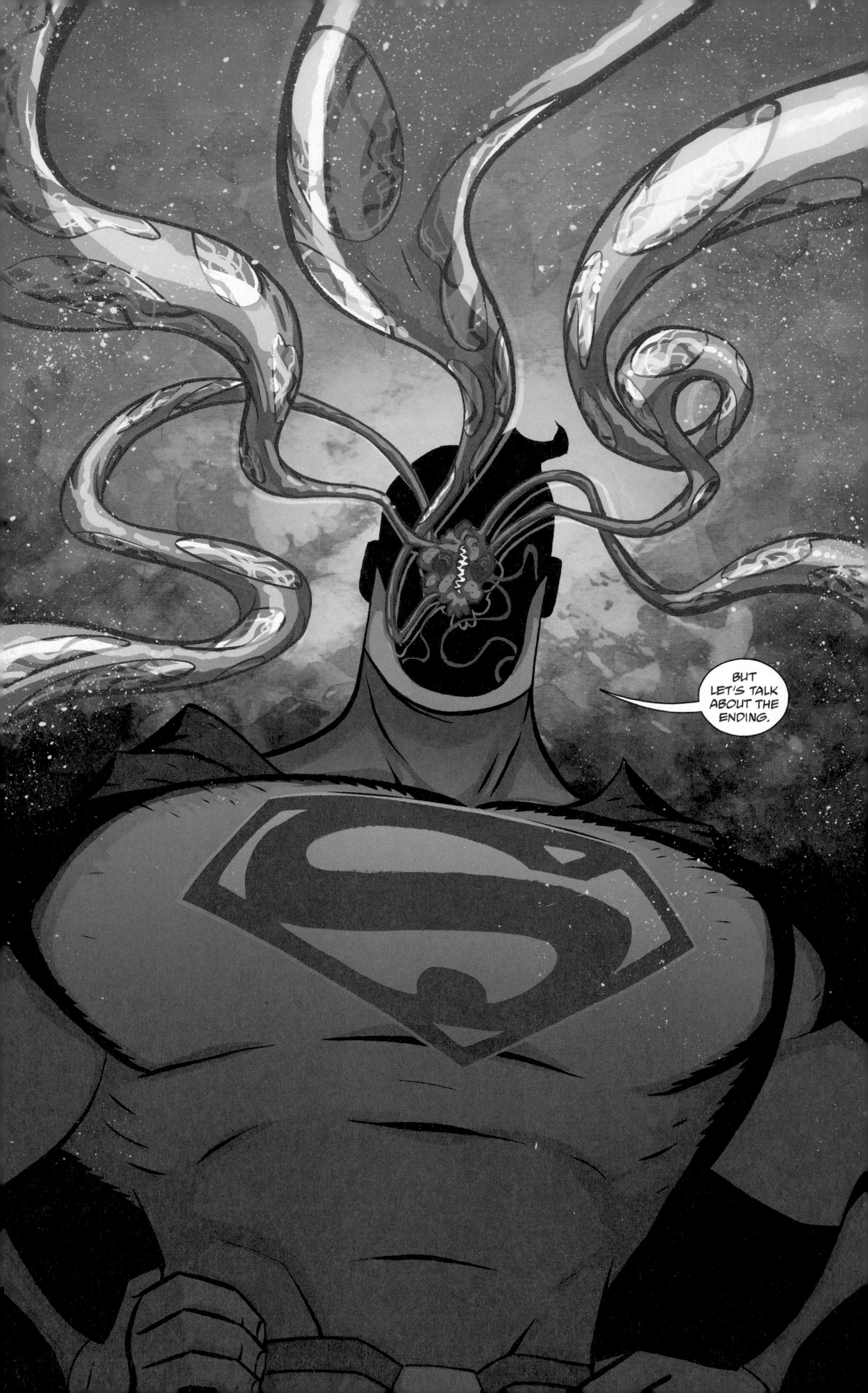
BUT LET'S TALK ABOUT THE ENDING.

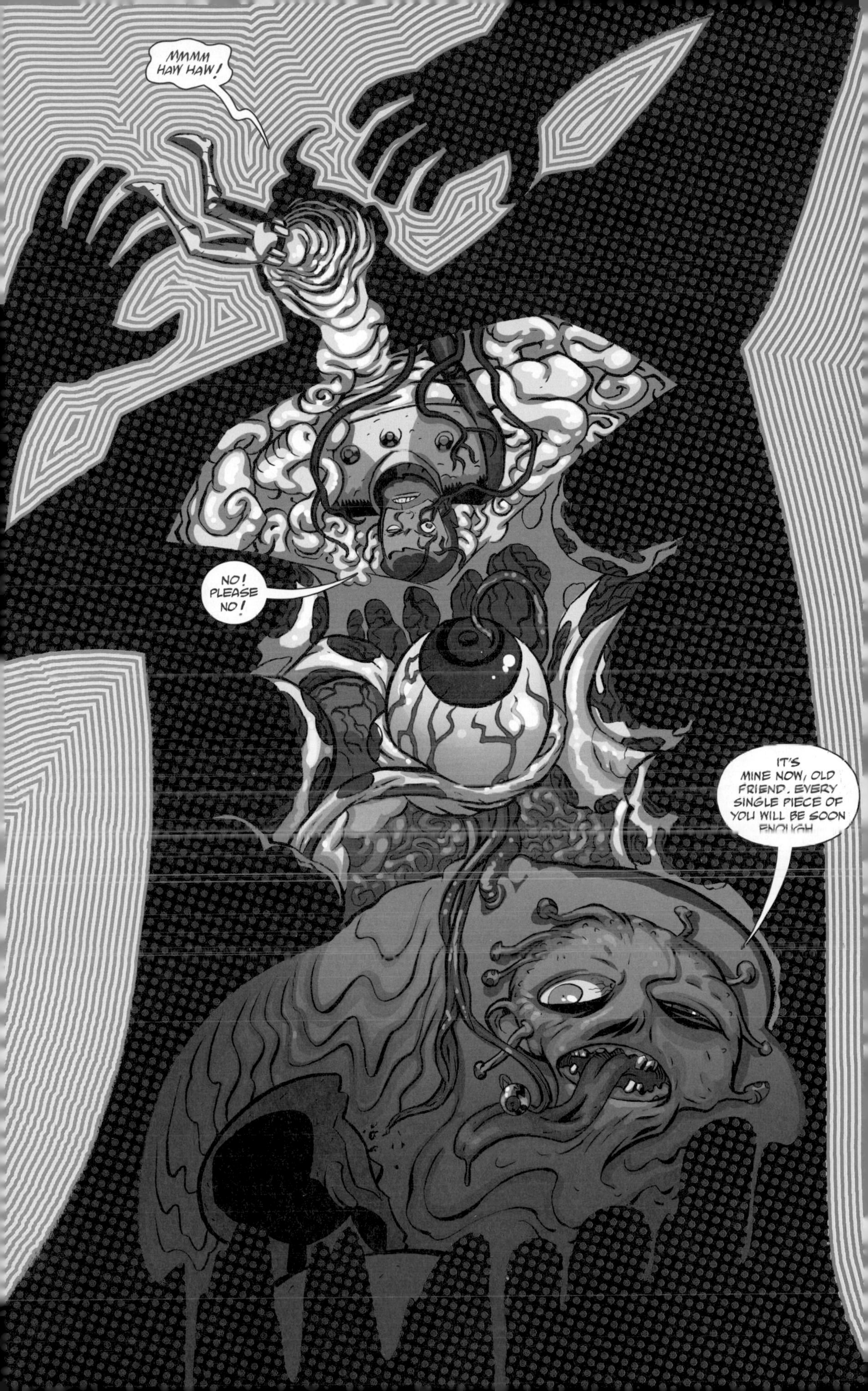
MMMM HAW HAW!
NO! PLEASE NO!
IT'S MINE NOW, OLD FRIEND. EVERY SINGLE PIECE OF YOU WILL BE SOON ENOUGH.

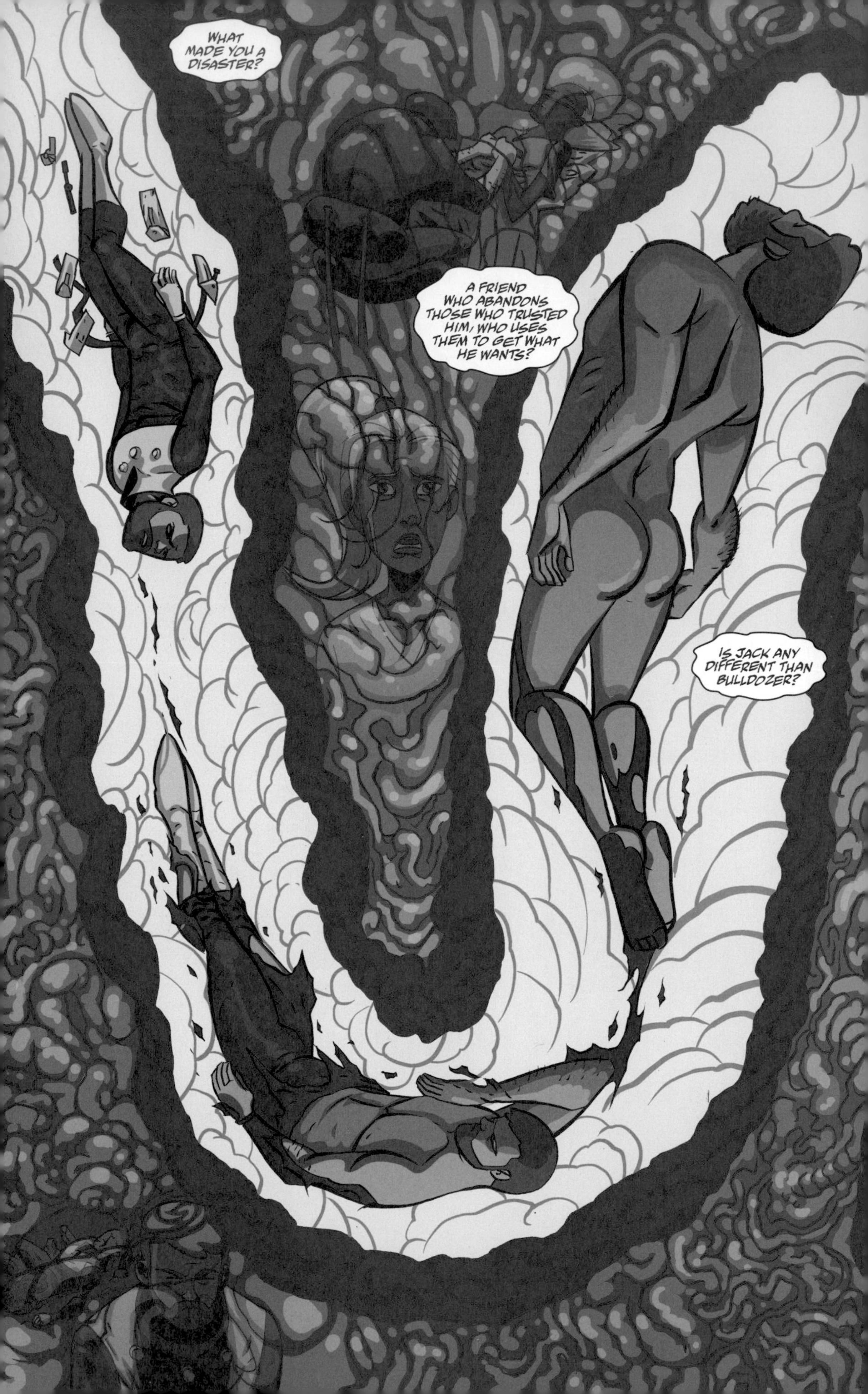
WHAT MADE YOU A DISASTER?
A FRIEND WHO ABANDONS THOSE WHO TRUSTED HIM, WHO USES THEM TO GET WHAT HE WANTS?
IS JACK ANY DIFFERENT THAN BULLDOZER?

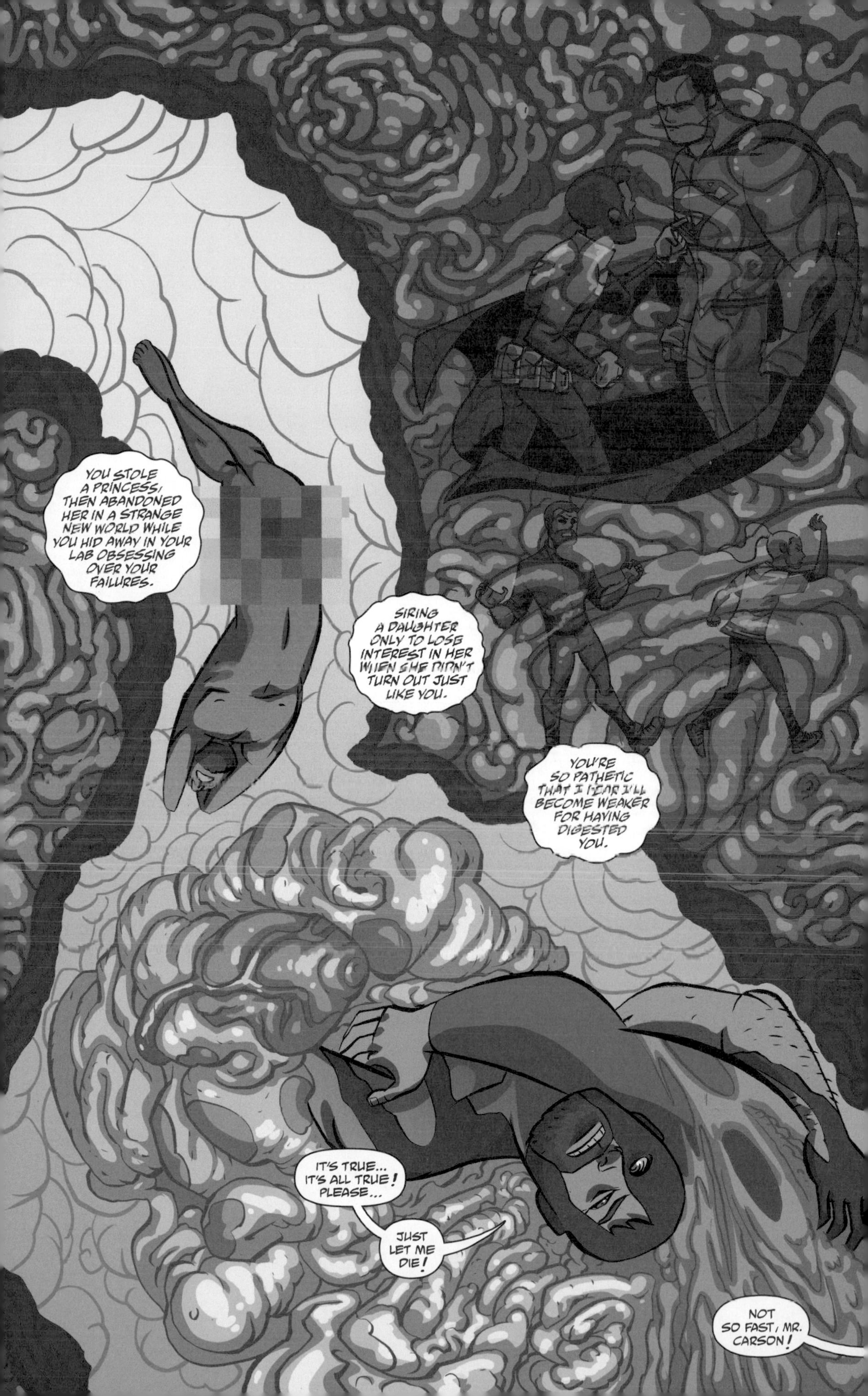
YOU STOLE A PRINCESS, THEN ABANDONED HER IN A STRANGE NEW WORLD WHILE YOU HID AWAY IN YOUR LAB OBSESSING OVER YOUR FAILURES.
SIRING A DAUGHTER ONLY TO LOSE INTEREST IN HER WHEN SHE DIDN'T TURN OUT JUST LIKE YOU.
YOU'RE SO PATHETIC THAT I FEAR I'LL BECOME WEAKER FOR HAVING DIGESTED YOU.
IT'S TRUE... IT'S ALL TRUE! PLEASE...
JUST LET ME DIE!
NOT SO FAST, MR. CARSON!

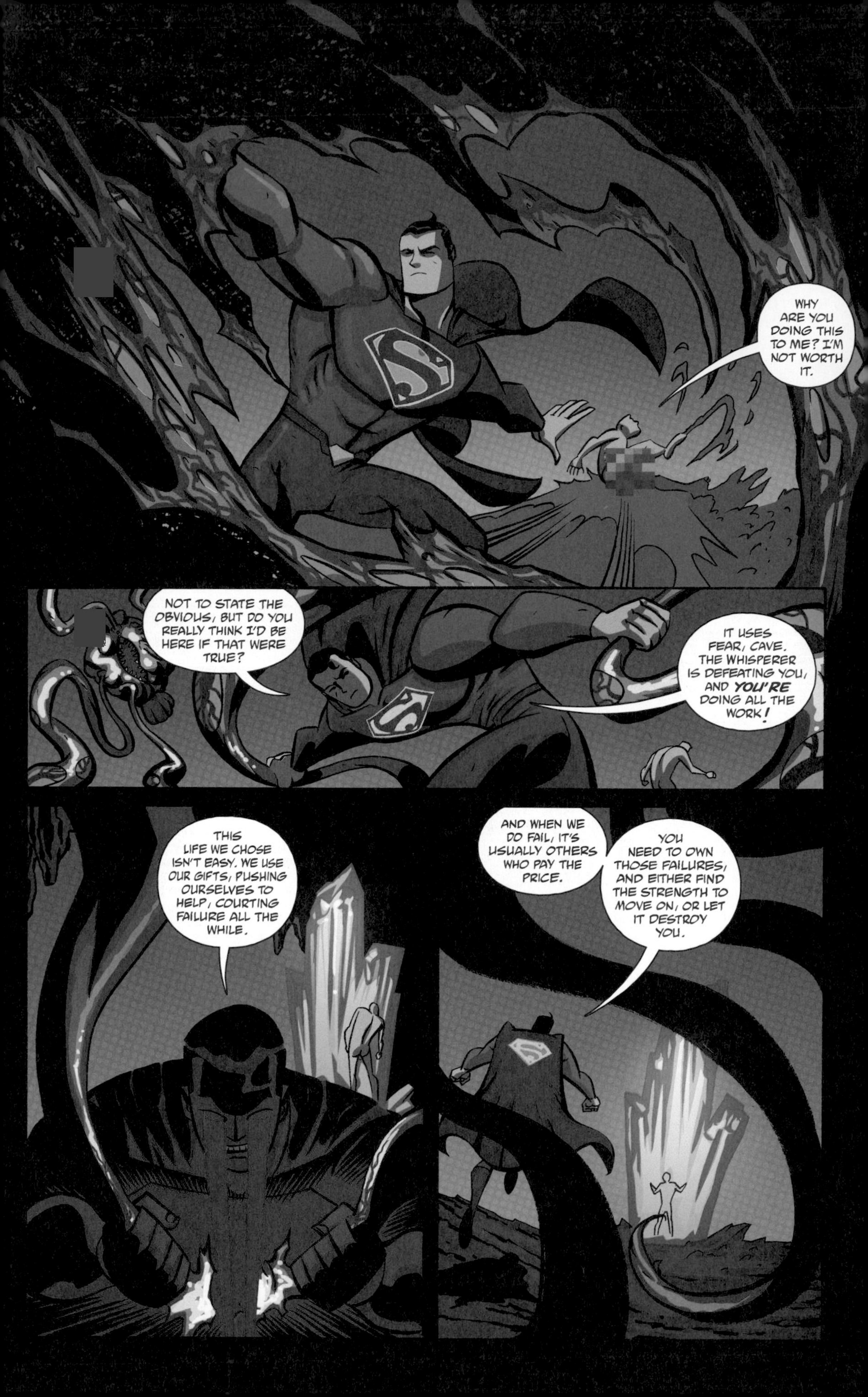

WHY ARE YOU DOING THIS TO ME? I'M NOT WORTH IT.
NOT TO STATE THE OBVIOUS, BUT DO YOU REALLY THINK I'D BE HERE IF THAT WERE TRUE?
IT USES FEAR, CAVE. THE WHISPERER IS DEFEATING YOU, AND ***YOU'RE*** DOING ALL THE WORK!
THIS LIFE WE CHOSE ISN'T EASY. WE USE OUR GIFTS, PUSHING OURSELVES TO HELP, COURTING FAILURE ALL THE WHILE.
AND WHEN WE DO FAIL, IT'S USUALLY OTHERS WHO PAY THE PRICE.
YOU NEED TO OWN THOSE FAILURES, AND EITHER FIND THE STRENGTH TO MOVE ON, OR LET IT DESTROY YOU.

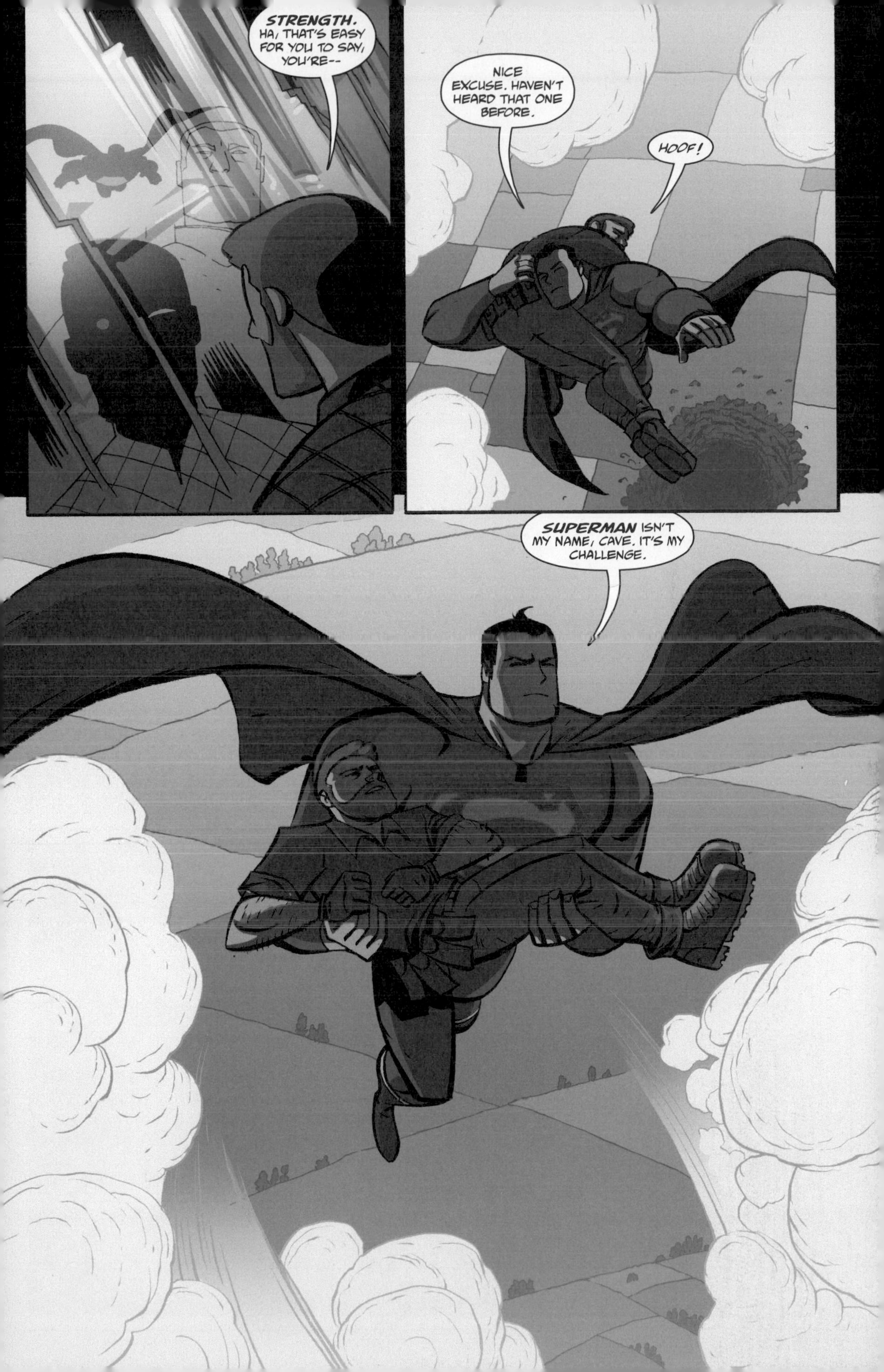
STRENGTH. HA, THAT'S EASY FOR YOU TO SAY, YOU'RE--
NICE EXCUSE. HAVEN'T HEARD THAT ONE BEFORE.
HOOF!
SUPERMAN ISN'T MY NAME, CAVE. IT'S MY CHALLENGE.

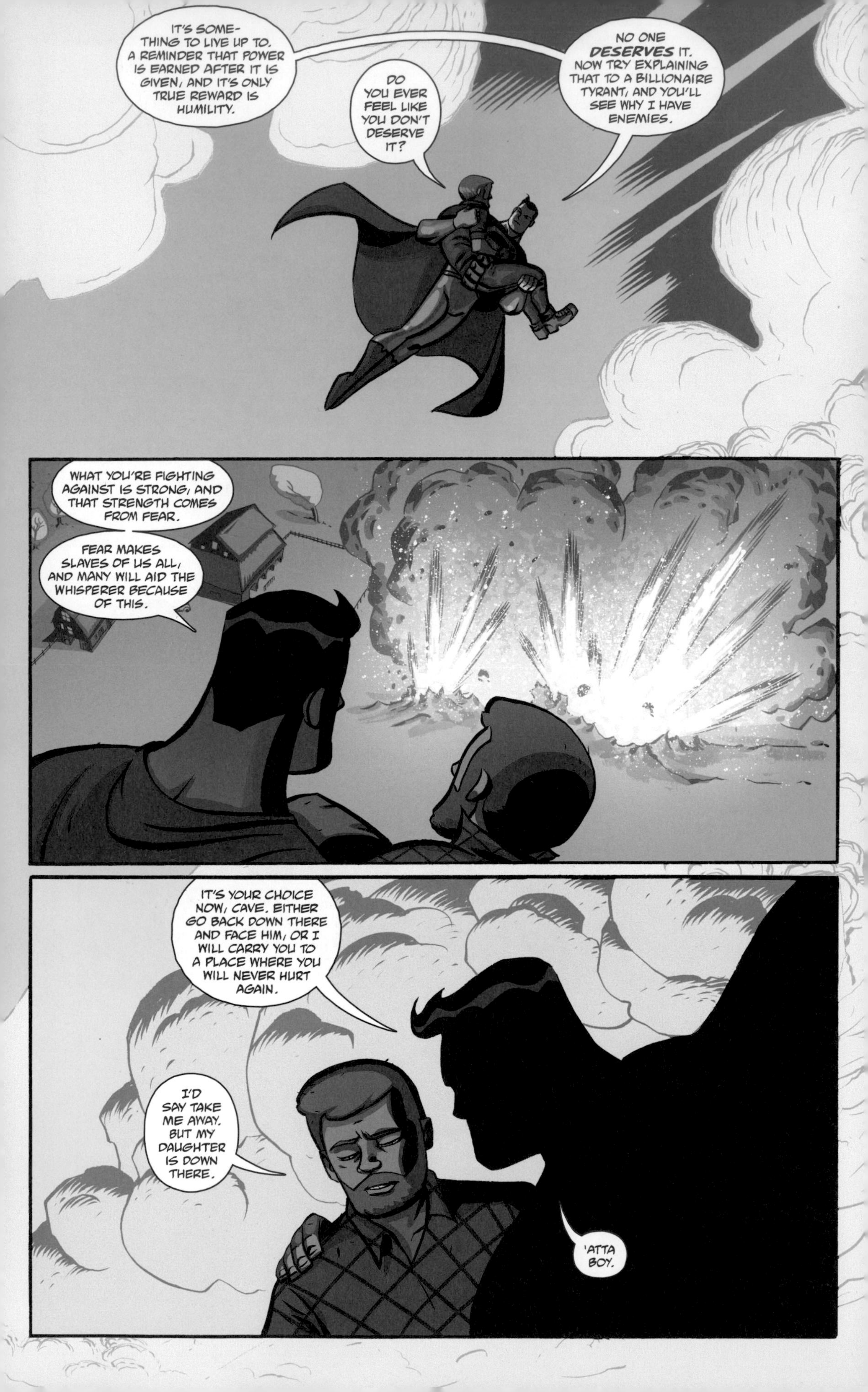

IT'S SOMETHING TO LIVE UP TO. A REMINDER THAT POWER IS EARNED AFTER IT IS GIVEN, AND IT'S ONLY TRUE REWARD IS HUMILITY.
DO YOU EVER FEEL LIKE YOU DON'T DESERVE IT?
NO ONE **DESERVES** IT. NOW TRY EXPLAINING THAT TO A BILLIONAIRE TYRANT, AND YOU'LL SEE WHY I HAVE ENEMIES.
WHAT YOU'RE FIGHTING AGAINST IS STRONG, AND THAT STRENGTH COMES FROM FEAR.
FEAR MAKES SLAVES OF US ALL, AND MANY WILL AID THE WHISPERER BECAUSE OF THIS.
IT'S YOUR CHOICE NOW, CAVE. EITHER GO BACK DOWN THERE AND FACE HIM, OR I WILL CARRY YOU TO A PLACE WHERE YOU WILL NEVER HURT AGAIN.
I'D SAY TAKE ME AWAY. BUT MY DAUGHTER IS DOWN THERE.
'ATTA BOY.

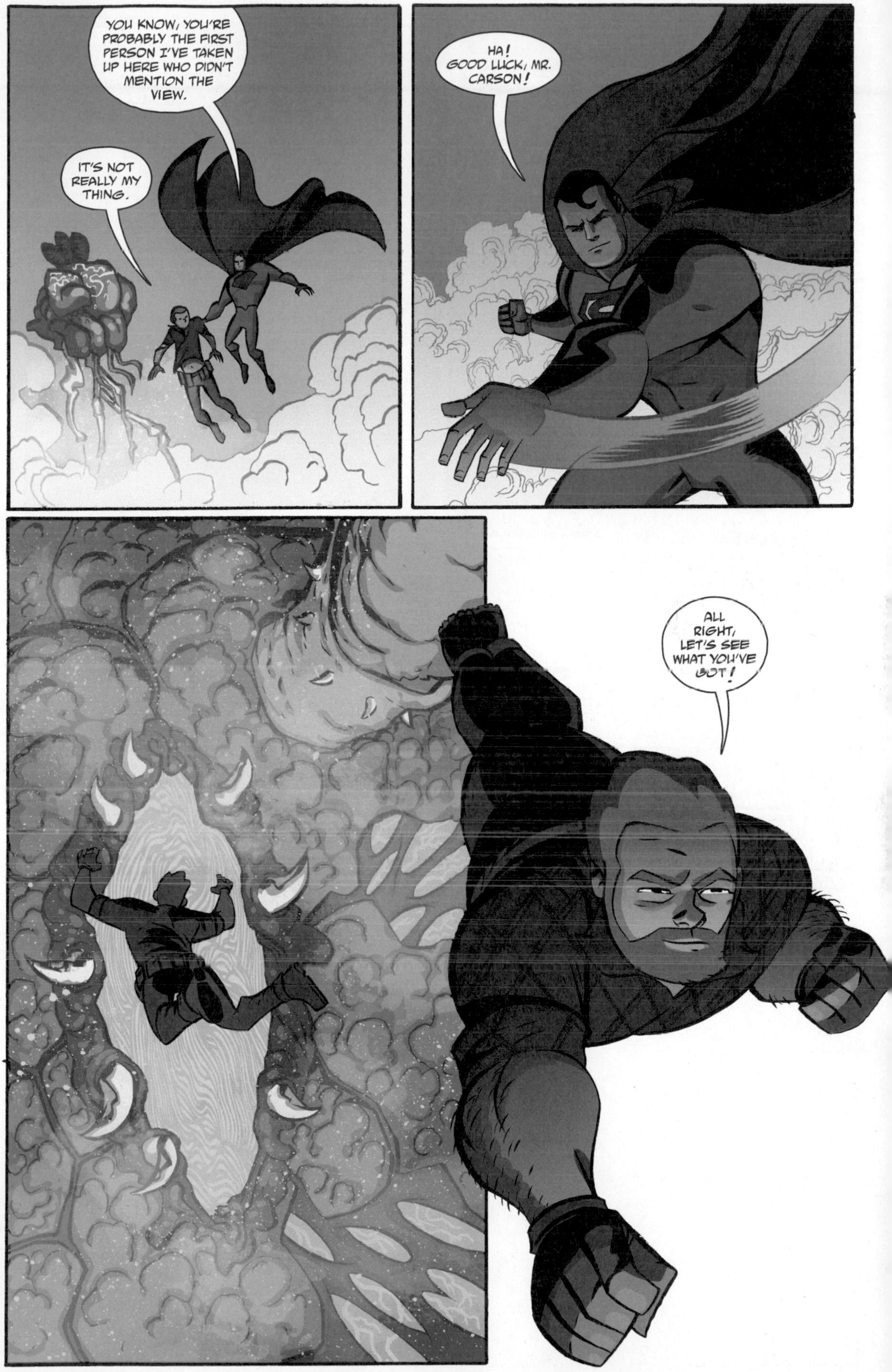
YOU KNOW, YOU'RE PROBABLY THE FIRST PERSON I'VE TAKEN UP HERE WHO DIDN'T MENTION THE VIEW.
IT'S NOT REALLY MY THING.
HA! GOOD LUCK, MR. CARSON!
ALL RIGHT, LET'S SEE WHAT YOU'VE GOT!

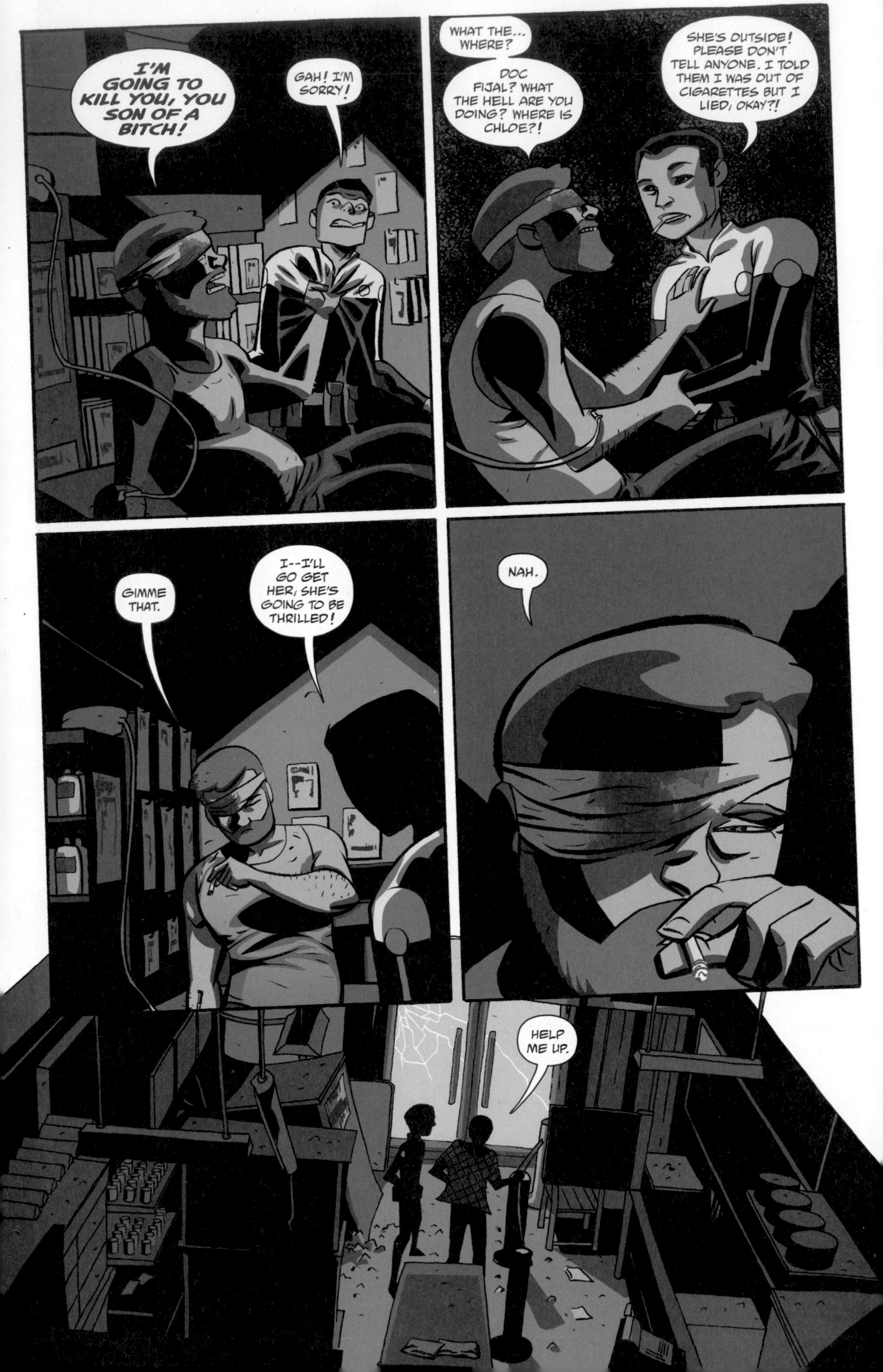
I'M GOING TO KILL YOU, YOU SON OF A BITCH!
GAH! I'M SORRY!
WHAT THE... WHERE?
DOC FIJAL? WHAT THE HELL ARE YOU DOING? WHERE IS CHLOE?!
SHE'S OUTSIDE! PLEASE DON'T TELL ANYONE. I TOLD THEM I WAS OUT OF CIGARETTES BUT I LIED, OKAY?!
GIMME THAT.
I--I'LL GO GET HER, SHE'S GOING TO BE THRILLED!
NAH.
HELP ME UP.

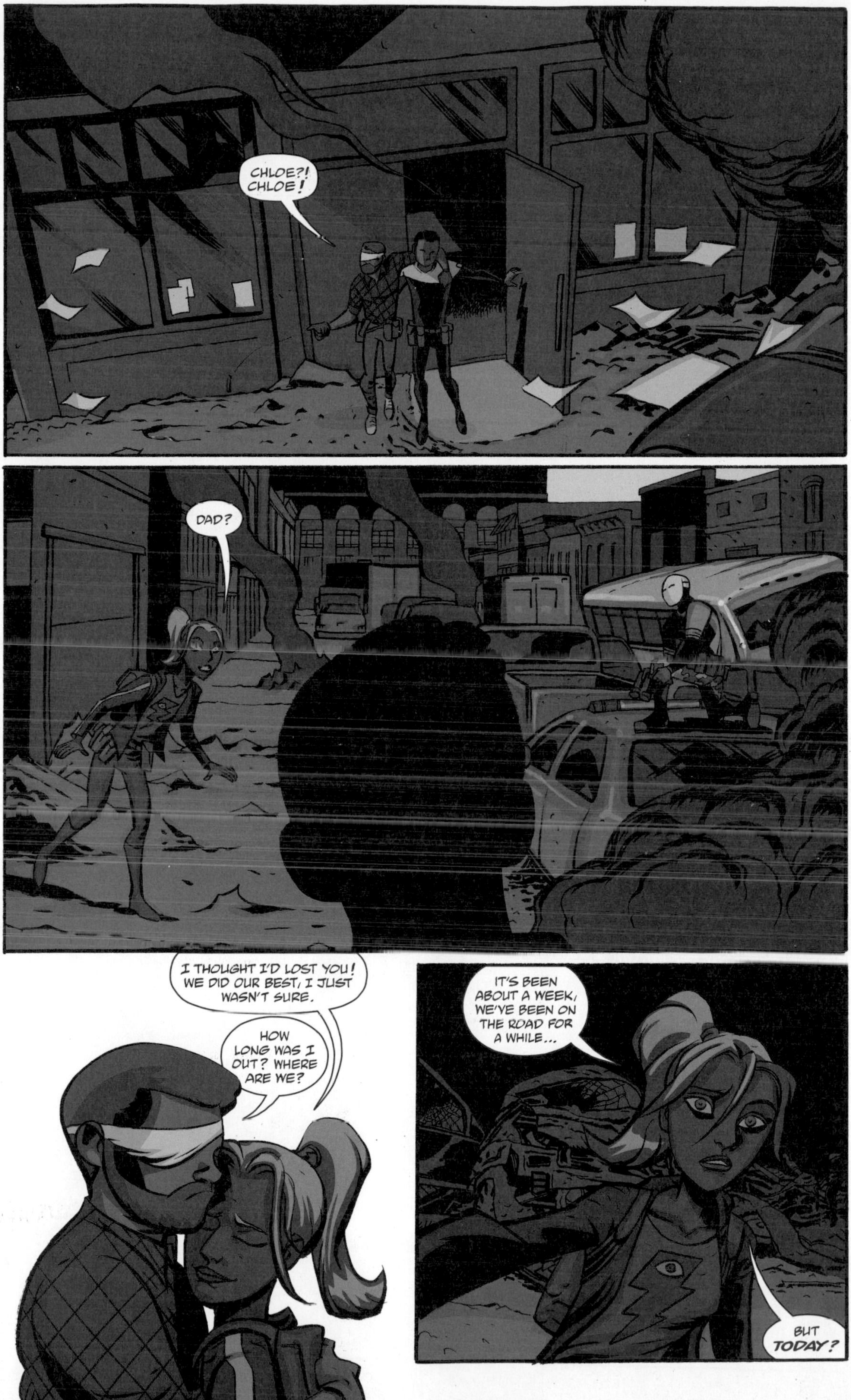
CHLOE?! CHLOE!
DAD?
I THOUGHT I'D LOST YOU! WE DID OUR BEST, I JUST WASN'T SURE.
HOW LONG WAS I OUT? WHERE ARE WE?
IT'S BEEN ABOUT A WEEK, WE'VE BEEN ON THE ROAD FOR A WHILE...
BUT TODAY?

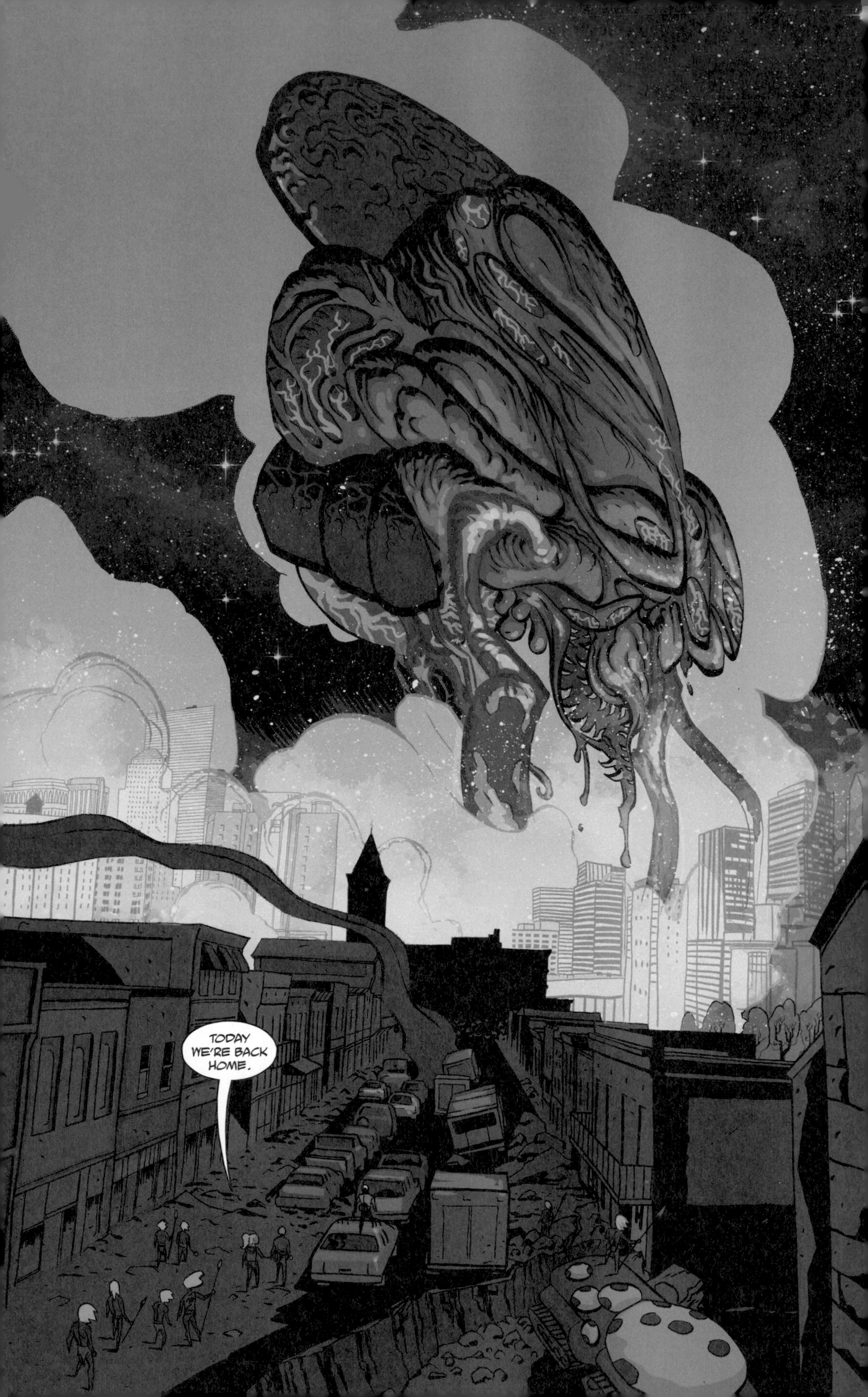
TODAY WE'RE BACK HOME.

# The Wonderful World of Rocks!

With Professor Marc Bartow

# "THE MONK PUMICE"

A porous stone infused with radioactive crystals, the pumice's crystals emit and absorb one another's energy the same way the synapses of the human brain do. Therefore, the Monk Pumice may be the world's only conscious stone, though—like its namesake—it has taken a vow of silence.

# The Universe Is Stable and Undying

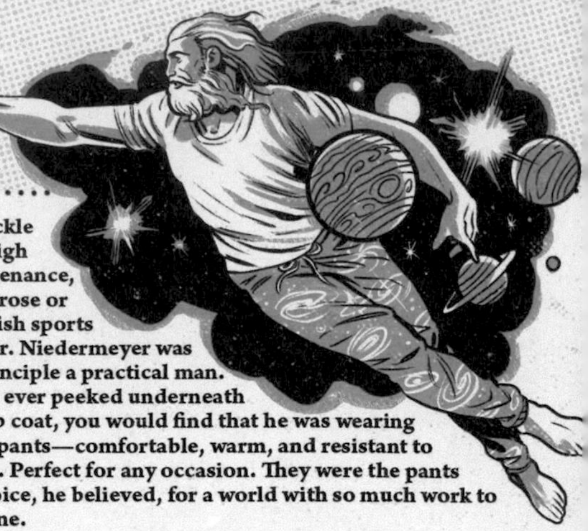

**The great** Herbert Niedermeyer died last year. He was not only a close friend, but a fellow scientist. As a geologist, I study rocks. As an astrophysicist, he also studied rocks, albeit ones hurtling through space. Before he died, we had planned to write a book together called, *Rocks and Their Relationships*, which we felt was all anyone really needed to know about the universe. I attended his funeral, even though I dislike funerals, where the genuinely bereaved mix with those pretending to be sad. I don't know who I pity more.

"We are gathered to mourn the loss of Dr. Herbert Niedermeyer," the officiating priest said. "Afterward, there will be a reception with deviled eggs."

The priest spoke a few reassuring words about the work of Dr. Niedermeyer's life being at an end, as if the work of a great mind is something to be avoided. "Only rest in perfect slumber awaits him now," the priest continued, "in a world untainted by death, the natural consequence of the corruption of man."

As one of his closest friends, I was then invited to speak. As I took the podium, I realized that my dear friend lie in a coffin made from marbled black onyx. He would have hated that. He found onyx to be beautiful, but fickle and high maintenance, like a rose or a British sports car. Dr. Niedermeyer was by principle a practical man. If you ever peeked underneath his lab coat, you would find that he was wearing sweatpants—comfortable, warm, and resistant to abuse. Perfect for any occasion. They were the pants of choice, he believed, for a world with so much work to be done.

In the front pew sat his grieving widow. I briefly considered saying something to her about the coffin-gaffe, but decided against it. Instead, I stood before her and the assembled mourners and announced:

**"The universe is stable and undying."**

This is a theory Dr. Niedermeyer and I had been working on before his untimely death. I could see on their faces that they did not understand.

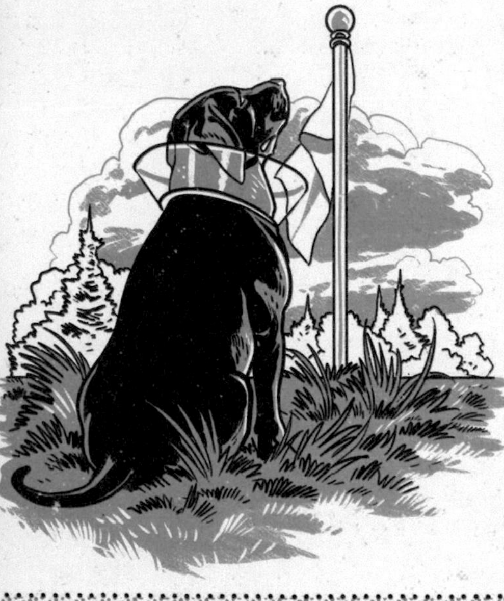

**"Imagine that you are a dog** with a cone around your head," I said. "You come to a flagpole. Because of the cone, you can only see the bottom of the flagpole, so you start there and look upward until you can see the top. Just because you can now only see the top half of the flagpole doesn't mean the base of the flagpole has ceased to exist. It's just that you are a dog with a cone around his head and this is the only way you can experience a flagpole."

**I could see they were still confused, so I explained further.**

"So it is with life. We can only experience it one moment at a time, so it appears to us as though what hasn't happened is yet to come and what has passed is no more. But this is an illusion imposed on us by the cone around our head. Our lives have always existed and always will," I told them. "The Universe is a four-dimensional object."

At this point, I could see the priest internally debating whether to intervene.

**"Humanity is a patch of fabric** in which our lives are threads, weaving together at some points, splitting off at others. The threads do not vanish merely because they have end points. It is not that Dr. Niedermeyer is gone. He has not ceased to exist. It's just that we now know where his thread ends. But his life, his work, the way his thread holds ours in place, is forever part of the four-dimensional object we call the Universe. His thread remains forever woven together with ours, deep within the sweatpants of God."

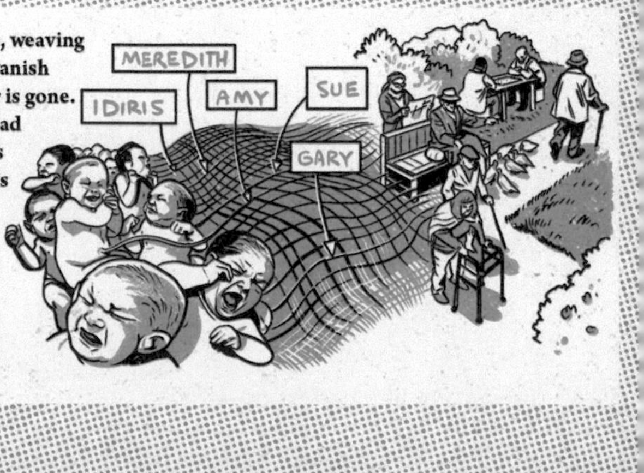
MEREDITH
IDIRIS
AMY
SUE
GARY

After my speech, the priest led us in some ridiculous hymn and then abruptly ended the service. I don't know if Herbert's widow took solace in these words, as she did not stay for the reception. But, nonetheless, I believe our theory to be wholesome and sound.

Words by Mark Russell
Art by Benjamin Dewey

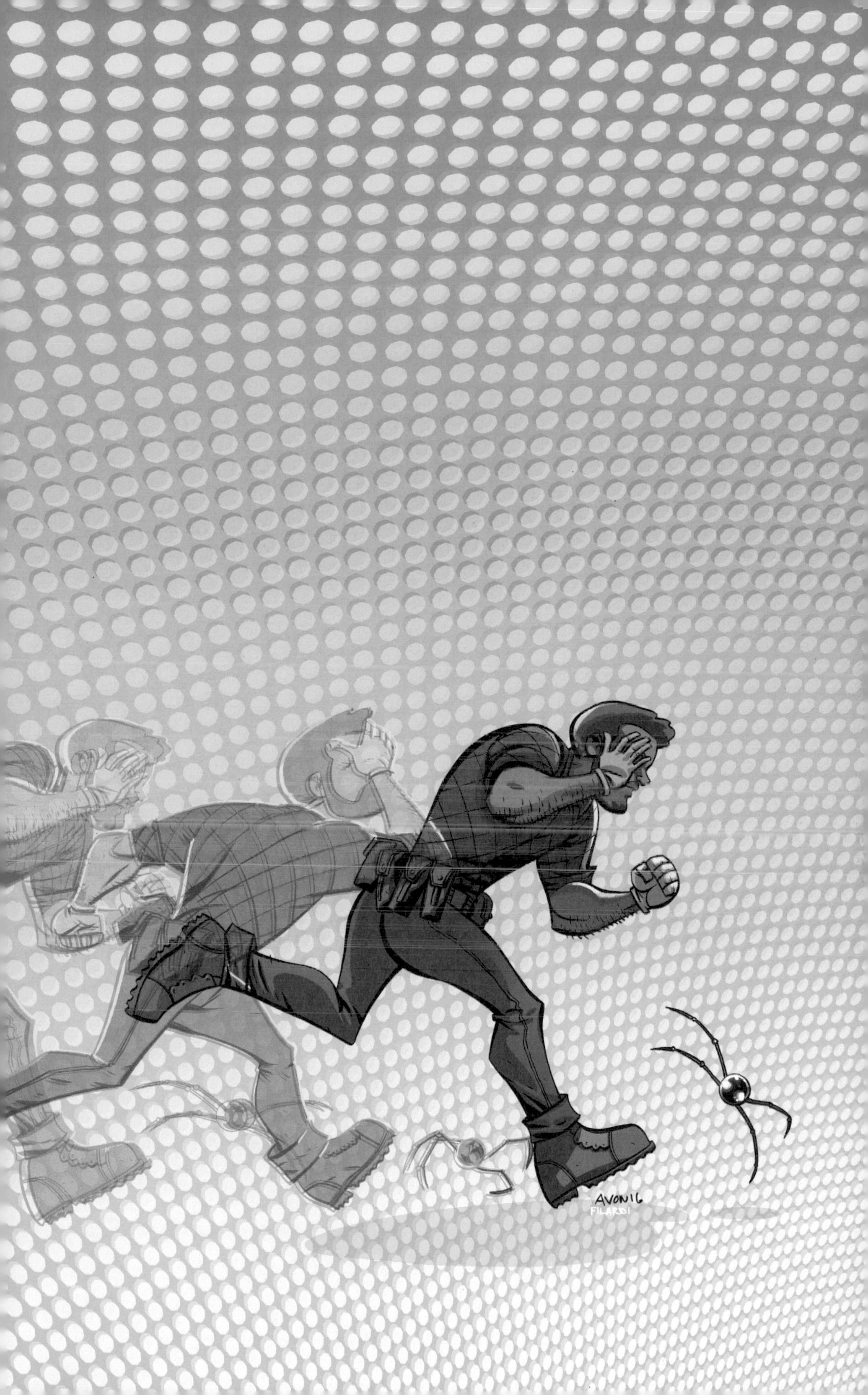
AVON 16
FILARDI

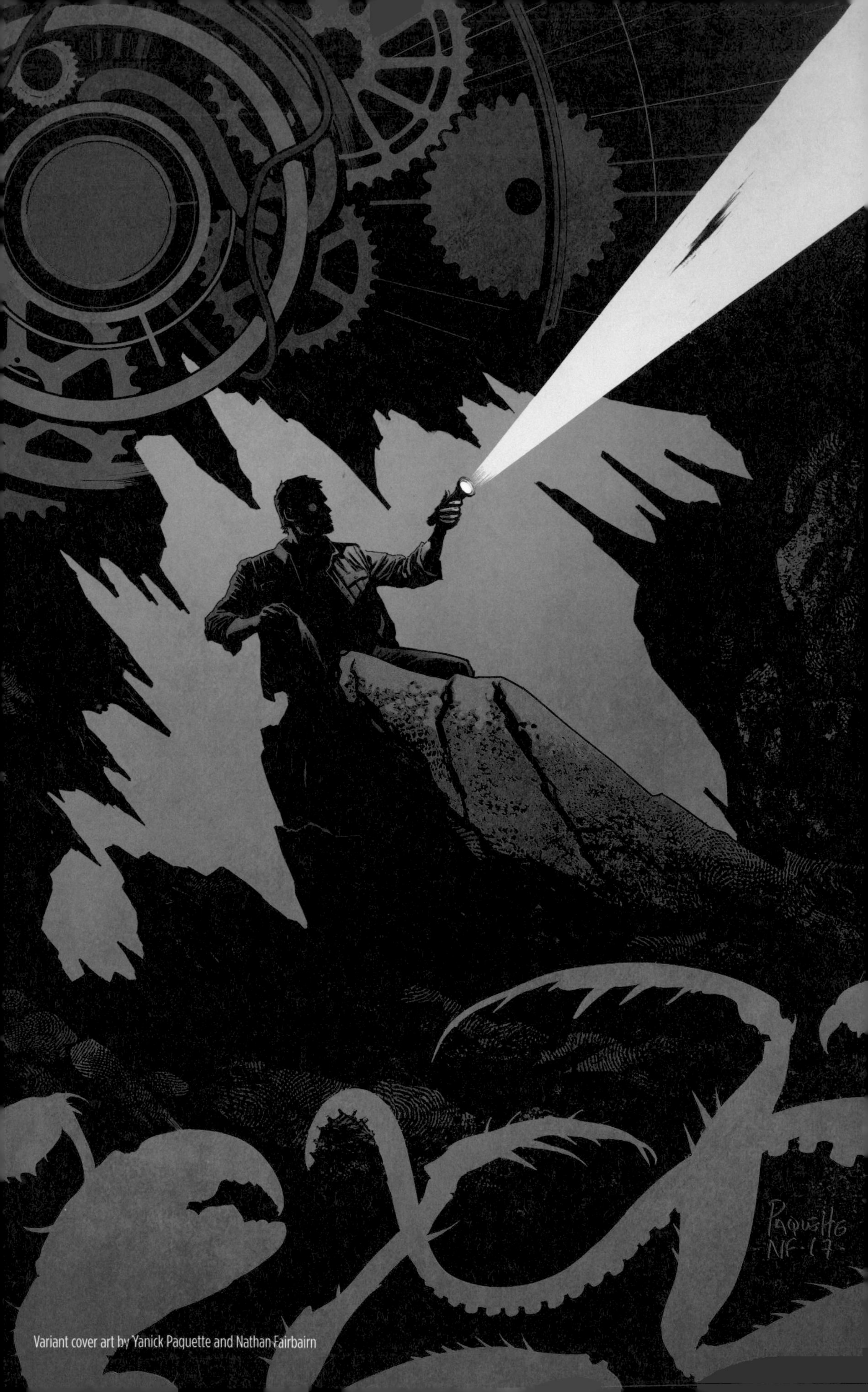
PAQUETTE
NF-17

Variant cover art by Yanick Paquette and Nathan Fairbairn

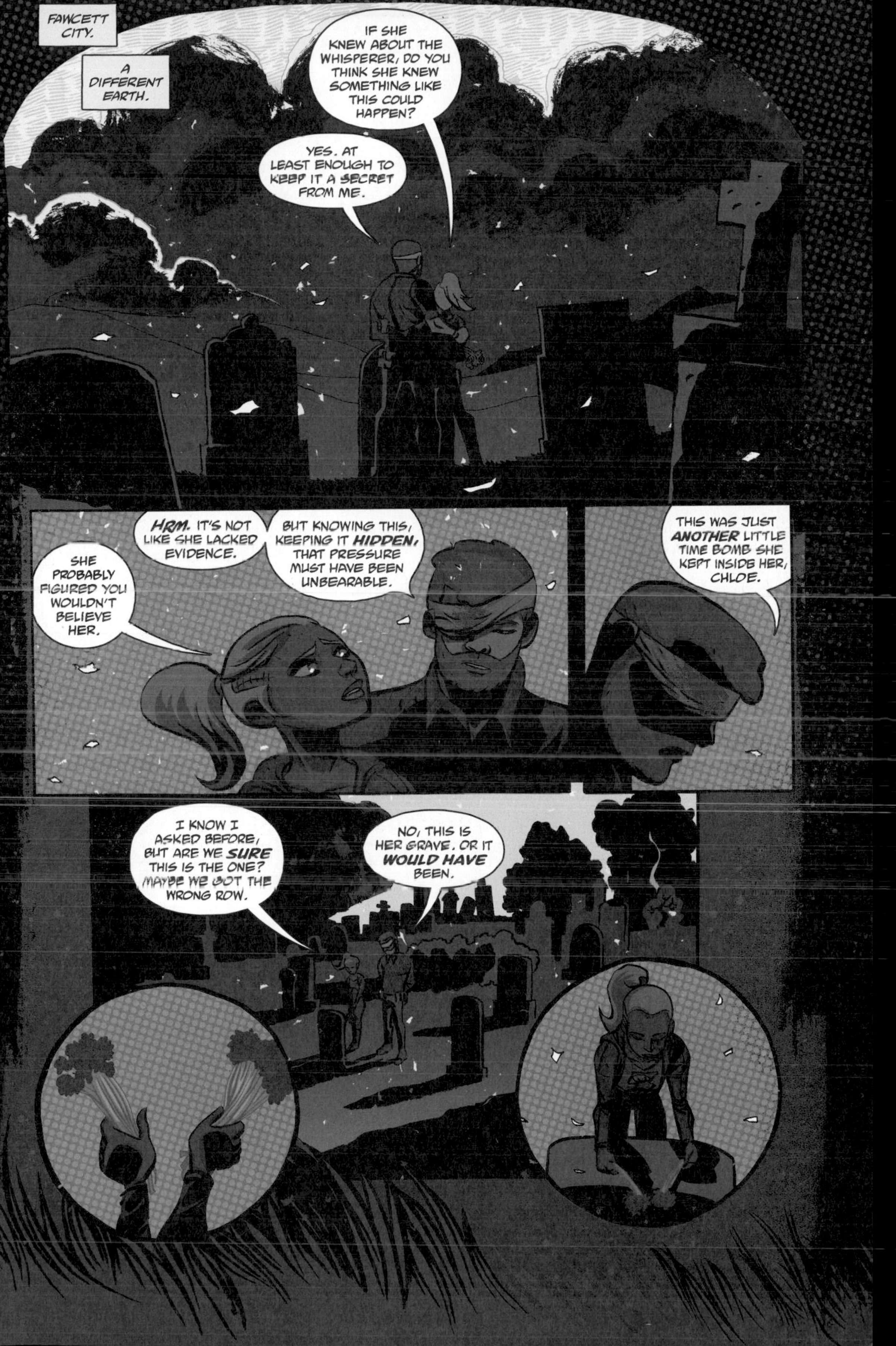
FAWCETT CITY.
A DIFFERENT EARTH.
IF SHE KNEW ABOUT THE WHISPERER, DO YOU THINK SHE KNEW SOMETHING LIKE THIS COULD HAPPEN?
YES. AT LEAST ENOUGH TO KEEP IT A SECRET FROM ME.
HRM. IT'S NOT LIKE SHE LACKED EVIDENCE.
SHE PROBABLY FIGURED YOU WOULDN'T BELIEVE HER.
BUT KNOWING THIS, KEEPING IT HIDDEN, THAT PRESSURE MUST HAVE BEEN UNBEARABLE.
THIS WAS JUST ANOTHER LITTLE TIME BOMB SHE KEPT INSIDE HER, CHLOE.
I KNOW I ASKED BEFORE, BUT ARE WE SURE THIS IS THE ONE? MAYBE WE GOT THE WRONG ROW.
NO, THIS IS HER GRAVE. OR IT WOULD HAVE BEEN.

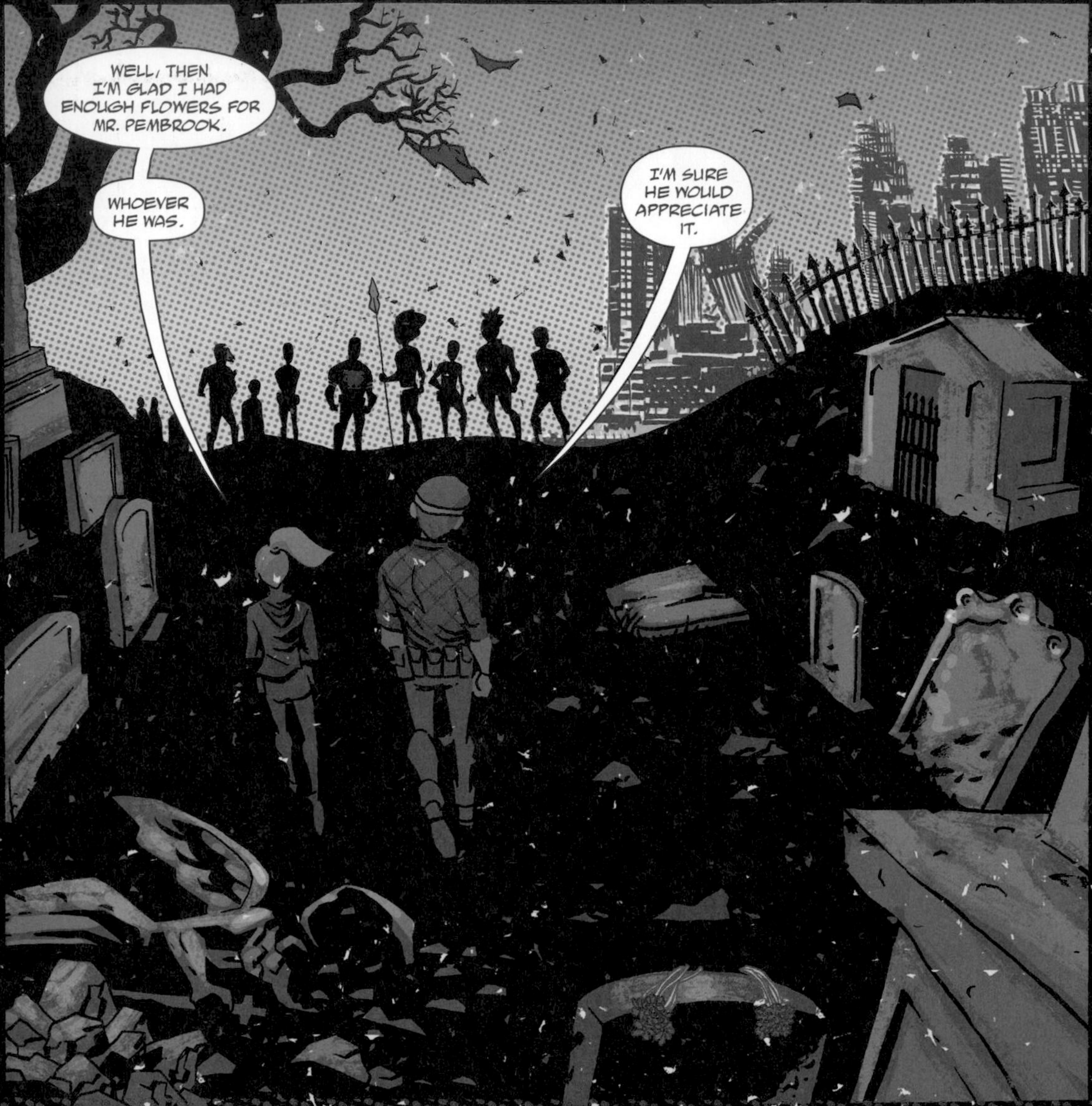
WELL, THEN I'M GLAD I HAD ENOUGH FLOWERS FOR MR. PEMBROOK.
WHOEVER HE WAS.
I'M SURE HE WOULD APPRECIATE IT.

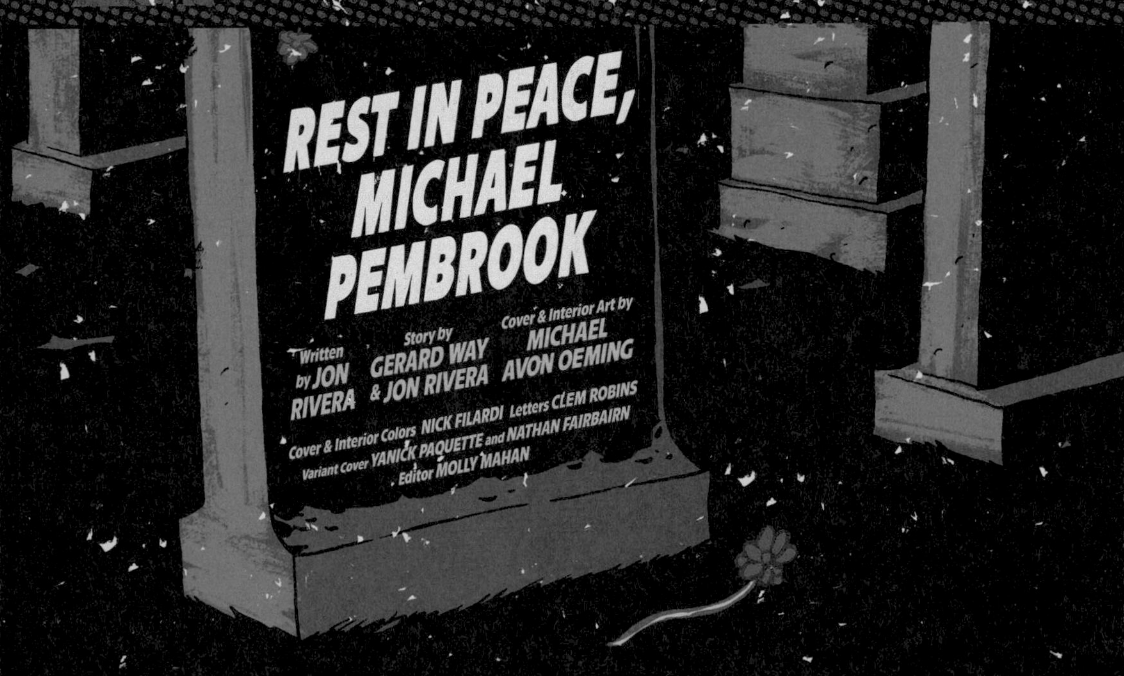
REST IN PEACE, MICHAEL PEMBROOK
Written by JON RIVERA
Story by GERARD WAY & JON RIVERA
Cover & Interior Art by MICHAEL AVON OEMING
Cover & Interior Colors NICK FILARDI Letters CLEM ROBINS
Variant Cover YANICK PAQUETTE and NATHAN FAIRBAIRN
Editor MOLLY MAHAN

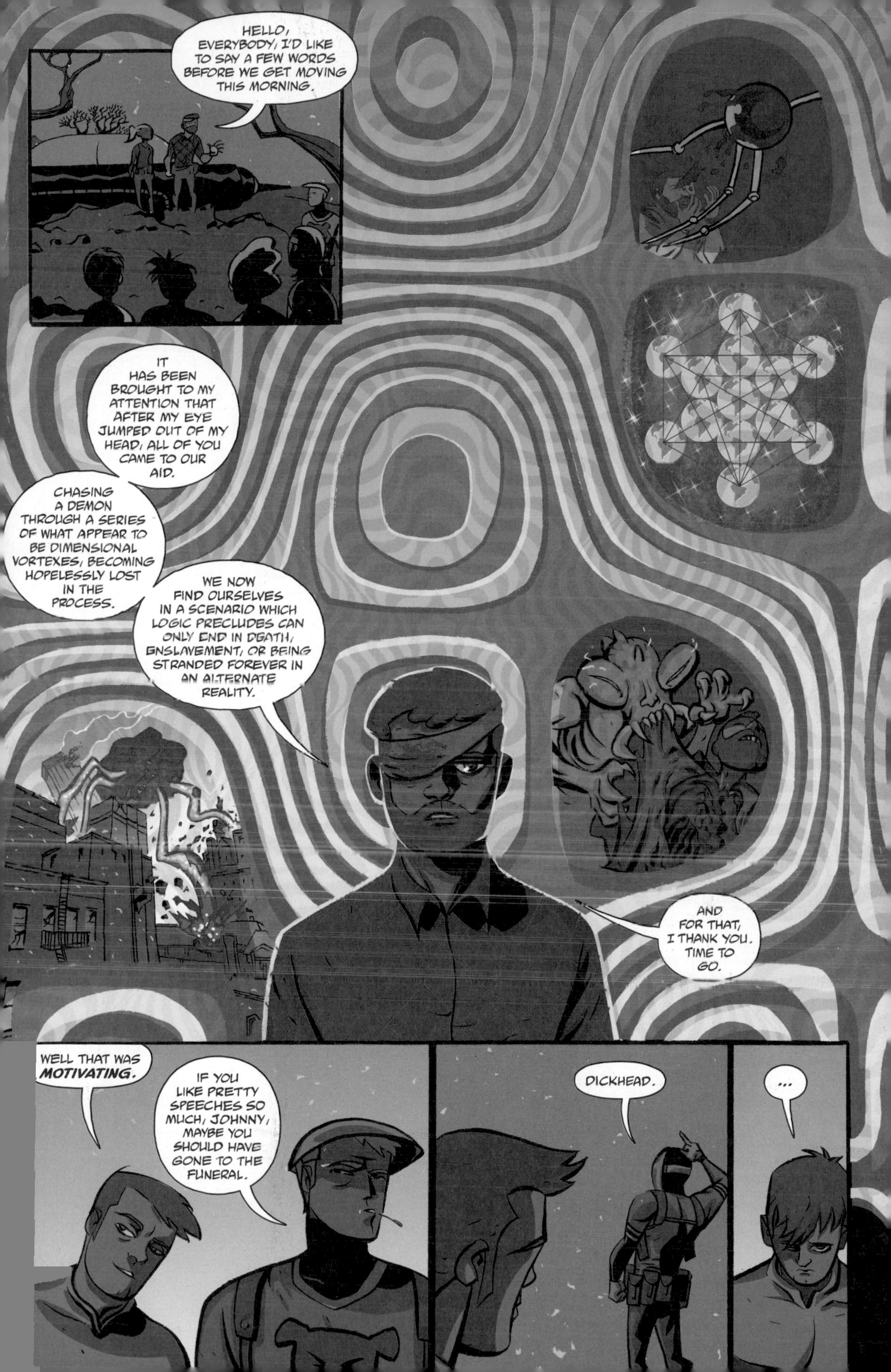
HELLO, EVERYBODY, I'D LIKE TO SAY A FEW WORDS BEFORE WE GET MOVING THIS MORNING.
IT HAS BEEN BROUGHT TO MY ATTENTION THAT AFTER MY EYE JUMPED OUT OF MY HEAD, ALL OF YOU CAME TO OUR AID.
CHASING A DEMON THROUGH A SERIES OF WHAT APPEAR TO BE DIMENSIONAL VORTEXES, BECOMING HOPELESSLY LOST IN THE PROCESS.
WE NOW FIND OURSELVES IN A SCENARIO WHICH LOGIC PRECLUDES CAN ONLY END IN DEATH, ENSLAVEMENT, OR BEING STRANDED FOREVER IN AN ALTERNATE REALITY.
AND FOR THAT, I THANK YOU. TIME TO GO.
WELL THAT WAS *MOTIVATING.*
IF YOU LIKE PRETTY SPEECHES SO MUCH, JOHNNY, MAYBE YOU SHOULD HAVE GONE TO THE FUNERAL.
DICKHEAD.
...

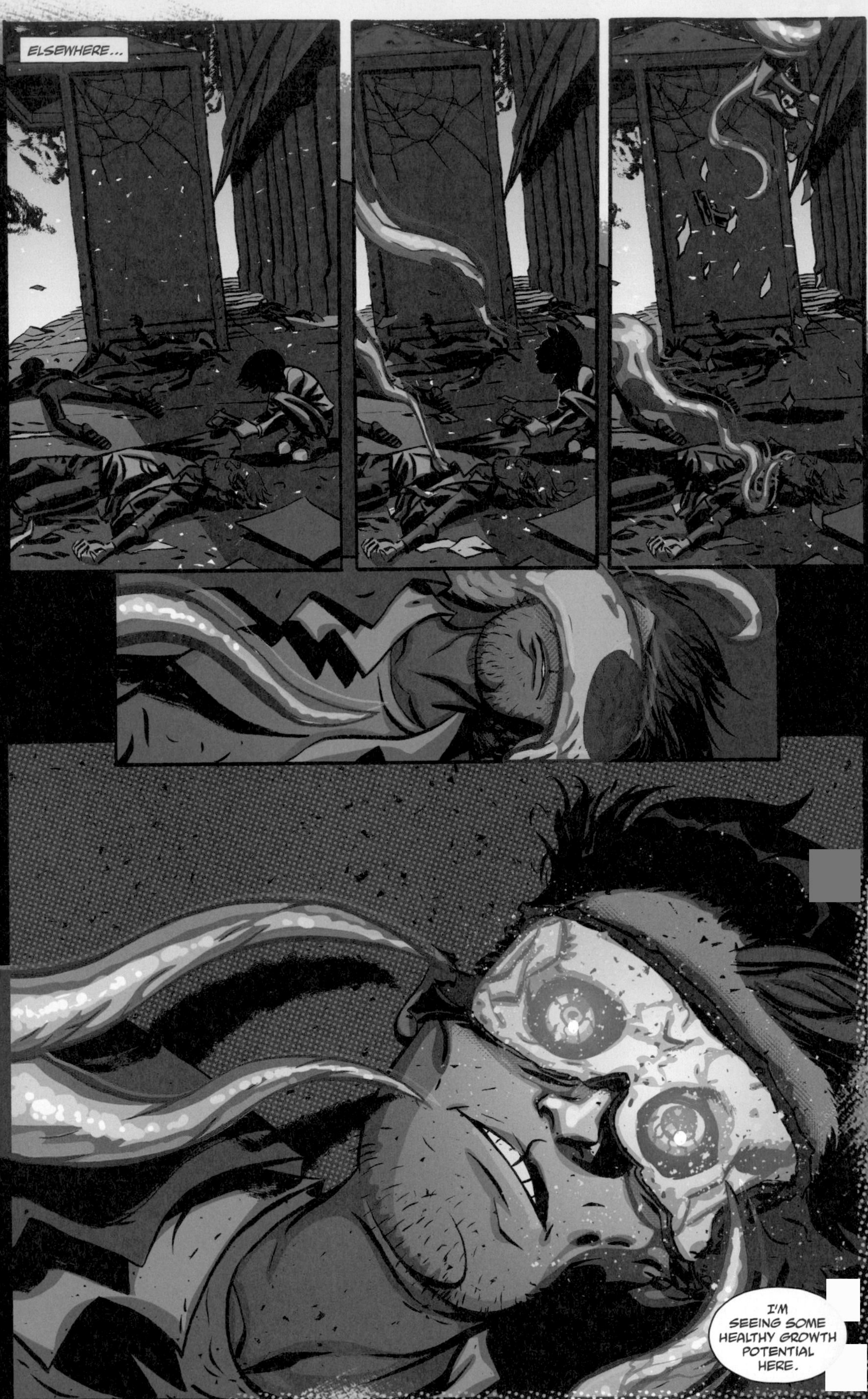
ELSEWHERE...
I'M SEEING SOME HEALTHY GROWTH POTENTIAL HERE.

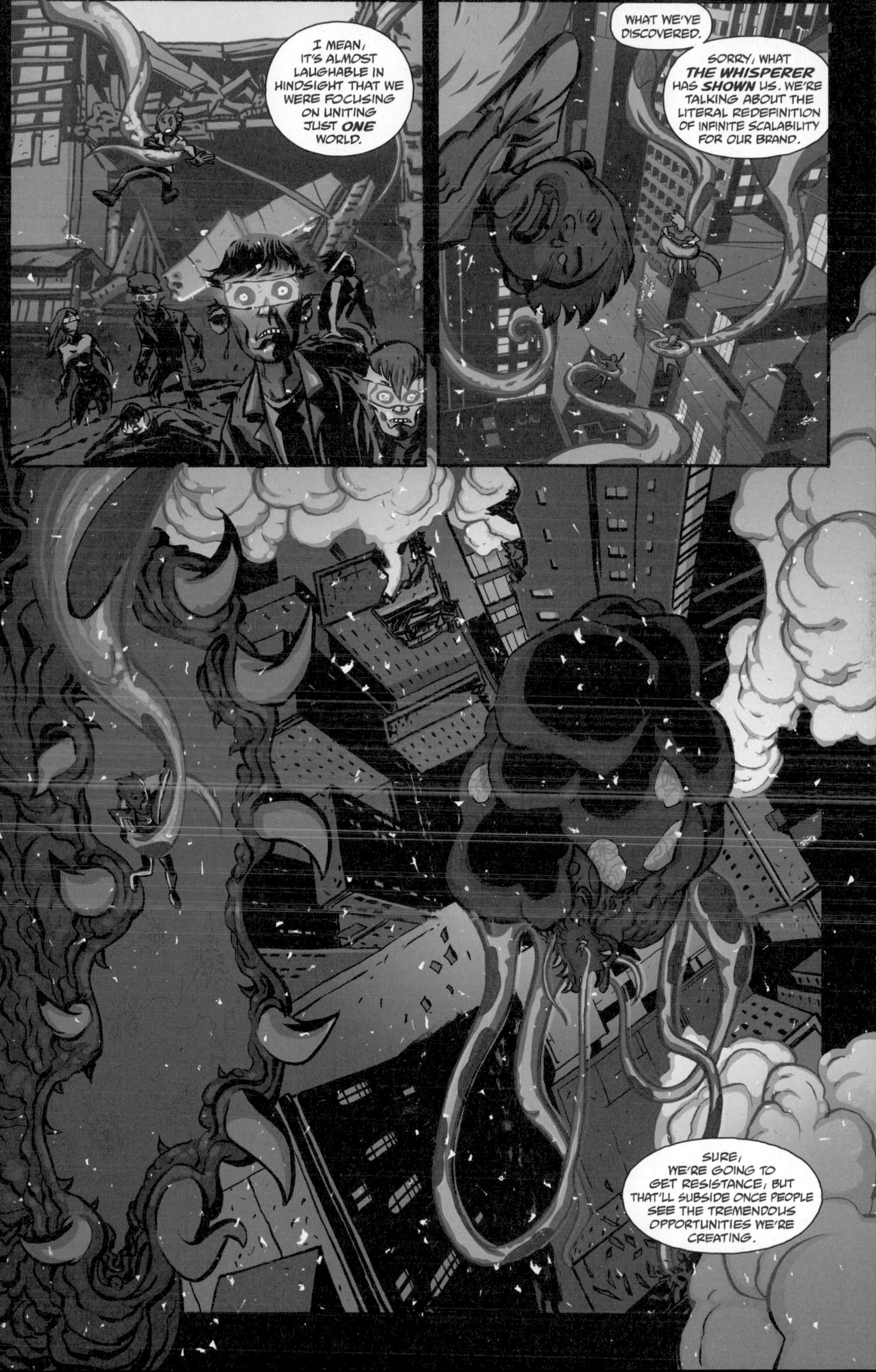
I MEAN, IT'S ALMOST LAUGHABLE IN HINDSIGHT THAT WE WERE FOCUSING ON UNITING JUST ONE WORLD.
WHAT WE'VE DISCOVERED.
SORRY, WHAT THE WHISPERER HAS SHOWN US. WE'RE TALKING ABOUT THE LITERAL REDEFINITION OF INFINITE SCALABILITY FOR OUR BRAND.
SURE, WE'RE GOING TO GET RESISTANCE, BUT THAT'LL SUBSIDE ONCE PEOPLE SEE THE TREMENDOUS OPPORTUNITIES WE'RE CREATING.

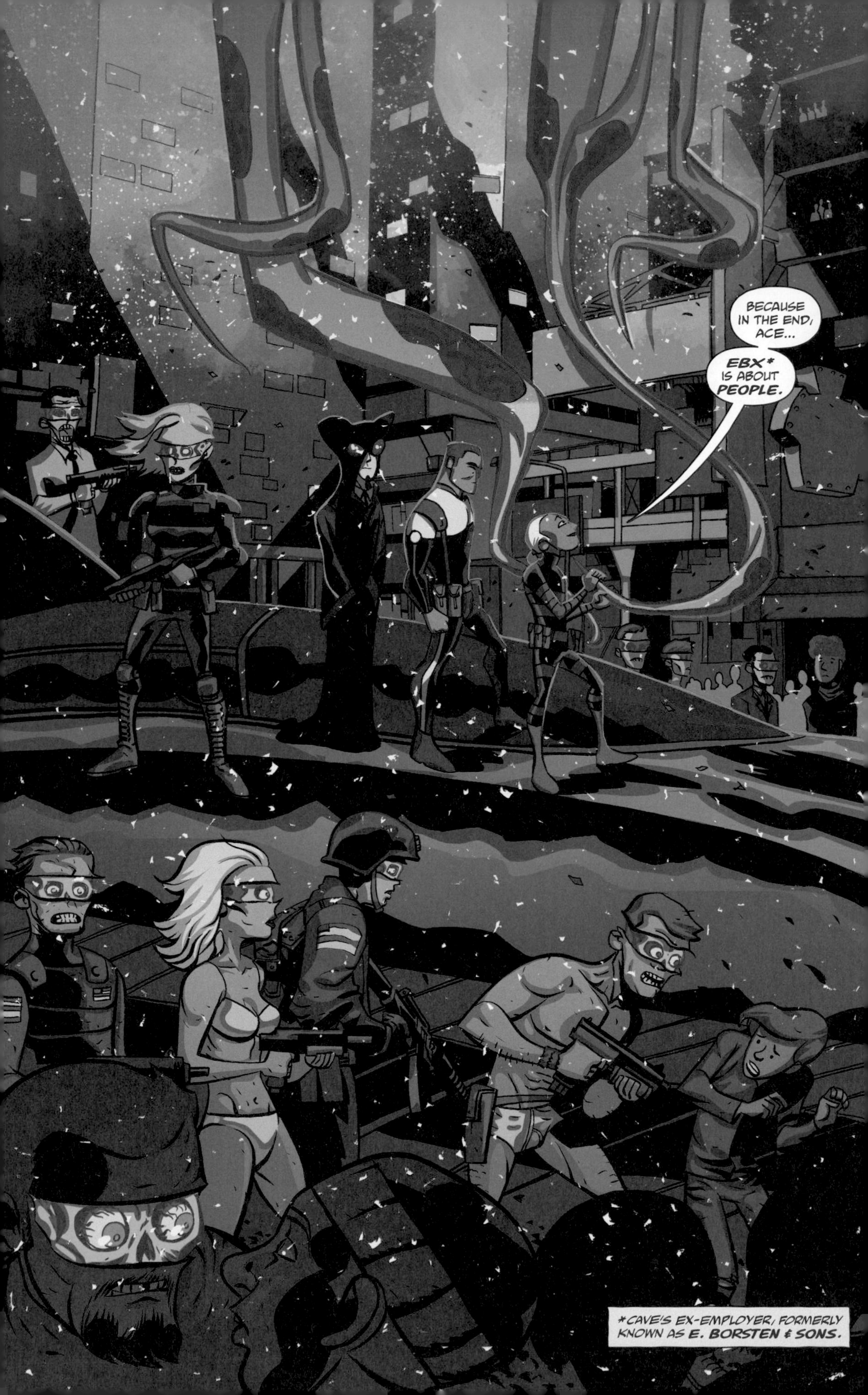
BECAUSE IN THE END, ACE...
EBX* IS ABOUT PEOPLE.
*CAVE'S EX-EMPLOYER, FORMERLY KNOWN AS E. BORSTEN & SONS.

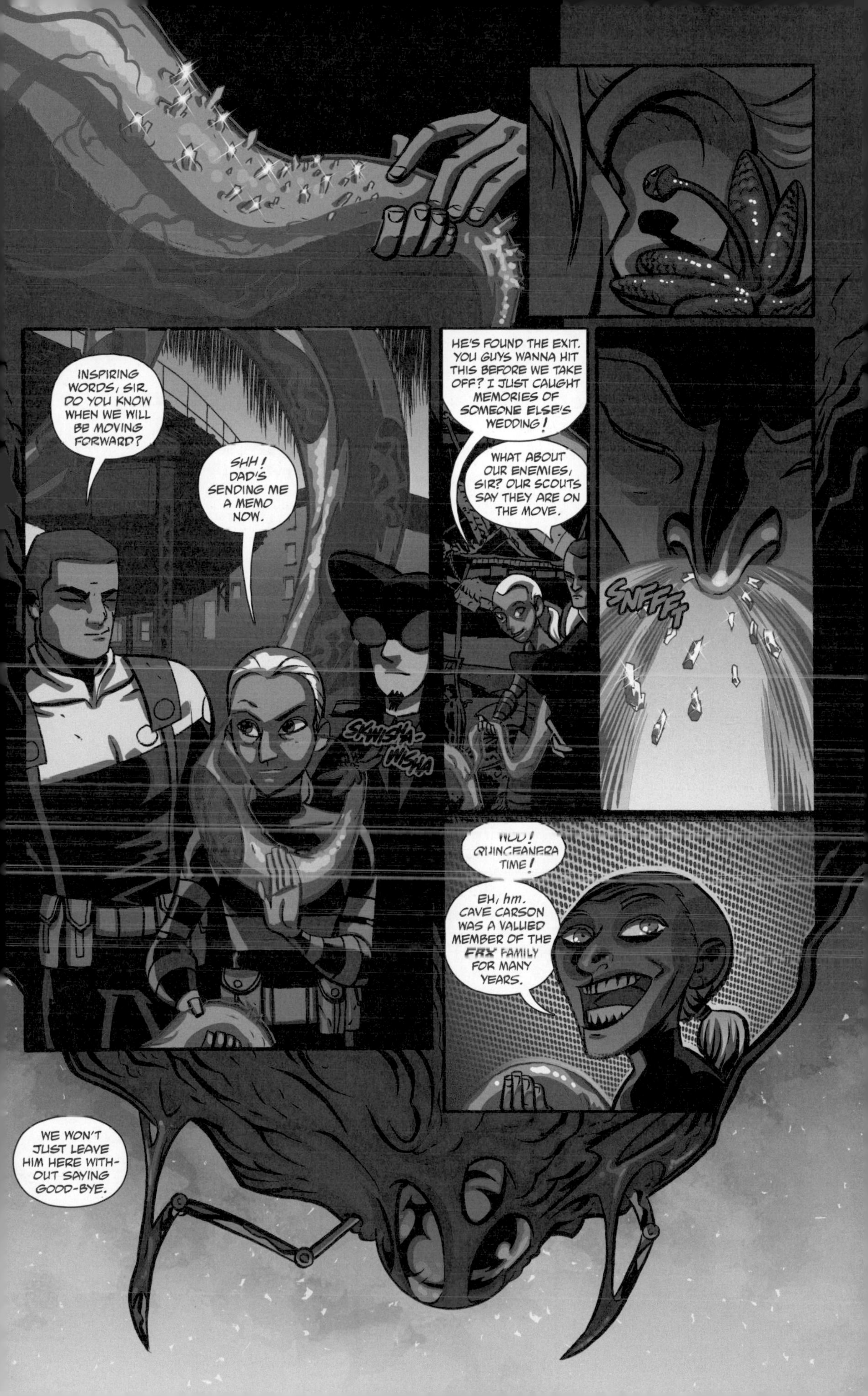
INSPIRING WORDS, SIR. DO YOU KNOW WHEN WE WILL BE MOVING FORWARD?
SHH! DAD'S SENDING ME A MEMO NOW.
SKWISHA-WISHA
HE'S FOUND THE EXIT. YOU GUYS WANNA HIT THIS BEFORE WE TAKE OFF? I JUST CAUGHT MEMORIES OF SOMEONE ELSE'S WEDDING!
WHAT ABOUT OUR ENEMIES, SIR? OUR SCOUTS SAY THEY ARE ON THE MOVE.
SNFFFT
WOO! QUINCEAÑERA TIME!
EH, hm. CAVE CARSON WAS A VALUED MEMBER OF THE ERX FAMILY FOR MANY YEARS.
WE WON'T JUST LEAVE HIM HERE WITHOUT SAYING GOOD-BYE.

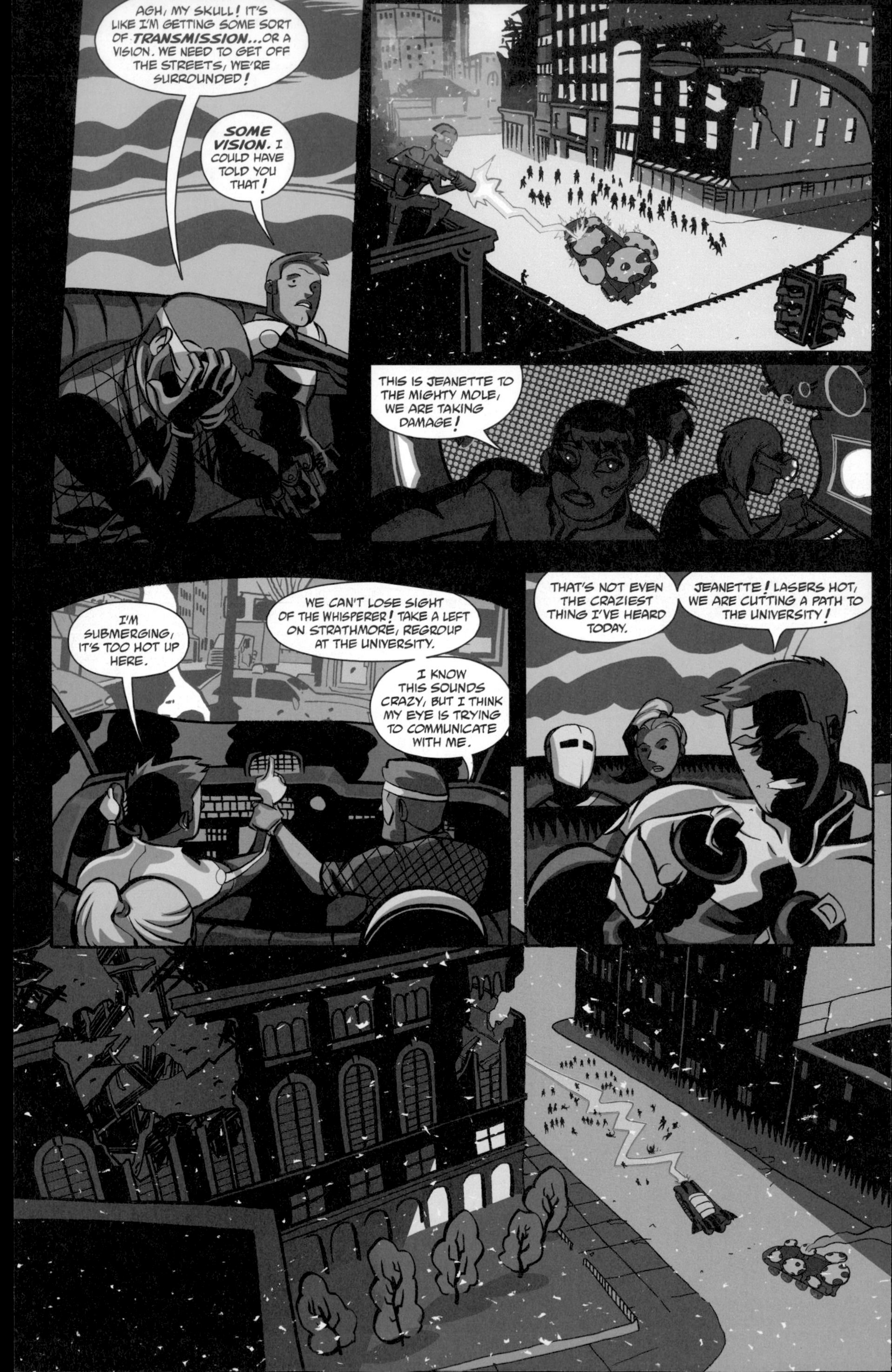
AGH, MY SKULL! IT'S LIKE I'M GETTING SOME SORT OF TRANSMISSION...OR A VISION. WE NEED TO GET OFF THE STREETS, WE'RE SURROUNDED!
SOME VISION. I COULD HAVE TOLD YOU THAT!
THIS IS JEANETTE TO THE MIGHTY MOLE, WE ARE TAKING DAMAGE!
I'M SUBMERGING, IT'S TOO HOT UP HERE.
WE CAN'T LOSE SIGHT OF THE WHISPERER! TAKE A LEFT ON STRATHMORE, REGROUP AT THE UNIVERSITY.
I KNOW THIS SOUNDS CRAZY, BUT I THINK MY EYE IS TRYING TO COMMUNICATE WITH ME.
THAT'S NOT EVEN THE CRAZIEST THING I'VE HEARD TODAY.
JEANETTE! LASERS HOT, WE ARE CUTTING A PATH TO THE UNIVERSITY!

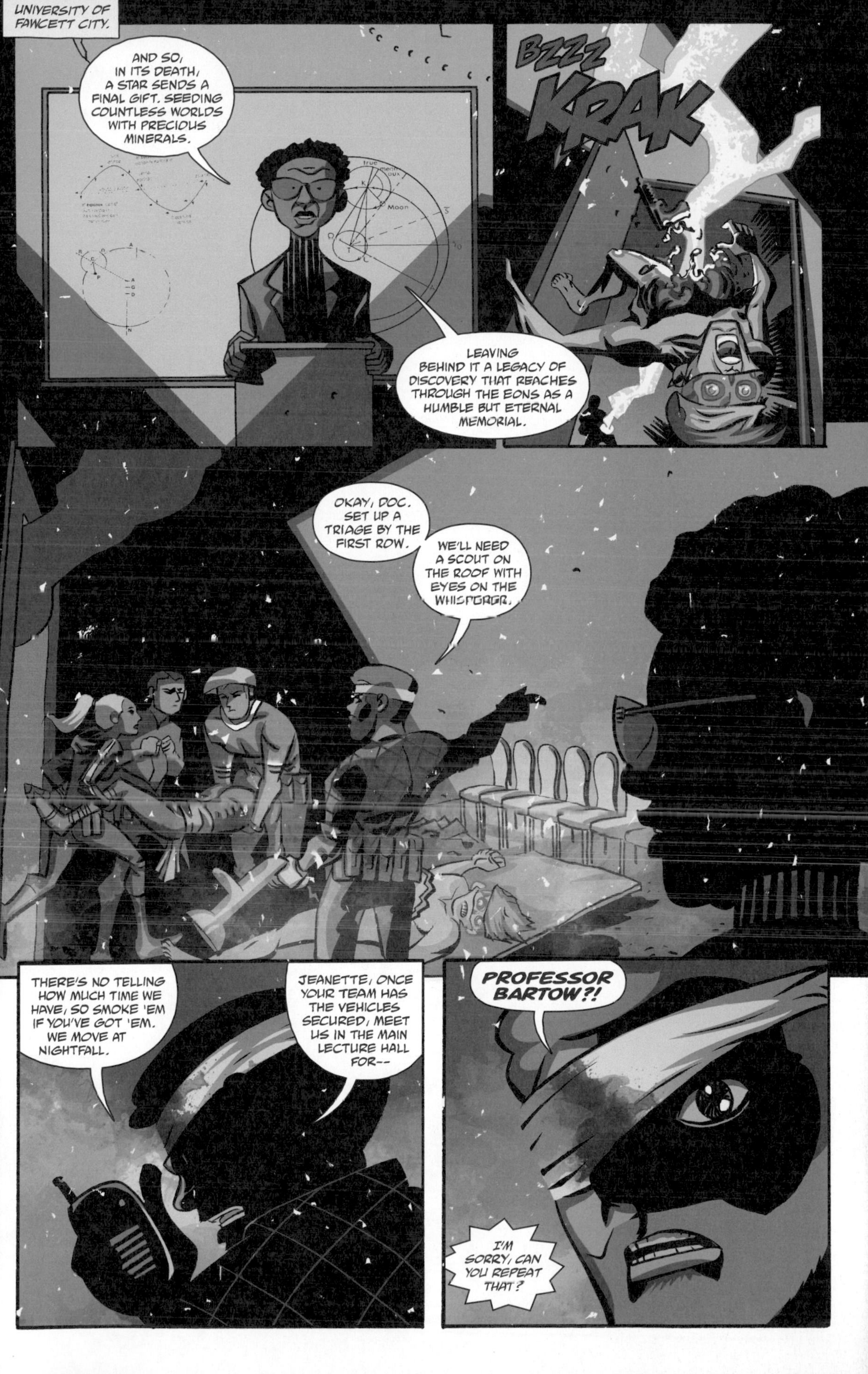
UNIVERSITY OF FAWCETT CITY.
AND SO, IN ITS DEATH, A STAR SENDS A FINAL GIFT. SEEDING COUNTLESS WORLDS WITH PRECIOUS MINERALS.
BZZZ
KRAK
LEAVING BEHIND IT A LEGACY OF DISCOVERY THAT REACHES THROUGH THE EONS AS A HUMBLE BUT ETERNAL MEMORIAL.
OKAY, DOC. SET UP A TRIAGE BY THE FIRST ROW.
WE'LL NEED A SCOUT ON THE ROOF WITH EYES ON THE WHISPERER.
THERE'S NO TELLING HOW MUCH TIME WE HAVE, SO SMOKE 'EM IF YOU'VE GOT 'EM. WE MOVE AT NIGHTFALL.
JEANETTE, ONCE YOUR TEAM HAS THE VEHICLES SECURED, MEET US IN THE MAIN LECTURE HALL FOR--
PROFESSOR BARTOW?!
I'M SORRY, CAN YOU REPEAT THAT?

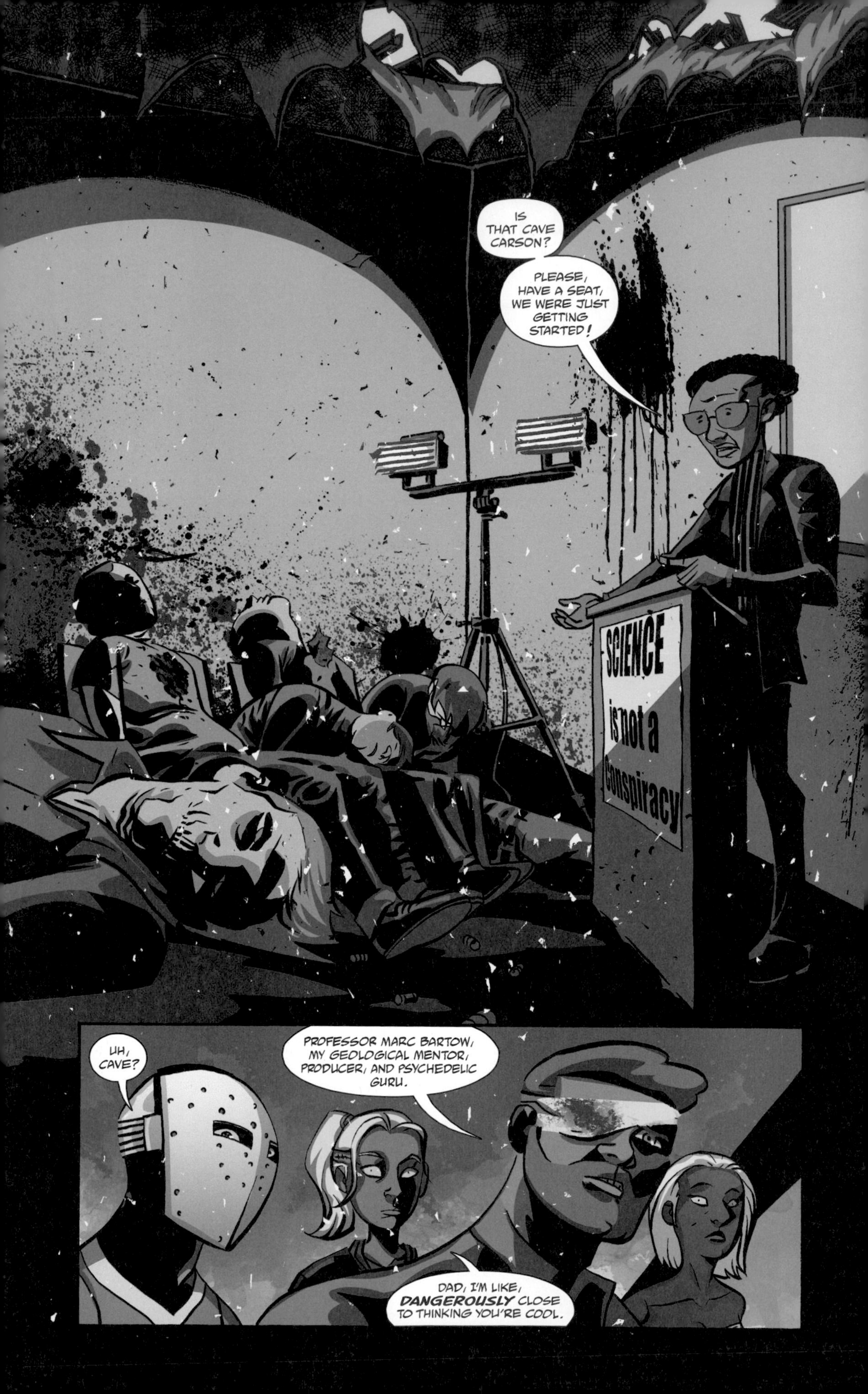

IS THAT CAVE CARSON?
PLEASE, HAVE A SEAT, WE WERE JUST GETTING STARTED!
SCIENCE is not a Conspiracy
UH, CAVE?
PROFESSOR MARC BARTOW, MY GEOLOGICAL MENTOR, PRODUCER, AND PSYCHEDELIC GURU.
DAD, I'M LIKE, DANGEROUSLY CLOSE TO THINKING YOU'RE COOL.

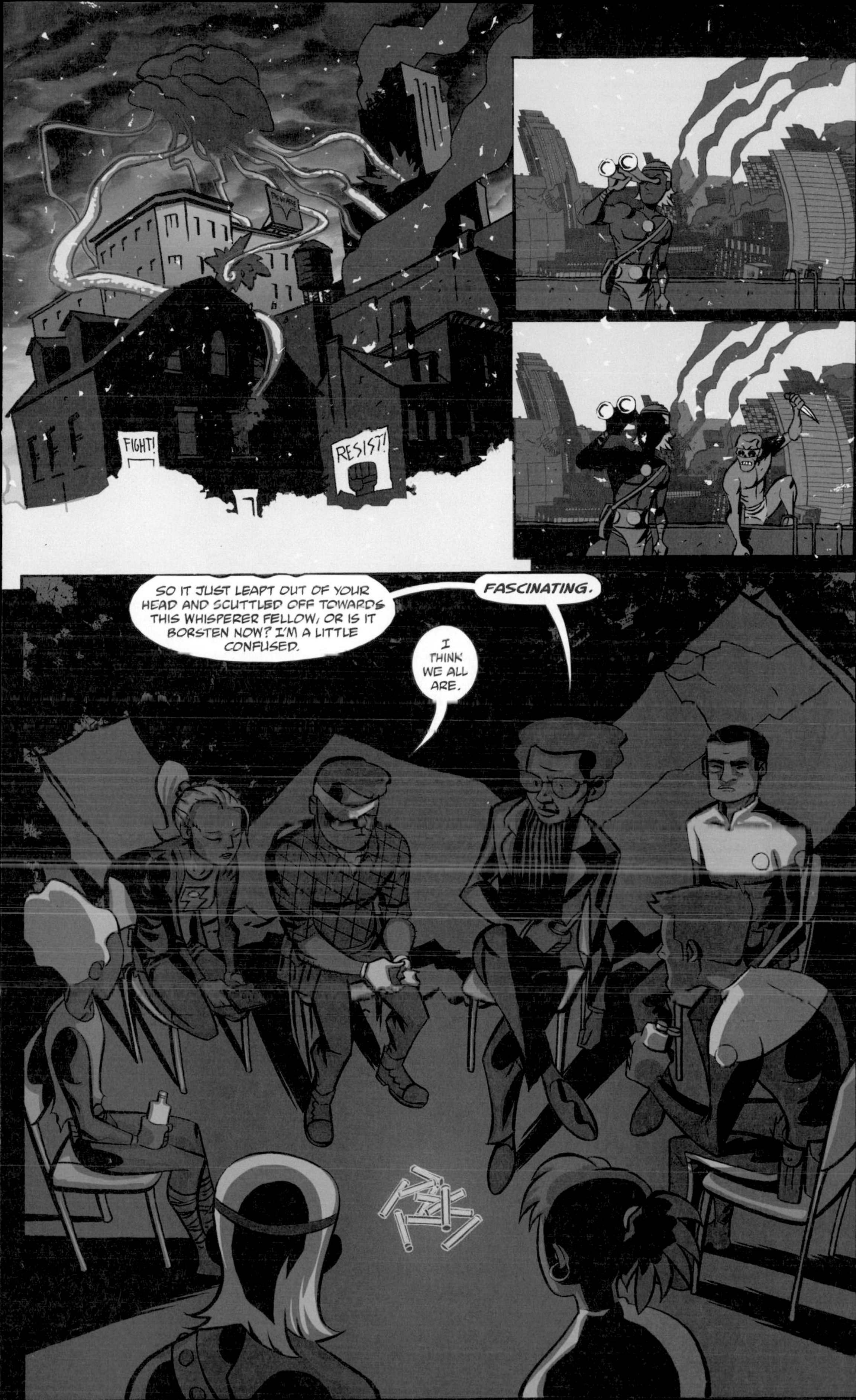
FIGHT!
RESIST!
SO IT JUST LEAPT OUT OF YOUR HEAD AND SCUTTLED OFF TOWARDS THIS WHISPERER FELLOW, OR IS IT BORSTEN NOW? I'M A LITTLE CONFUSED.
FASCINATING.
I THINK WE ALL ARE.

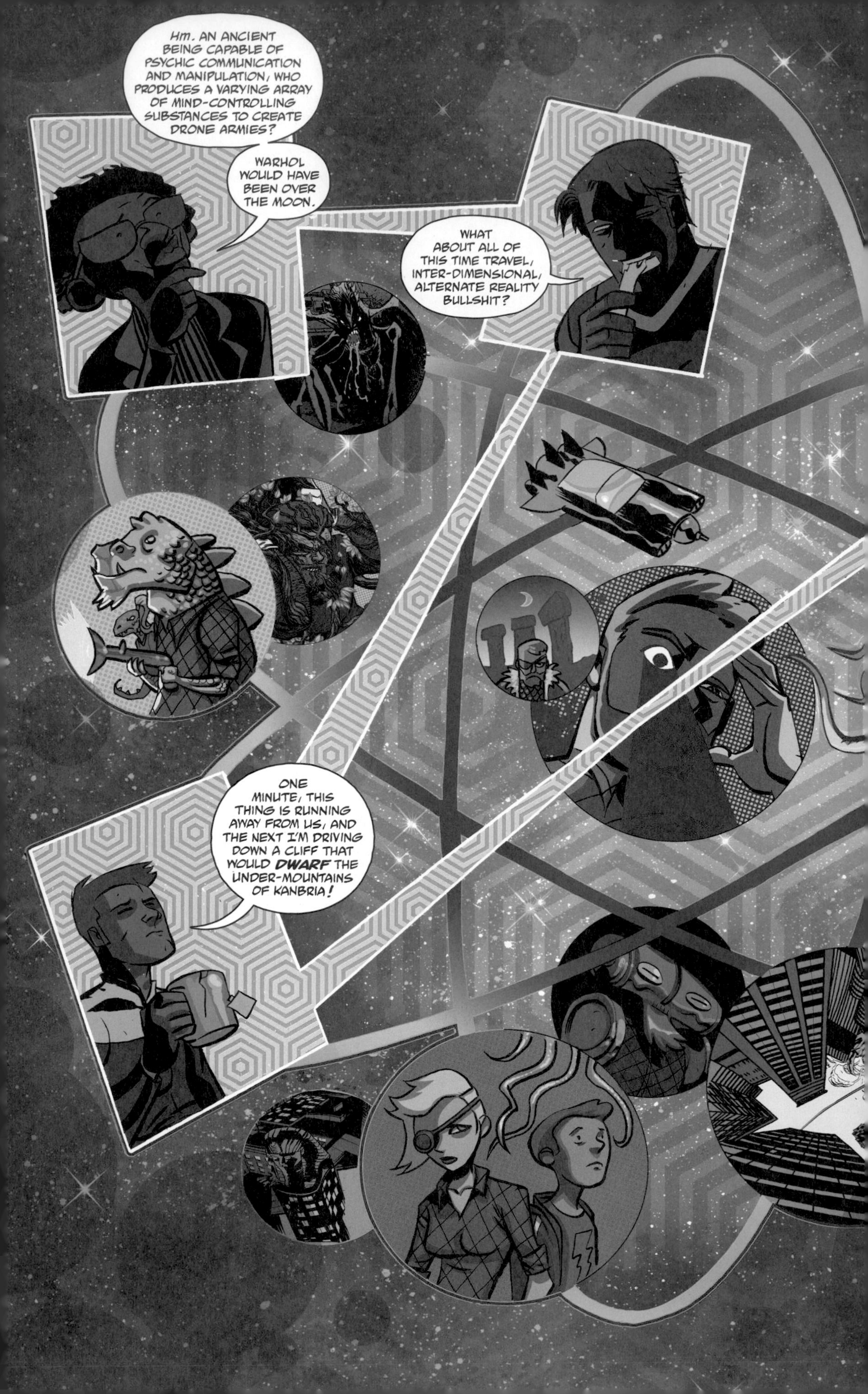
Hm. AN ANCIENT BEING CAPABLE OF PSYCHIC COMMUNICATION AND MANIPULATION, WHO PRODUCES A VARYING ARRAY OF MIND-CONTROLLING SUBSTANCES TO CREATE DRONE ARMIES?
WARHOL WOULD HAVE BEEN OVER THE MOON.
WHAT ABOUT ALL OF THIS TIME TRAVEL, INTER-DIMENSIONAL, ALTERNATE REALITY BULLSHIT?
ONE MINUTE, THIS THING IS RUNNING AWAY FROM US, AND THE NEXT I'M DRIVING DOWN A CLIFF THAT WOULD DWARF THE UNDER-MOUNTAINS OF KANBRIA!

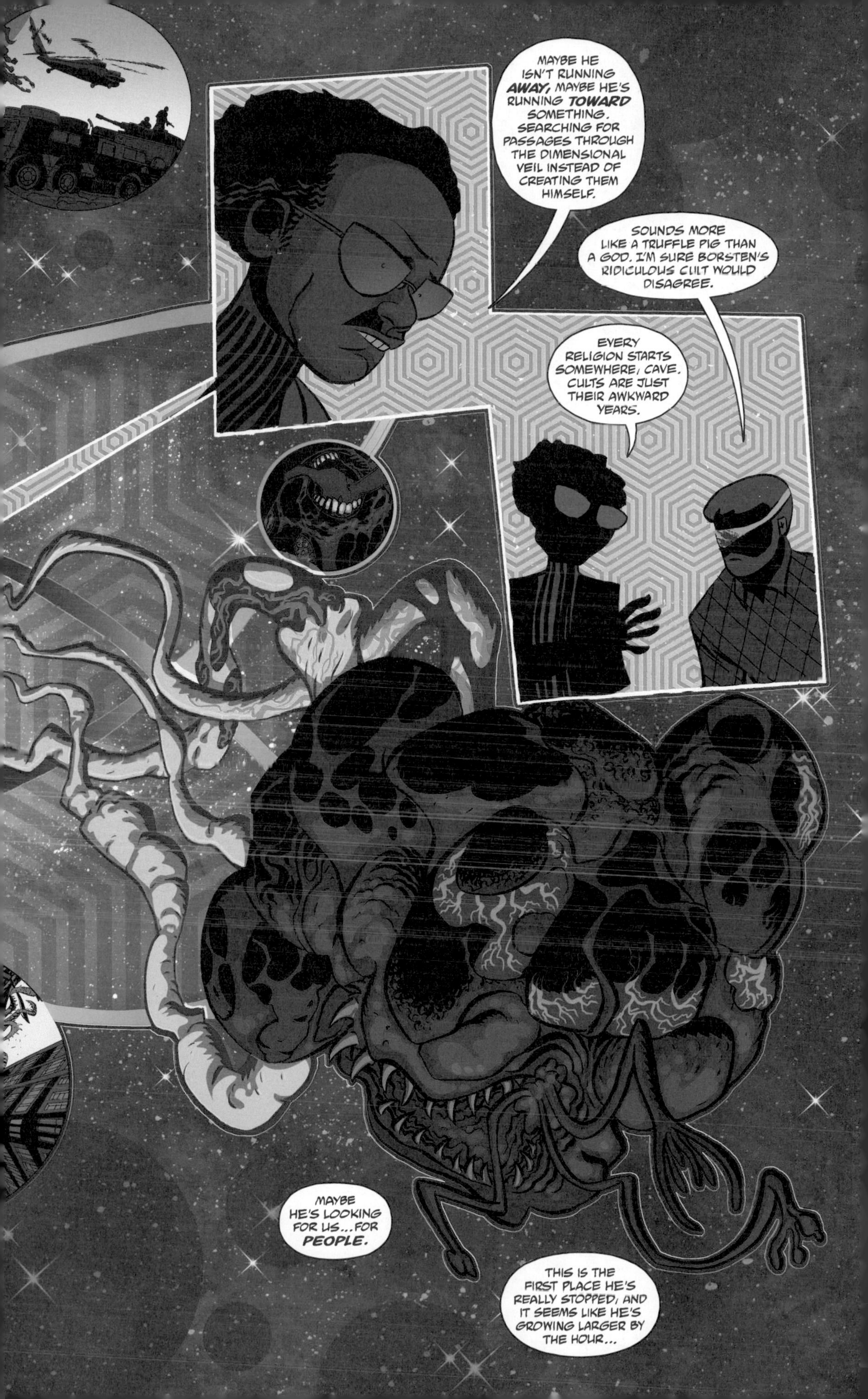
MAYBE HE ISN'T RUNNING **AWAY,** MAYBE HE'S RUNNING **TOWARD** SOMETHING. SEARCHING FOR PASSAGES THROUGH THE DIMENSIONAL VEIL INSTEAD OF CREATING THEM HIMSELF.
SOUNDS MORE LIKE A TRUFFLE PIG THAN A GOD. I'M SURE BORSTEN'S RIDICULOUS CULT WOULD DISAGREE.
EVERY RELIGION STARTS SOMEWHERE, CAVE. CULTS ARE JUST THEIR AWKWARD YEARS.
MAYBE HE'S LOOKING FOR US...FOR **PEOPLE.**
THIS IS THE FIRST PLACE HE'S REALLY STOPPED, AND IT SEEMS LIKE HE'S GROWING LARGER BY THE HOUR...

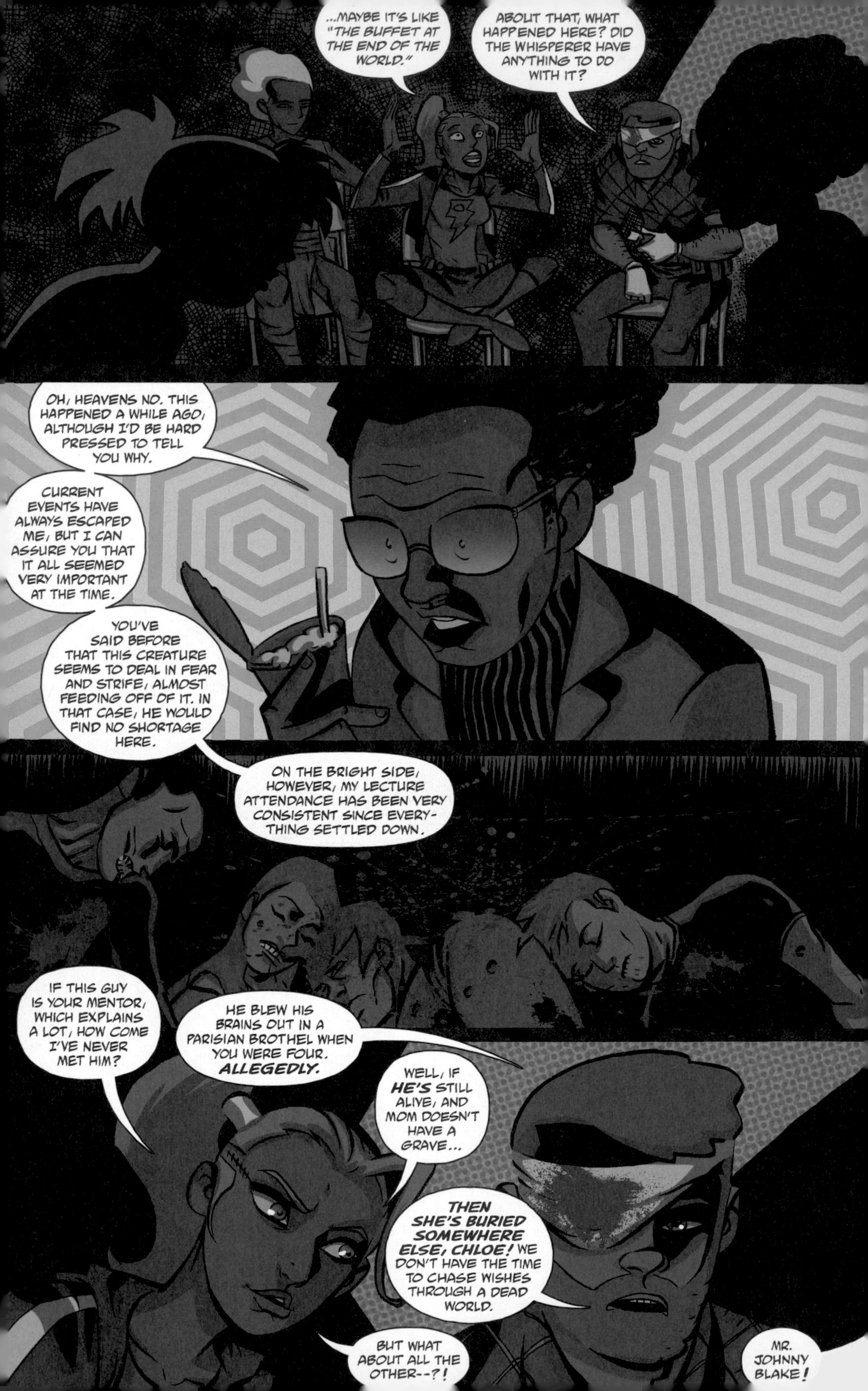
...MAYBE IT'S LIKE "THE BUFFET AT THE END OF THE WORLD."
ABOUT THAT, WHAT HAPPENED HERE? DID THE WHISPERER HAVE ANYTHING TO DO WITH IT?
OH, HEAVENS NO. THIS HAPPENED A WHILE AGO, ALTHOUGH I'D BE HARD PRESSED TO TELL YOU WHY.
CURRENT EVENTS HAVE ALWAYS ESCAPED ME, BUT I CAN ASSURE YOU THAT IT ALL SEEMED VERY IMPORTANT AT THE TIME.
YOU'VE SAID BEFORE THAT THIS CREATURE SEEMS TO DEAL IN FEAR AND STRIFE, ALMOST FEEDING OFF OF IT. IN THAT CASE, HE WOULD FIND NO SHORTAGE HERE.
ON THE BRIGHT SIDE, HOWEVER, MY LECTURE ATTENDANCE HAS BEEN VERY CONSISTENT SINCE EVERYTHING SETTLED DOWN.
IF THIS GUY IS YOUR MENTOR, WHICH EXPLAINS A LOT, HOW COME I'VE NEVER MET HIM?
HE BLEW HIS BRAINS OUT IN A PARISIAN BROTHEL WHEN YOU WERE FOUR. ***ALLEGEDLY.***
WELL, IF ***HE'S*** STILL ALIVE, AND MOM DOESN'T HAVE A GRAVE...
***THEN SHE'S BURIED SOMEWHERE ELSE, CHLOE!*** WE DON'T HAVE THE TIME TO CHASE WISHES THROUGH A DEAD WORLD.
BUT WHAT ABOUT ALL THE OTHER--?!
MR. JOHNNY BLAKE!

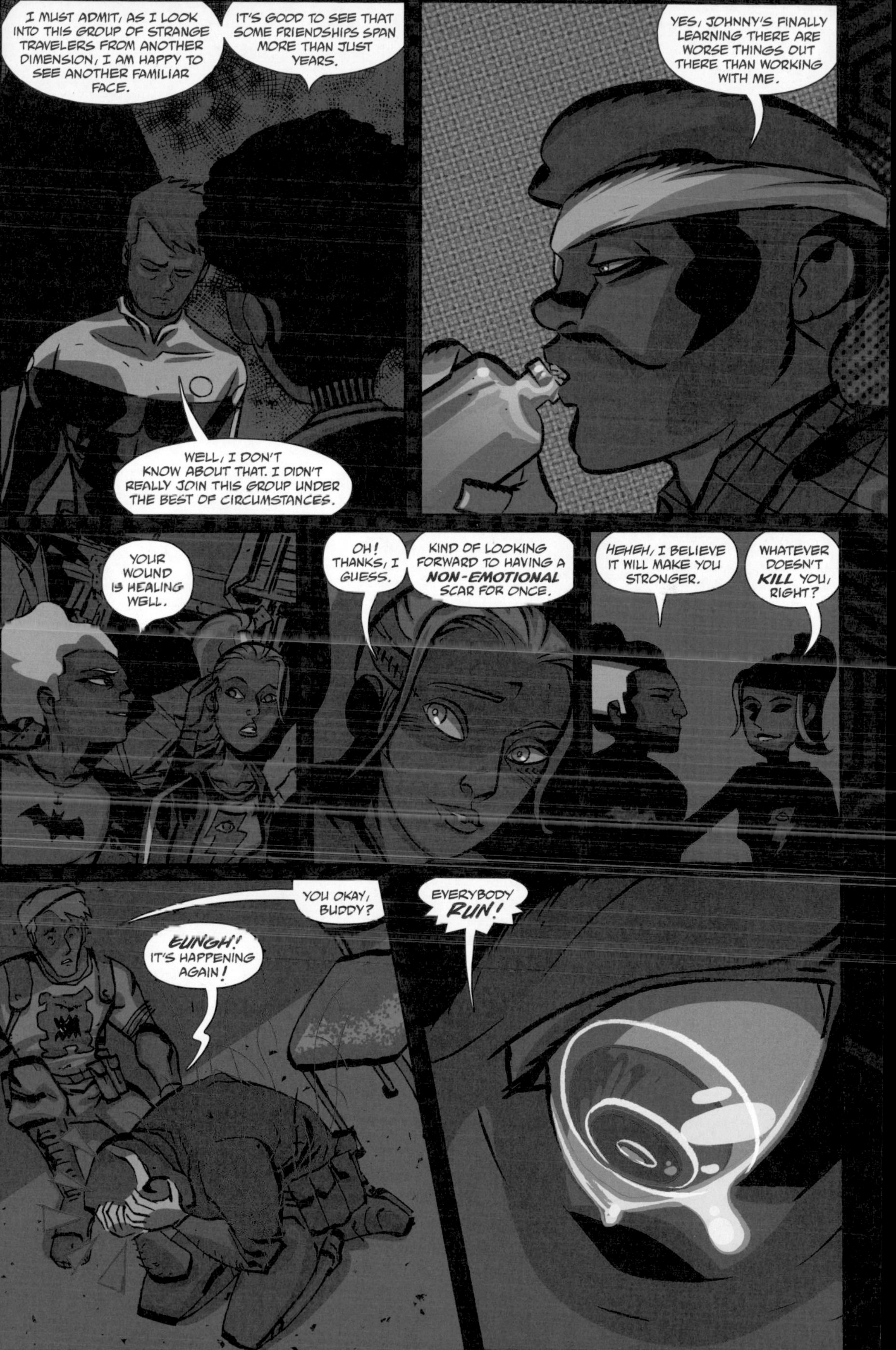
I MUST ADMIT, AS I LOOK INTO THIS GROUP OF STRANGE TRAVELERS FROM ANOTHER DIMENSION, I AM HAPPY TO SEE ANOTHER FAMILIAR FACE.
IT'S GOOD TO SEE THAT SOME FRIENDSHIPS SPAN MORE THAN JUST YEARS.
WELL, I DON'T KNOW ABOUT THAT. I DIDN'T REALLY JOIN THIS GROUP UNDER THE BEST OF CIRCUMSTANCES.
YES, JOHNNY'S FINALLY LEARNING THERE ARE WORSE THINGS OUT THERE THAN WORKING WITH ME.
YOUR WOUND IS HEALING WELL.
OH! THANKS, I GUESS.
KIND OF LOOKING FORWARD TO HAVING A NON-EMOTIONAL SCAR FOR ONCE.
HEHEH, I BELIEVE IT WILL MAKE YOU STRONGER.
WHATEVER DOESN'T KILL YOU, RIGHT?
YOU OKAY, BUDDY?
EUNGH! IT'S HAPPENING AGAIN!
EVERYBODY RUN!

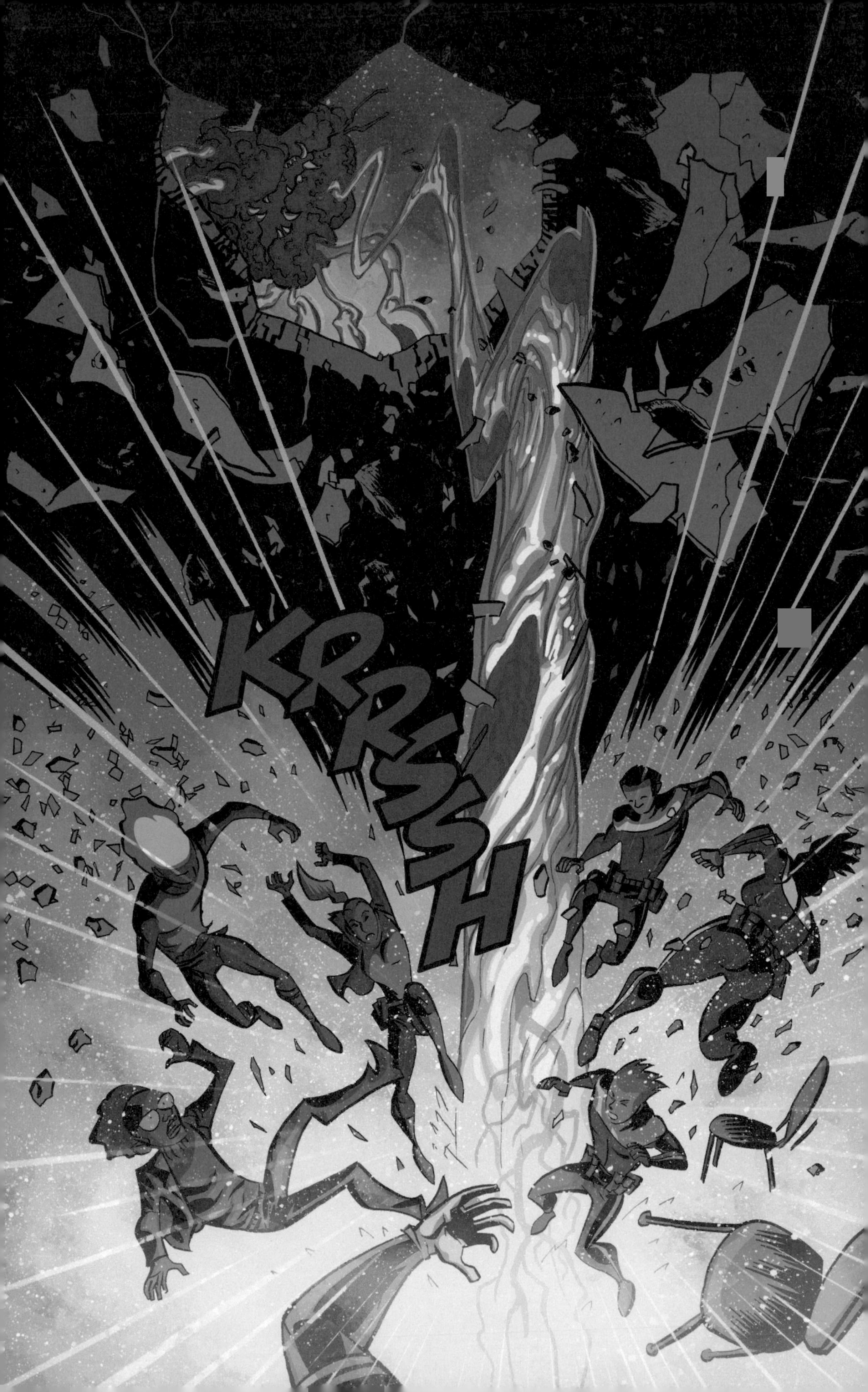
KRRSSSH

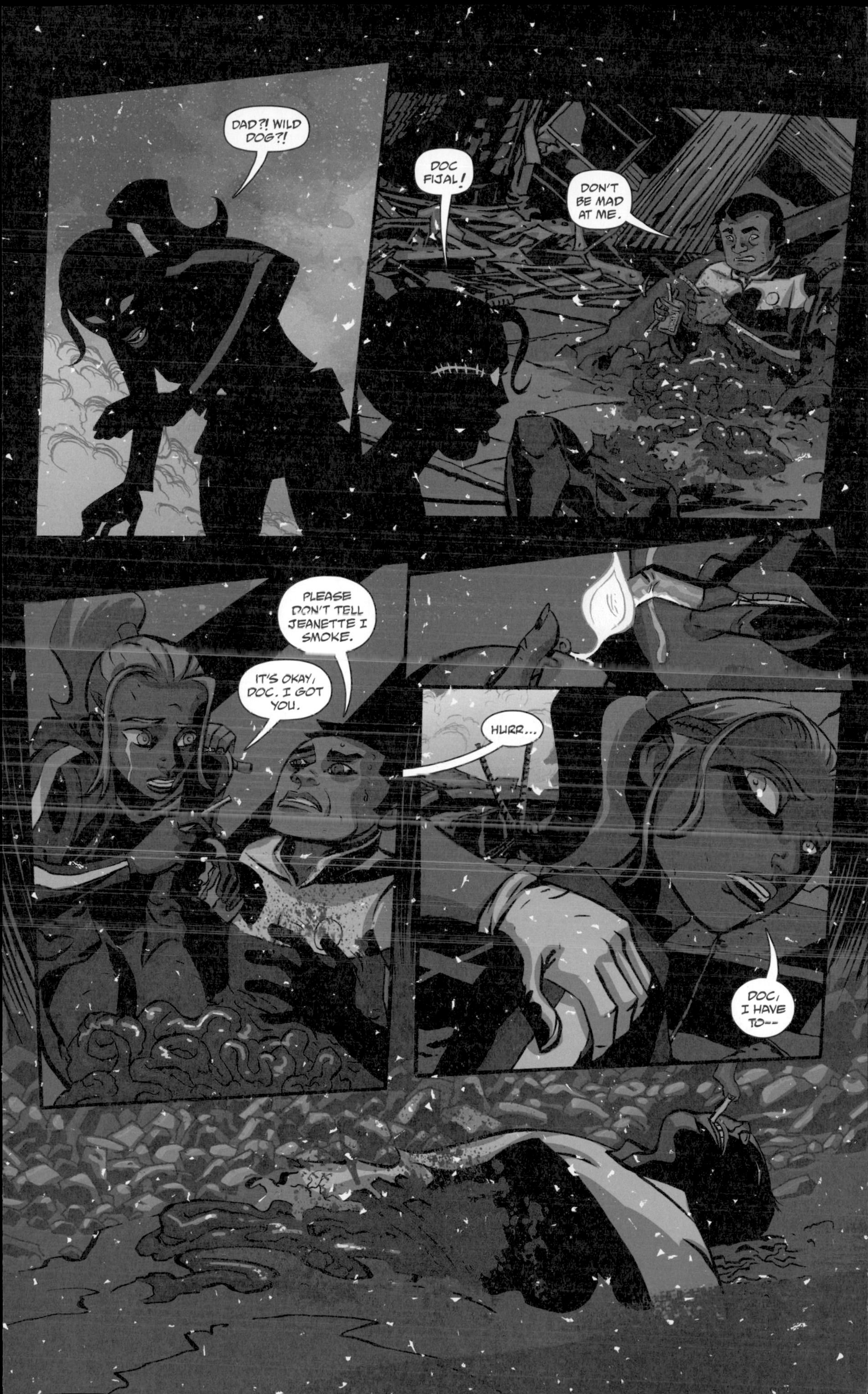
DAD?! WILD DOG?!
DOC FIJAL!
DON'T BE MAD AT ME.
PLEASE DON'T TELL JEANETTE I SMOKE.
IT'S OKAY, DOC. I GOT YOU.
HURR...
DOC, I HAVE TO--

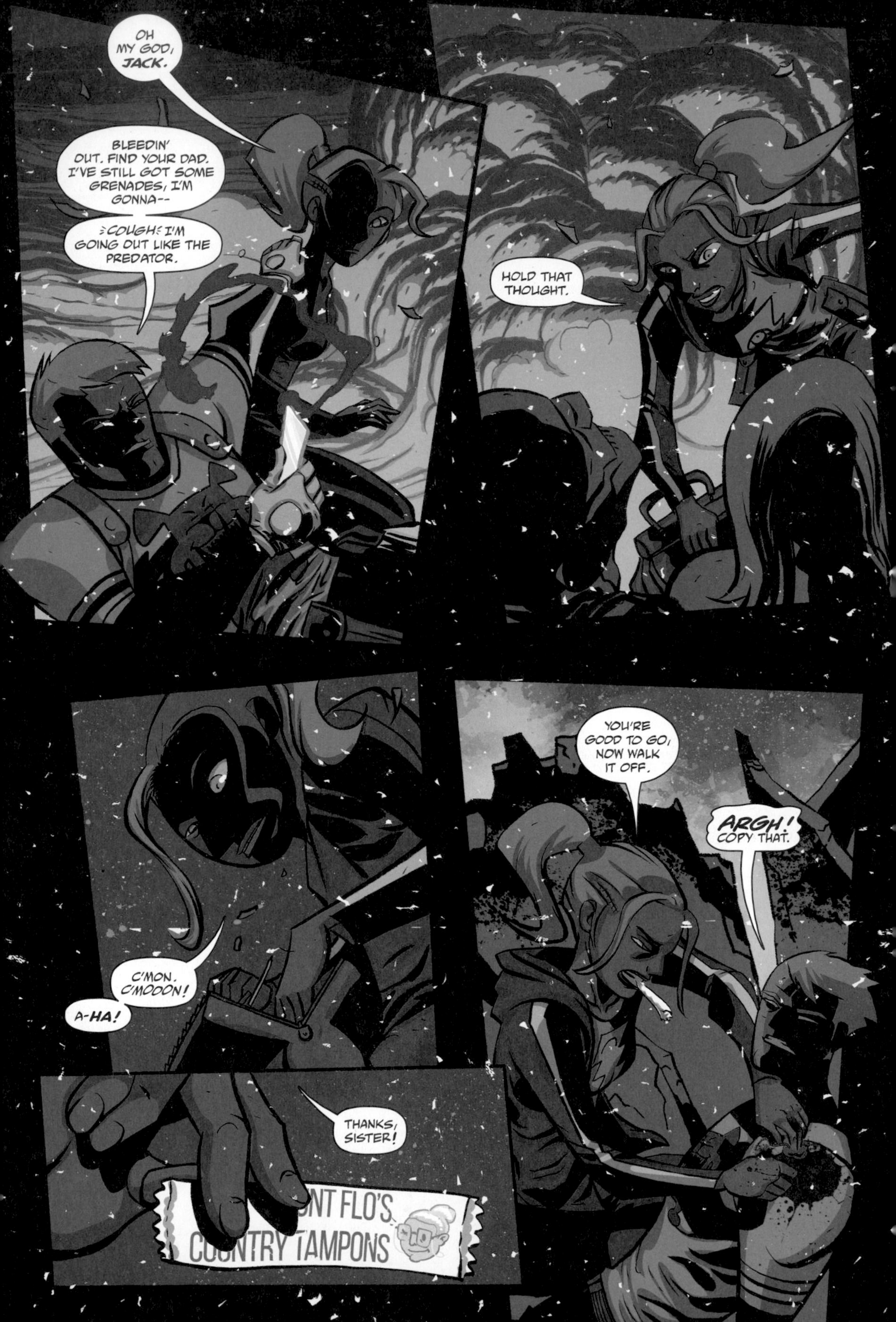
OH MY GOD, JACK.
BLEEDIN' OUT. FIND YOUR DAD. I'VE STILL GOT SOME GRENADES, I'M GONNA--
*COUGH* I'M GOING OUT LIKE THE PREDATOR.
HOLD THAT THOUGHT.
C'MON. C'MOOON!
A-HA!
THANKS, SISTER!
...NT FLO'S COUNTRY TAMPONS
YOU'RE GOOD TO GO, NOW WALK IT OFF.
ARGH! COPY THAT.

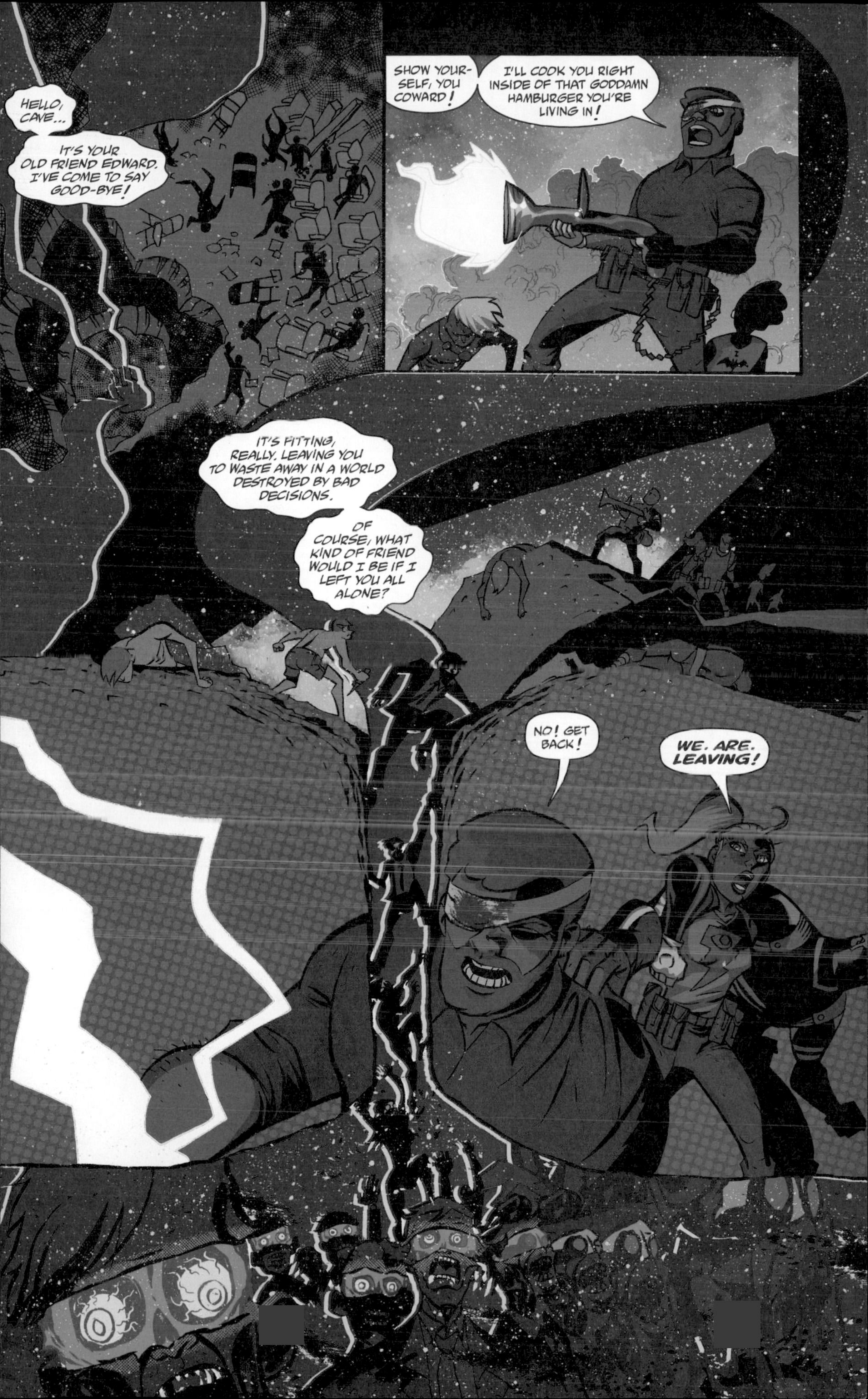
HELLO, CAVE...
IT'S YOUR OLD FRIEND EDWARD. I'VE COME TO SAY GOOD-BYE!
SHOW YOURSELF, YOU COWARD!
I'LL COOK YOU RIGHT INSIDE OF THAT GODDAMN HAMBURGER YOU'RE LIVING IN!
IT'S FITTING, REALLY. LEAVING YOU TO WASTE AWAY IN A WORLD DESTROYED BY BAD DECISIONS.
OF COURSE, WHAT KIND OF FRIEND WOULD I BE IF I LEFT YOU ALL ALONE?
NO! GET BACK!
WE. ARE. LEAVING!

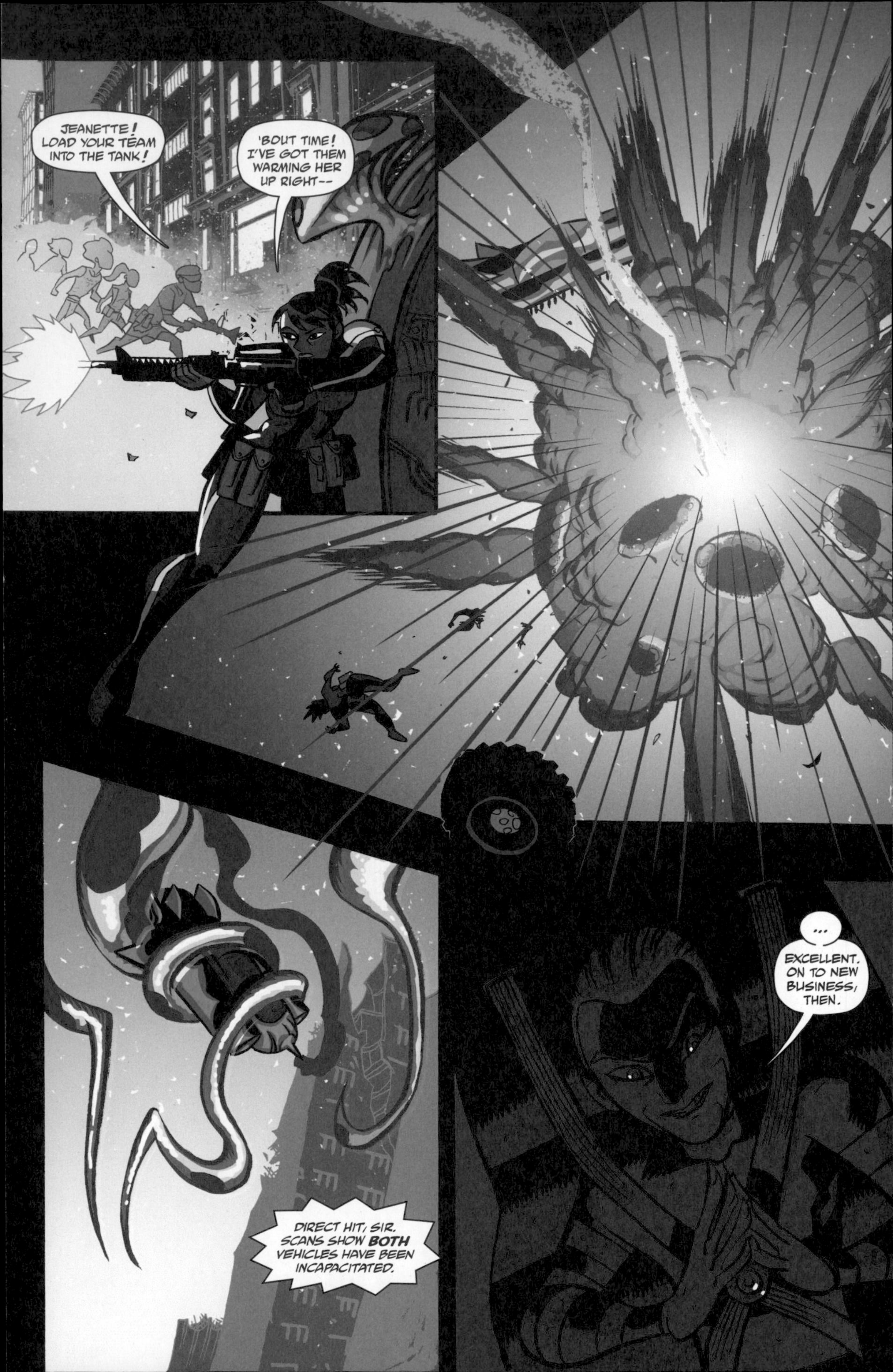
JEANETTE! LOAD YOUR TEAM INTO THE TANK!
'BOUT TIME! I'VE GOT THEM WARMING HER UP RIGHT--
DIRECT HIT, SIR. SCANS SHOW BOTH VEHICLES HAVE BEEN INCAPACITATED.
...
EXCELLENT. ON TO NEW BUSINESS, THEN.

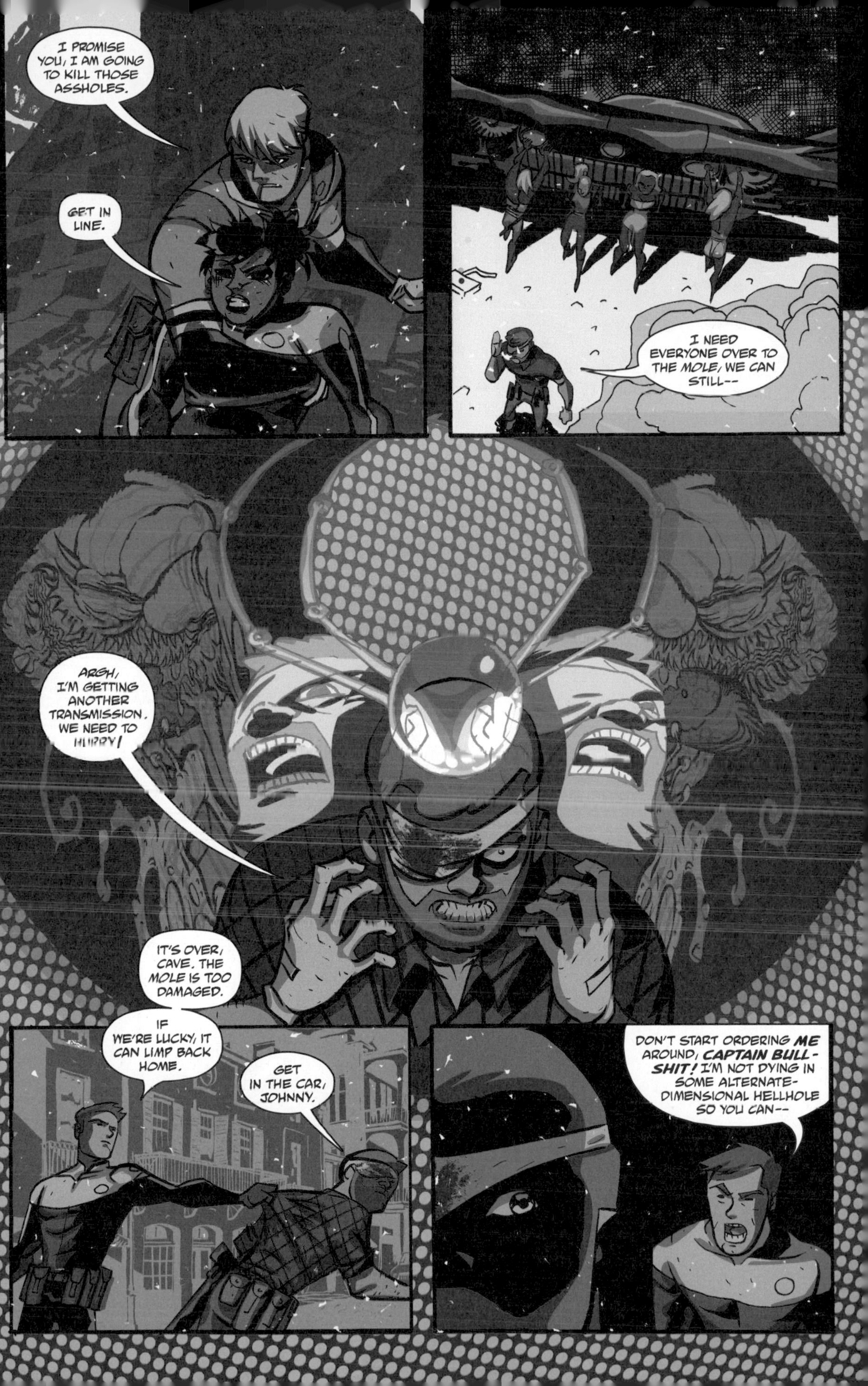
I PROMISE YOU, I AM GOING TO KILL THOSE ASSHOLES.
GET IN LINE.
I NEED EVERYONE OVER TO THE MOLE, WE CAN STILL--
ARGH, I'M GETTING ANOTHER TRANSMISSION. WE NEED TO HURRY!
IT'S OVER, CAVE. THE MOLE IS TOO DAMAGED.
IF WE'RE LUCKY, IT CAN LIMP BACK HOME.
GET IN THE CAR, JOHNNY.
DON'T START ORDERING ME AROUND, CAPTAIN BULL-SHIT! I'M NOT DYING IN SOME ALTERNATE-DIMENSIONAL HELLHOLE SO YOU CAN--

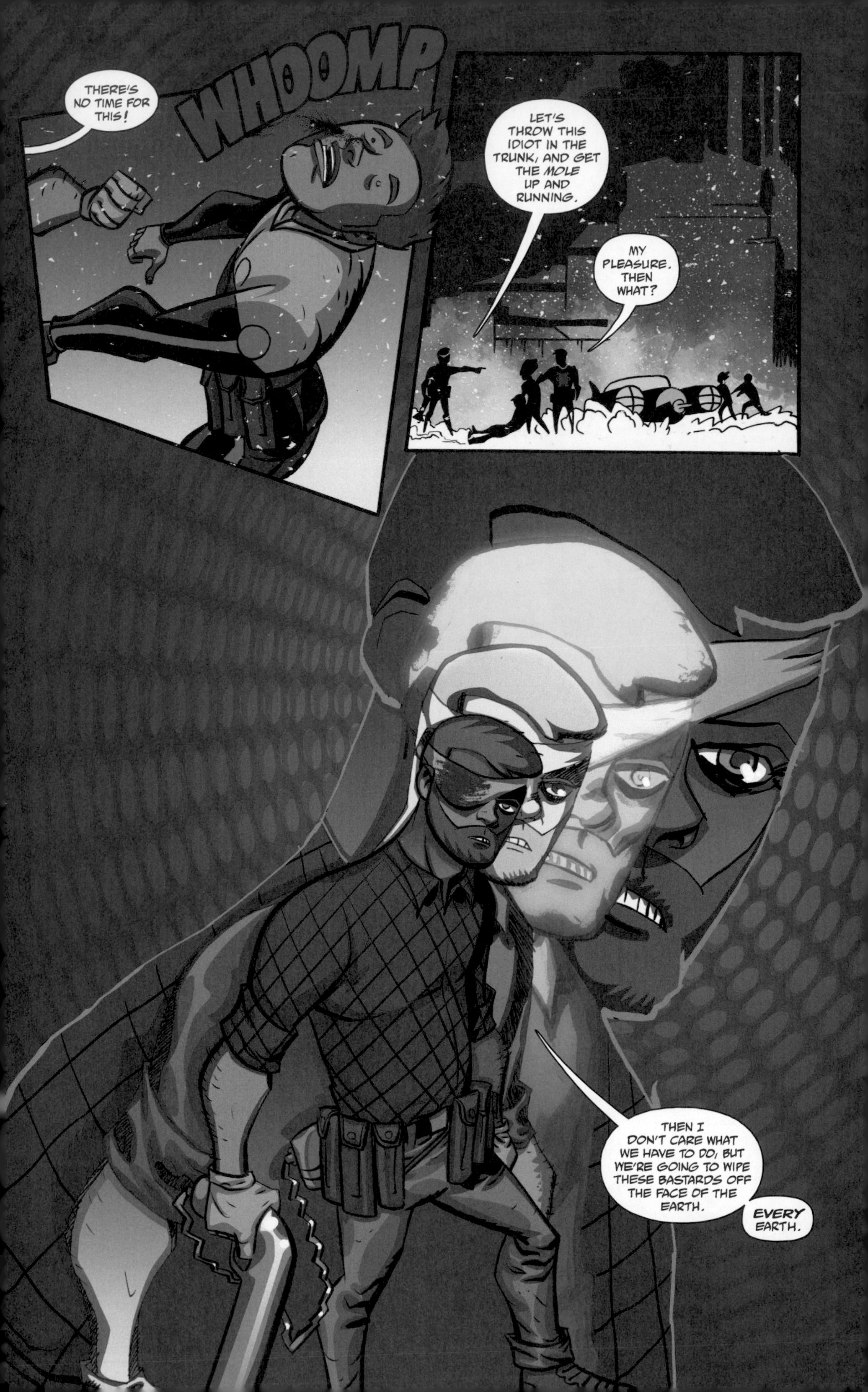
THERE'S NO TIME FOR THIS!
WHOOMP
LET'S THROW THIS IDIOT IN THE TRUNK, AND GET THE *MOLE* UP AND RUNNING.
MY PLEASURE. THEN WHAT?
THEN I DON'T CARE WHAT WE HAVE TO DO, BUT WE'RE GOING TO WIPE THESE BASTARDS OFF THE FACE OF THE EARTH.
**EVERY** EARTH.

# The Wonderful World of Rocks!

With Professor Marc Bartow

# "ROCHE CREVETTE"

Formed two hundred million years ago when sedimentary layers of salt were pressurized and fused with schools of dead ancient krill, Roche Crevette is an unusual rock in that it is edible. Discovered in 1847 by French miners trapped in a cave-in, the miners survived for forty-five days eating nothing but Roche Crevette. Their only complaint was that it came without a white wine pairing.

# Geologists Are the True Explorers of the Universe

**As young scientists,** Dr. Niedermeyer and myself both began our careers at SETI (the Search for Extra-Terrestrial Intelligence). We considered ourselves as much explorers as scientists. And we both felt that exploration of the universe was the real work of the human race. Stationed at the Arecibo telescope in Puerto Rico, we frequently met for breakfast at El Gato Flojo, the local cantina, to discuss our theories and our dreams from the night before, as that was where most of our theories came from.

The day after I announced my decision to leave SETI to pursue a career as an experimental geologist, we met at El Gato Flojo for one last breakfast. I could tell right away that Dr. Niedermeyer did not approve of my decision. He was wearing his black sweatpants, as if in mourning.

**"Why are you doing this?"** Dr Niedermeyer asked me. From the tone in his voice, you'd think I was leaving to become a human cannonball.

"Why would you become a geologist just to be stacked on top of the world's pile of geologists? This is where the real action is. If the human race ever changes course, it will be because of what we find here," he said. "You can't just give up on that."

I explained, as best I could, that I hadn't given up, but had decided that geologists are the true explorers of the universe.

"What percentage of solar systems in the galaxy do you think contain Class I habitable planets capable of supporting liquid water and life on the surface of the planet?" I asked. "One in a thousand? One in a hundred thousand?"

"But guess what percentage of these solar systems contain frozen rocky planets or moons with liquid water under the surface heated by geothermal energy? Almost every single goddamn one," I continued.

I told him that our search for life on habitable planets like our own was like a man who grew up next to the Eiffel Tower and therefore searches for alien life by looking only for planets that have an Eiffel Tower.

The cosmic deck is overwhelmingly stacked in favor of extra-terrestrial life being underground, locked in subterranean caverns or oceans powered by the geothermal energy of its planetary core. Therefore, if anyone ever makes contact with extra-terrestrial life, it will almost certainly be a geologist.

Having said these words, our breakfast arrived. As we ate, I told him of the dream I'd had the night before. I dreamed that I was an alien astronaut, from a subterranean species, who made history by being the first of my kind to step onto the surface of our planet.

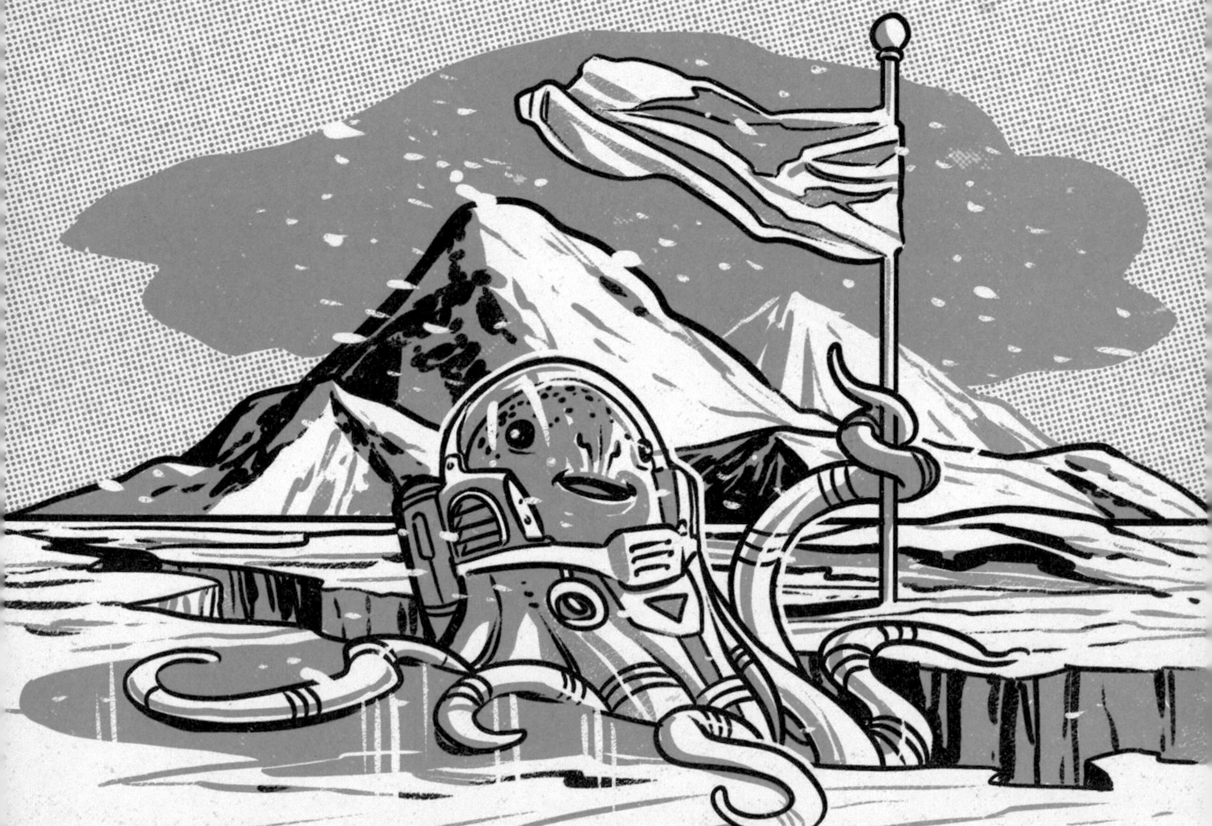

Words by Mark Russell
Art by Benjamin Dewey

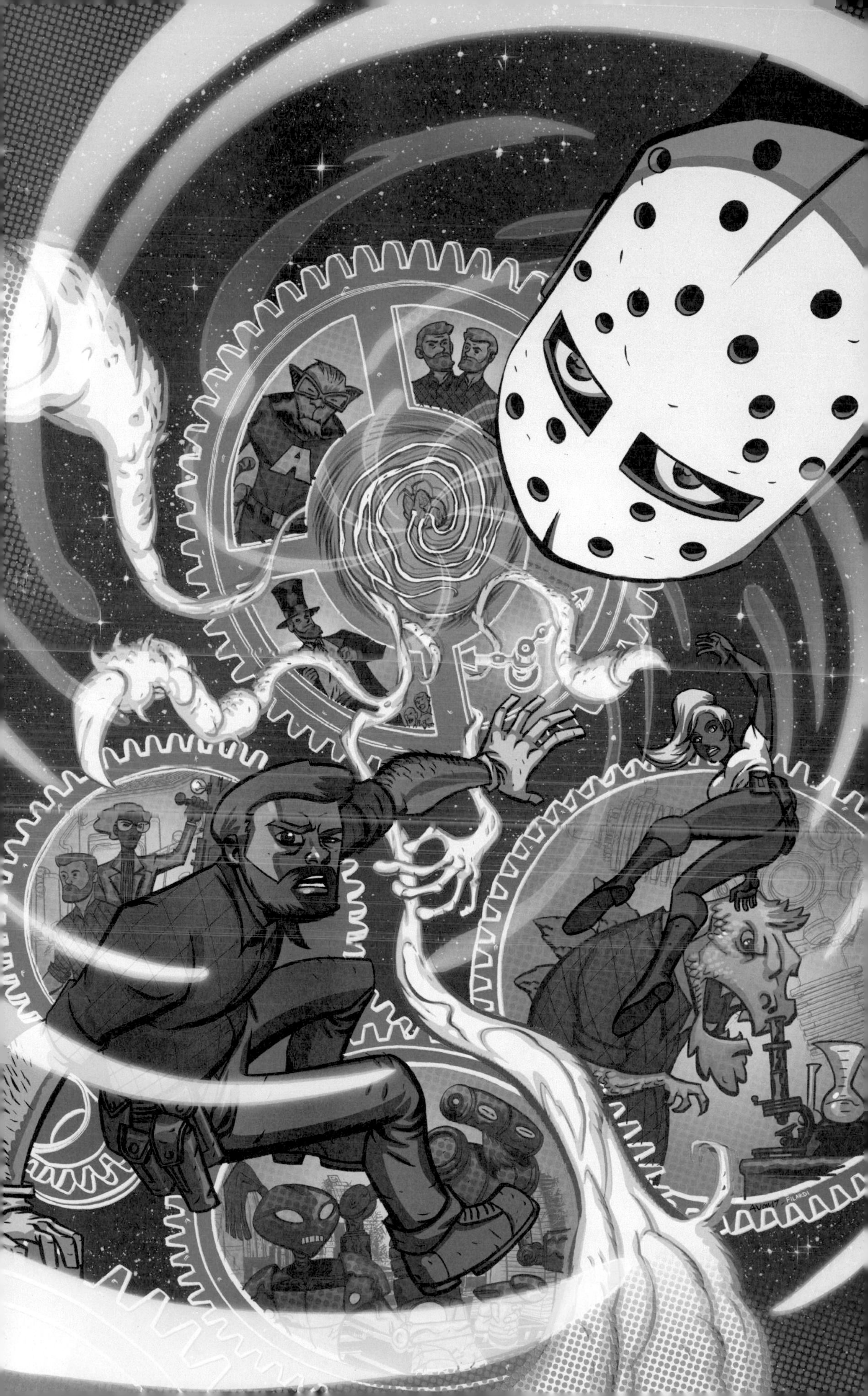

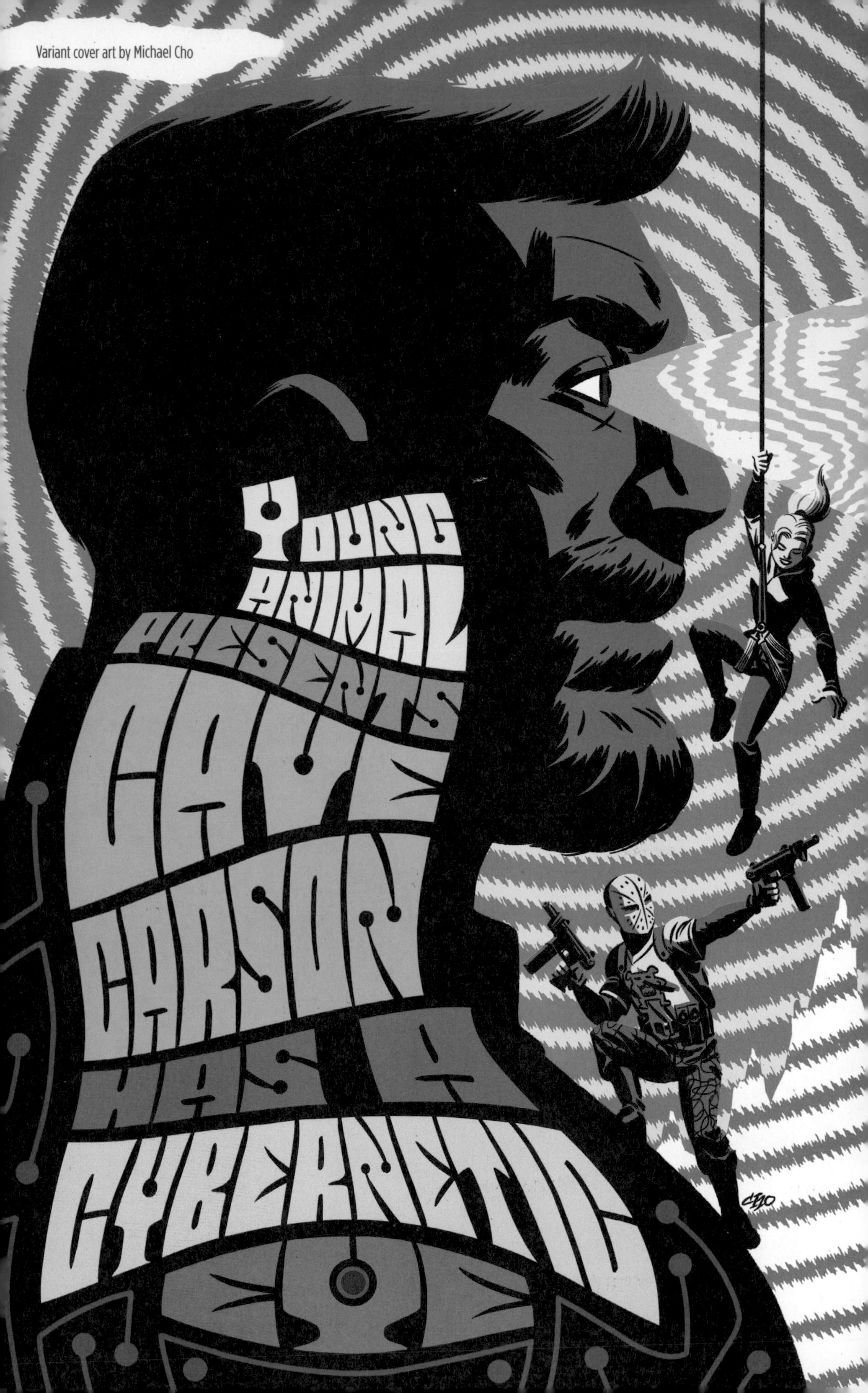
YOUNG
ANIMAL
PRESENTS
CAVE
CARSON
HAS A
CYBERNETIC
CHO
Variant cover art by Michael Cho

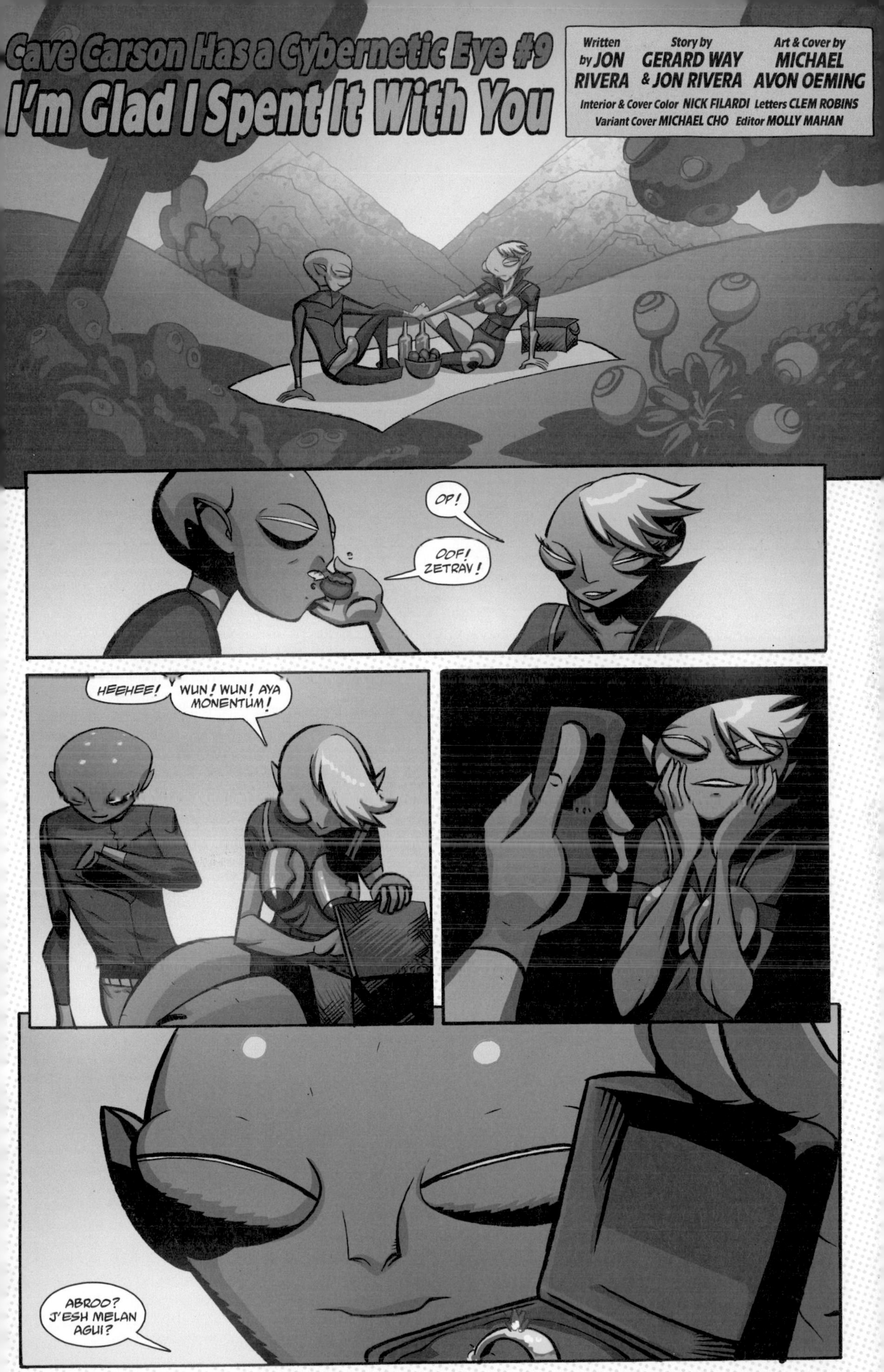
Cave Carson Has a Cybernetic Eye #9
I'm Glad I Spent It With You
Written by JON RIVERA
Story by GERARD WAY & JON RIVERA
Art & Cover by MICHAEL AVON OEMING
Interior & Cover Color NICK FILARDI Letters CLEM ROBINS
Variant Cover MICHAEL CHO Editor MOLLY MAHAN
OP!
OOF! ZETRAV!
HEEHEE!
WUN! WUN! AYA MONENTUM!
ABROO? J'ESH MELAN AGUI?

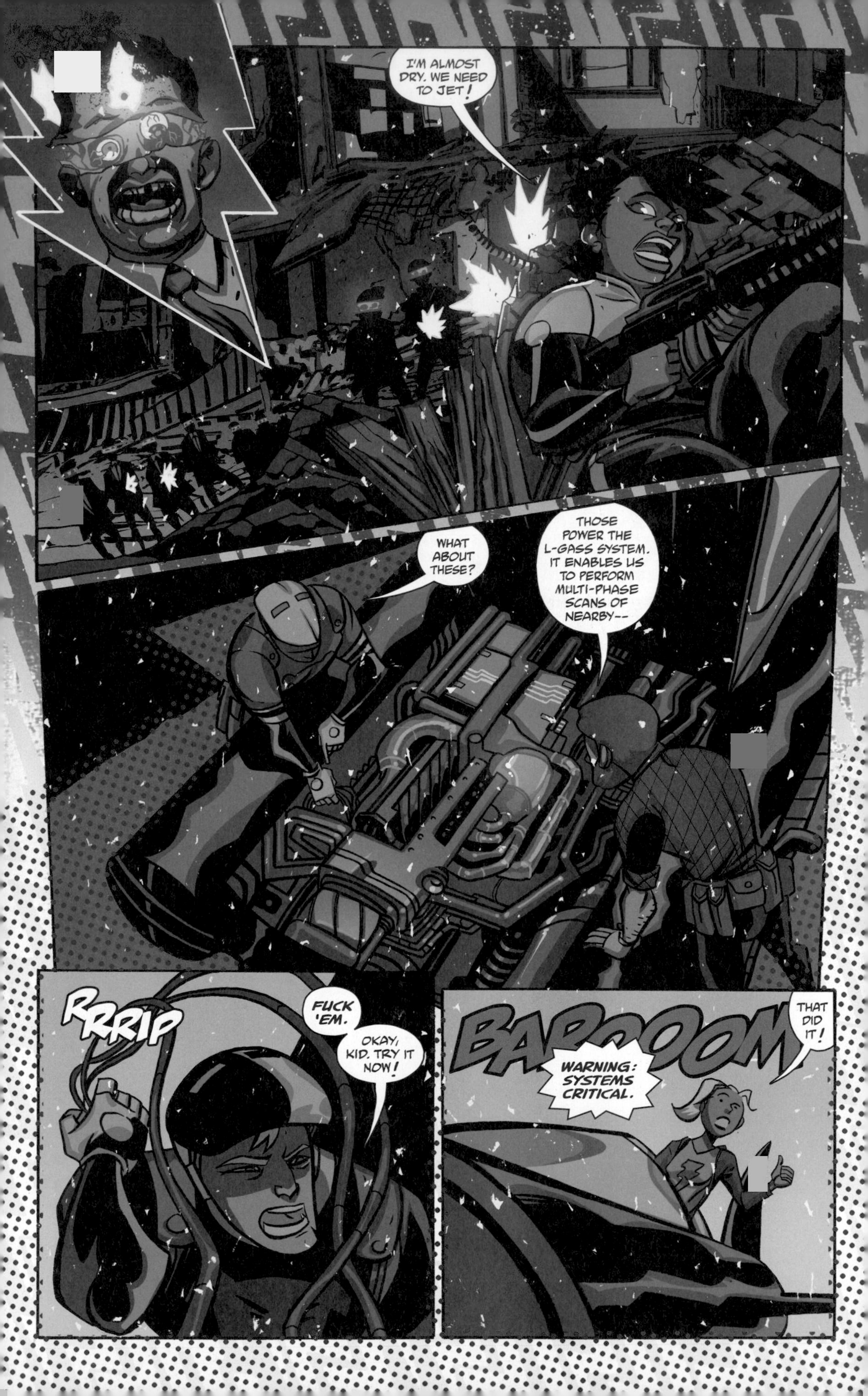
I'M ALMOST DRY. WE NEED TO JET!
WHAT ABOUT THESE?
THOSE POWER THE L-GASS SYSTEM. IT ENABLES US TO PERFORM MULTI-PHASE SCANS OF NEARBY--
RRRIP
FUCK 'EM.
OKAY, KID. TRY IT NOW!
BARROOOM
THAT DID IT!
WARNING: SYSTEMS CRITICAL.

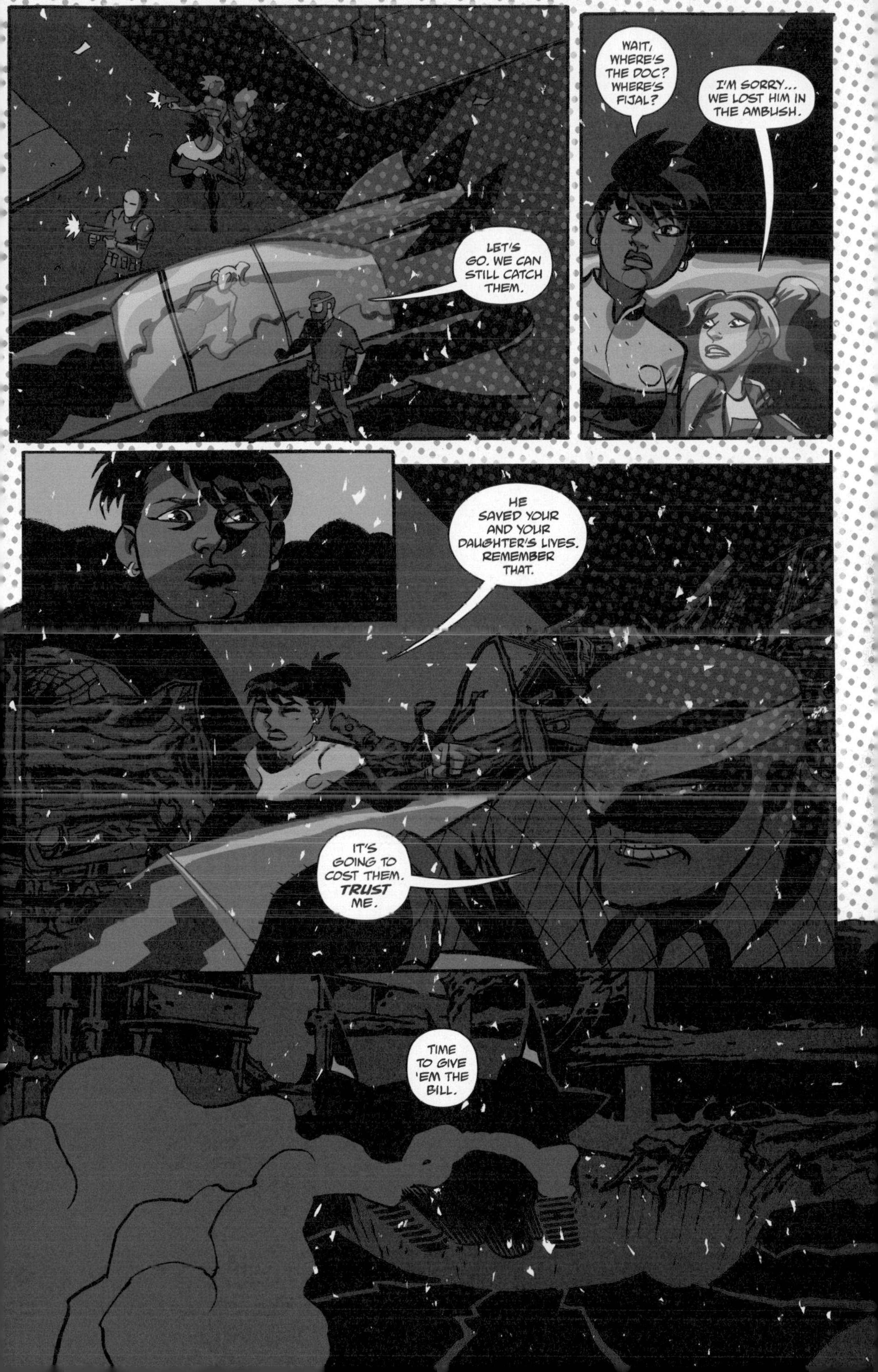
LET'S GO. WE CAN STILL CATCH THEM.
WAIT, WHERE'S THE DOC? WHERE'S FIJAL?
I'M SORRY... WE LOST HIM IN THE AMBUSH.
HE SAVED YOUR AND YOUR DAUGHTER'S LIVES. REMEMBER THAT.
IT'S GOING TO COST THEM. TRUST ME.
TIME TO GIVE 'EM THE BILL.

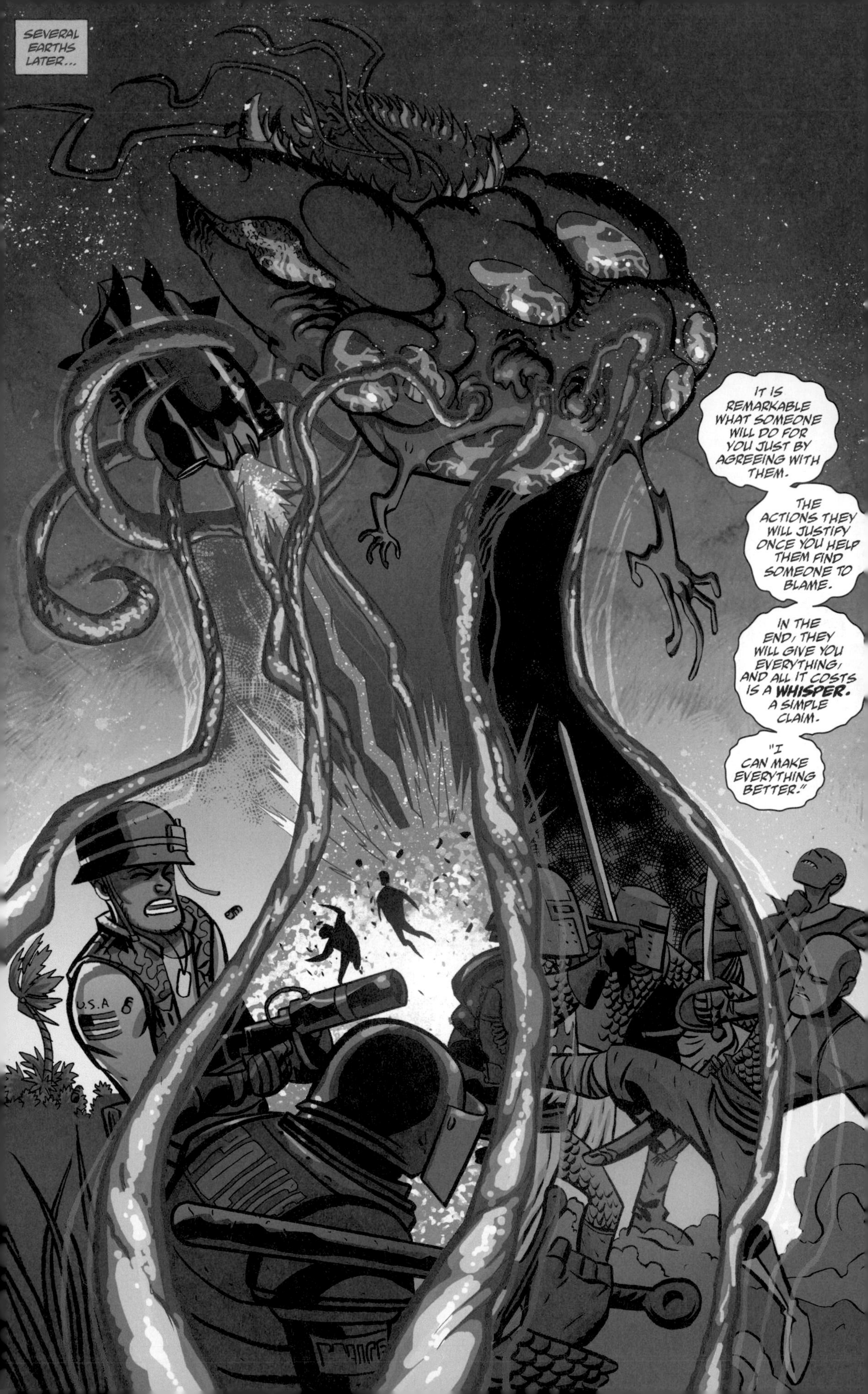
SEVERAL EARTHS LATER...
IT IS REMARKABLE WHAT SOMEONE WILL DO FOR YOU JUST BY AGREEING WITH THEM.
THE ACTIONS THEY WILL JUSTIFY ONCE YOU HELP THEM FIND SOMEONE TO BLAME.
IN THE END, THEY WILL GIVE YOU EVERYTHING, AND ALL IT COSTS IS A **WHISPER.** A SIMPLE CLAIM.
"I CAN MAKE EVERYTHING BETTER."
U.S.A

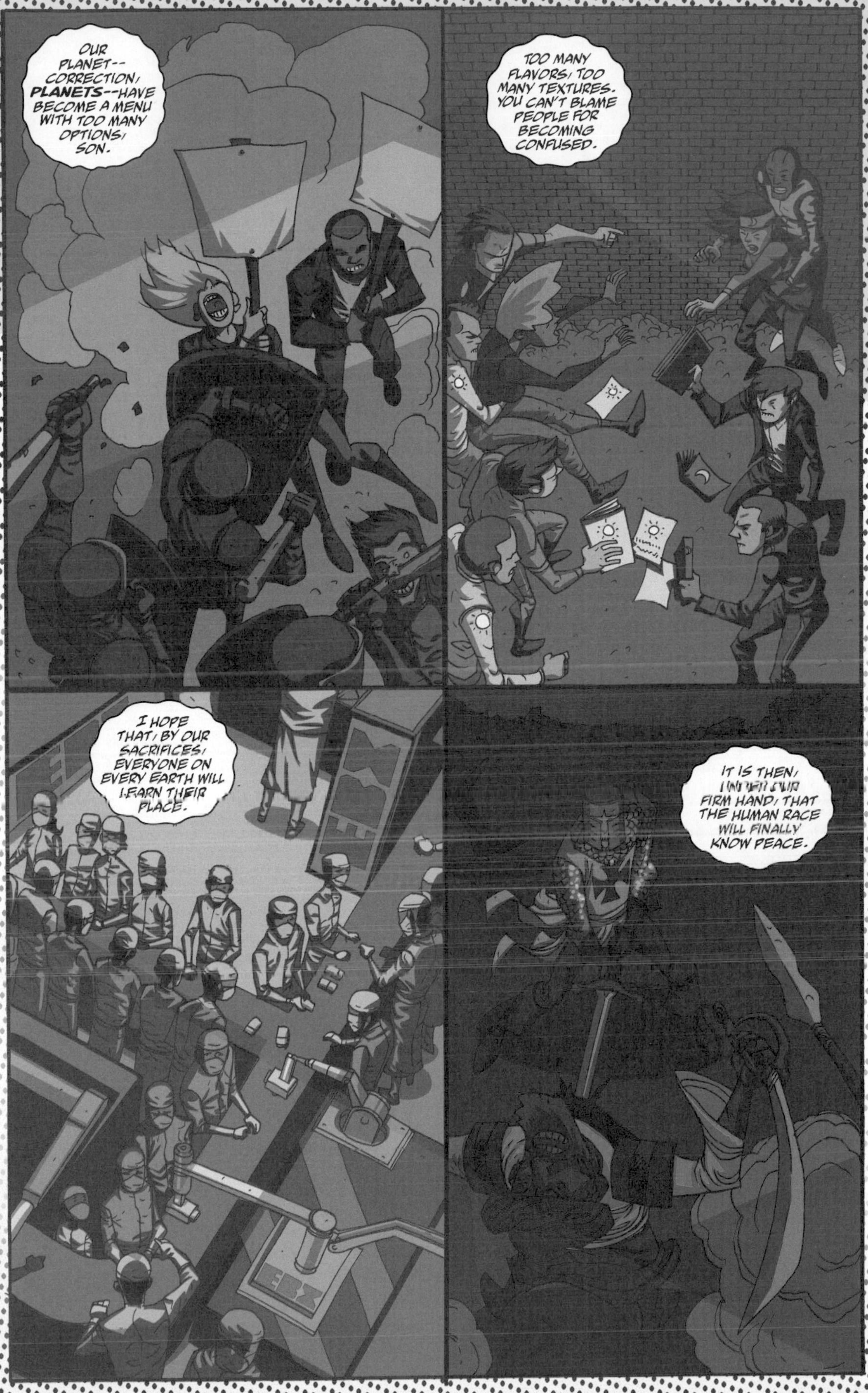
OUR PLANET-- CORRECTION, **PLANETS**--HAVE BECOME A MENU WITH TOO MANY OPTIONS, SON.
TOO MANY FLAVORS, TOO MANY TEXTURES. YOU CAN'T BLAME PEOPLE FOR BECOMING CONFUSED.
I HOPE THAT, BY OUR SACRIFICES, EVERYONE ON EVERY EARTH WILL LEARN THEIR PLACE.
IT IS THEN,
FIRM HAND, THAT THE HUMAN RACE WILL FINALLY KNOW PEACE.

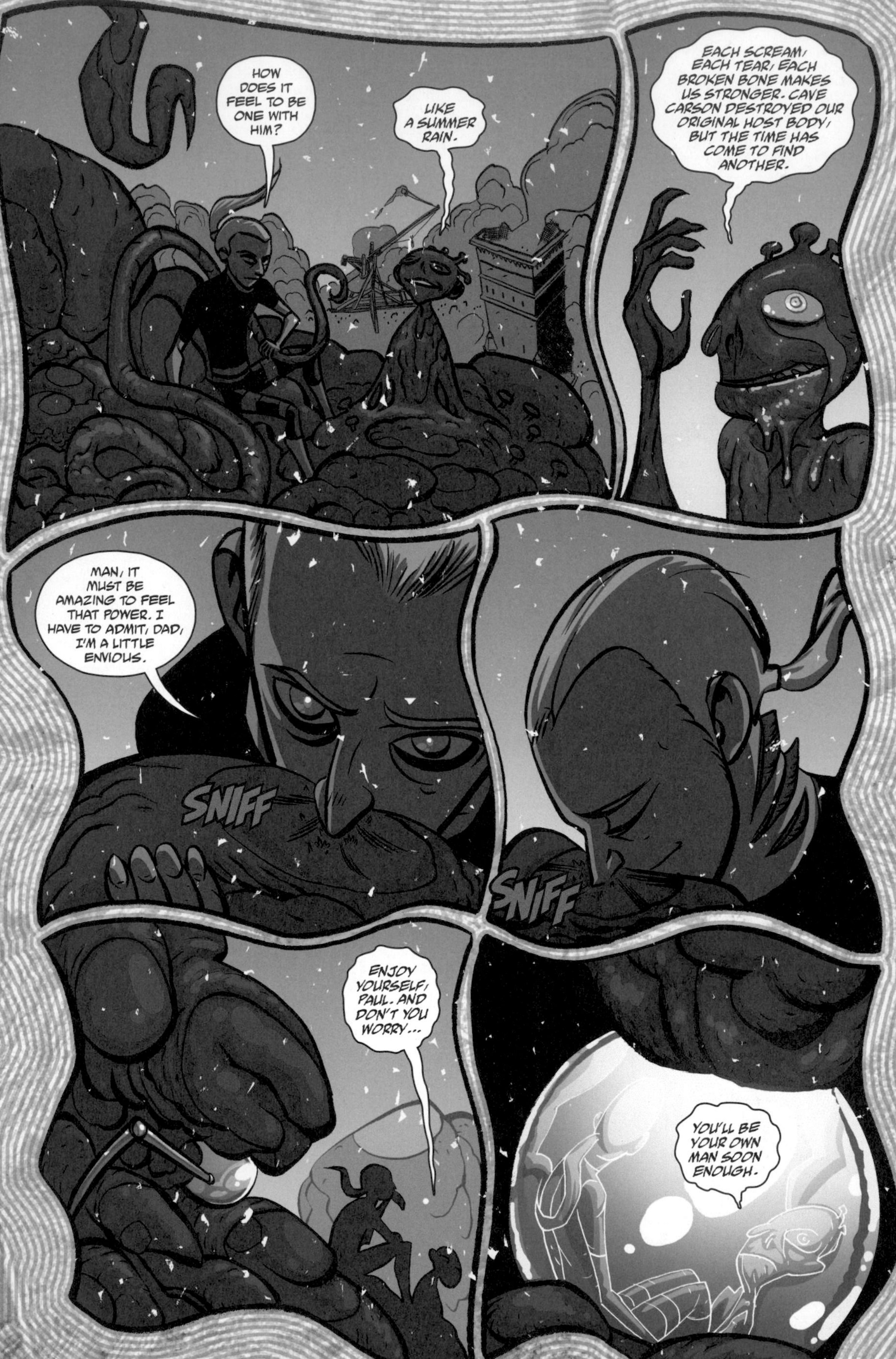
HOW DOES IT FEEL TO BE ONE WITH HIM?
LIKE A SUMMER RAIN.
EACH SCREAM, EACH TEAR, EACH BROKEN BONE MAKES US STRONGER. CAVE CARSON DESTROYED OUR ORIGINAL HOST BODY, BUT THE TIME HAS COME TO FIND ANOTHER.
MAN, IT MUST BE AMAZING TO FEEL THAT POWER. I HAVE TO ADMIT, DAD, I'M A LITTLE ENVIOUS.
SNIFF
SNIFF
ENJOY YOURSELF, PAUL. AND DON'T YOU WORRY...
YOU'LL BE YOUR OWN MAN SOON ENOUGH.

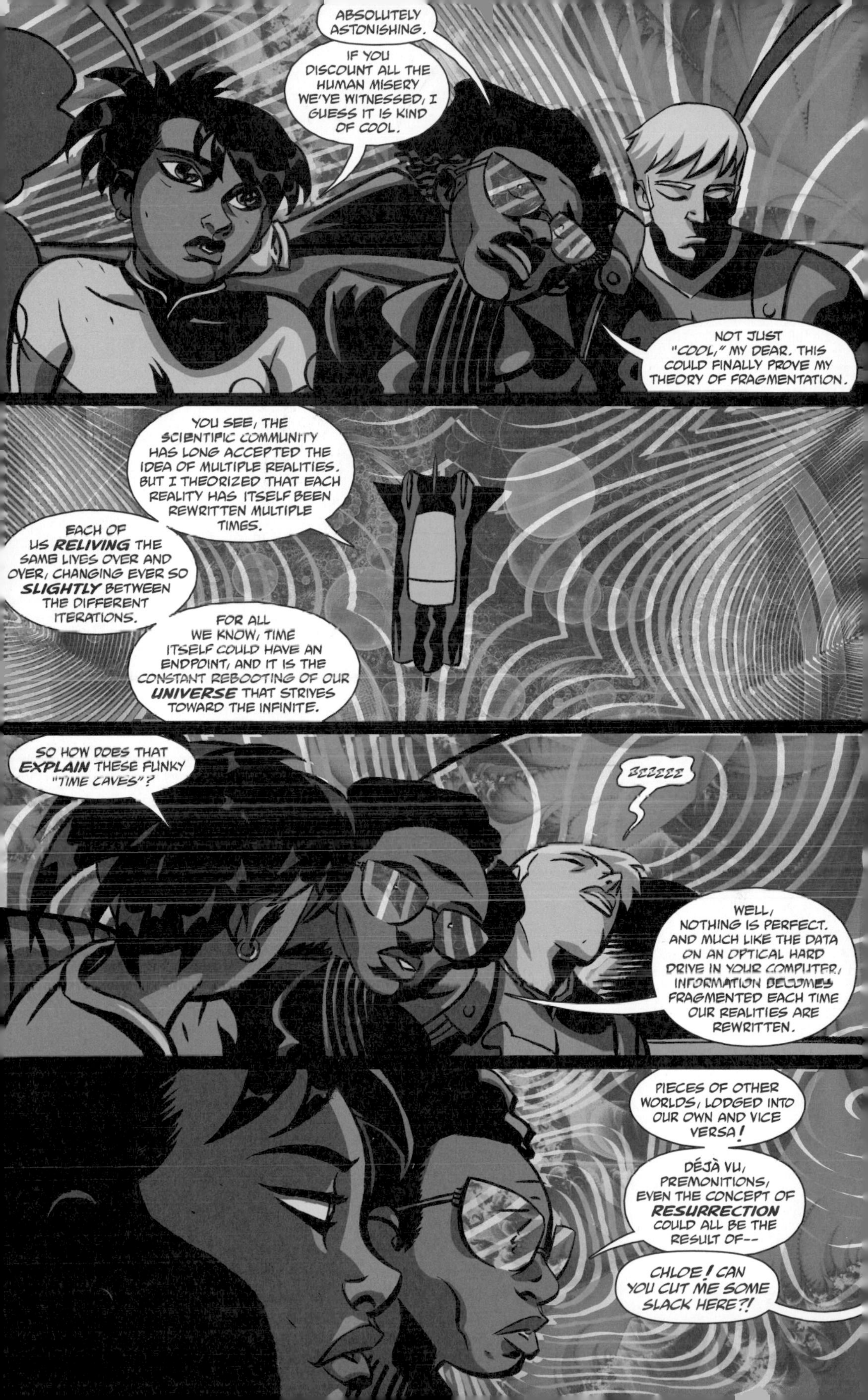

ABSOLUTELY ASTONISHING.
IF YOU DISCOUNT ALL THE HUMAN MISERY WE'VE WITNESSED, I GUESS IT IS KIND OF COOL.
NOT JUST "COOL," MY DEAR. THIS COULD FINALLY PROVE MY THEORY OF FRAGMENTATION.
YOU SEE, THE SCIENTIFIC COMMUNITY HAS LONG ACCEPTED THE IDEA OF MULTIPLE REALITIES. BUT I THEORIZED THAT EACH REALITY HAS ITSELF BEEN REWRITTEN MULTIPLE TIMES.
EACH OF US RELIVING THE SAME LIVES OVER AND OVER, CHANGING EVER SO SLIGHTLY BETWEEN THE DIFFERENT ITERATIONS.
FOR ALL WE KNOW, TIME ITSELF COULD HAVE AN ENDPOINT, AND IT IS THE CONSTANT REBOOTING OF OUR UNIVERSE THAT STRIVES TOWARD THE INFINITE.
SO HOW DOES THAT EXPLAIN THESE FUNKY "TIME CAVES"?
ZEEEEE
WELL, NOTHING IS PERFECT. AND MUCH LIKE THE DATA ON AN OPTICAL HARD DRIVE IN YOUR COMPUTER, INFORMATION BECOMES FRAGMENTED EACH TIME OUR REALITIES ARE REWRITTEN.
PIECES OF OTHER WORLDS, LODGED INTO OUR OWN AND VICE VERSA!
DÉJÀ VU, PREMONITIONS, EVEN THE CONCEPT OF RESURRECTION COULD ALL BE THE RESULT OF--
CHLOE! CAN YOU CUT ME SOME SLACK HERE?!

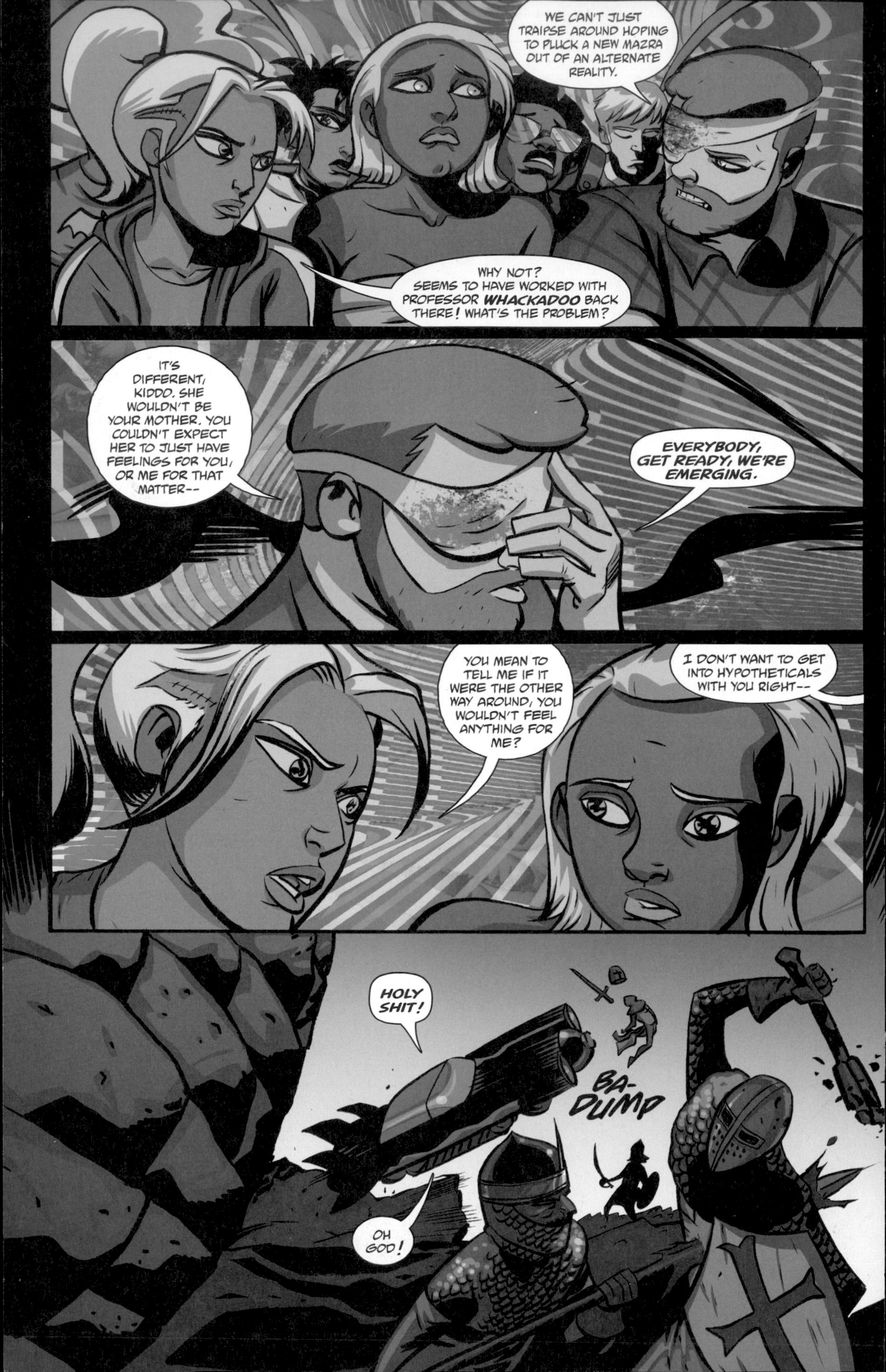
WE CAN'T JUST TRAIPSE AROUND HOPING TO PLUCK A NEW MAZRA OUT OF AN ALTERNATE REALITY.
WHY NOT? SEEMS TO HAVE WORKED WITH PROFESSOR **WHACKADOO** BACK THERE! WHAT'S THE PROBLEM?
IT'S DIFFERENT, KIDDO. SHE WOULDN'T BE YOUR MOTHER. YOU COULDN'T EXPECT HER TO JUST HAVE FEELINGS FOR YOU, OR ME FOR THAT MATTER--
EVERYBODY, GET READY, WE'RE EMERGING.
YOU MEAN TO TELL ME IF IT WERE THE OTHER WAY AROUND, YOU WOULDN'T FEEL ANYTHING FOR ME?
I DON'T WANT TO GET INTO HYPOTHETICALS WITH YOU RIGHT--
HOLY SHIT!
BA-DUMP
OH GOD!

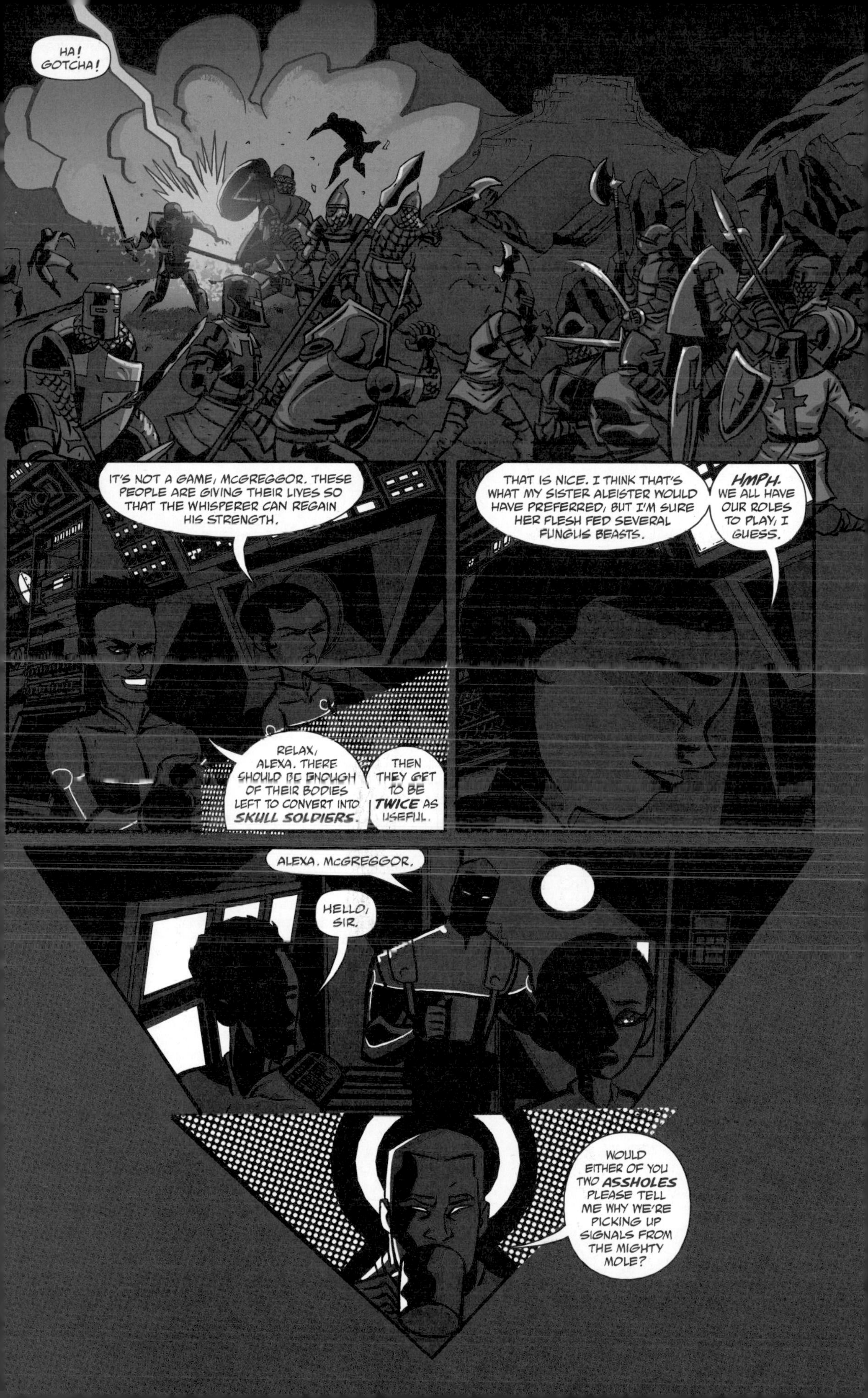
HA! GOTCHA!
IT'S NOT A GAME, MCGREGGOR. THESE PEOPLE ARE GIVING THEIR LIVES SO THAT THE WHISPERER CAN REGAIN HIS STRENGTH.
RELAX, ALEXA. THERE SHOULD BE ENOUGH OF THEIR BODIES LEFT TO CONVERT INTO SKULL SOLDIERS.
THEN THEY GET TO BE TWICE AS USEFUL.
THAT IS NICE. I THINK THAT'S WHAT MY SISTER ALEISTER WOULD HAVE PREFERRED, BUT I'M SURE HER FLESH FED SEVERAL FUNGUS BEASTS.
HMPH. WE ALL HAVE OUR ROLES TO PLAY, I GUESS.
ALEXA. MCGREGGOR.
HELLO, SIR.
WOULD EITHER OF YOU TWO ASSHOLES PLEASE TELL ME WHY WE'RE PICKING UP SIGNALS FROM THE MIGHTY MOLE?

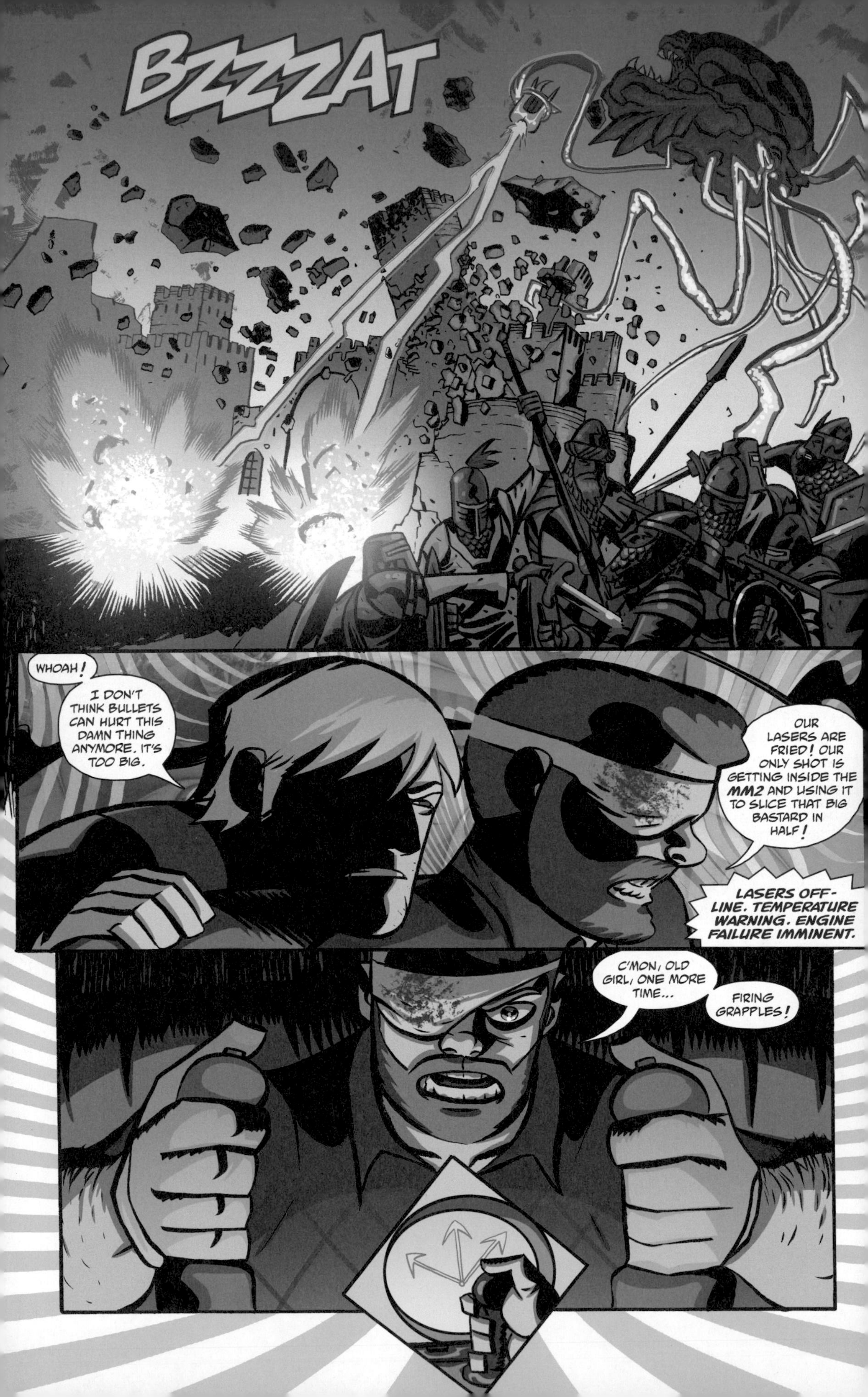
BZZZAT
WHOAH!
I DON'T THINK BULLETS CAN HURT THIS DAMN THING ANYMORE. IT'S TOO BIG.
OUR LASERS ARE FRIED! OUR ONLY SHOT IS GETTING INSIDE THE MM2 AND USING IT TO SLICE THAT BIG BASTARD IN HALF!
LASERS OFF-LINE. TEMPERATURE WARNING. ENGINE FAILURE IMMINENT.
C'MON, OLD GIRL, ONE MORE TIME...
FIRING GRAPPLES!

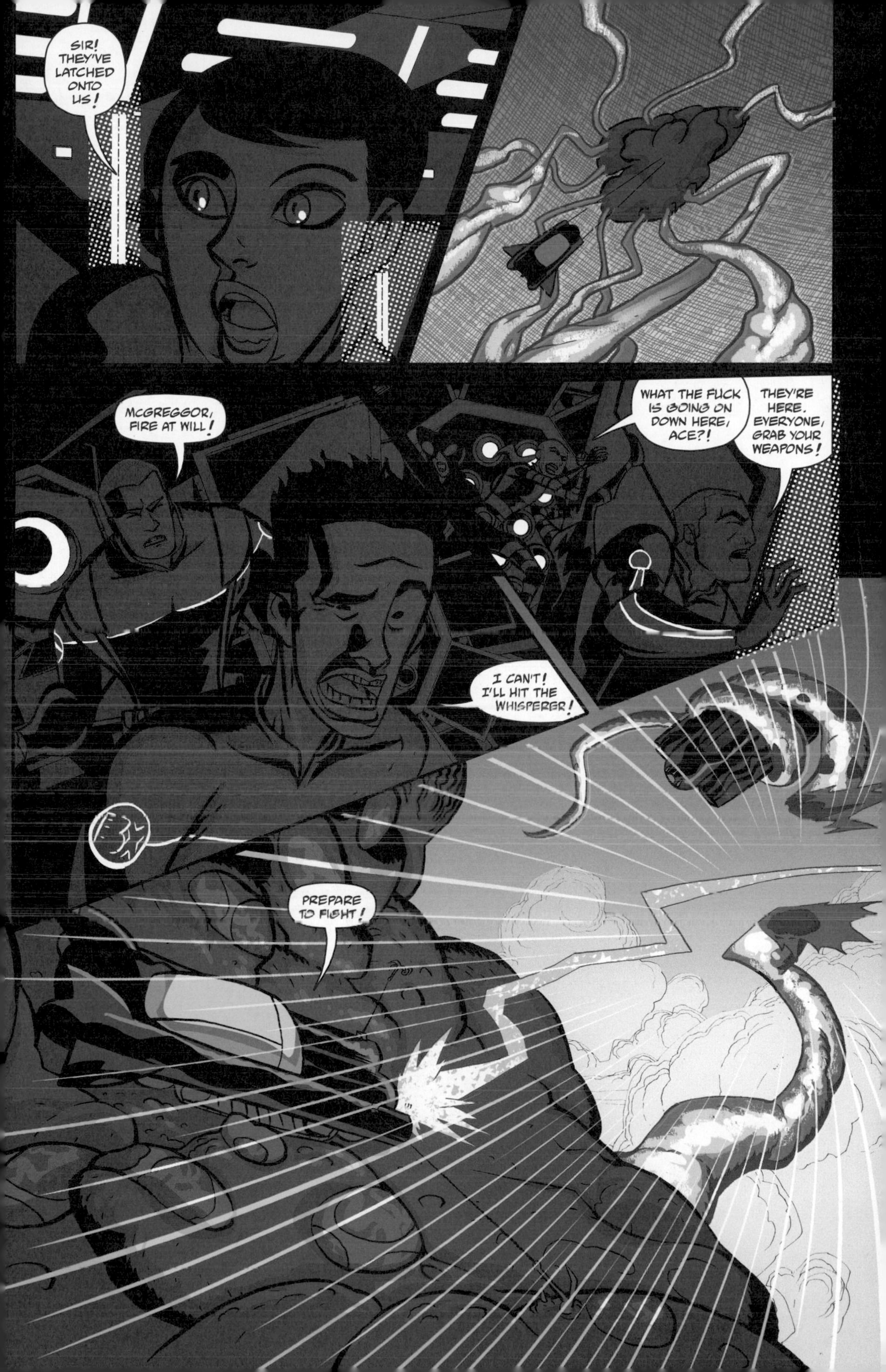
SIR! THEY'VE LATCHED ONTO US!
McGREGGOR, FIRE AT WILL!
WHAT THE FUCK IS GOING ON DOWN HERE, ACE?!
THEY'RE HERE. EVERYONE, GRAB YOUR WEAPONS!
I CAN'T! I'LL HIT THE WHISPERER!
PREPARE TO FIGHT!

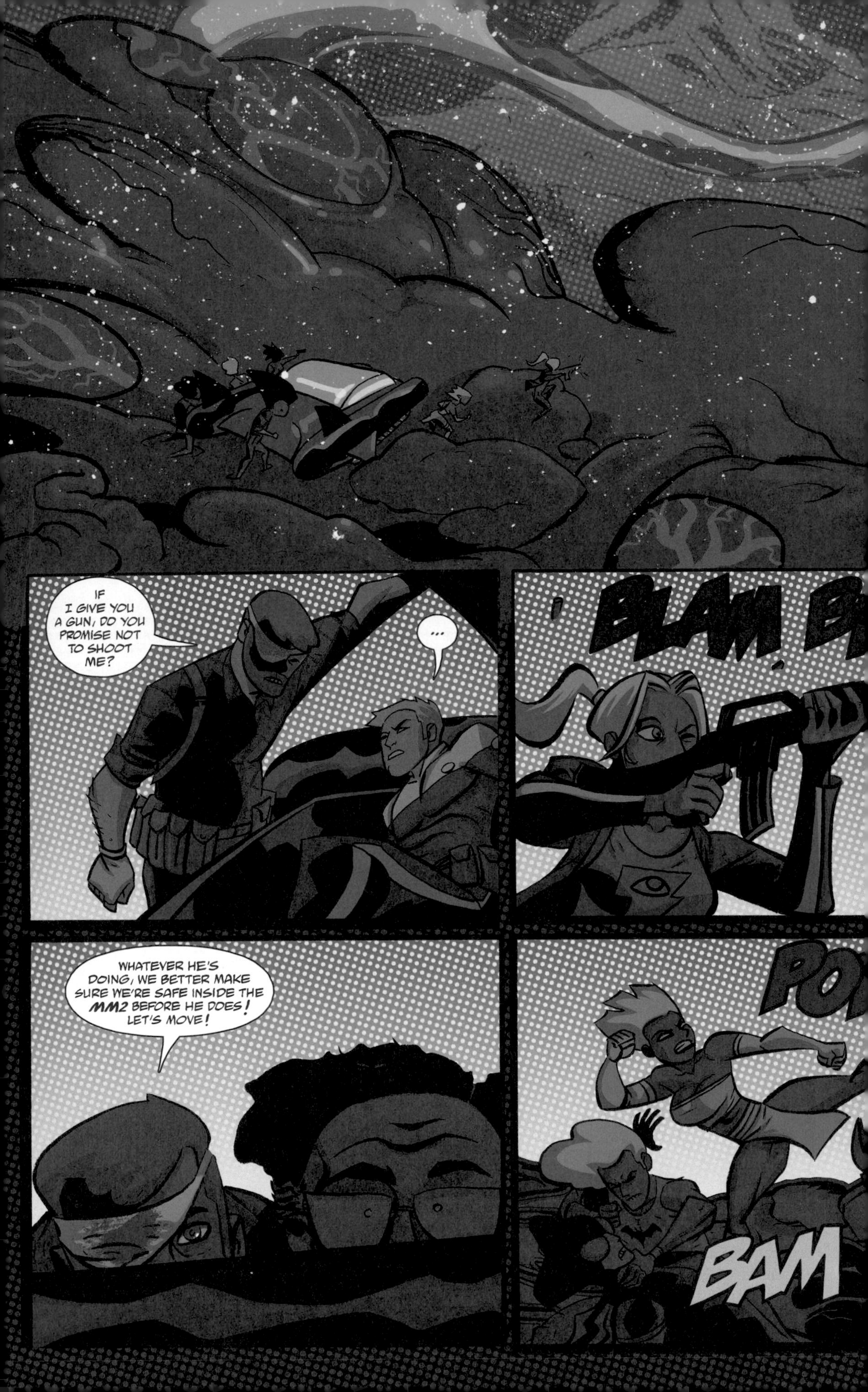

IF I GIVE YOU A GUN, DO YOU PROMISE NOT TO SHOOT ME?
...
BLAM
WHATEVER HE'S DOING, WE BETTER MAKE SURE WE'RE SAFE INSIDE THE MM2 BEFORE HE DOES! LET'S MOVE!
BAM

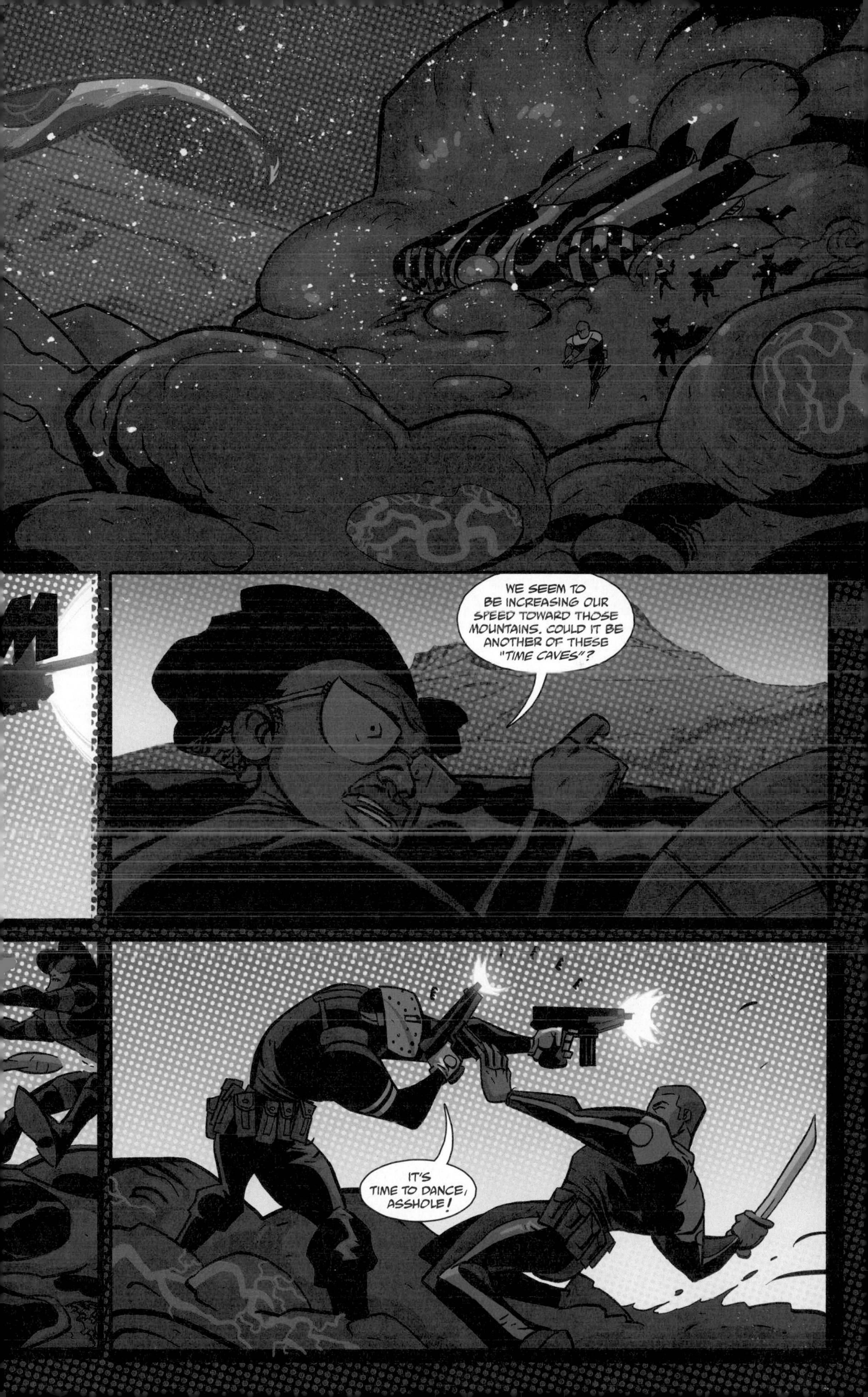
WE SEEM TO BE INCREASING OUR SPEED TOWARD THOSE MOUNTAINS. COULD IT BE ANOTHER OF THESE "TIME CAVES"?
IT'S TIME TO DANCE, ASSHOLE!

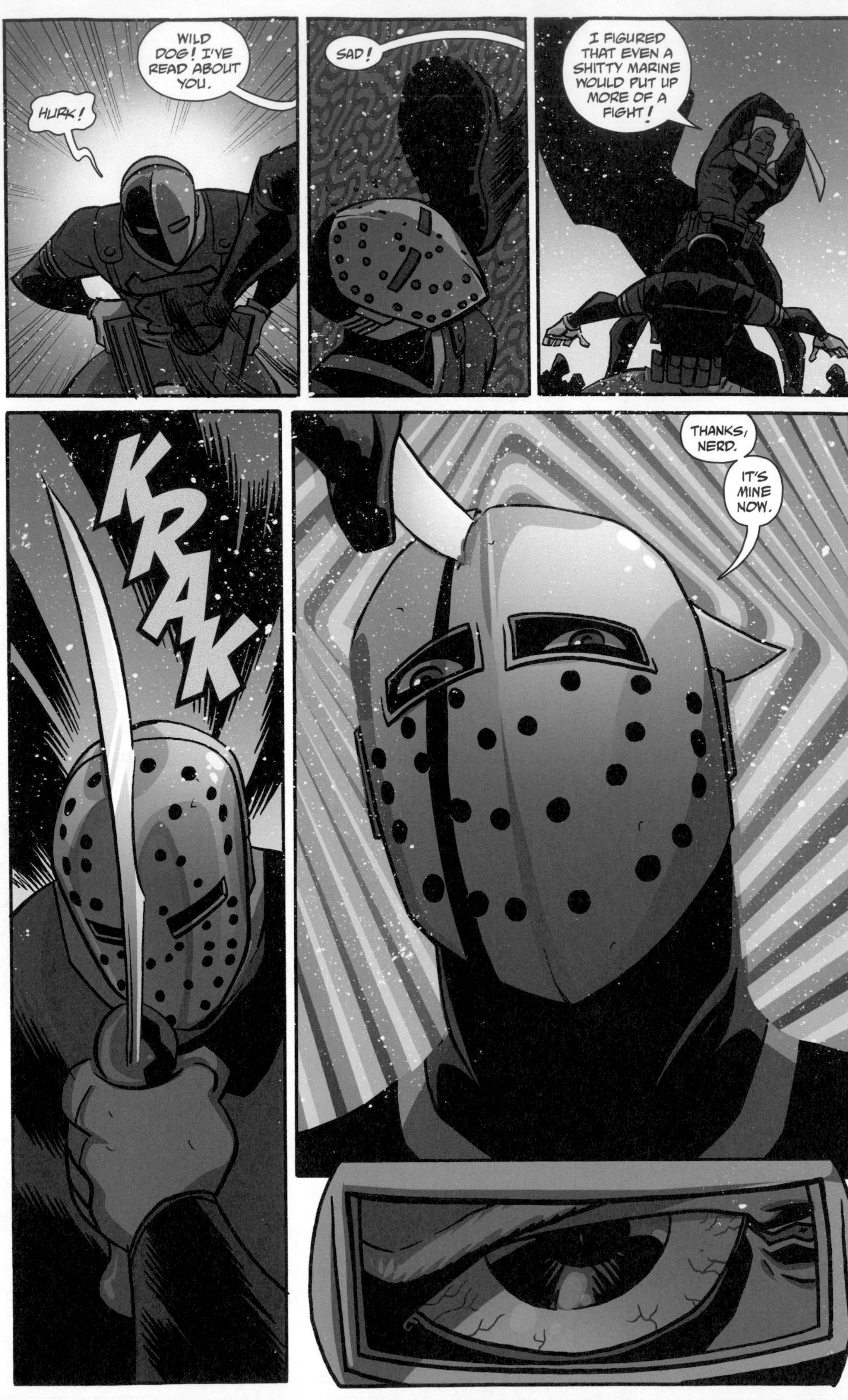
WILD DOG! I'VE READ ABOUT YOU.
HURK!
SAD!
I FIGURED THAT EVEN A SHITTY MARINE WOULD PUT UP MORE OF A FIGHT!
KRAK
THANKS, NERD.
IT'S MINE NOW.

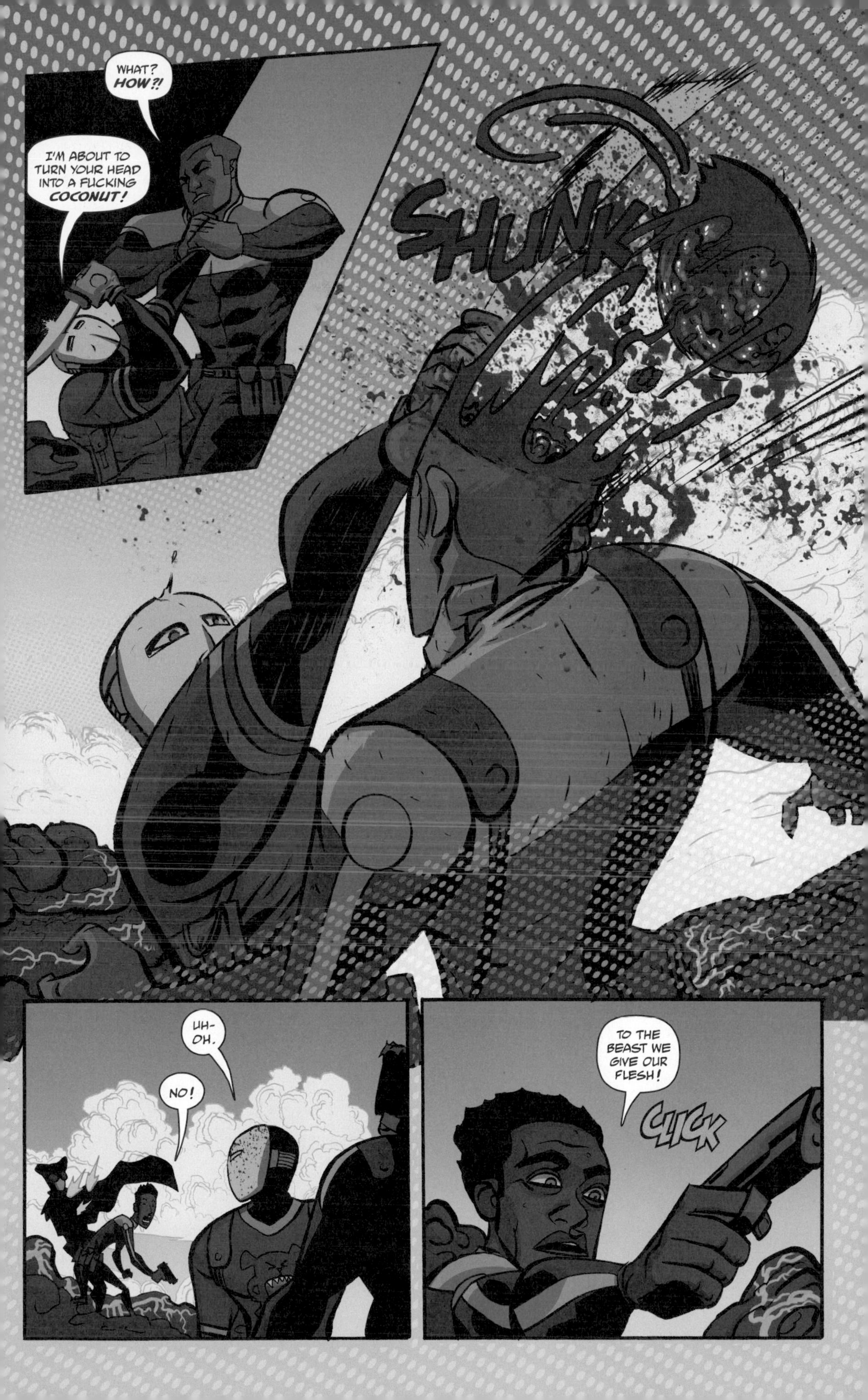
WHAT? HOW?!
I'M ABOUT TO TURN YOUR HEAD INTO A FUCKING COCONUT!
SHUNK
UH-OH.
NO!
TO THE BEAST WE GIVE OUR FLESH!
CLICK

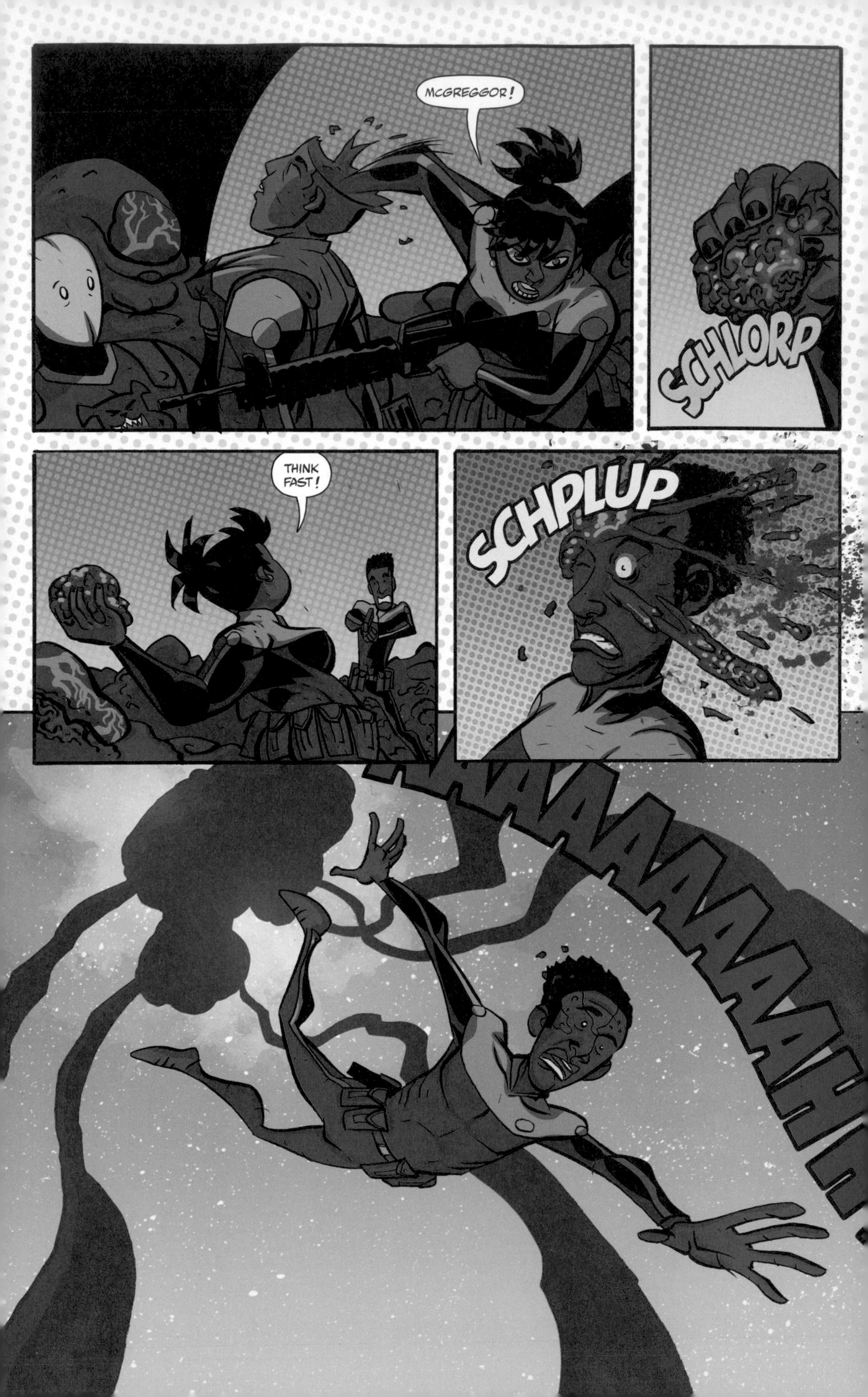
MCGREGGOR!
SCHLORP
THINK FAST!
SCHPLUP
AAAAAAAAAAAAH!!

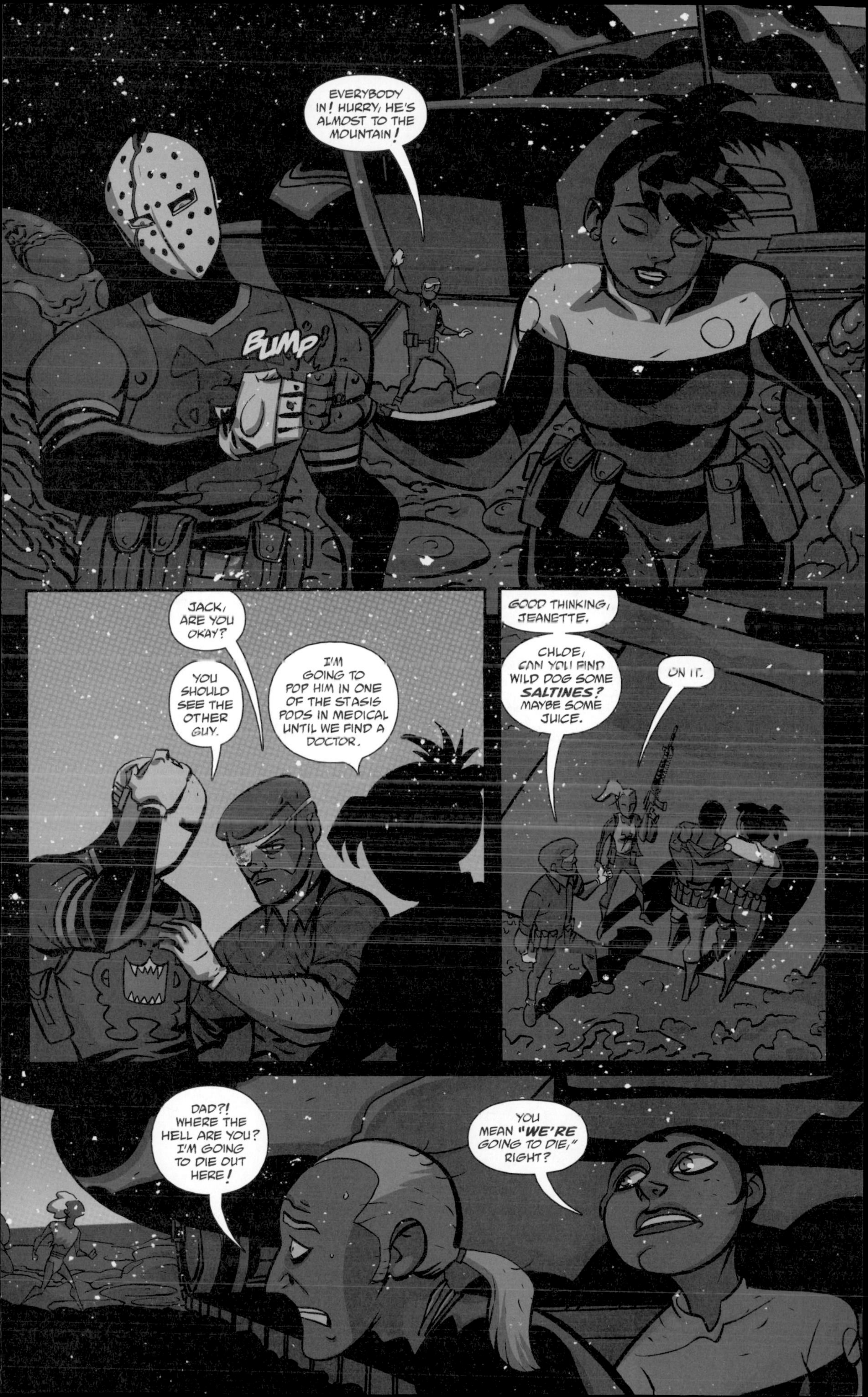
EVERYBODY IN! HURRY, HE'S ALMOST TO THE MOUNTAIN!
BUMP
JACK, ARE YOU OKAY?
YOU SHOULD SEE THE OTHER GUY.
I'M GOING TO POP HIM IN ONE OF THE STASIS PODS IN MEDICAL UNTIL WE FIND A DOCTOR.
GOOD THINKING, JEANETTE.
CHLOE, CAN YOU FIND WILD DOG SOME SALTINES? MAYBE SOME JUICE.
ON IT.
DAD?! WHERE THE HELL ARE YOU? I'M GOING TO DIE OUT HERE!
YOU MEAN "WE'RE GOING TO DIE," RIGHT?

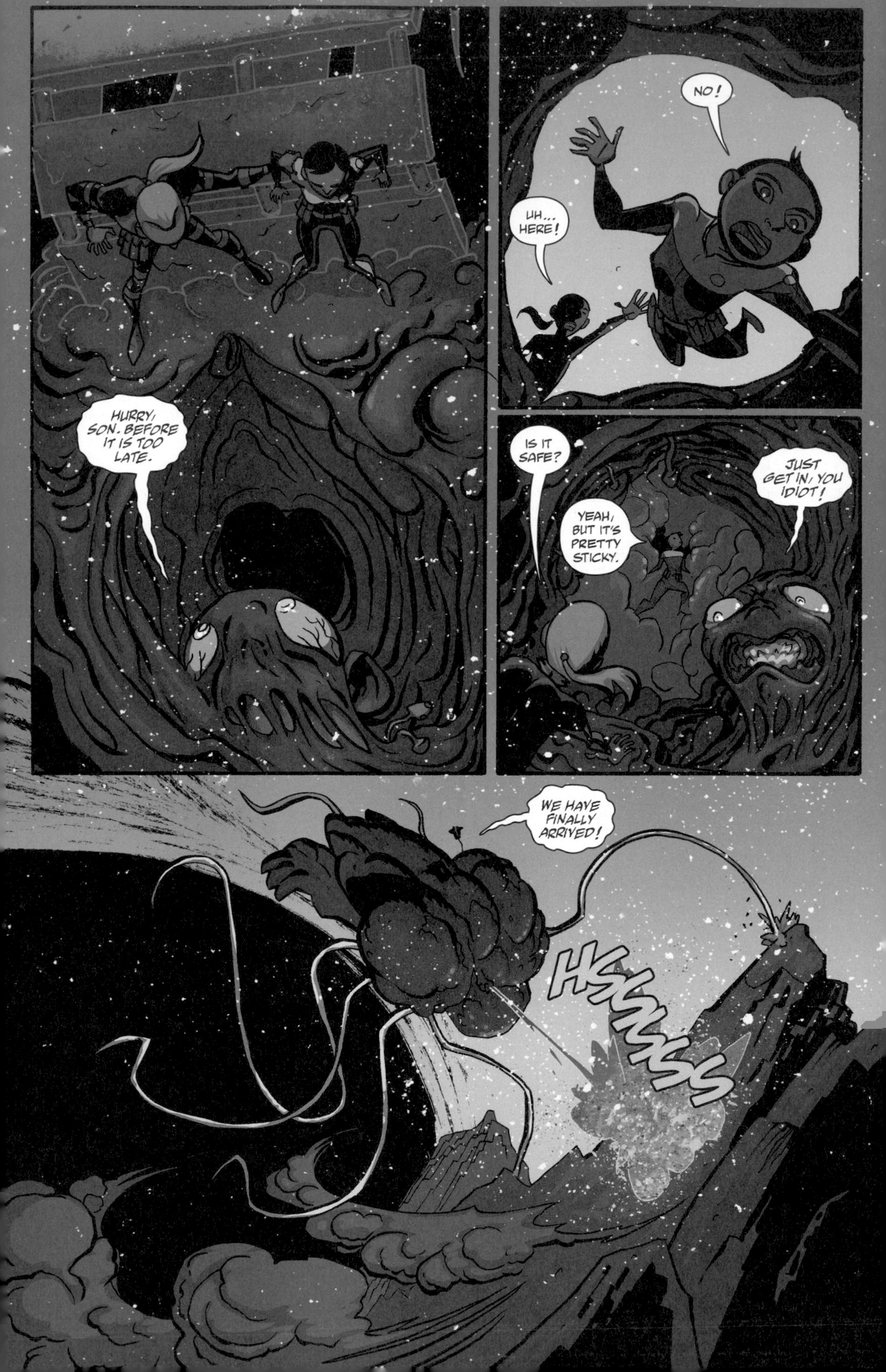
HURRY, SON. BEFORE IT IS TOO LATE.
NO!
UH... HERE!
IS IT SAFE?
YEAH, BUT IT'S PRETTY STICKY.
JUST GET IN, YOU IDIOT!
WE HAVE FINALLY ARRIVED!
HSSSSSS

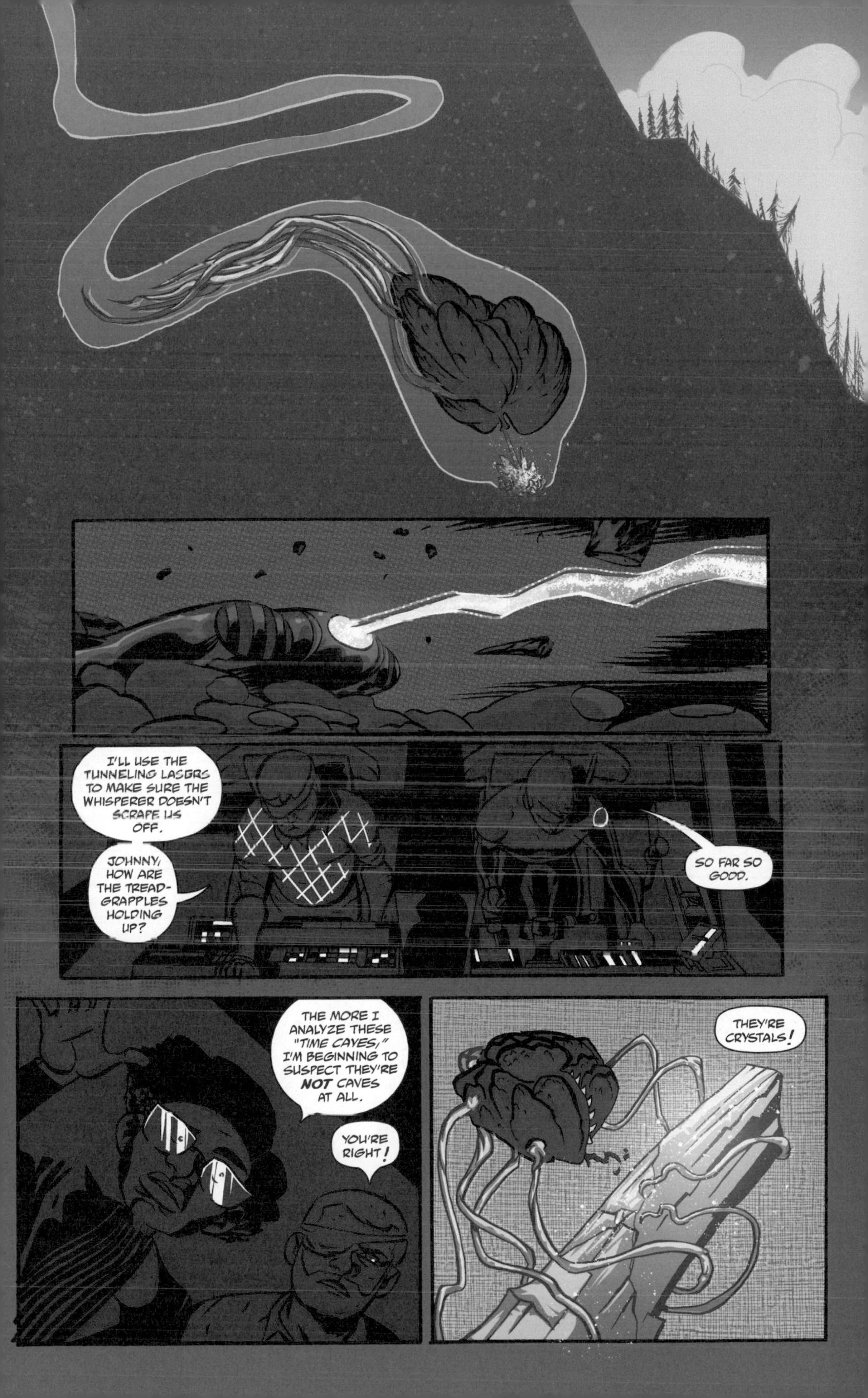
I'LL USE THE TUNNELING LASERS TO MAKE SURE THE WHISPERER DOESN'T SCRAPE US OFF.
JOHNNY, HOW ARE THE TREAD-GRAPPLES HOLDING UP?
SO FAR SO GOOD.
THE MORE I ANALYZE THESE "TIME CAVES," I'M BEGINNING TO SUSPECT THEY'RE NOT CAVES AT ALL.
YOU'RE RIGHT!
THEY'RE CRYSTALS!

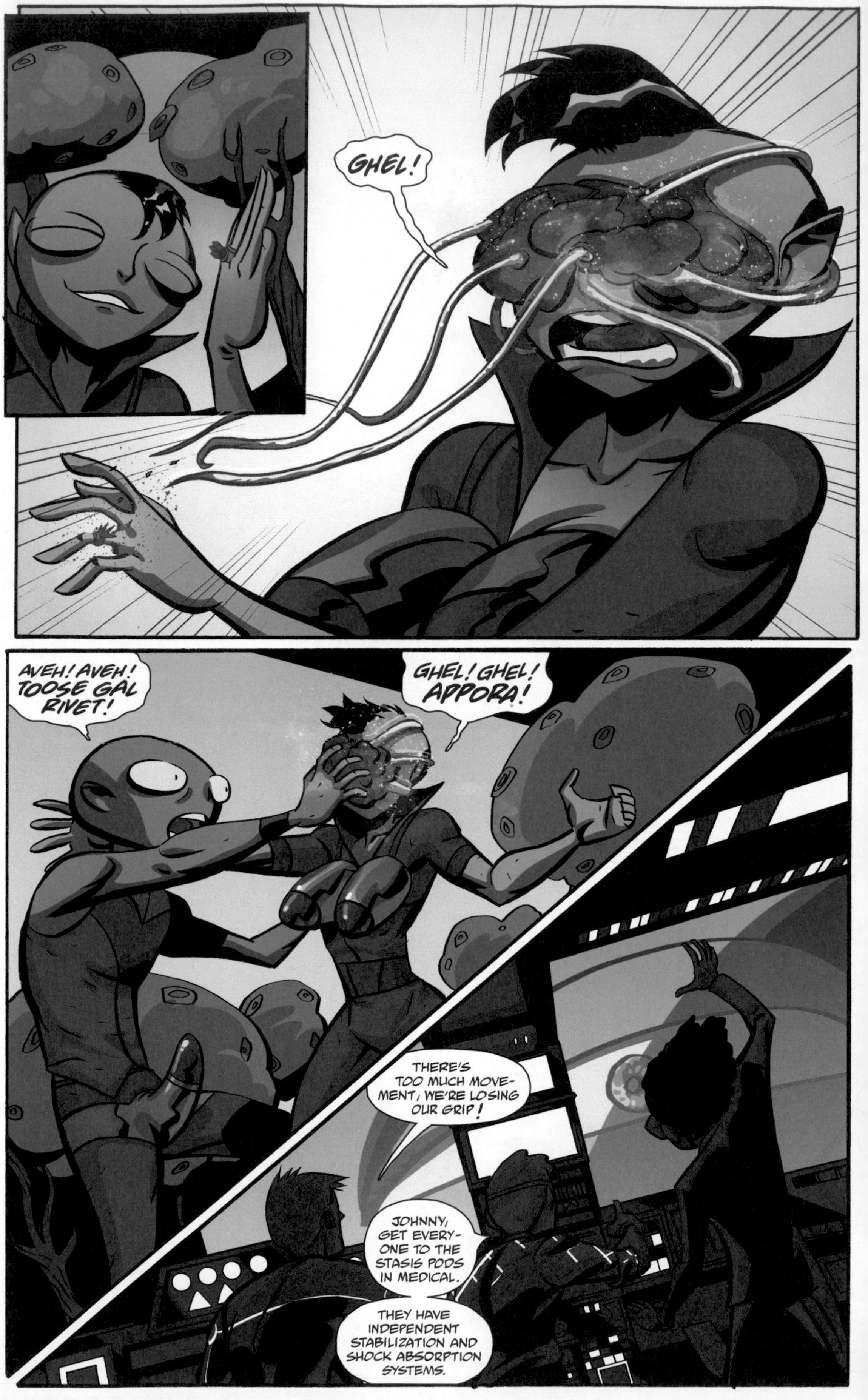
GHEL!
AVEH! AVEH! TOOSE GAL RIVET!
GHEL! GHEL! APPORA!
THERE'S TOO MUCH MOVEMENT, WE'RE LOSING OUR GRIP!
JOHNNY, GET EVERYONE TO THE STASIS PODS IN MEDICAL.
THEY HAVE INDEPENDENT STABILIZATION AND SHOCK ABSORPTION SYSTEMS.

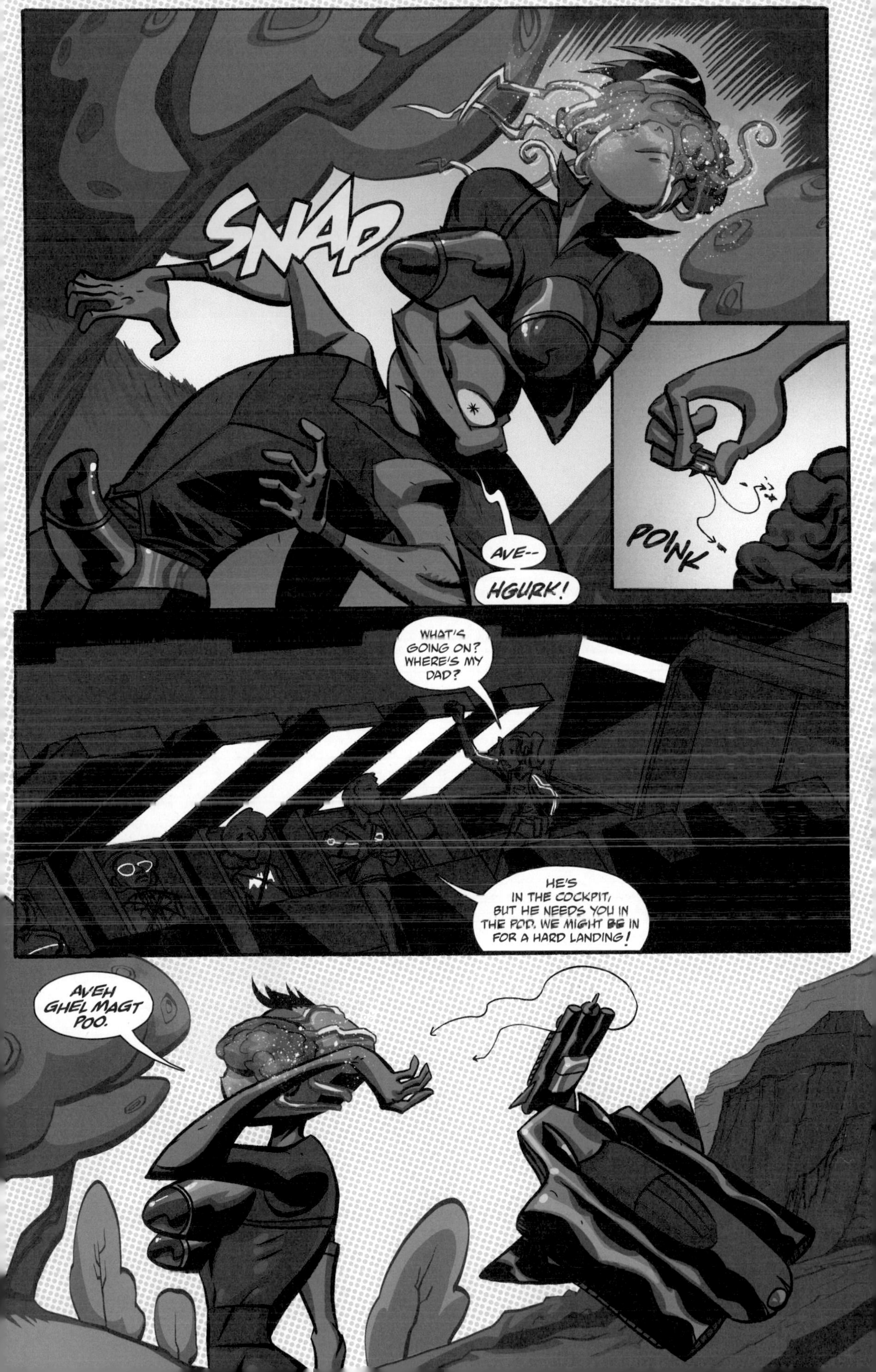
SNAP
AVE--
HGURK!
POINK
WHAT'S GOING ON? WHERE'S MY DAD?
HE'S IN THE COCKPIT, BUT HE NEEDS YOU IN THE POD. WE MIGHT BE IN FOR A HARD LANDING!
AVEH GHEL MAGT POO.

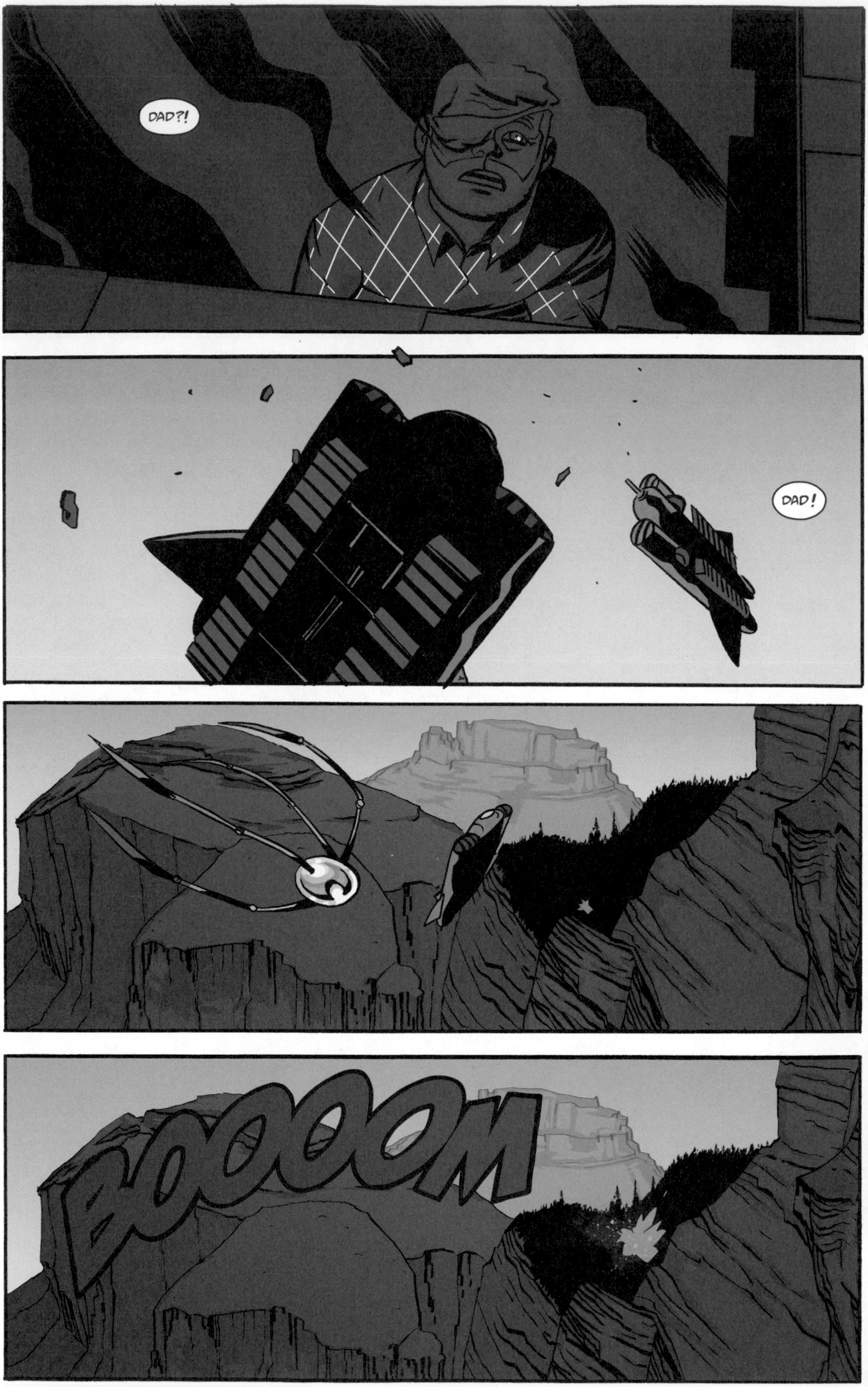
DAD?!
DAD!
BOOOOM

# Hey! Your Universe Is Leaking

**The nature of human consciousness** has always puzzled me. Human beings have been around for over 200,000 years, but for most of that time, we were duds. Content to eat a lizard, walk around a little, but never really creating or doing anything of interest. Then, about 75,000 years ago, something changed. Our brains exploded. Suddenly we began filling the world with cave paintings, music, and little ivory action figures to worship and play with. But why? Why all of a sudden? Why at all? Nobody knows. My good friend Herbert Niedermeyer and I have had many conversations on the subject, none of which had ended with any better guesses than when we started.

When Dr. Niedermeyer got engaged to be married, I took a trip to Puerto Rico to pay him a visit at the SETI Institute and meet Olga, his bride-to-be.

We were both avid art collectors and would often buy each other the weirdest works of art we could find just to dazzle each other with what could be found in the strange and darkened corners in the mind of an artist.

For their wedding present, I gave Herbert and Olga a painting of a desert landscape, over which people were flying inside cat heads. This is the moment I began to suspect that she didn't like me very much.

## "Where in the hell did that come from?"

Herbert asked, clearly impressed. What he meant was, why would a human mind produce something like that?

The next day, I attended a lecture Dr. Niedermeyer was giving on a new theory of his, which he called "Galactic Leakage."

"You may not have realized it when you were showering this morning," he said, "but you are all involved in one of the worst head-on collisions in history." What he was referring to, of course, was the fact that our galaxy, the Milky Way, has for eons been locked in a head-on collision with the Andromeda Galaxy. "Though, for the most part, the galaxies aren't colliding so much as they are just sort of leaking into each other." His point, ultimately, was that the larger an entity, the more prone it was to "leakage," and that conversely, the tinier a part of that entity you are, the less likely you are to be aware that anything unusual is happening. Leakage being his term for how we collide with forces too big for us to notice.

After the lecture, we had our traditional brunch at El Gato Flojo.

"What if leakage is not merely a galactic phenomenon?" I asked. "What do you mean?" he said, grappling with his breakfast burrito. "Well, as you know, our universe is just one small zipcode in a Multiverse." "Of course," Dr. Niedermeyer replied. "And most of these other universes, unlike ours, will be immaterial. They won't have solid matter, but will instead be made purely of energy." "Obviously," he agreed. "Even our universe is virtually empty. Matter is just an accounting error of the Big Bang. Is your hot sauce working?" I passed him the hot sauce. "So how do you think one of these non-corporeal universes would go about leaking into ours?" When he realized what I was getting at, he dropped his breakfast burrito onto the patio cement.

I was speaking, of course, about human consciousness. That about 75,000 years ago, another universe began leaking into ours. Through our minds. Our thoughts may not be free or random. In fact, they may not be ours at all, but merely the holes in the dike through which a nonmaterial universe, the spirit world, you might say, leaks into ours.

Words by Mark Russell
Art by Benjamin Dewey

# The Wonderful World of Rocks!

With Professor Marc Bartow

# "THE DIAMOND PLANET"

The largest rock in the known universe, "Olga" is a single diamond five times the size of Earth. Discovered by Dr. Herbert Niedermeyer while investigating the pulsar around which it orbits, he presented the Diamond Planet to his wife at their wedding, as he was too poor to buy her a ring on his astronomer's salary.

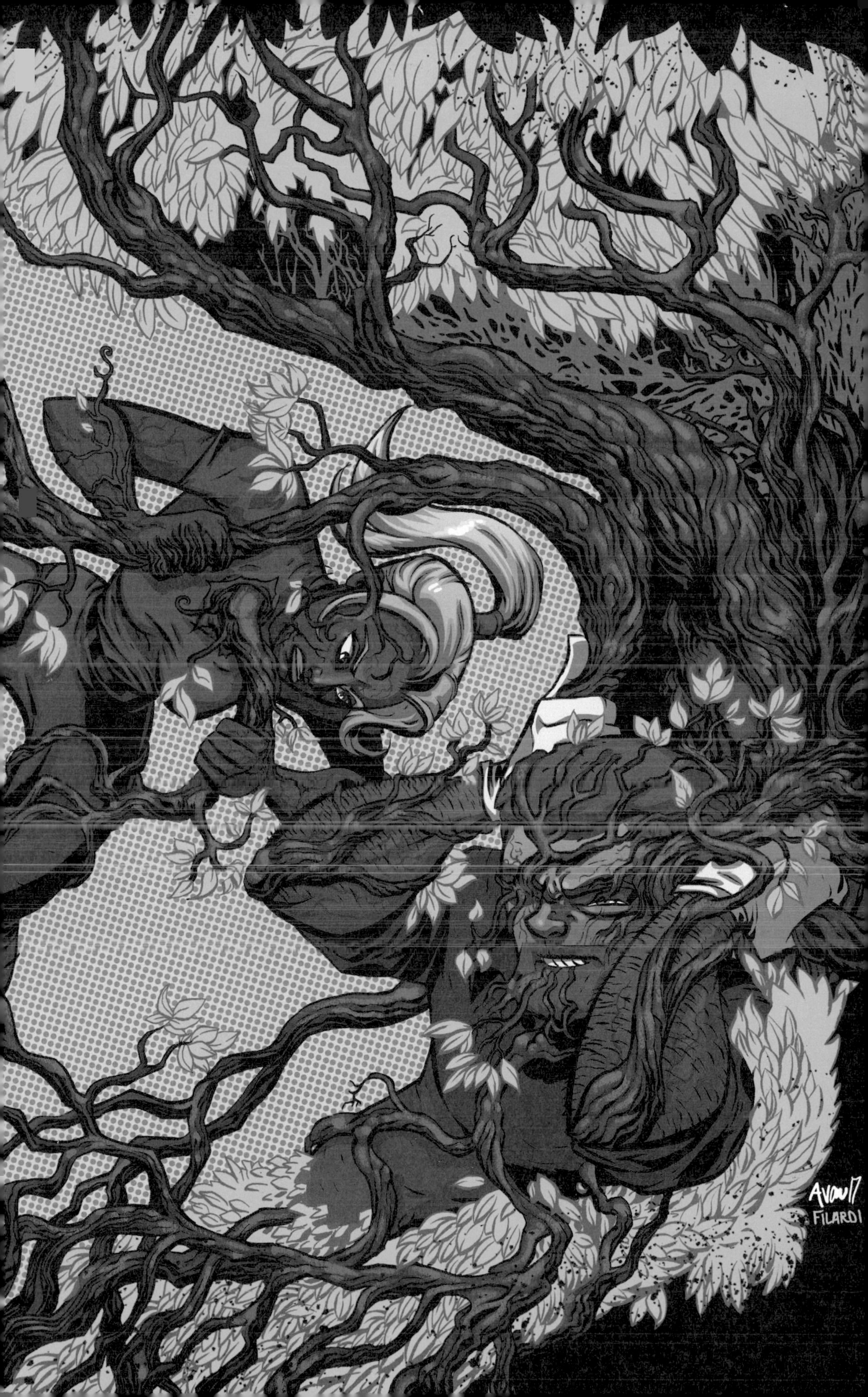
FILARDI

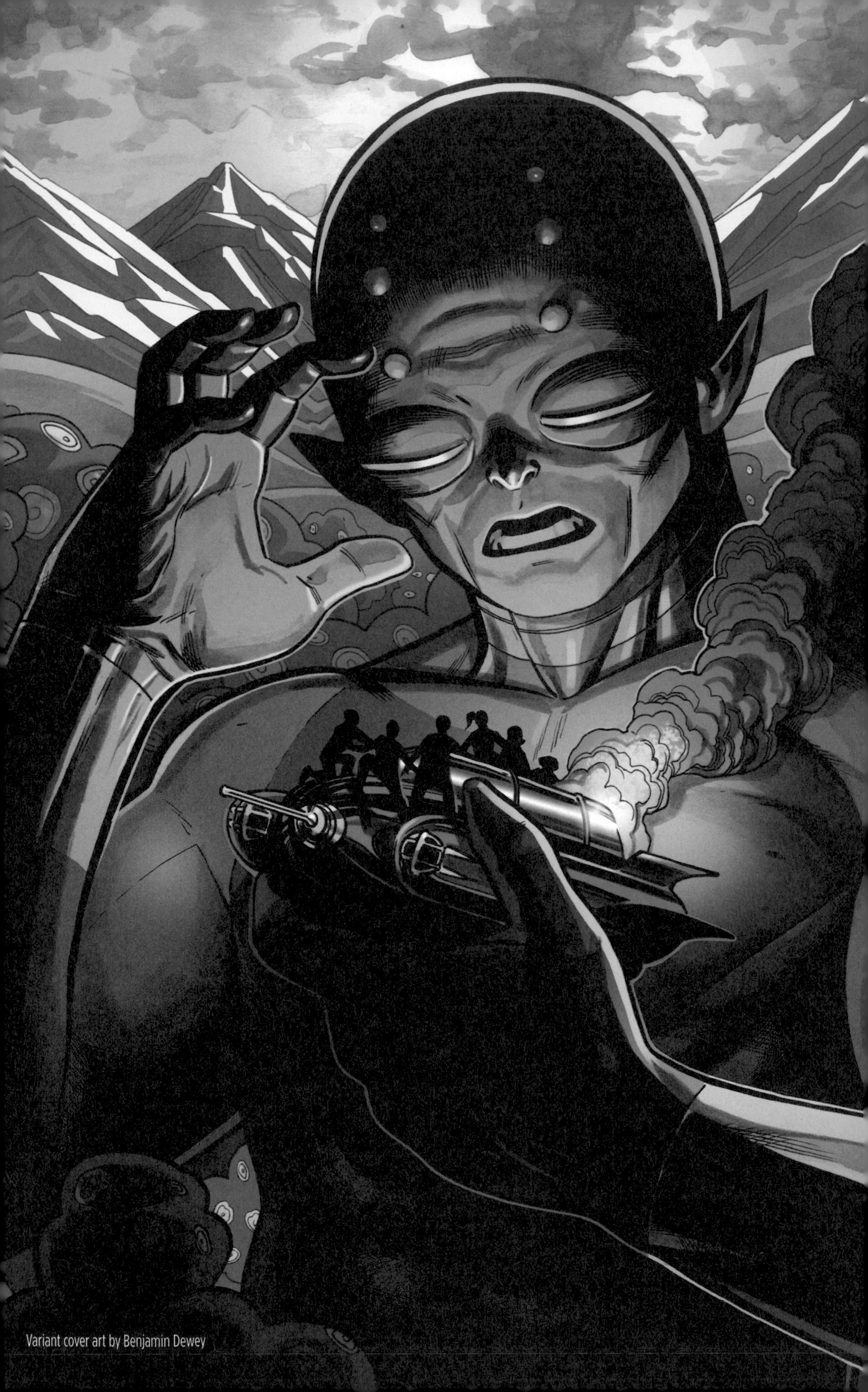

Variant cover art by Benjamin Dewey

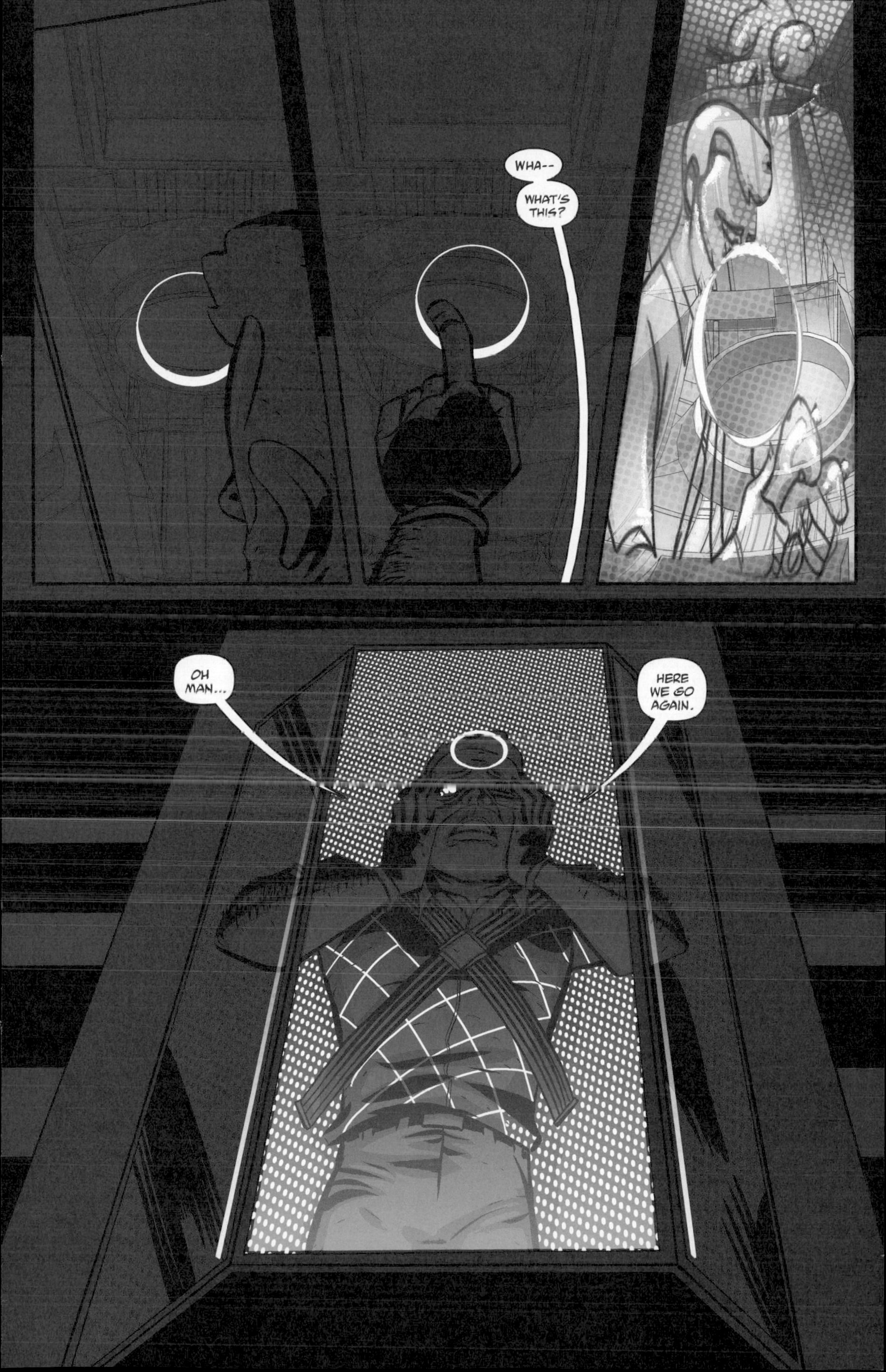
WHA--
WHAT'S THIS?
OH MAN...
HERE WE GO AGAIN.

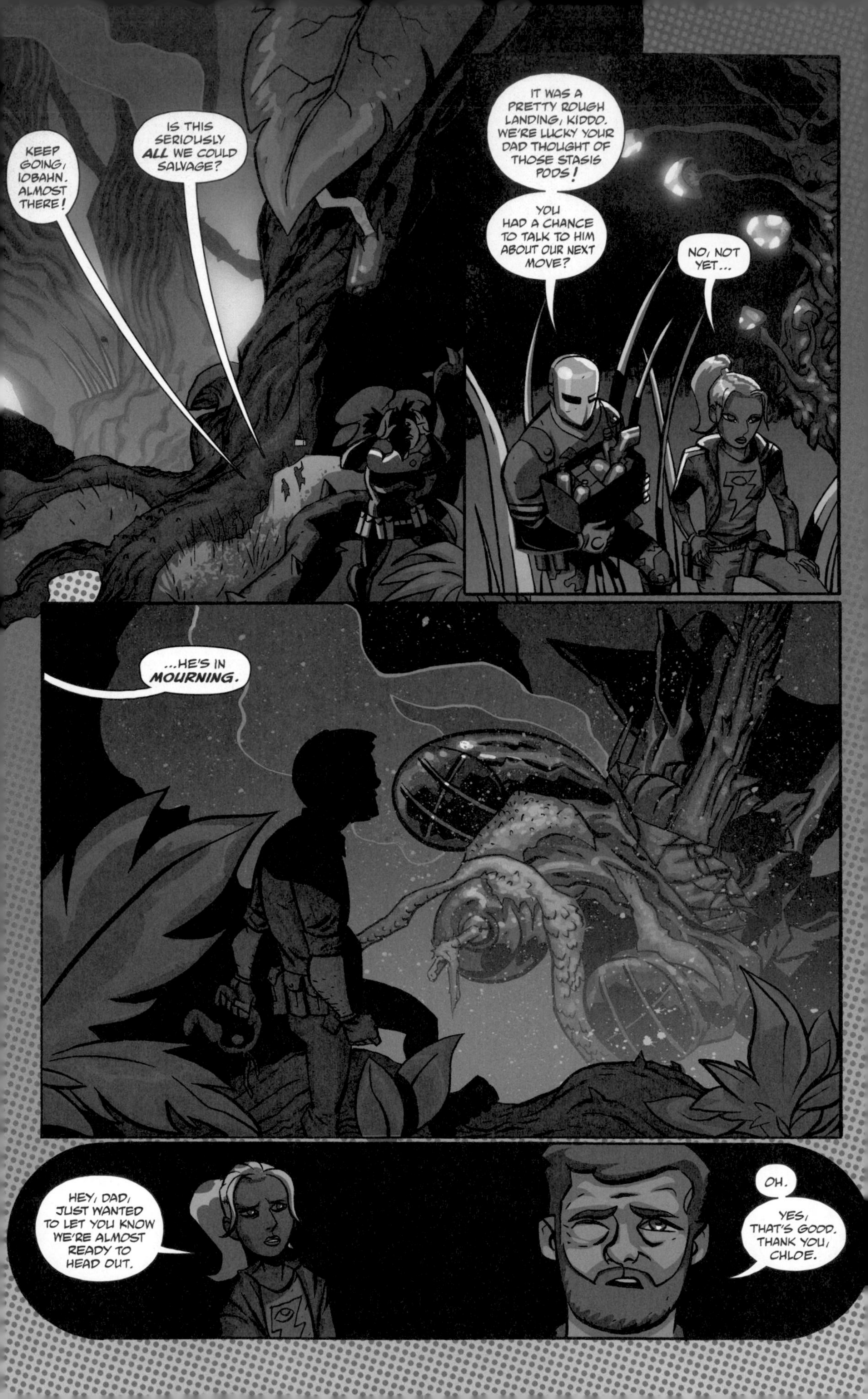
KEEP GOING, IOBAHN. ALMOST THERE!
IS THIS SERIOUSLY ALL WE COULD SALVAGE?
IT WAS A PRETTY ROUGH LANDING, KIDDO. WE'RE LUCKY YOUR DAD THOUGHT OF THOSE STASIS PODS!
YOU HAD A CHANCE TO TALK TO HIM ABOUT OUR NEXT MOVE?
NO, NOT YET...
...HE'S IN MOURNING.
HEY, DAD, JUST WANTED TO LET YOU KNOW WE'RE ALMOST READY TO HEAD OUT.
OH.
YES, THAT'S GOOD. THANK YOU, CHLOE.

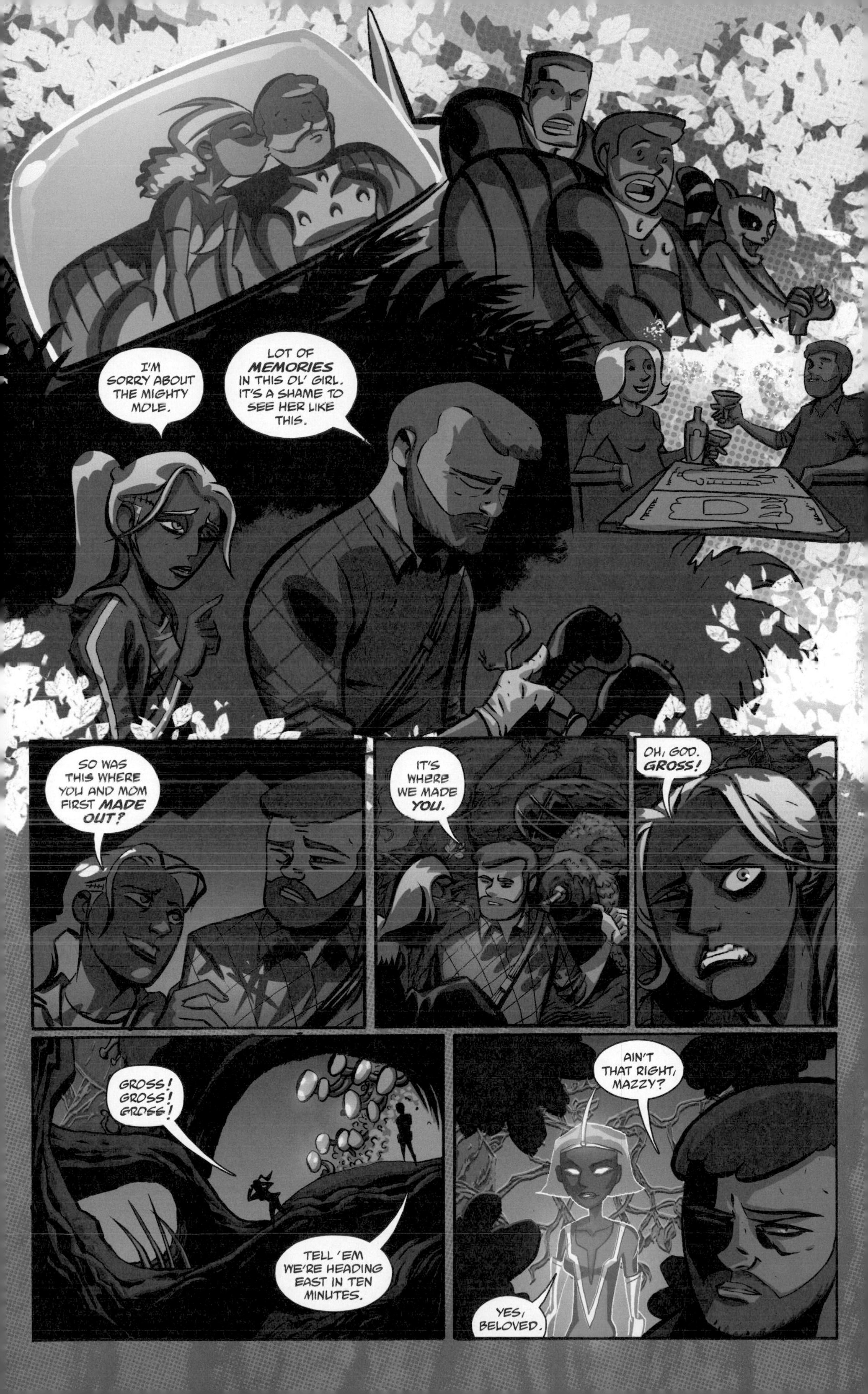
I'M SORRY ABOUT THE MIGHTY MOLE.
LOT OF MEMORIES IN THIS OL' GIRL. IT'S A SHAME TO SEE HER LIKE THIS.
SO WAS THIS WHERE YOU AND MOM FIRST MADE OUT?
IT'S WHERE WE MADE YOU.
OH, GOD. GROSS!
GROSS! GROSS! GROSS!
TELL 'EM WE'RE HEADING EAST IN TEN MINUTES.
AIN'T THAT RIGHT, MAZZY?
YES, BELOVED.

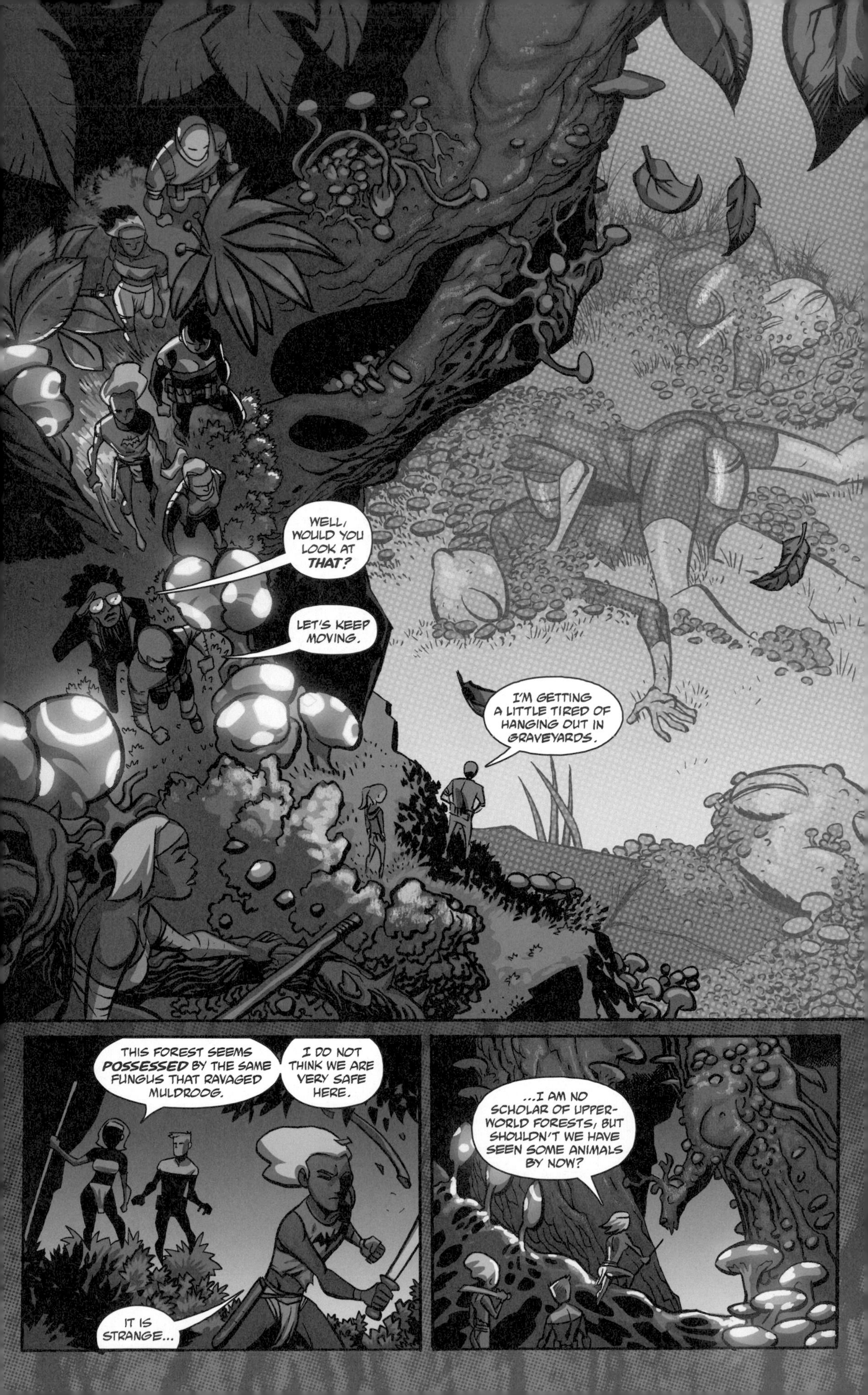
WELL, WOULD YOU LOOK AT THAT?
LET'S KEEP MOVING.
I'M GETTING A LITTLE TIRED OF HANGING OUT IN GRAVEYARDS.
THIS FOREST SEEMS POSSESSED BY THE SAME FUNGUS THAT RAVAGED MULDROOG.
I DO NOT THINK WE ARE VERY SAFE HERE.
IT IS STRANGE...
...I AM NO SCHOLAR OF UPPER-WORLD FORESTS, BUT SHOULDN'T WE HAVE SEEN SOME ANIMALS BY NOW?

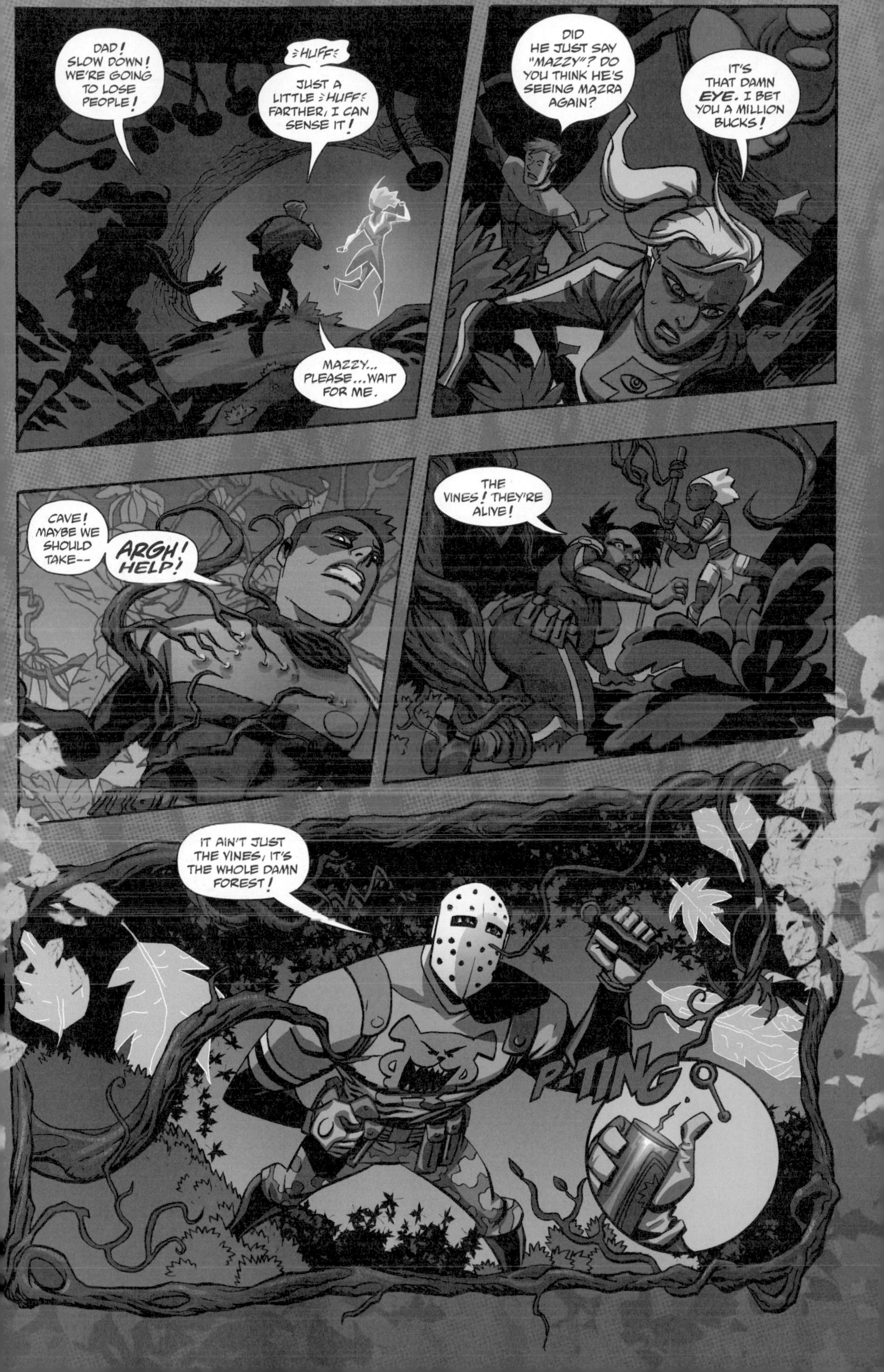
DAD! SLOW DOWN! WE'RE GOING TO LOSE PEOPLE!
HUFF
JUST A LITTLE HUFF FARTHER, I CAN SENSE IT!
MAZZY... PLEASE...WAIT FOR ME.
DID HE JUST SAY "MAZZY"? DO YOU THINK HE'S SEEING MAZRA AGAIN?
IT'S THAT DAMN EYE. I BET YOU A MILLION BUCKS!
CAVE! MAYBE WE SHOULD TAKE--
ARGH! HELP!
THE VINES! THEY'RE ALIVE!
IT AIN'T JUST THE VINES, IT'S THE WHOLE DAMN FOREST!
P-TING

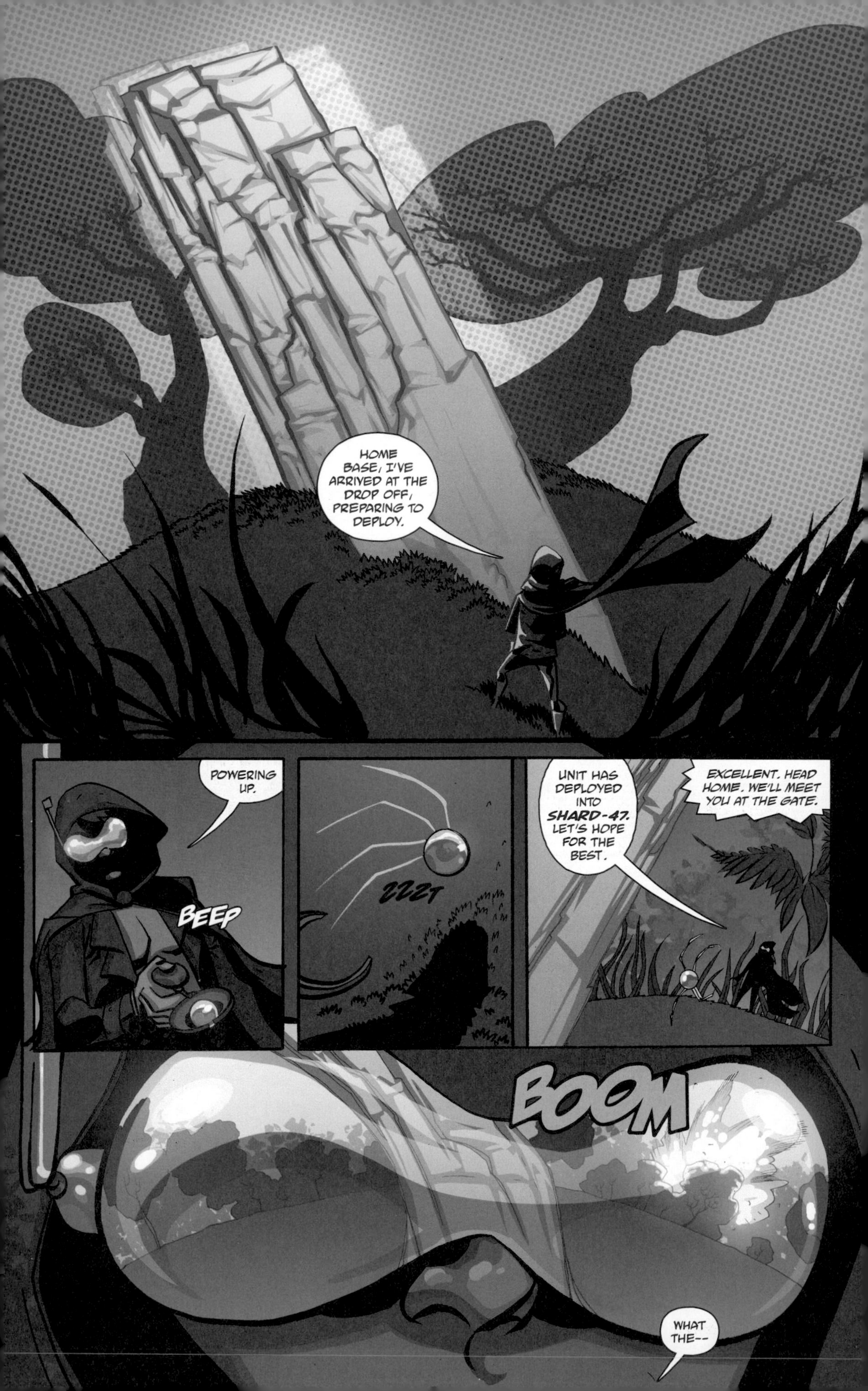
HOME BASE, I'VE ARRIVED AT THE DROP OFF, PREPARING TO DEPLOY.
POWERING UP.
BEEP
ZZZT
UNIT HAS DEPLOYED INTO SHARD-47. LET'S HOPE FOR THE BEST.
EXCELLENT. HEAD HOME. WE'LL MEET YOU AT THE GATE.
BOOM
WHAT THE--

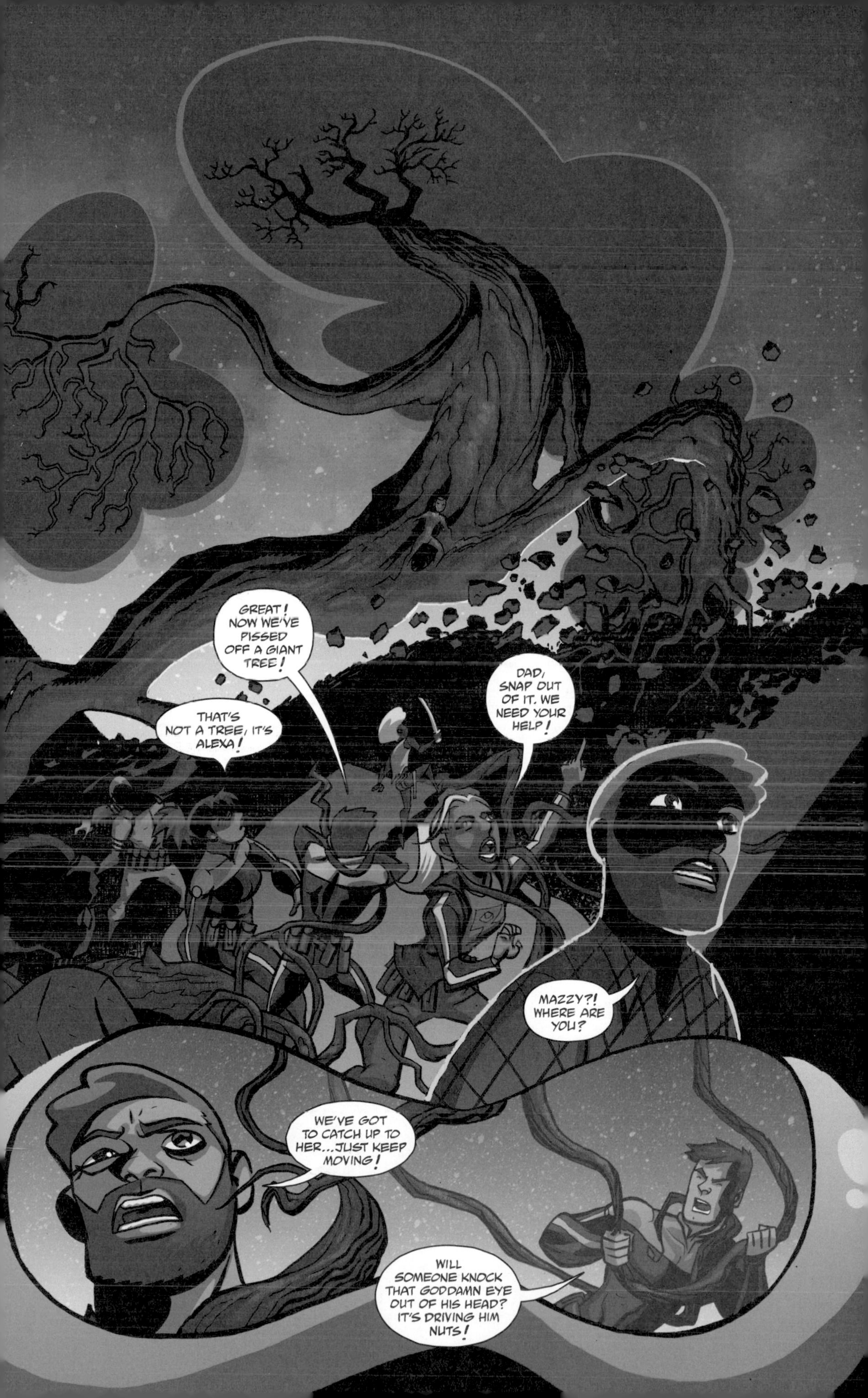
GREAT! NOW WE'VE PISSED OFF A GIANT TREE!
THAT'S NOT A TREE, IT'S ALEXA!
DAD, SNAP OUT OF IT. WE NEED YOUR HELP!
MAZZY?! WHERE ARE YOU?
WE'VE GOT TO CATCH UP TO HER...JUST KEEP MOVING!
WILL SOMEONE KNOCK THAT GODDAMN EYE OUT OF HIS HEAD? IT'S DRIVING HIM NUTS!

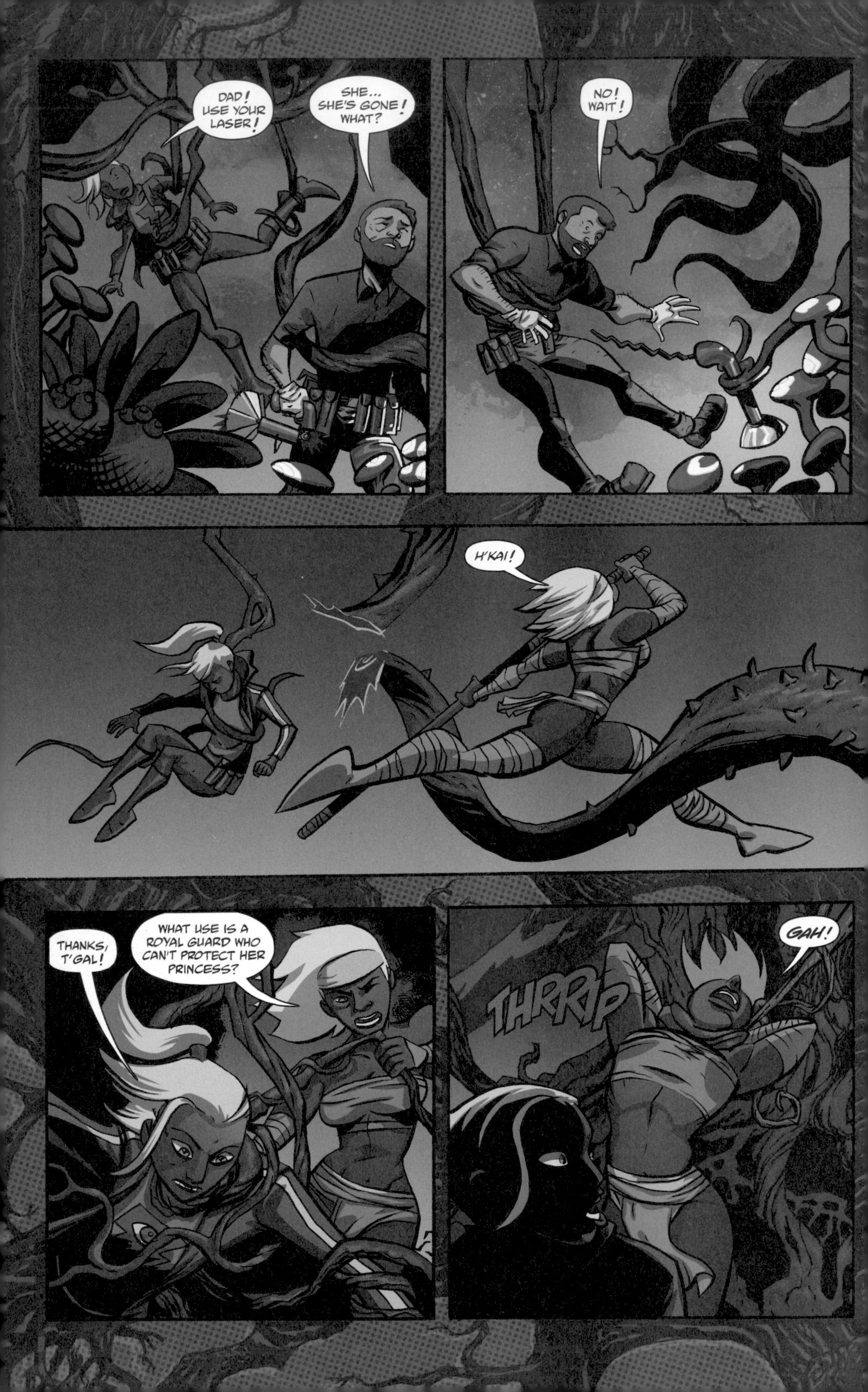
DAD! USE YOUR LASER!
SHE... SHE'S GONE! WHAT?
NO! WAIT!
H'KAI!
THANKS, T'GAL!
WHAT USE IS A ROYAL GUARD WHO CAN'T PROTECT HER PRINCESS?
THRRIP
GAH!

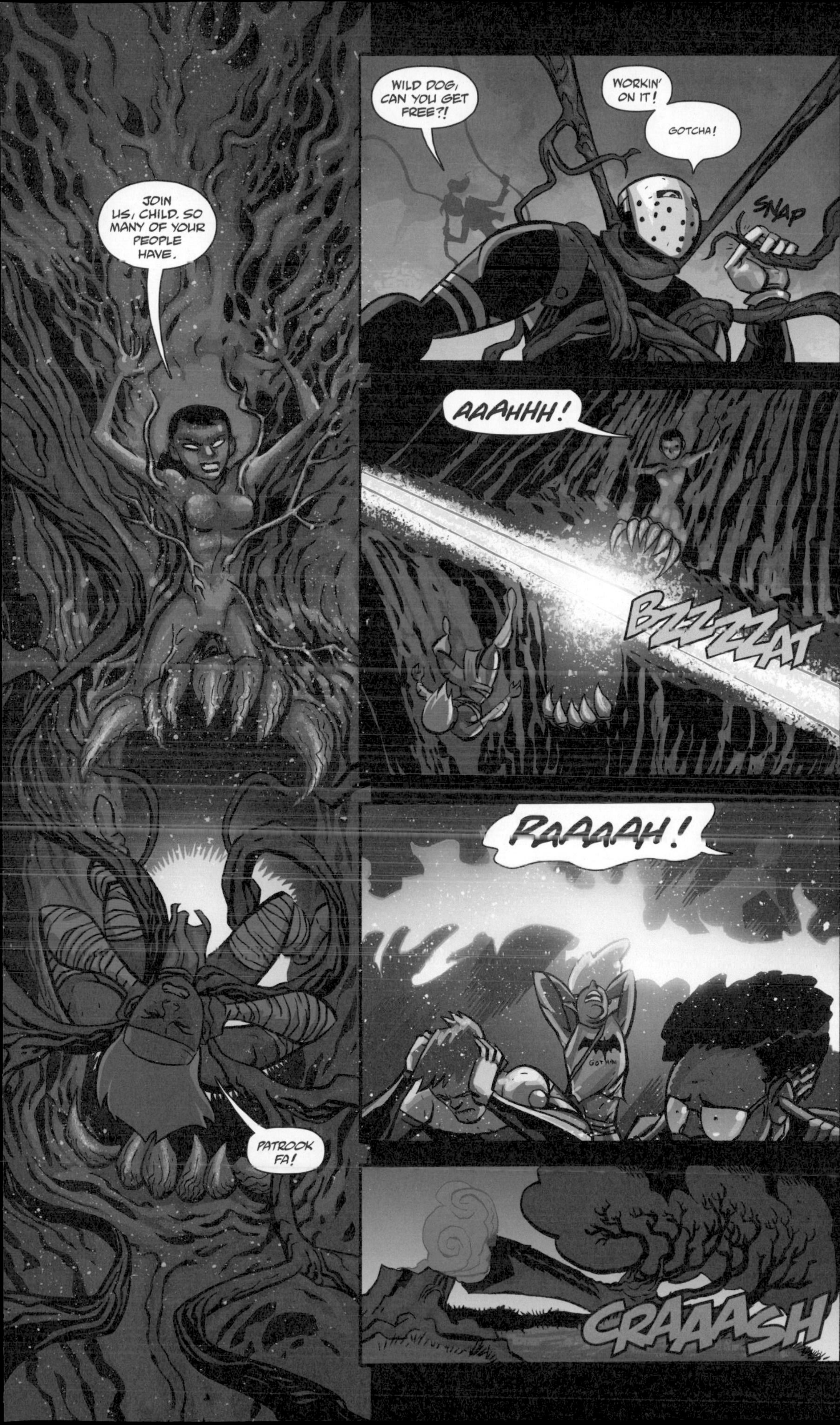
JOIN US, CHILD. SO MANY OF YOUR PEOPLE HAVE.
PATROOK FA!
WILD DOG, CAN YOU GET FREE?!
WORKIN' ON IT!
GOTCHA!
SNAP
AAAHHH!
BZZZZAT
RAAAAH!
GOTHAM
CRAAASH

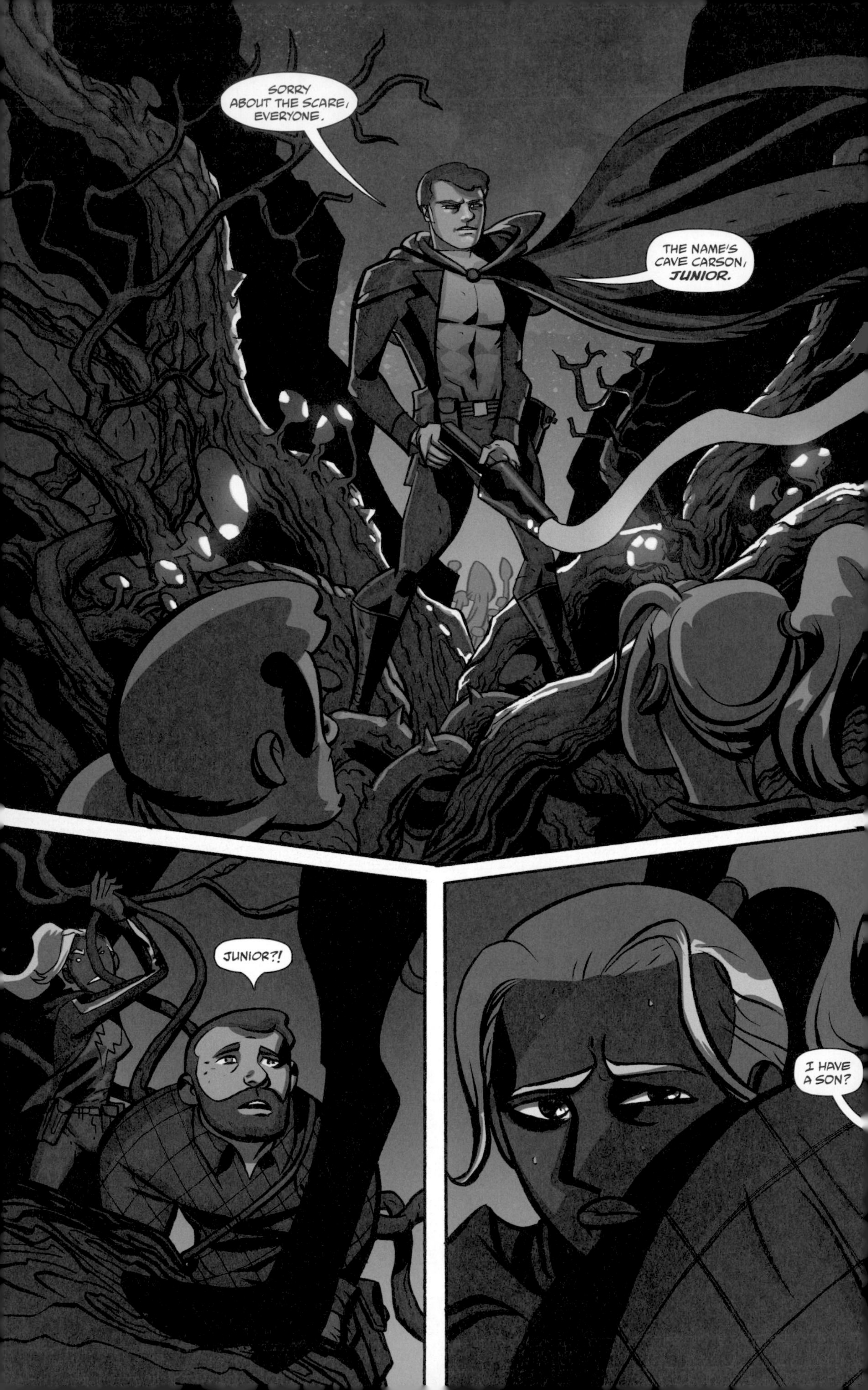
SORRY ABOUT THE SCARE, EVERYONE.
THE NAME'S CAVE CARSON, JUNIOR.
JUNIOR?!
I HAVE A SON?

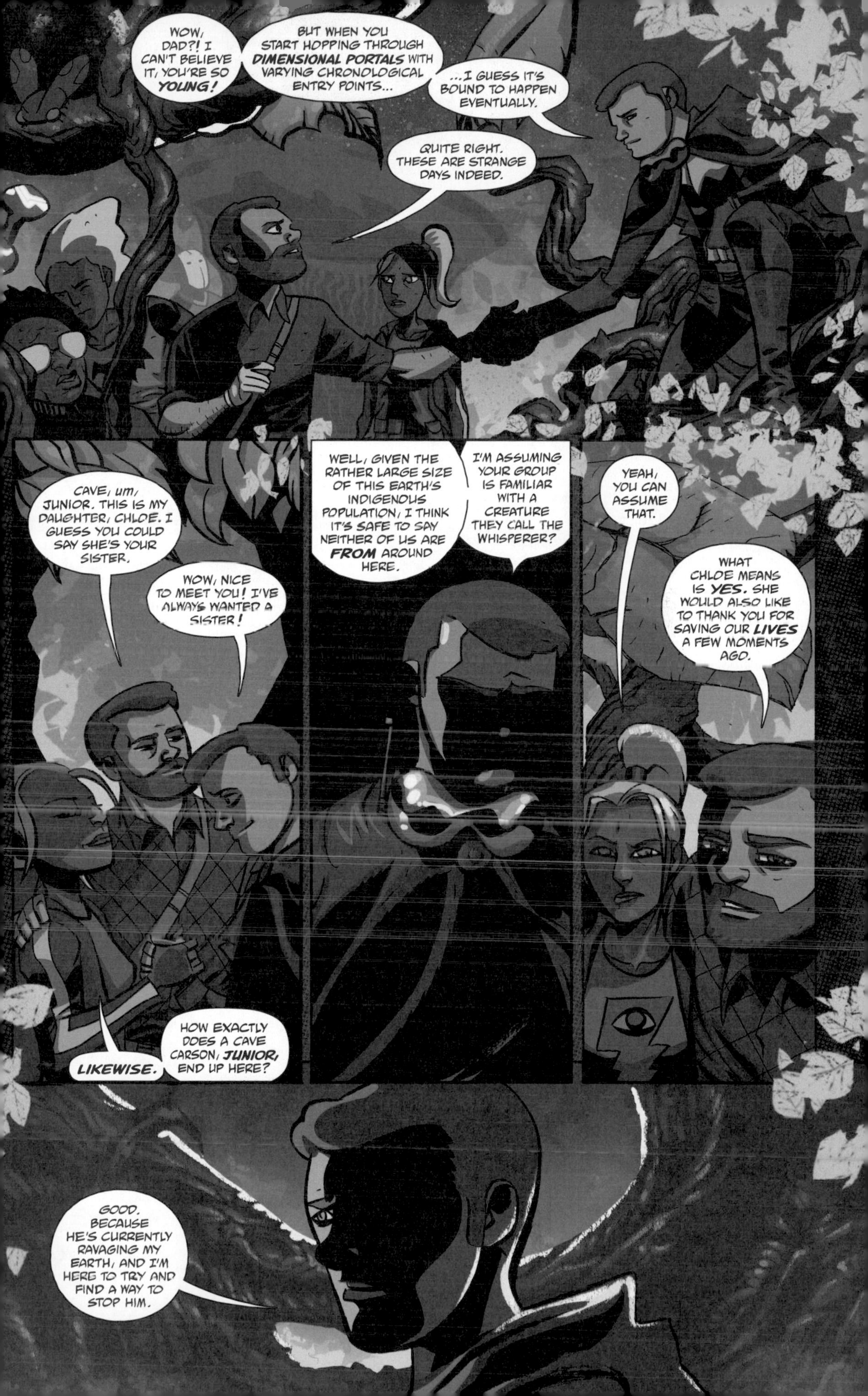
WOW, DAD?! I CAN'T BELIEVE IT, YOU'RE SO YOUNG!
BUT WHEN YOU START HOPPING THROUGH DIMENSIONAL PORTALS WITH VARYING CHRONOLOGICAL ENTRY POINTS...
...I GUESS IT'S BOUND TO HAPPEN EVENTUALLY.
QUITE RIGHT. THESE ARE STRANGE DAYS INDEED.
CAVE, um, JUNIOR. THIS IS MY DAUGHTER, CHLOE. I GUESS YOU COULD SAY SHE'S YOUR SISTER.
WOW, NICE TO MEET YOU! I'VE ALWAYS WANTED A SISTER!
LIKEWISE.
HOW EXACTLY DOES A CAVE CARSON, JUNIOR, END UP HERE?
WELL, GIVEN THE RATHER LARGE SIZE OF THIS EARTH'S INDIGENOUS POPULATION, I THINK IT'S SAFE TO SAY NEITHER OF US ARE FROM AROUND HERE.
I'M ASSUMING YOUR GROUP IS FAMILIAR WITH A CREATURE THEY CALL THE WHISPERER?
YEAH, YOU CAN ASSUME THAT.
WHAT CHLOE MEANS IS YES. SHE WOULD ALSO LIKE TO THANK YOU FOR SAVING OUR LIVES A FEW MOMENTS AGO.
GOOD. BECAUSE HE'S CURRENTLY RAVAGING MY EARTH, AND I'M HERE TO TRY AND FIND A WAY TO STOP HIM.

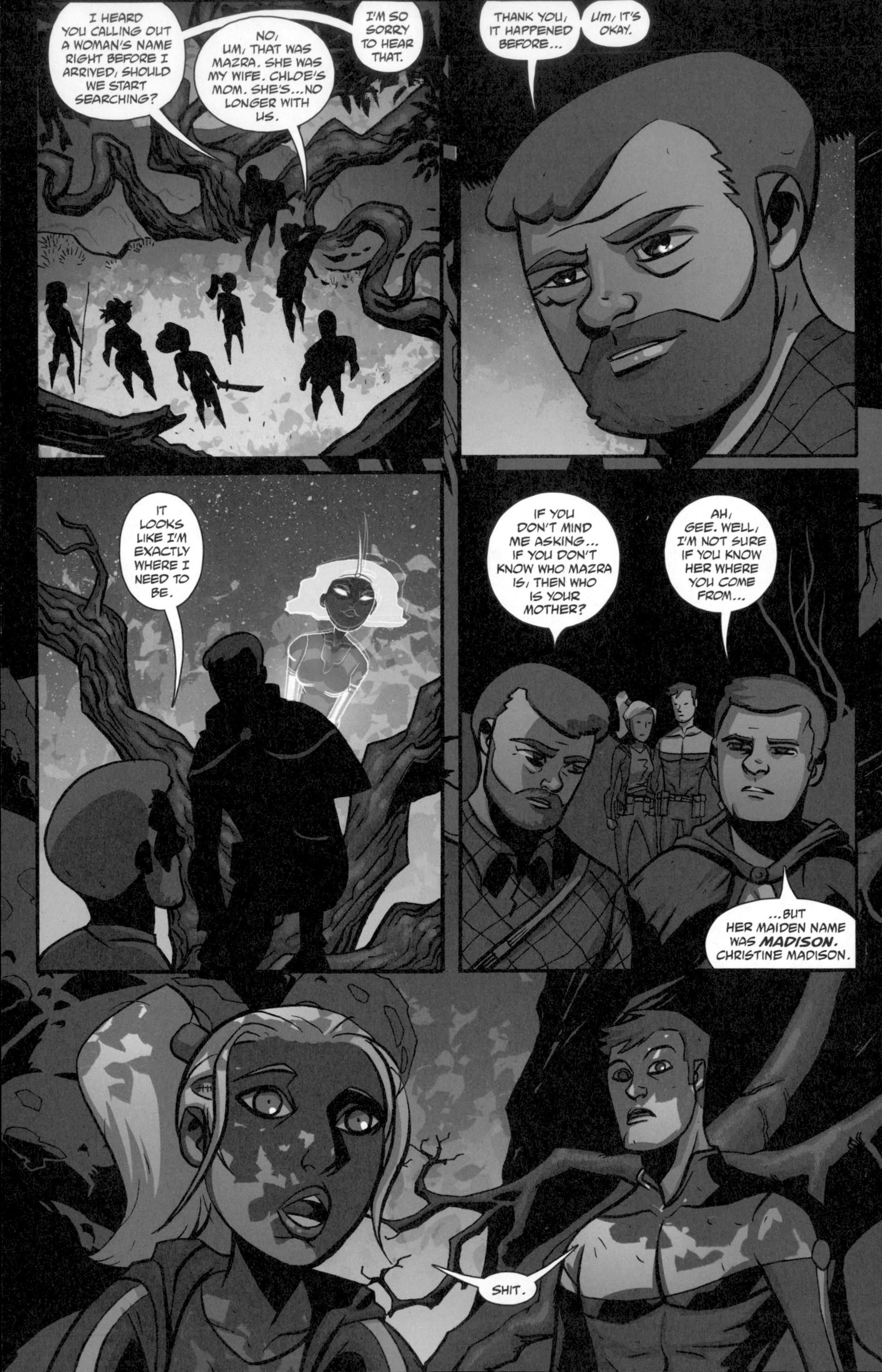
I HEARD YOU CALLING OUT A WOMAN'S NAME RIGHT BEFORE I ARRIVED, SHOULD WE START SEARCHING?
NO, UM, THAT WAS MAZRA. SHE WAS MY WIFE. CHLOE'S MOM. SHE'S...NO LONGER WITH US.
I'M SO SORRY TO HEAR THAT.
THANK YOU, IT HAPPENED BEFORE...
UM, IT'S OKAY.
IT LOOKS LIKE I'M EXACTLY WHERE I NEED TO BE.
IF YOU DON'T MIND ME ASKING... IF YOU DON'T KNOW WHO MAZRA IS, THEN WHO IS YOUR MOTHER?
AH, GEE. WELL, I'M NOT SURE IF YOU KNOW HER WHERE YOU COME FROM...
...BUT HER MAIDEN NAME WAS MADISON. CHRISTINE MADISON.
SHIT.

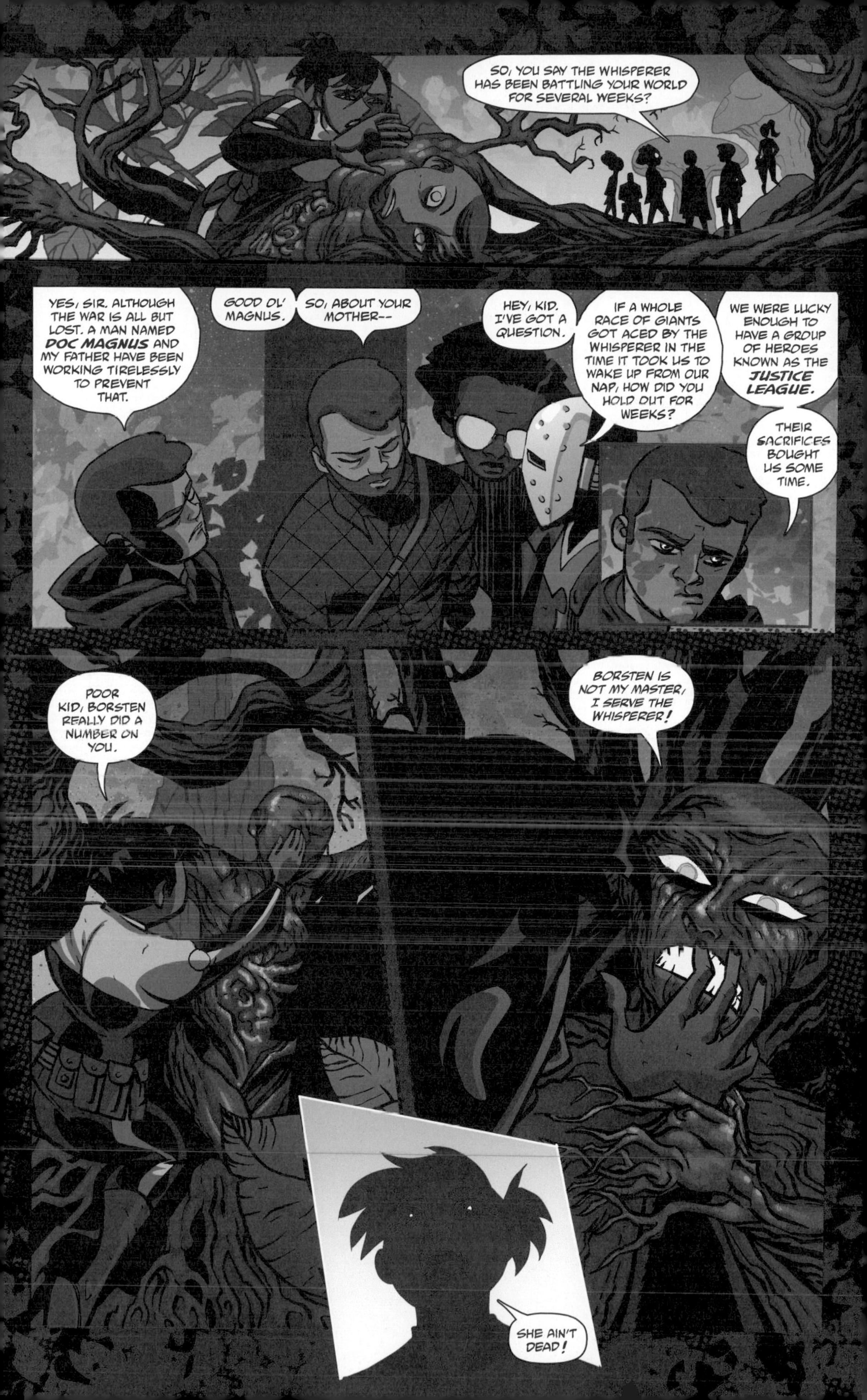
SO, YOU SAY THE WHISPERER HAS BEEN BATTLING YOUR WORLD FOR SEVERAL WEEKS?
YES, SIR. ALTHOUGH THE WAR IS ALL BUT LOST. A MAN NAMED DOC MAGNUS AND MY FATHER HAVE BEEN WORKING TIRELESSLY TO PREVENT THAT.
GOOD OL' MAGNUS.
SO, ABOUT YOUR MOTHER--
HEY, KID. I'VE GOT A QUESTION.
IF A WHOLE RACE OF GIANTS GOT ACED BY THE WHISPERER IN THE TIME IT TOOK US TO WAKE UP FROM OUR NAP, HOW DID YOU HOLD OUT FOR WEEKS?
WE WERE LUCKY ENOUGH TO HAVE A GROUP OF HEROES KNOWN AS THE JUSTICE LEAGUE.
THEIR SACRIFICES BOUGHT US SOME TIME.
POOR KID, BORSTEN REALLY DID A NUMBER ON YOU.
BORSTEN IS NOT MY MASTER, I SERVE THE WHISPERER!
SHE AIN'T DEAD!

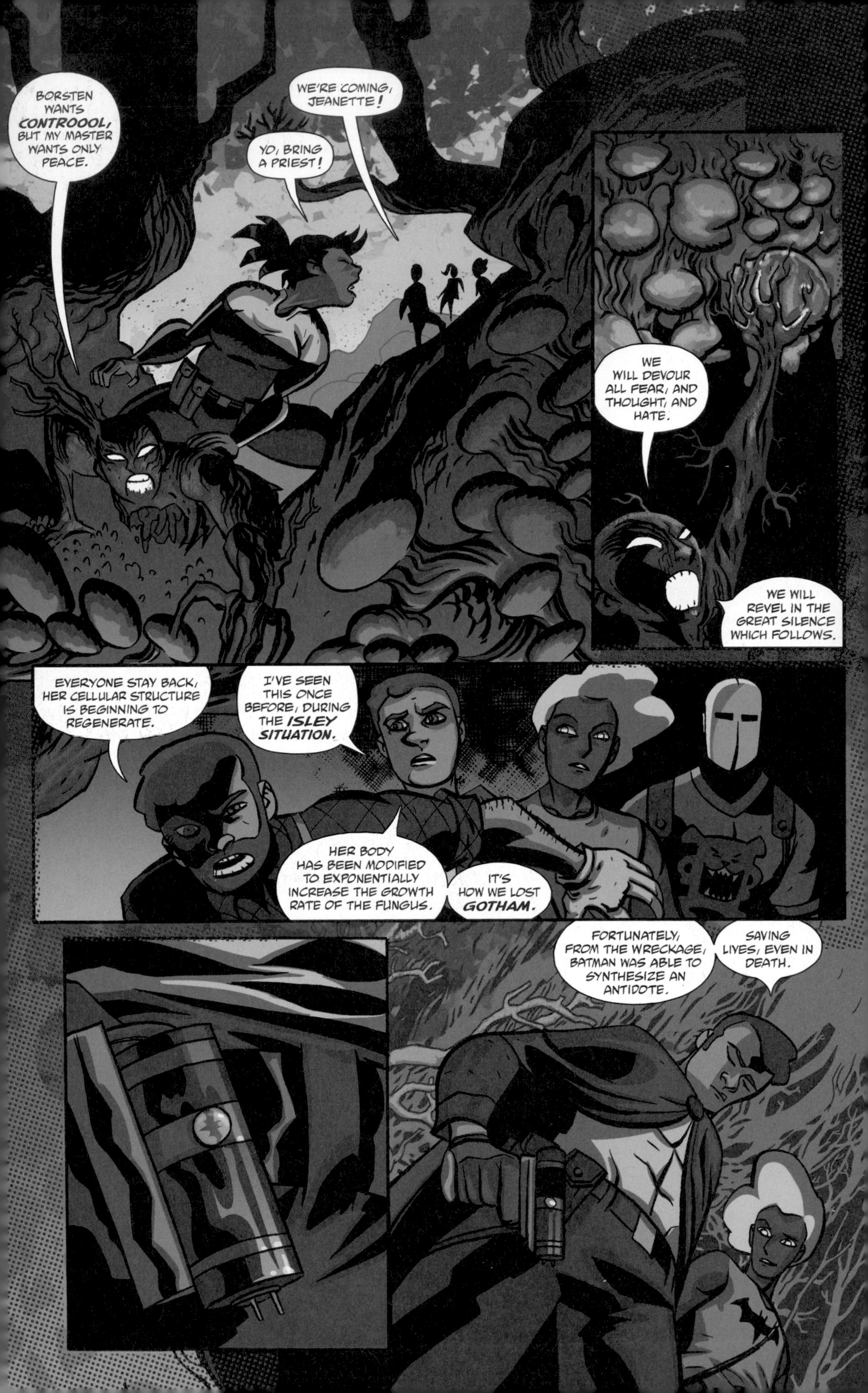
BORSTEN WANTS CONTROOOL, BUT MY MASTER WANTS ONLY PEACE.
WE'RE COMING, JEANETTE!
YO, BRING A PRIEST!
WE WILL DEVOUR ALL FEAR, AND THOUGHT, AND HATE.
WE WILL REVEL IN THE GREAT SILENCE WHICH FOLLOWS.
EVERYONE STAY BACK, HER CELLULAR STRUCTURE IS BEGINNING TO REGENERATE.
I'VE SEEN THIS ONCE BEFORE, DURING THE ISLEY SITUATION.
HER BODY HAS BEEN MODIFIED TO EXPONENTIALLY INCREASE THE GROWTH RATE OF THE FUNGUS.
IT'S HOW WE LOST GOTHAM.
FORTUNATELY, FROM THE WRECKAGE, BATMAN WAS ABLE TO SYNTHESIZE AN ANTIDOTE.
SAVING LIVES, EVEN IN DEATH.

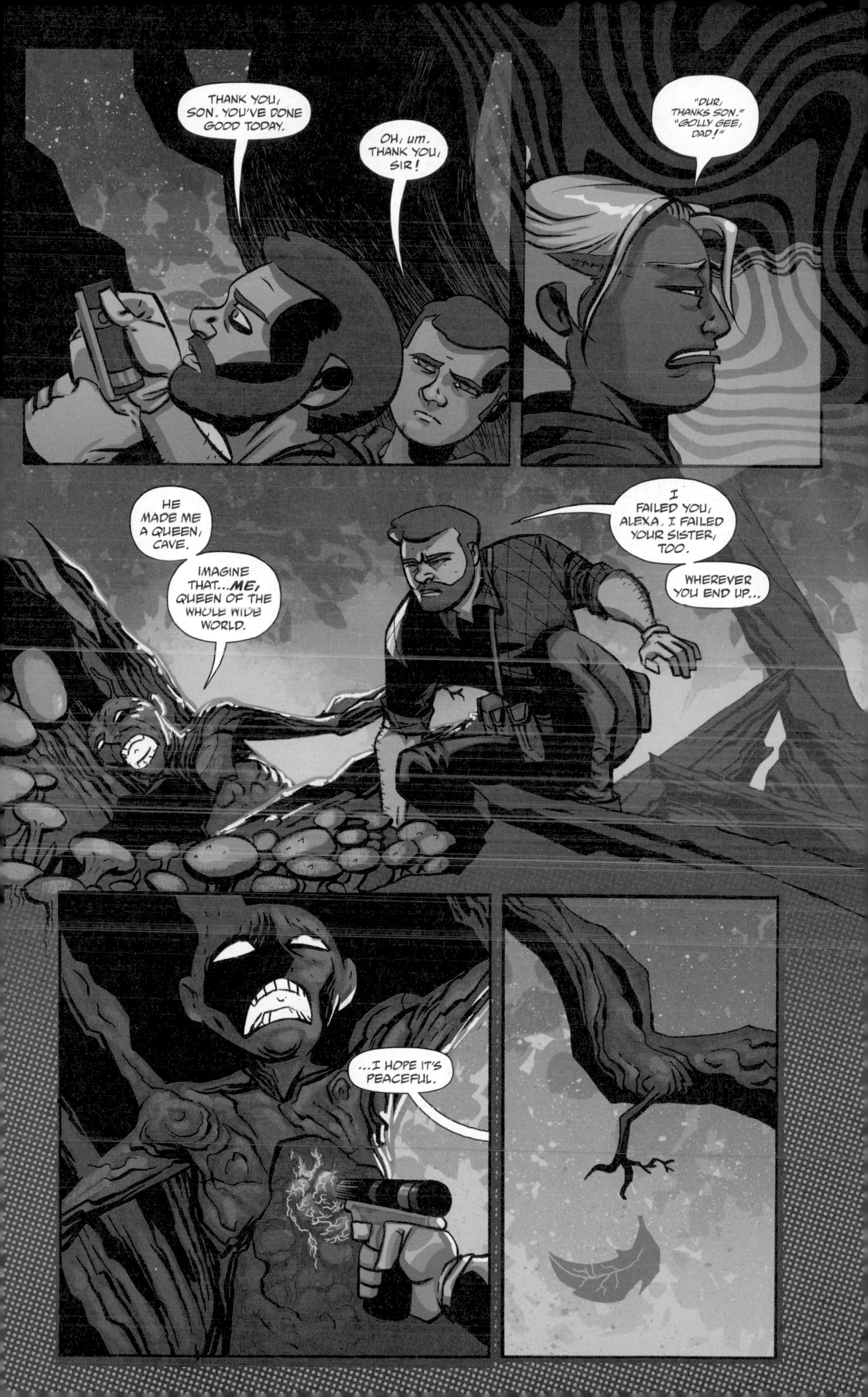
THANK YOU, SON. YOU'VE DONE GOOD TODAY.
OH, UM. THANK YOU, SIR!
"DUR, THANKS SON." "GOLLY GEE, DAD!"
HE MADE ME A QUEEN, CAVE.
IMAGINE THAT...ME, QUEEN OF THE WHOLE WIDE WORLD.
I FAILED YOU, ALEXA. I FAILED YOUR SISTER, TOO.
WHEREVER YOU END UP...
...I HOPE IT'S PEACEFUL.

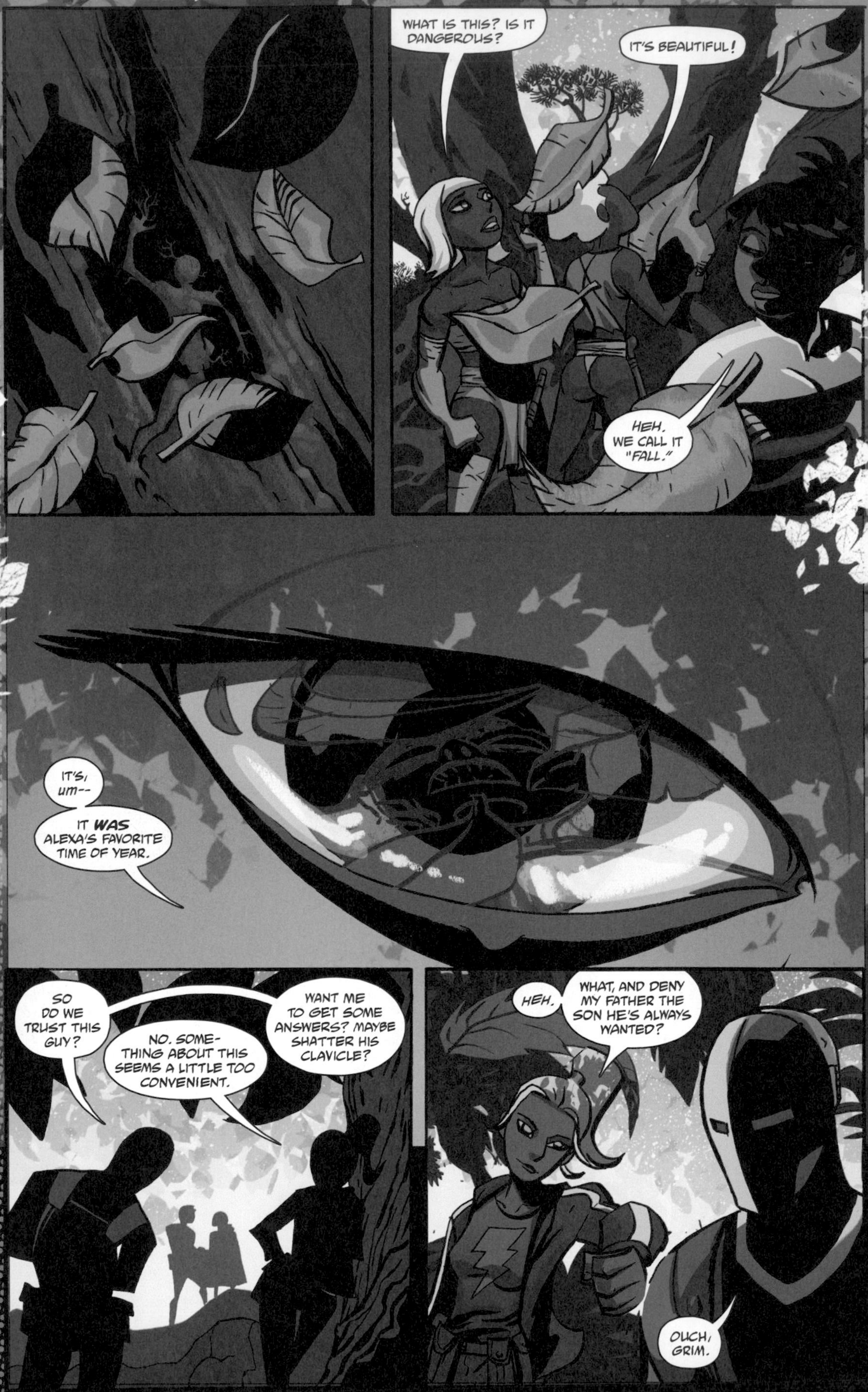
WHAT IS THIS? IS IT DANGEROUS?
IT'S BEAUTIFUL!
HEH. WE CALL IT "FALL."
IT'S, UM--
IT WAS ALEXA'S FAVORITE TIME OF YEAR.
SO DO WE TRUST THIS GUY?
NO. SOMETHING ABOUT THIS SEEMS A LITTLE TOO CONVENIENT.
WANT ME TO GET SOME ANSWERS? MAYBE SHATTER HIS CLAVICLE?
HEH.
WHAT, AND DENY MY FATHER THE SON HE'S ALWAYS WANTED?
OUCH, GRIM.

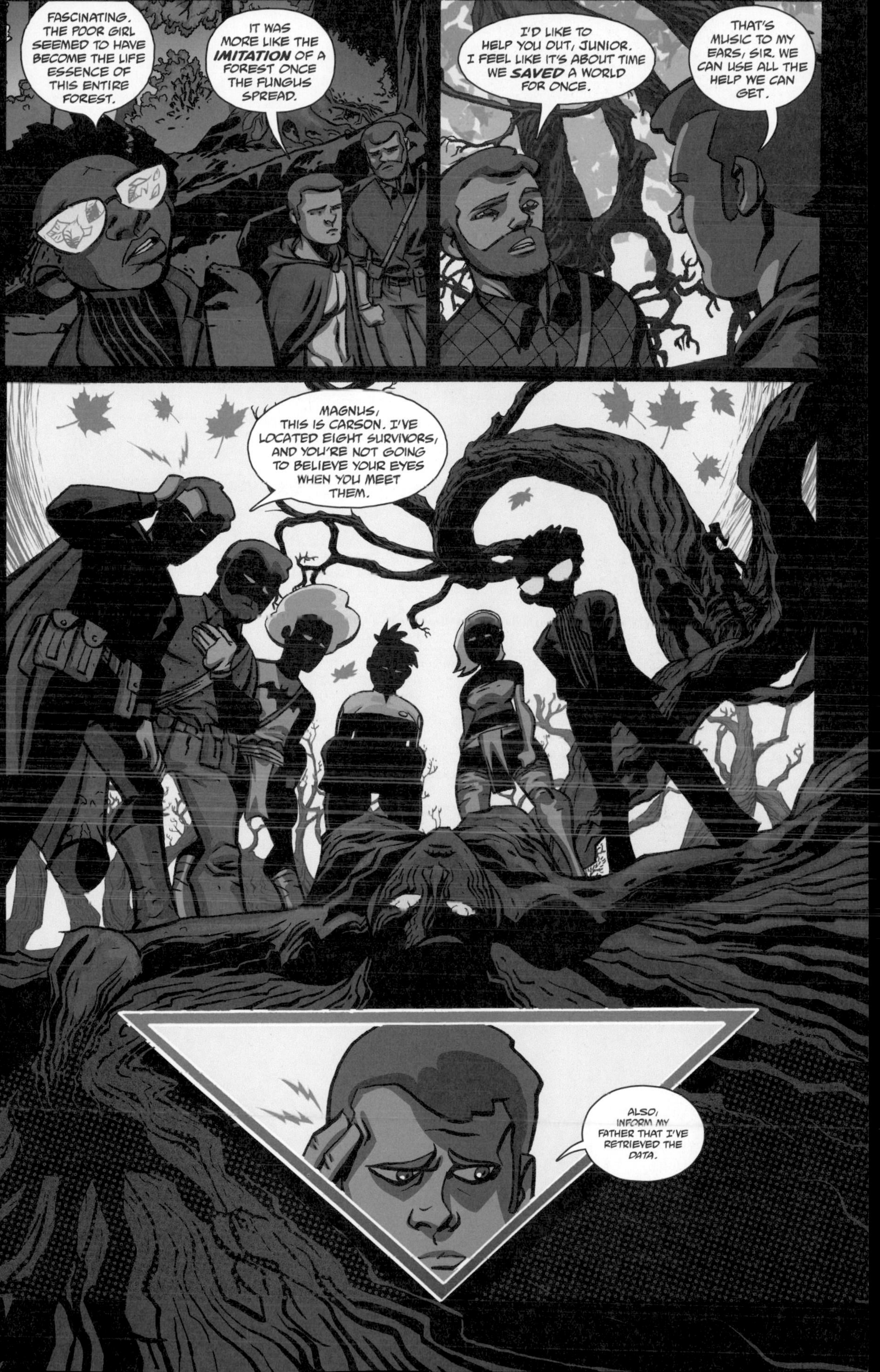
FASCINATING. THE POOR GIRL SEEMED TO HAVE BECOME THE LIFE ESSENCE OF THIS ENTIRE FOREST.
IT WAS MORE LIKE THE IMITATION OF A FOREST ONCE THE FUNGUS SPREAD.
I'D LIKE TO HELP YOU OUT, JUNIOR. I FEEL LIKE IT'S ABOUT TIME WE SAVED A WORLD FOR ONCE.
THAT'S MUSIC TO MY EARS, SIR. WE CAN USE ALL THE HELP WE CAN GET.
MAGNUS, THIS IS CARSON. I'VE LOCATED EIGHT SURVIVORS, AND YOU'RE NOT GOING TO BELIEVE YOUR EYES WHEN YOU MEET THEM.
ALSO, INFORM MY FATHER THAT I'VE RETRIEVED THE DATA.

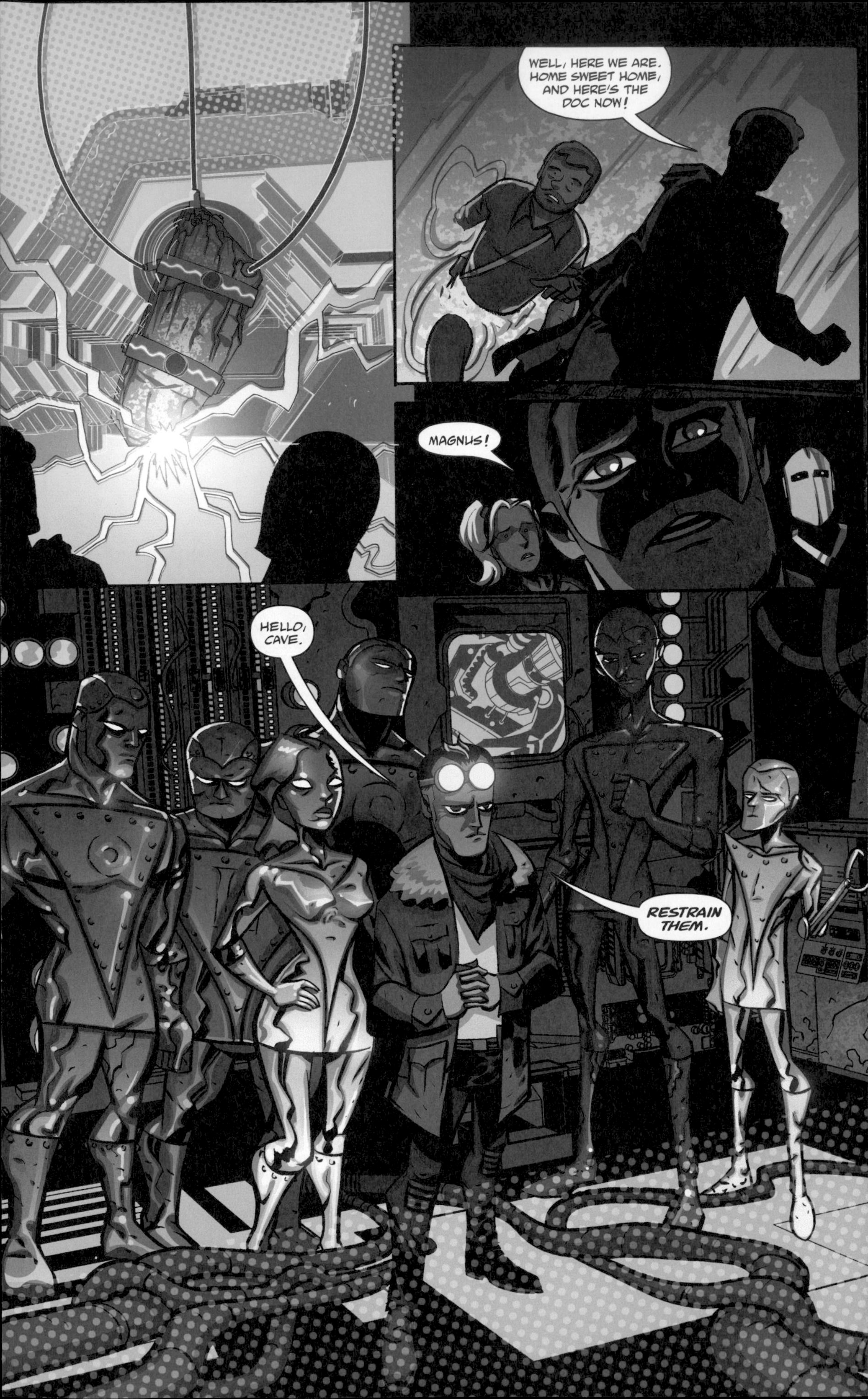
WELL, HERE WE ARE. HOME SWEET HOME, AND HERE'S THE DOC NOW!
MAGNUS!
HELLO, CAVE.
RESTRAIN THEM.

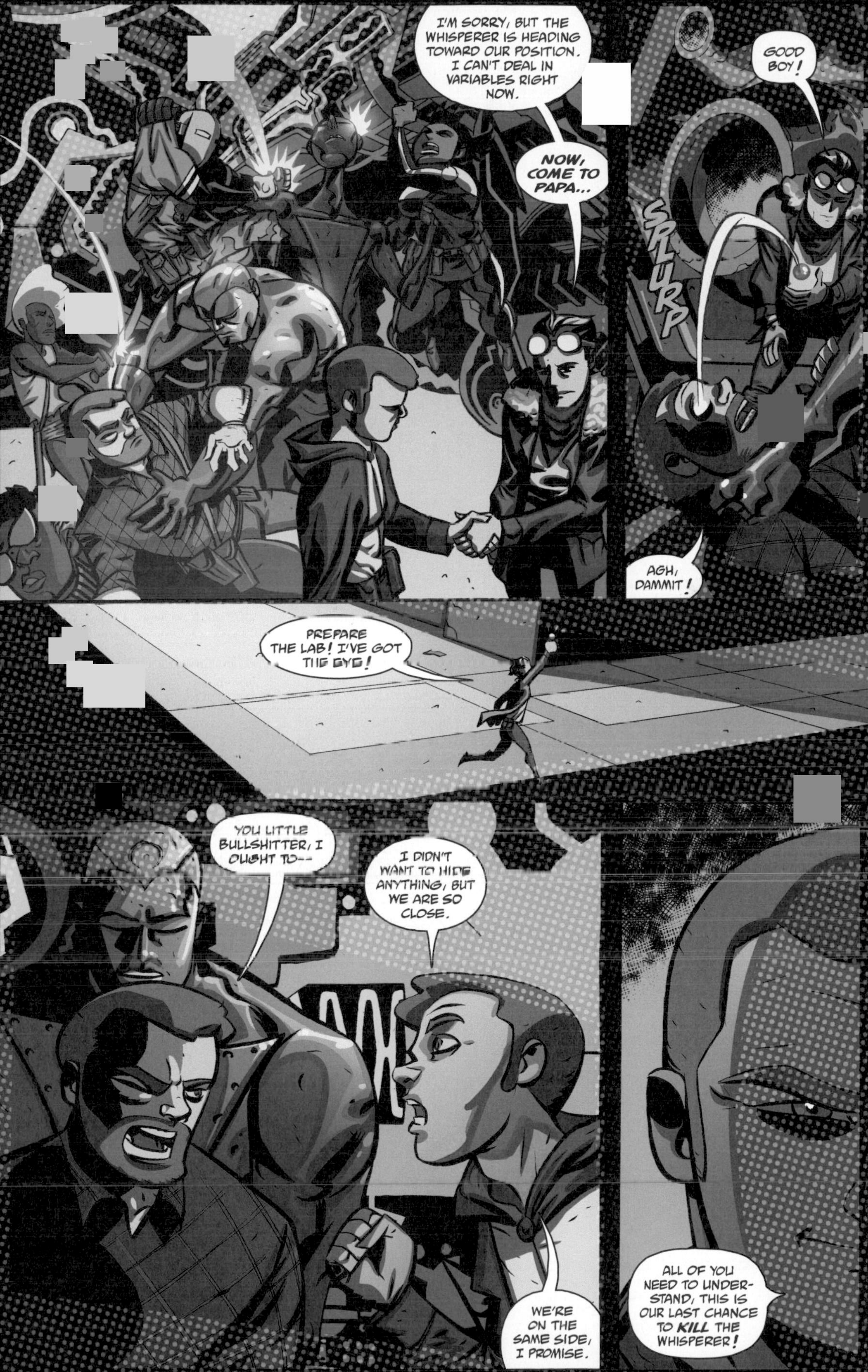

I'M SORRY, BUT THE WHISPERER IS HEADING TOWARD OUR POSITION. I CAN'T DEAL IN VARIABLES RIGHT NOW.
NOW, COME TO PAPA...
GOOD BOY!
SPLURP
AGH, DAMMIT!
PREPARE THE LAB! I'VE GOT THE EYE!
YOU LITTLE BULLSHITTER, I OUGHT TO--
I DIDN'T WANT TO HIDE ANYTHING, BUT WE ARE SO CLOSE.
WE'RE ON THE SAME SIDE, I PROMISE.
ALL OF YOU NEED TO UNDER-STAND, THIS IS OUR LAST CHANCE TO KILL THE WHISPERER!

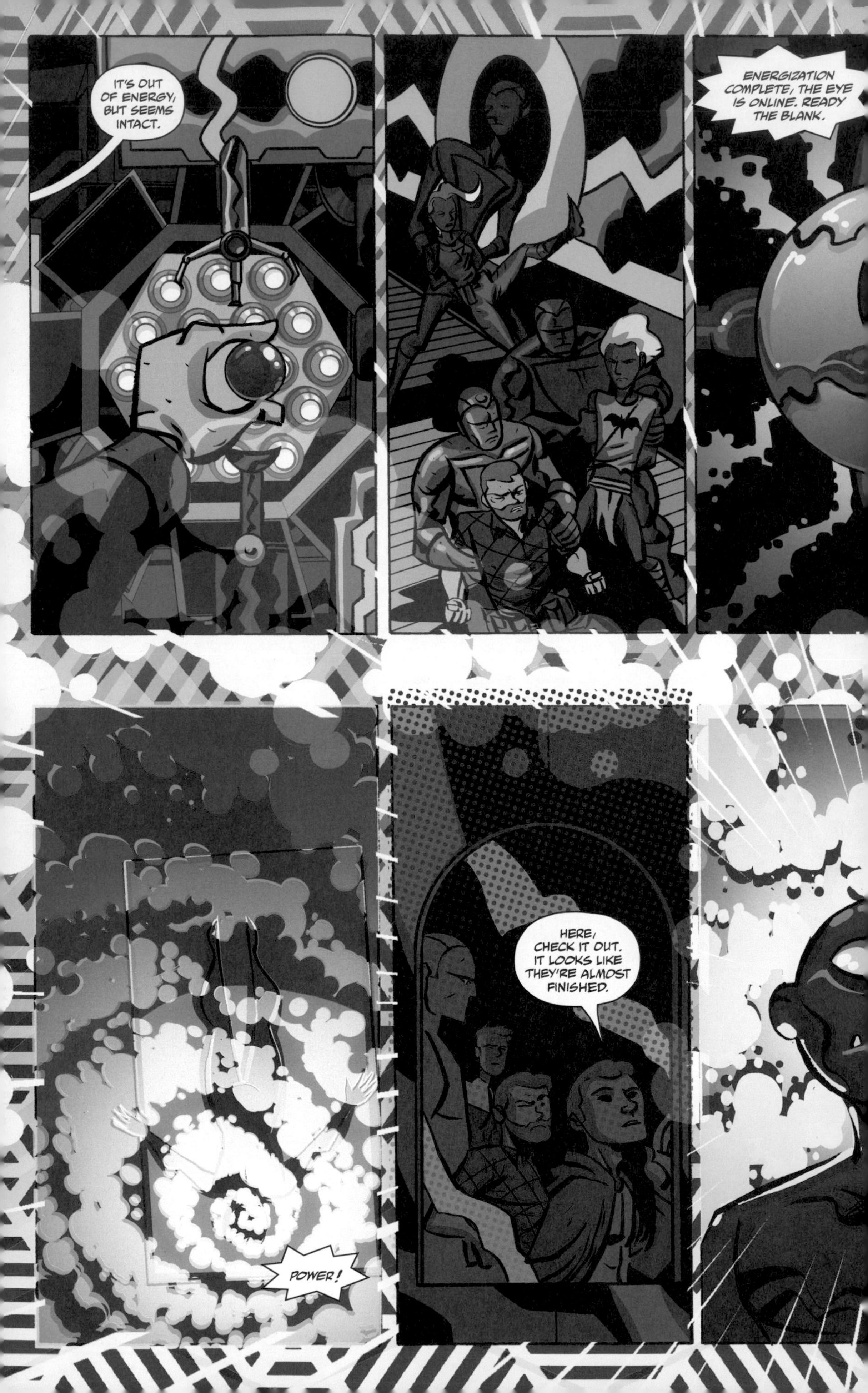
IT'S OUT OF ENERGY, BUT SEEMS INTACT.
ENERGIZATION COMPLETE, THE EYE IS ONLINE. READY THE BLANK.
POWER!
HERE, CHECK IT OUT. IT LOOKS LIKE THEY'RE ALMOST FINISHED.

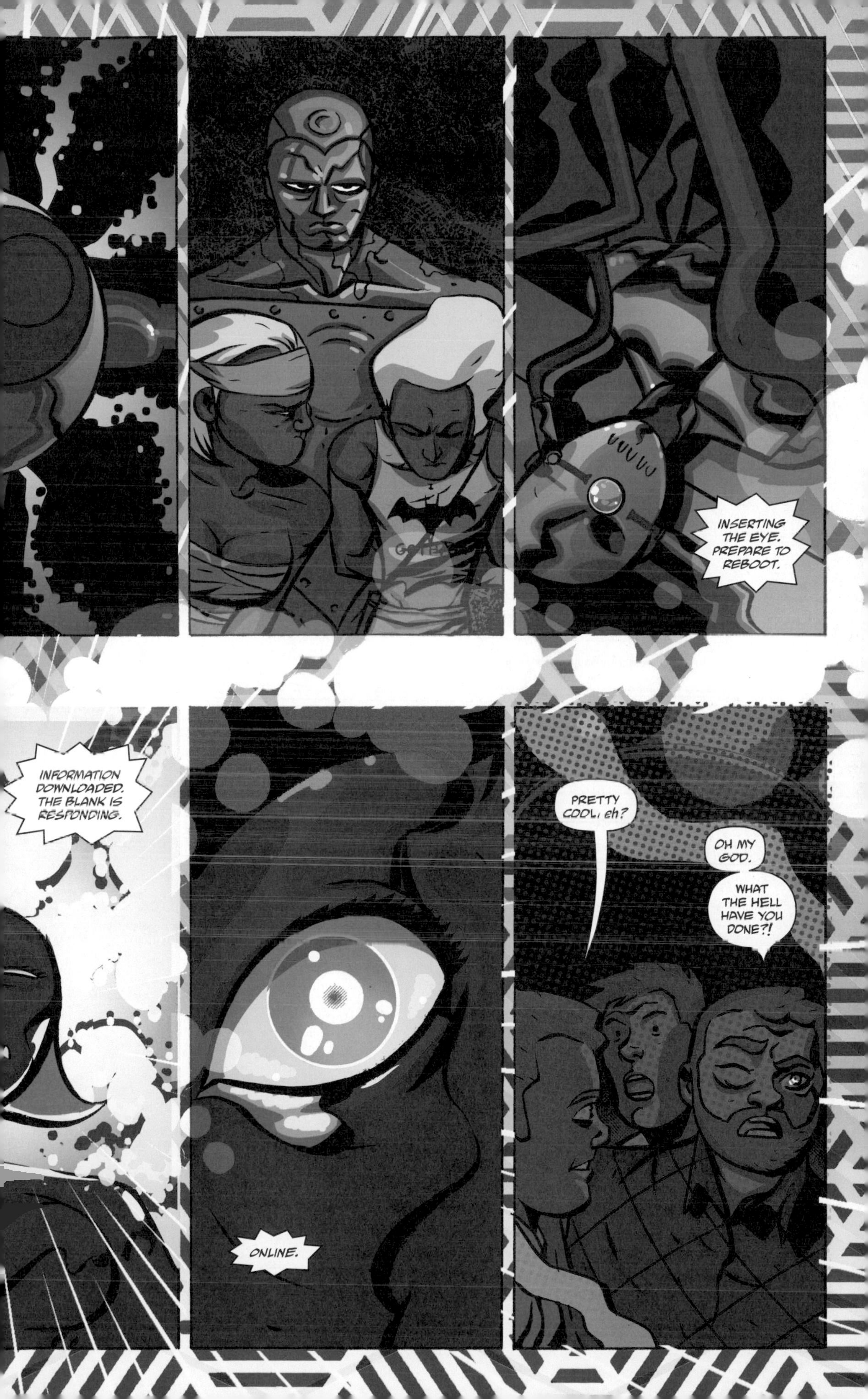
INSERTING THE EYE. PREPARE TO REBOOT.
INFORMATION DOWNLOADED. THE BLANK IS RESPONDING.
ONLINE.
PRETTY COOL, eh?
OH MY GOD.
WHAT THE HELL HAVE YOU DONE?!

# Cave Carson Has a Cybernetic Eye #10
# The Queen of Nothing

Written by JON RIVERA
Story by GERARD WAY & JON RIVERA
Art & Cover by MICHAEL AVON OEMING
Interior & Cover Color NICK FILARDI Letters CLEM ROBINS
Variant Cover BENJAMIN DEWEY Editor MOLLY MAHAN

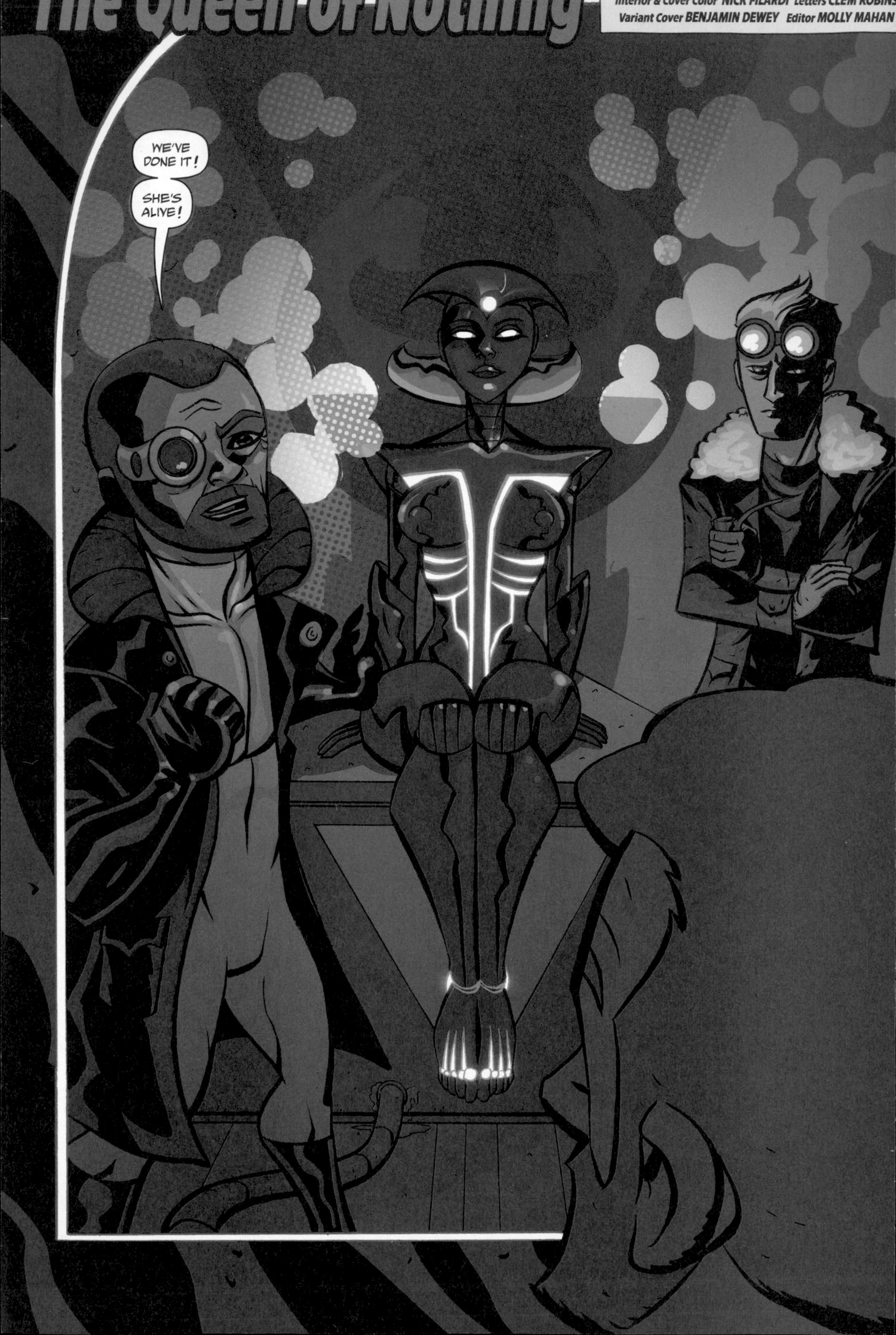
WE'VE DONE IT!
SHE'S ALIVE!

# The Wonderful World of Rocks!

With Professor Marc Bartow

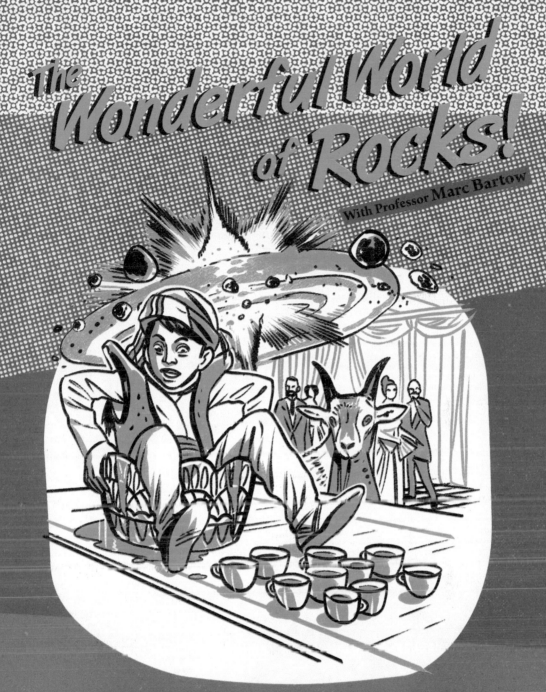

# "QUAZINITE"

**The mineral expulsion of dying quasars—collect enough quazinite in a room and it will form a small wormhole. This is only known to have happened once, in 1838, when a young Kurdish boy looking for a lost goat wandered into a cave laced with quazinite. The boy woke up 3,000 miles away inside a punchbowl at Queen Victoria's coronation. The goat was discovered two doors down in the coat room.**

ROCK ON! MAGAZINE vol 2, issue 4 JULY 19

# "Project Epitaph!"

I have always theorized about what sort of life might exist deep beneath the surface of the Earth. My fellow scientists thought I was crazy, but I imagined I would find microbial, perhaps even multi-celled, organisms in even the deepest caverns of the Earth. Once, while leading an expedition into the Krubera Cave, I encountered the exceedingly rare Monk Pummice, a rock whose radioactive crystals appear to "communicate," like the synapses of the human brain. Given their similarity to brain waves, I began to wonder if the electromagnetic pulsations within the Monk Pummice might actually be a form of consciousness, hitherto unknown on this planet.

In my youth, as a scientist at SETI, I worked on something called Project Epitaph. The idea was to preserve the things of the human race we felt worth saving and put it in a stable orbit around the Earth, so that future alien visitors would know something about us long after we go extinct. We collected all the usual stuff—Beethoven's Ninth Symphony (let's hope they have a record player), the collected works of Shakespeare, a bongo. Dr. Niedermeyer managed to sneak in a pair of sweatpants, and I slipped in a book of bad poetry I'd written in college. And this is all future alien civilizations will ever know of human art and culture.

While working on Project Epitaph, though, Dr. Niedermeyer and I became consumed with one minor problem—how the fudge are aliens supposed to read Shakespeare?! The solution we came up with was to create a book of simple pictures, illustrating the meaning of every word in the Shakespeare canon. In creating this picture book, I not only taught English to future generations of aliens, but I think I finally understood Hamlet for the first time.

One day, without warning, I was struck by the fickle lightning bolt of inspiration. It occurred to me that if I reversed the process, treating myself as the alien, I might be able to teach myself the language of the Monk Pummice. So I connected a brain wave translator to the pulsating rock, which interpreted its electromagnetic synapses into "images," which I used to construct the vocabulary of its brain waves. I then translated the pulses into an audio voice I could listen to through a pair of headphones. After several more years of eavesdropping on the thoughts of the Monk Pummice, I finally decided to introduce myself, greeting the rock in its own vibratory language.

After the screaming subsided (it had never been spoken to before), we actually settled into a nice conversation. Apparently, twelve million years of solitude left it a little starved for company. I told Fred (I named him Fred) that Earth was only one of many planets in a solar system, which was itself one of only hundreds of millions of solar systems in the galaxy. Fred told me that he'd been formed in the mantle of the Earth, but had been slowly pushed upward toward the crust by tectonic activity. He said that he remembered the day I took him out of the cave. He also apparently could tell how much I weighed and how tall I was by the size and distance of the vibrations of my footsteps.

"How is that possible?" I asked. "What could you possibly have to compare me to if I was the first living being you'd ever encountered?"

"Who says you were the first?" Fred replied. And what he told me next will forever change our understanding of life under the surface of this planet.

Words by Mark Russell
Art by Benjamin Dewey

ROCK ON! MAGAZINE vol 2, issue 4 JULY 19

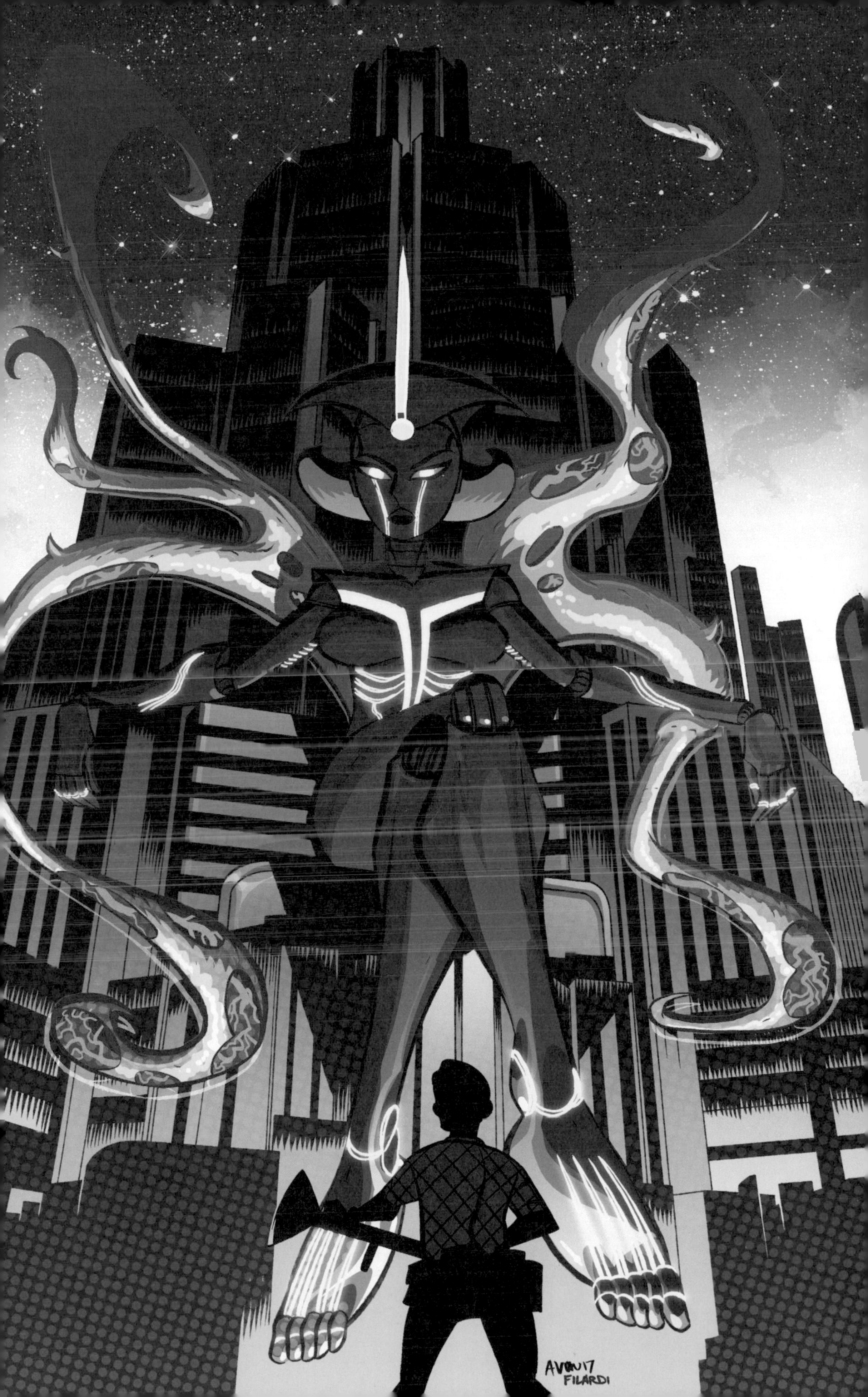
AVON17
FILARDI

Variant cover art by Javier Pulido

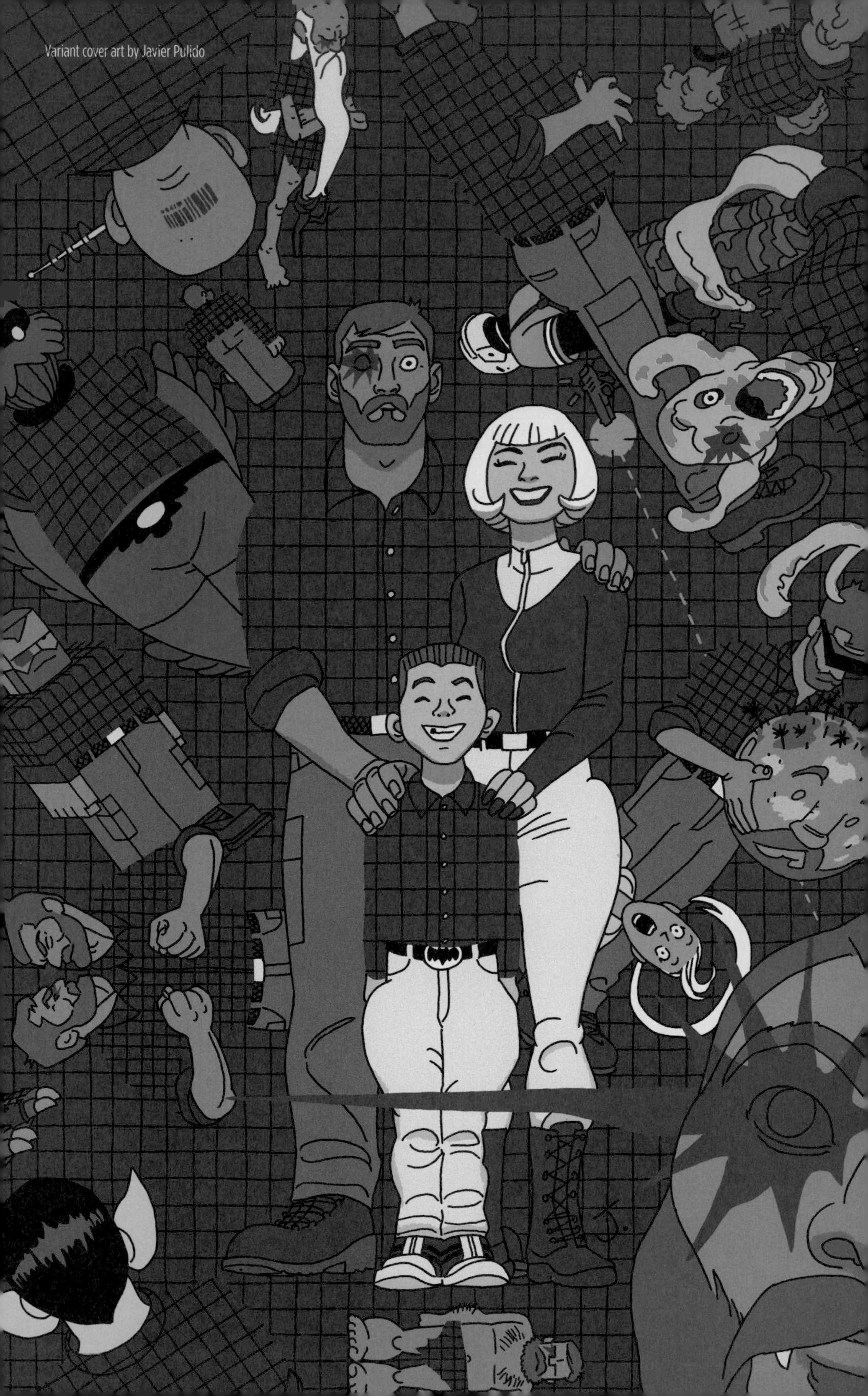

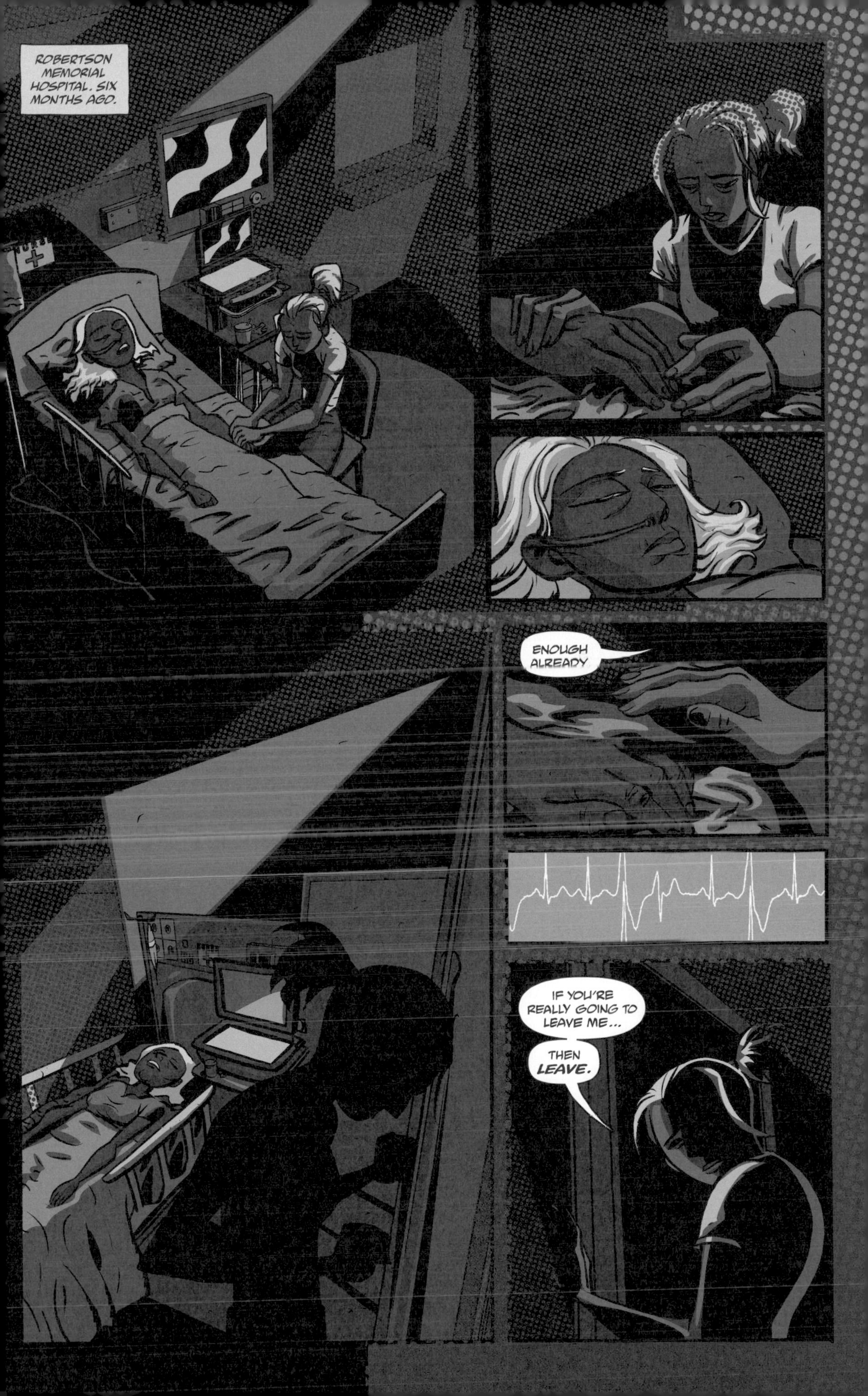
ROBERTSON MEMORIAL HOSPITAL. SIX MONTHS AGO.
ENOUGH ALREADY
IF YOU'RE REALLY GOING TO LEAVE ME...
THEN *LEAVE.*

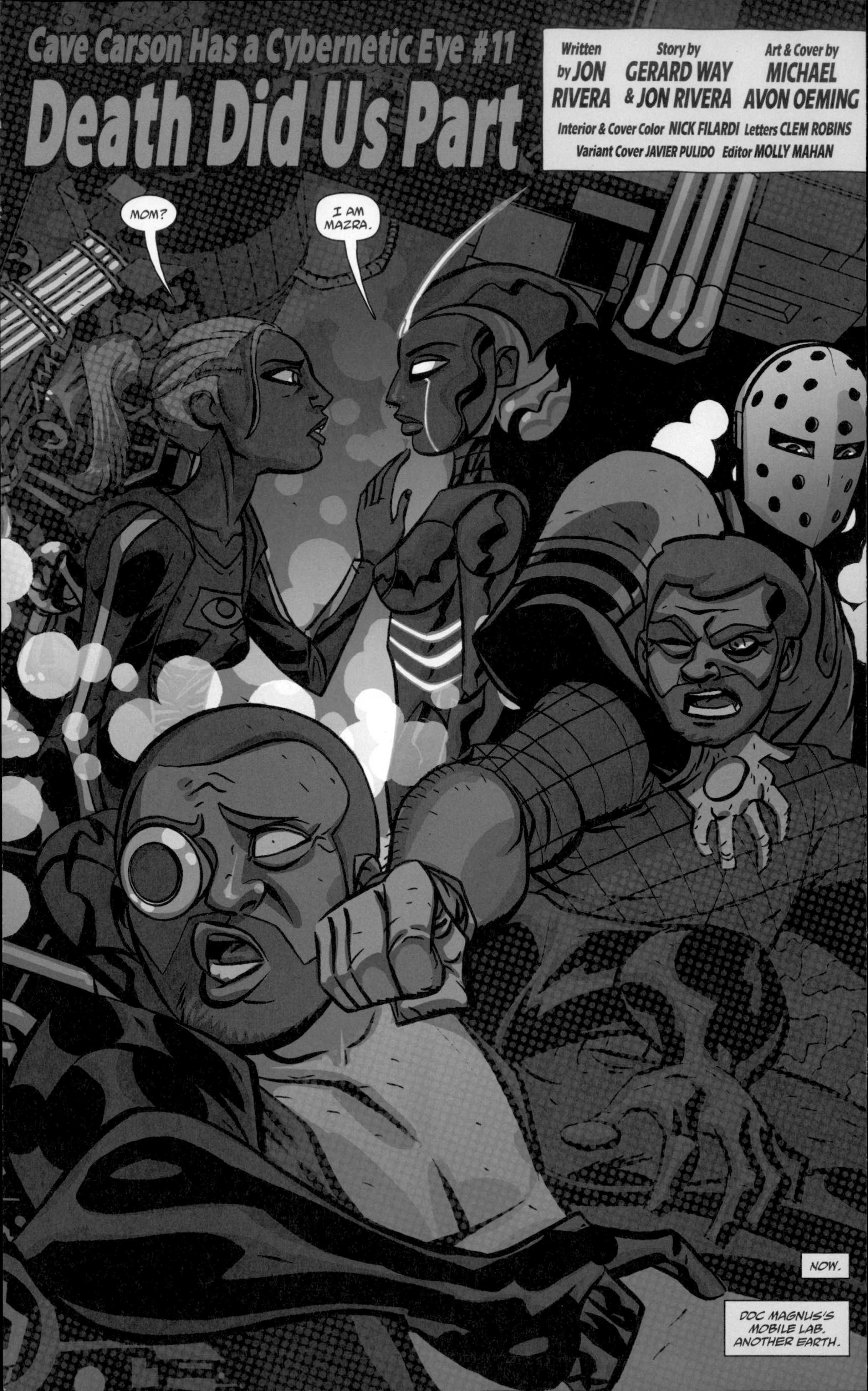
Cave Carson Has a Cybernetic Eye #11
Death Did Us Part
Written by JON RIVERA
Story by GERARD WAY & JON RIVERA
Art & Cover by MICHAEL AVON OEMING
Interior & Cover Color NICK FILARDI Letters CLEM ROBINS
Variant Cover JAVIER PULIDO Editor MOLLY MAHAN
MOM?
I AM MAZRA.
NOW.
DOC MAGNUS'S MOBILE LAB. ANOTHER EARTH.

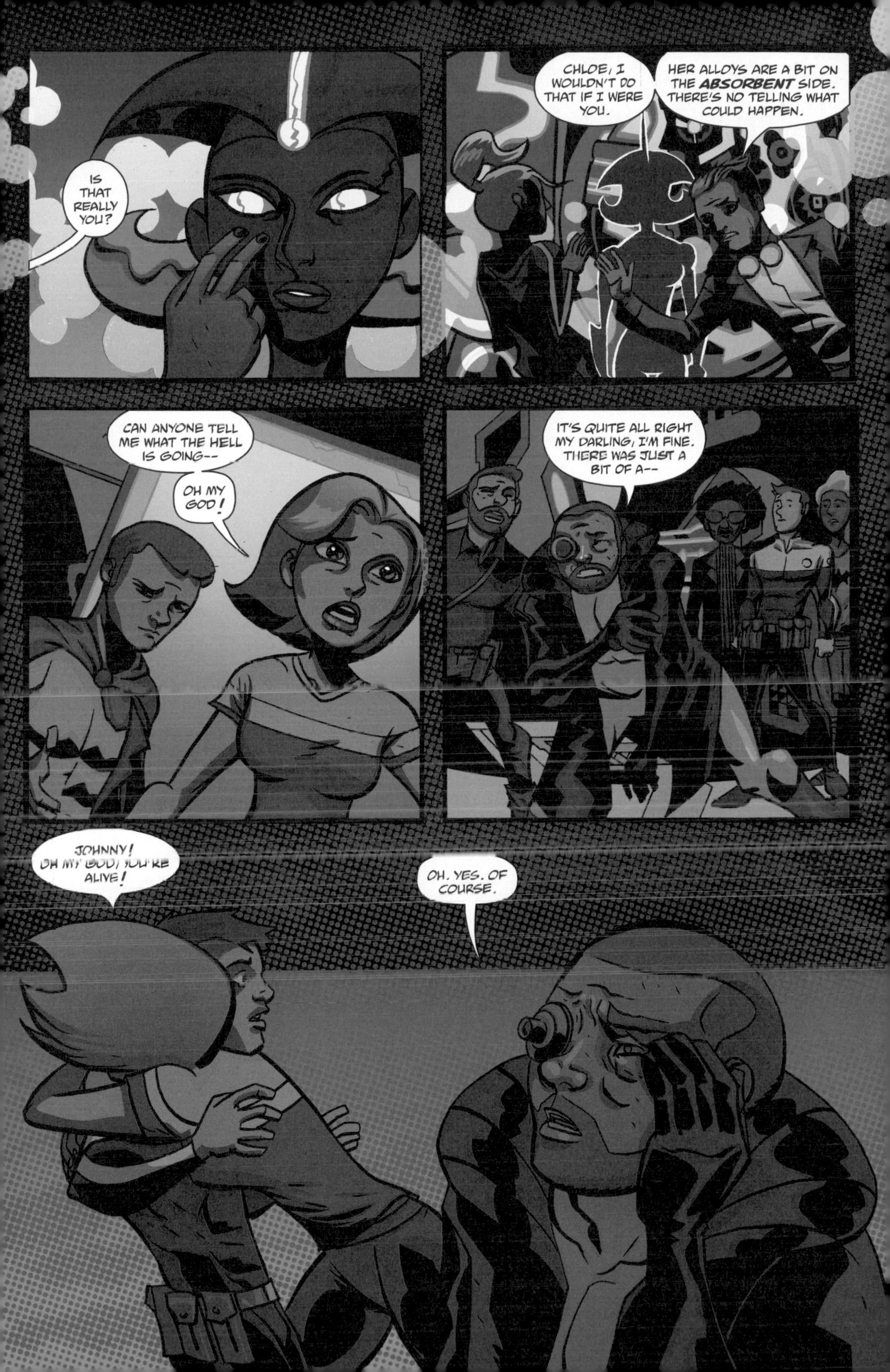
IS THAT REALLY YOU?
CHLOE, I WOULDN'T DO THAT IF I WERE YOU.
HER ALLOYS ARE A BIT ON THE **ABSORBENT** SIDE. THERE'S NO TELLING WHAT COULD HAPPEN.
CAN ANYONE TELL ME WHAT THE HELL IS GOING--
OH MY GOD!
IT'S QUITE ALL RIGHT MY DARLING, I'M FINE. THERE WAS JUST A BIT OF A--
JOHNNY! OH MY GOD, YOU'RE ALIVE!
OH. YES. OF COURSE.

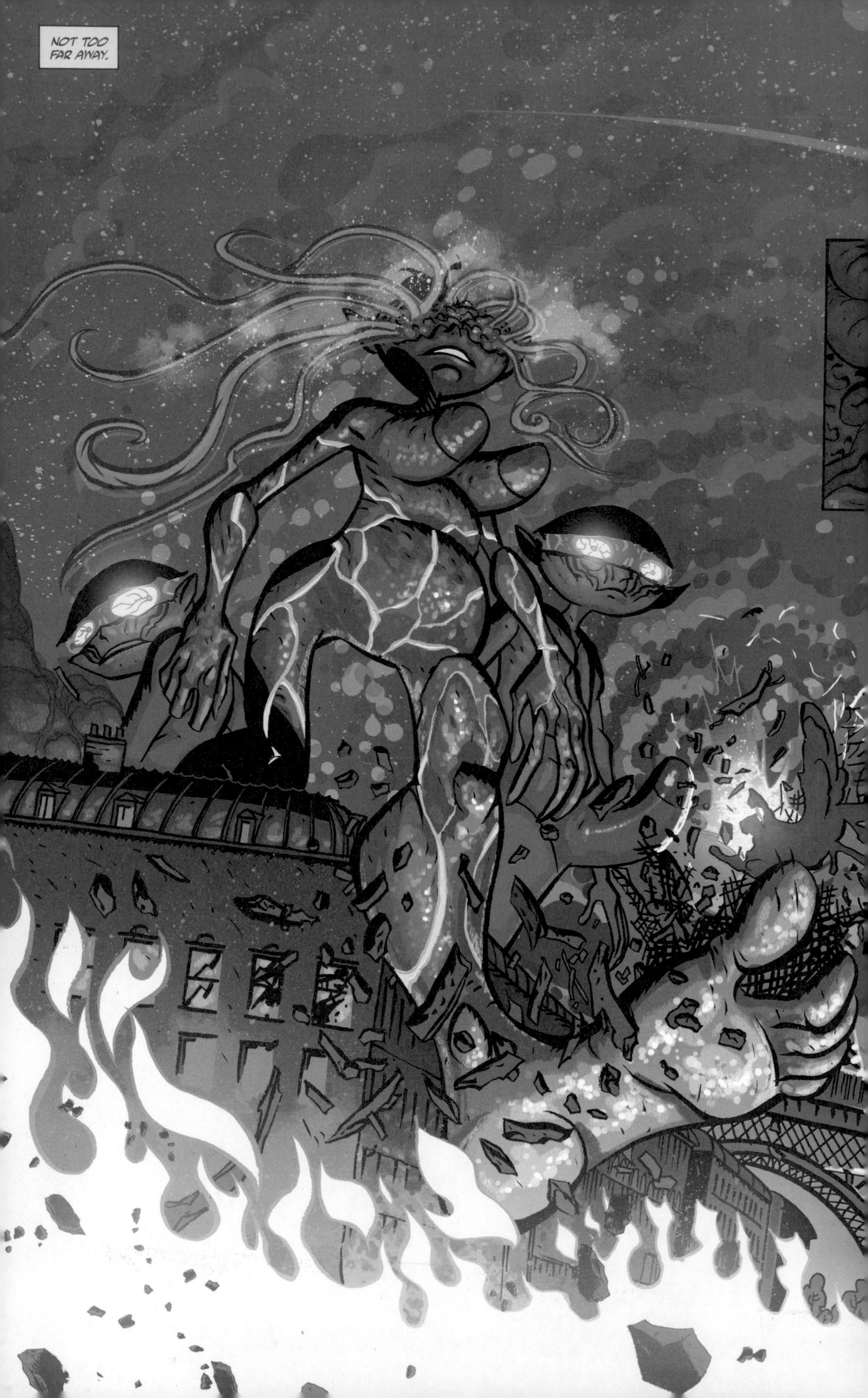
NOT TOO FAR AWAY.

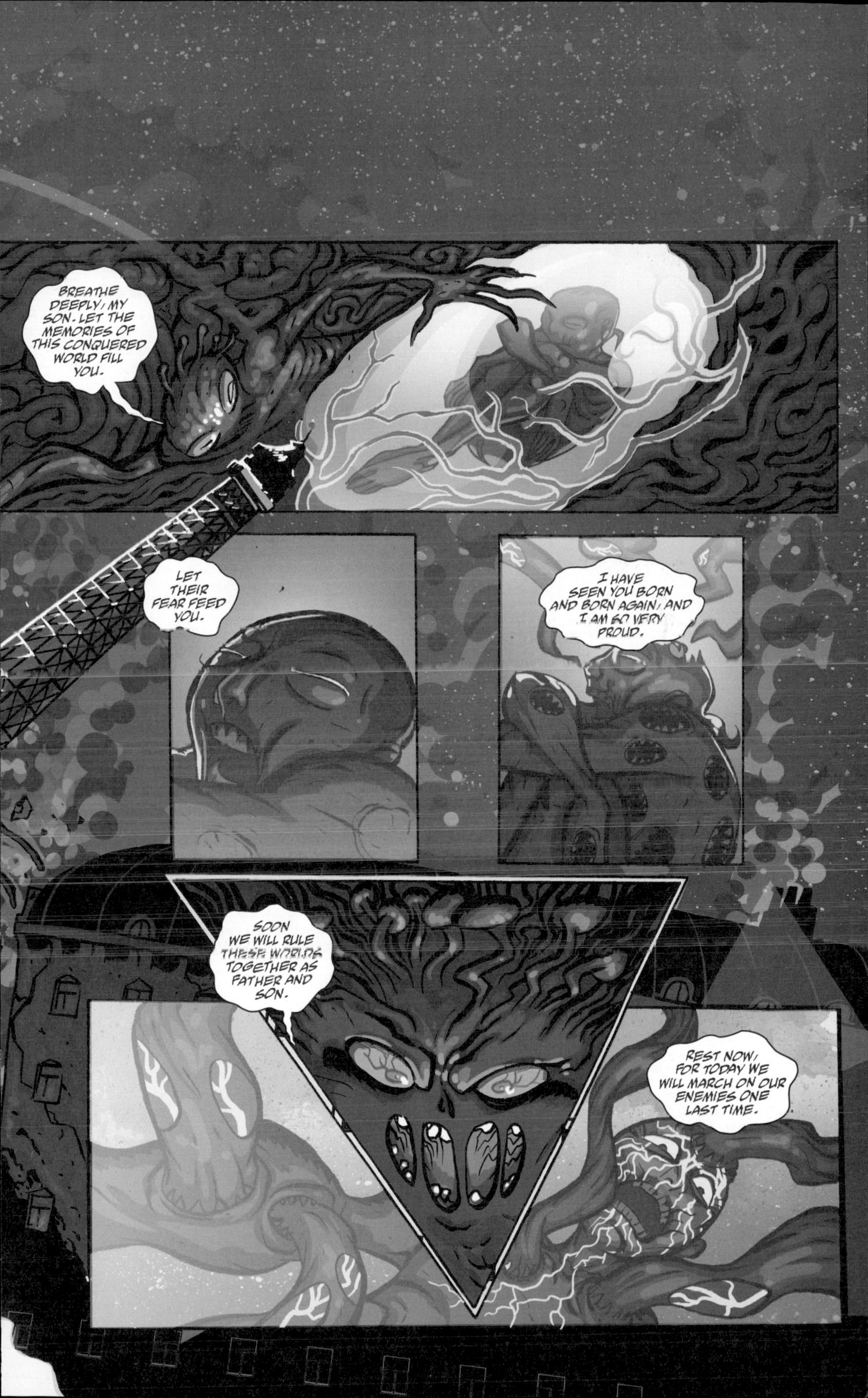
BREATHE DEEPLY, MY SON. LET THE MEMORIES OF THIS CONQUERED WORLD FILL YOU.
LET THEIR FEAR FEED YOU.
I HAVE SEEN YOU BORN AND BORN AGAIN, AND I AM SO VERY PROUD.
SOON WE WILL RULE THESE WORLDS TOGETHER AS FATHER AND SON.
REST NOW, FOR TODAY WE WILL MARCH ON OUR ENEMIES ONE LAST TIME.

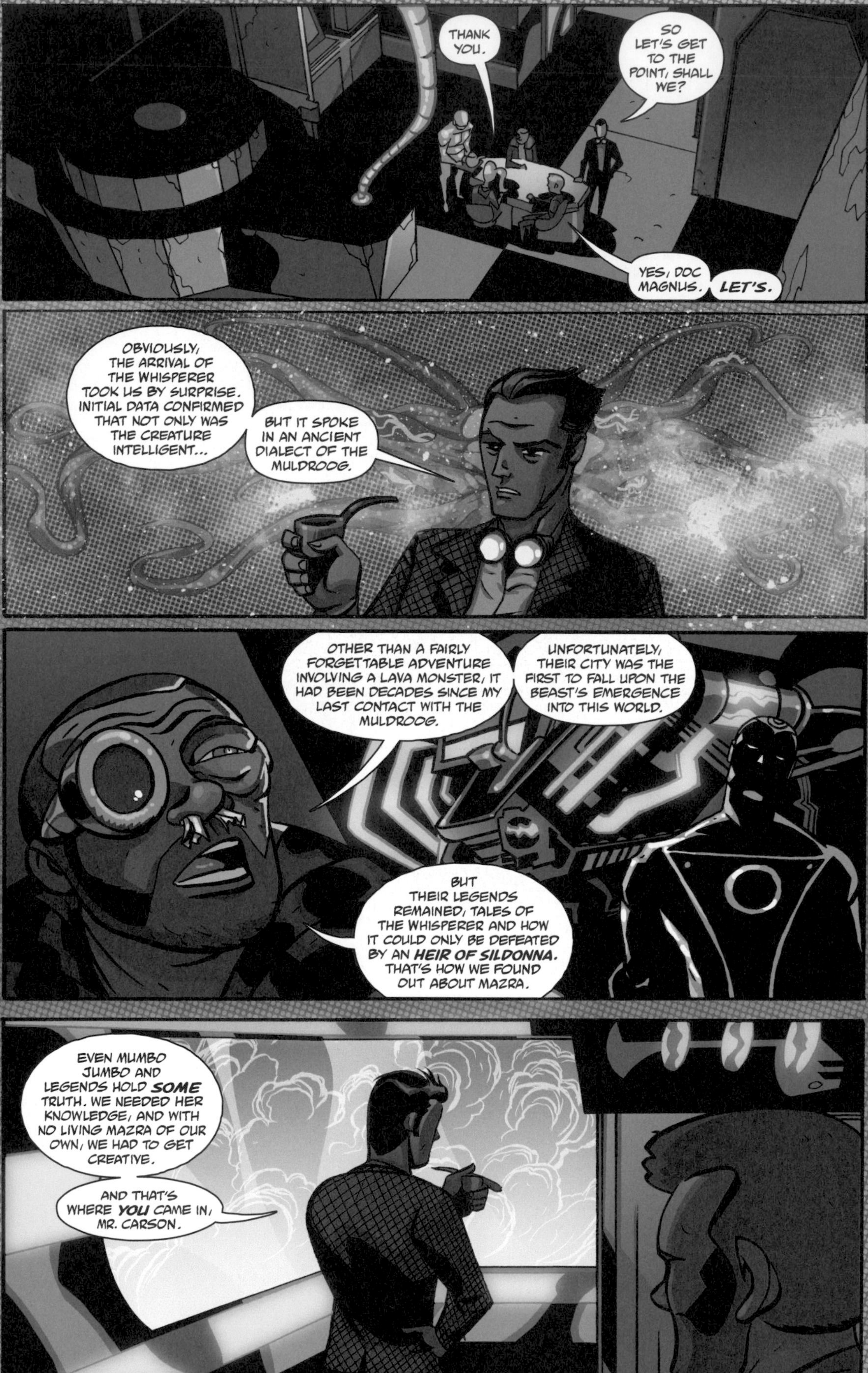
THANK YOU.
SO LET'S GET TO THE POINT, SHALL WE?
YES, DOC MAGNUS. LET'S.
OBVIOUSLY, THE ARRIVAL OF THE WHISPERER TOOK US BY SURPRISE. INITIAL DATA CONFIRMED THAT NOT ONLY WAS THE CREATURE INTELLIGENT...
BUT IT SPOKE IN AN ANCIENT DIALECT OF THE MULDROOG.
OTHER THAN A FAIRLY FORGETTABLE ADVENTURE INVOLVING A LAVA MONSTER, IT HAD BEEN DECADES SINCE MY LAST CONTACT WITH THE MULDROOG.
UNFORTUNATELY, THEIR CITY WAS THE FIRST TO FALL UPON THE BEAST'S EMERGENCE INTO THIS WORLD.
BUT THEIR LEGENDS REMAINED, TALES OF THE WHISPERER AND HOW IT COULD ONLY BE DEFEATED BY AN HEIR OF SILDONNA. THAT'S HOW WE FOUND OUT ABOUT MAZRA.
EVEN MUMBO JUMBO AND LEGENDS HOLD SOME TRUTH. WE NEEDED HER KNOWLEDGE, AND WITH NO LIVING MAZRA OF OUR OWN, WE HAD TO GET CREATIVE.
AND THAT'S WHERE YOU CAME IN, MR. CARSON.

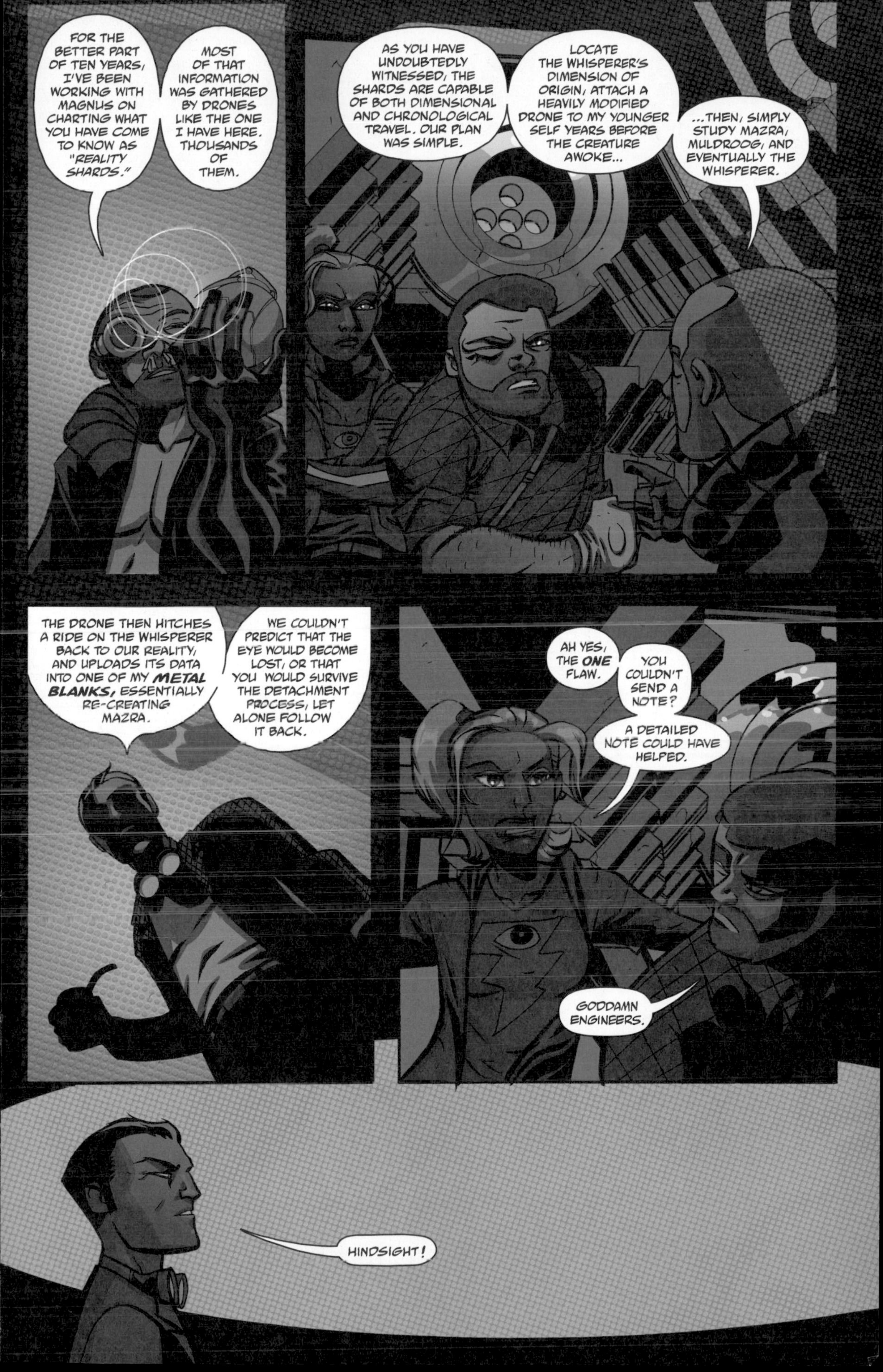
FOR THE BETTER PART OF TEN YEARS, I'VE BEEN WORKING WITH MAGNUS ON CHARTING WHAT YOU HAVE COME TO KNOW AS "REALITY SHARDS."
MOST OF THAT INFORMATION WAS GATHERED BY DRONES LIKE THE ONE I HAVE HERE. THOUSANDS OF THEM.
AS YOU HAVE UNDOUBTEDLY WITNESSED, THE SHARDS ARE CAPABLE OF BOTH DIMENSIONAL AND CHRONOLOGICAL TRAVEL. OUR PLAN WAS SIMPLE.
LOCATE THE WHISPERER'S DIMENSION OF ORIGIN, ATTACH A HEAVILY MODIFIED DRONE TO MY YOUNGER SELF YEARS BEFORE THE CREATURE AWOKE...
...THEN, SIMPLY STUDY MAZRA, MULDROOG, AND EVENTUALLY THE WHISPERER.
THE DRONE THEN HITCHES A RIDE ON THE WHISPERER BACK TO OUR REALITY, AND UPLOADS ITS DATA INTO ONE OF MY METAL BLANKS, ESSENTIALLY RE-CREATING MAZRA.
WE COULDN'T PREDICT THAT THE EYE WOULD BECOME LOST, OR THAT YOU WOULD SURVIVE THE DETACHMENT PROCESS, LET ALONE FOLLOW IT BACK.
AH YES, THE ONE FLAW.
YOU COULDN'T SEND A NOTE?
A DETAILED NOTE COULD HAVE HELPED.
GODDAMN ENGINEERS.
HINDSIGHT!

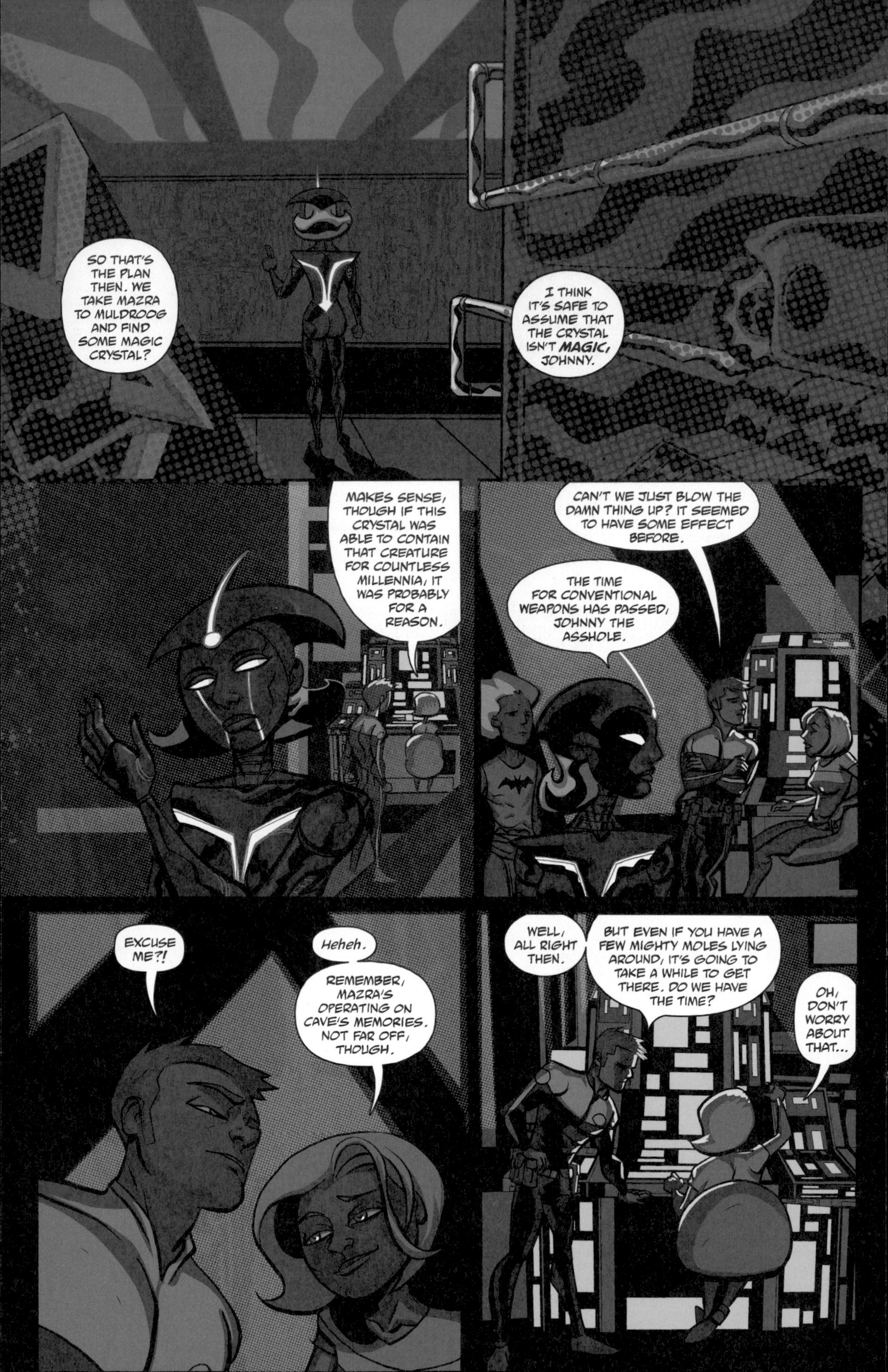

SO THAT'S THE PLAN THEN. WE TAKE MAZRA TO MULDROOG AND FIND SOME MAGIC CRYSTAL?
I THINK IT'S SAFE TO ASSUME THAT THE CRYSTAL ISN'T MAGIC, JOHNNY.
MAKES SENSE, THOUGH IF THIS CRYSTAL WAS ABLE TO CONTAIN THAT CREATURE FOR COUNTLESS MILLENNIA, IT WAS PROBABLY FOR A REASON.
CAN'T WE JUST BLOW THE DAMN THING UP? IT SEEMED TO HAVE SOME EFFECT BEFORE.
THE TIME FOR CONVENTIONAL WEAPONS HAS PASSED, JOHNNY THE ASSHOLE.
EXCUSE ME?!
Heheh.
REMEMBER, MAZRA'S OPERATING ON CAVE'S MEMORIES. NOT FAR OFF, THOUGH.
WELL, ALL RIGHT THEN.
BUT EVEN IF YOU HAVE A FEW MIGHTY MOLES LYING AROUND, IT'S GOING TO TAKE A WHILE TO GET THERE. DO WE HAVE THE TIME?
OH, DON'T WORRY ABOUT THAT...

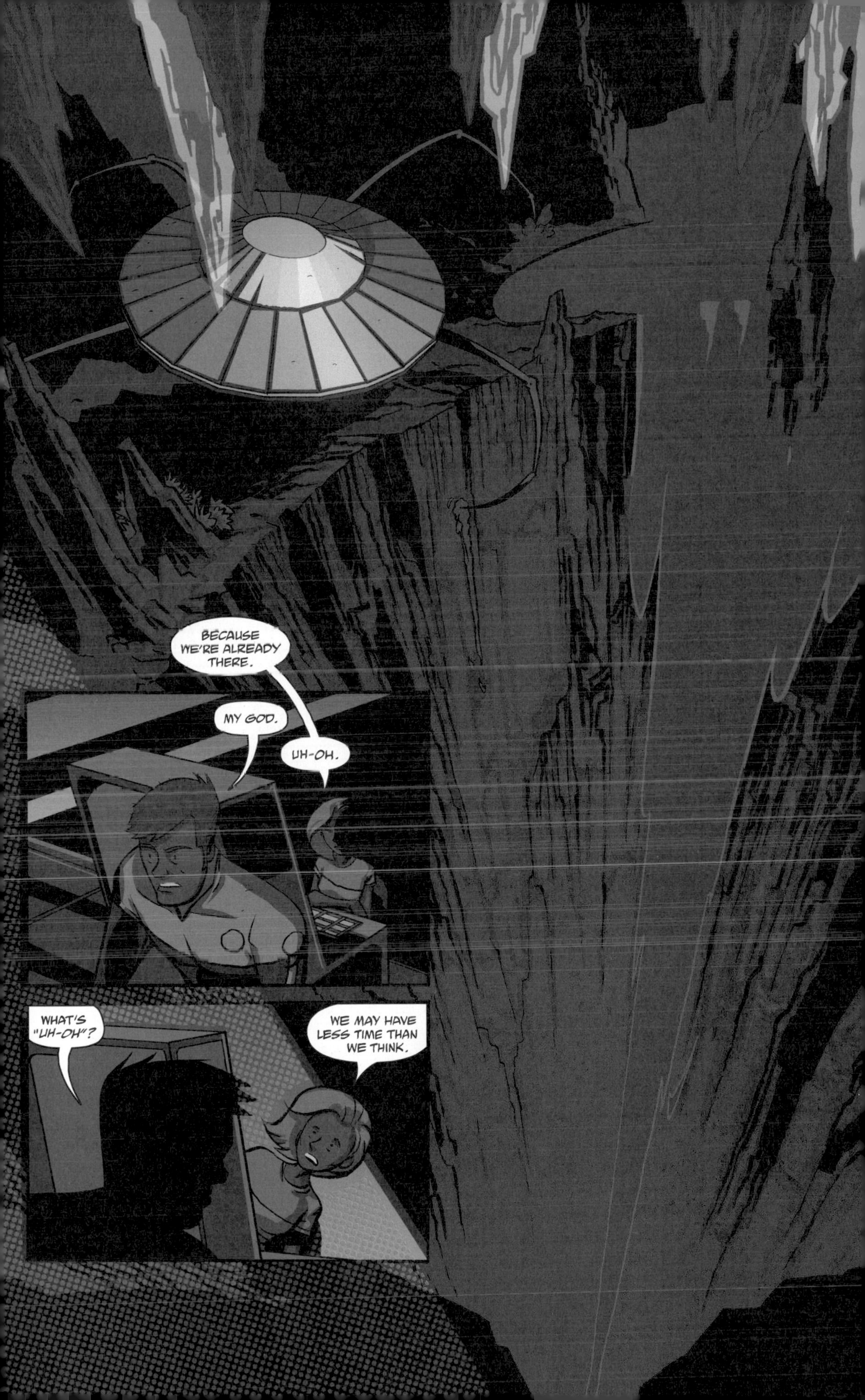
BECAUSE WE'RE ALREADY THERE.
MY GOD.
UH-OH.
WHAT'S "UH-OH"?
WE MAY HAVE LESS TIME THAN WE THINK.

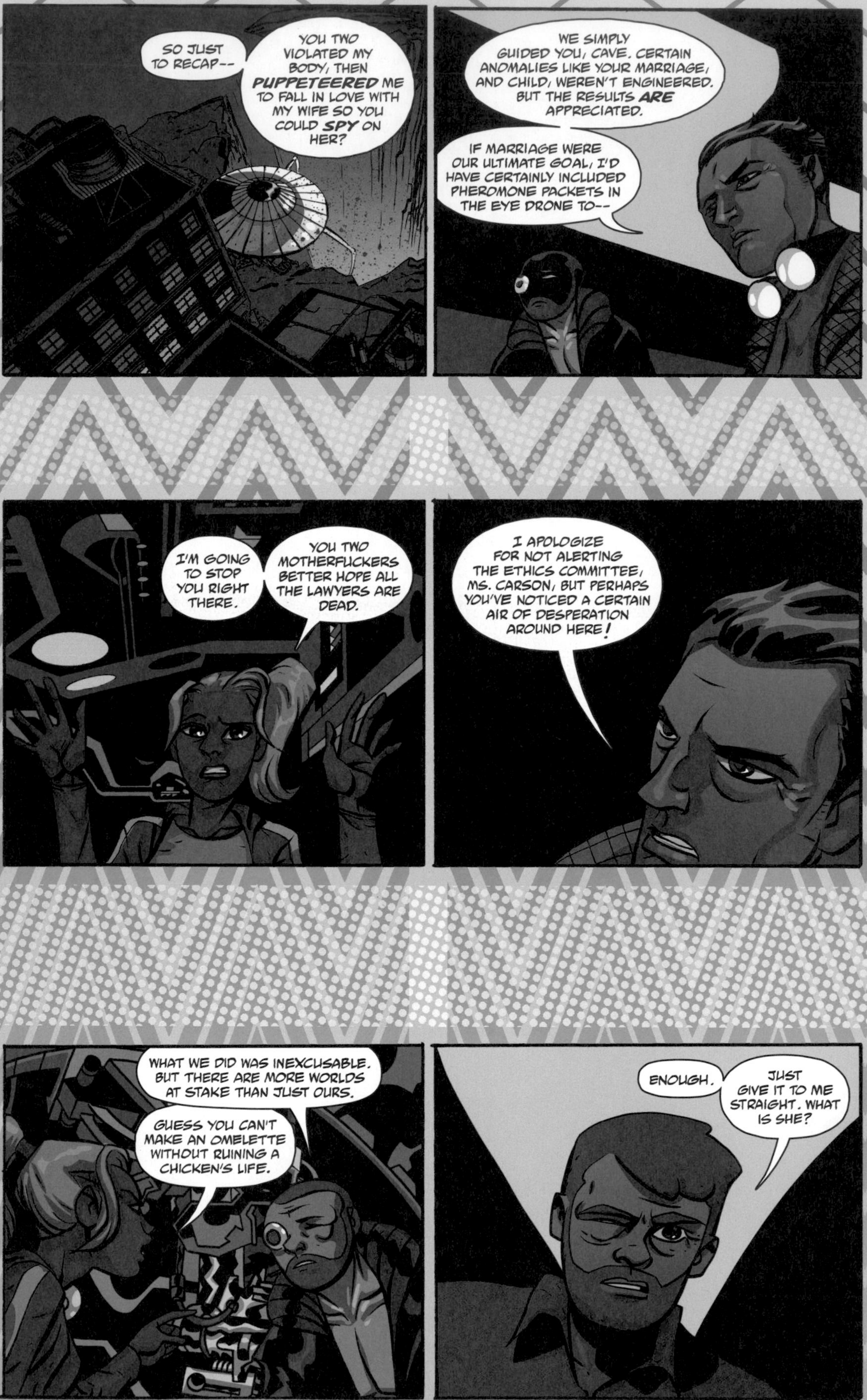
SO JUST TO RECAP--
YOU TWO VIOLATED MY BODY, THEN **PUPPETEERED** ME TO FALL IN LOVE WITH MY WIFE SO YOU COULD **SPY** ON HER?
WE SIMPLY GUIDED YOU, CAVE. CERTAIN ANOMALIES LIKE YOUR MARRIAGE, AND CHILD, WEREN'T ENGINEERED. BUT THE RESULTS **ARE** APPRECIATED.
IF MARRIAGE WERE OUR ULTIMATE GOAL, I'D HAVE CERTAINLY INCLUDED PHEROMONE PACKETS IN THE EYE DRONE TO--
I'M GOING TO STOP YOU RIGHT THERE.
YOU TWO MOTHERFUCKERS BETTER HOPE ALL THE LAWYERS ARE DEAD.
I APOLOGIZE FOR NOT ALERTING THE ETHICS COMMITTEE, MS. CARSON, BUT PERHAPS YOU'VE NOTICED A CERTAIN AIR OF DESPERATION AROUND HERE!
WHAT WE DID WAS INEXCUSABLE. BUT THERE ARE MORE WORLDS AT STAKE THAN JUST OURS.
GUESS YOU CAN'T MAKE AN OMELETTE WITHOUT RUINING A CHICKEN'S LIFE.
ENOUGH.
JUST GIVE IT TO ME STRAIGHT. WHAT IS SHE?

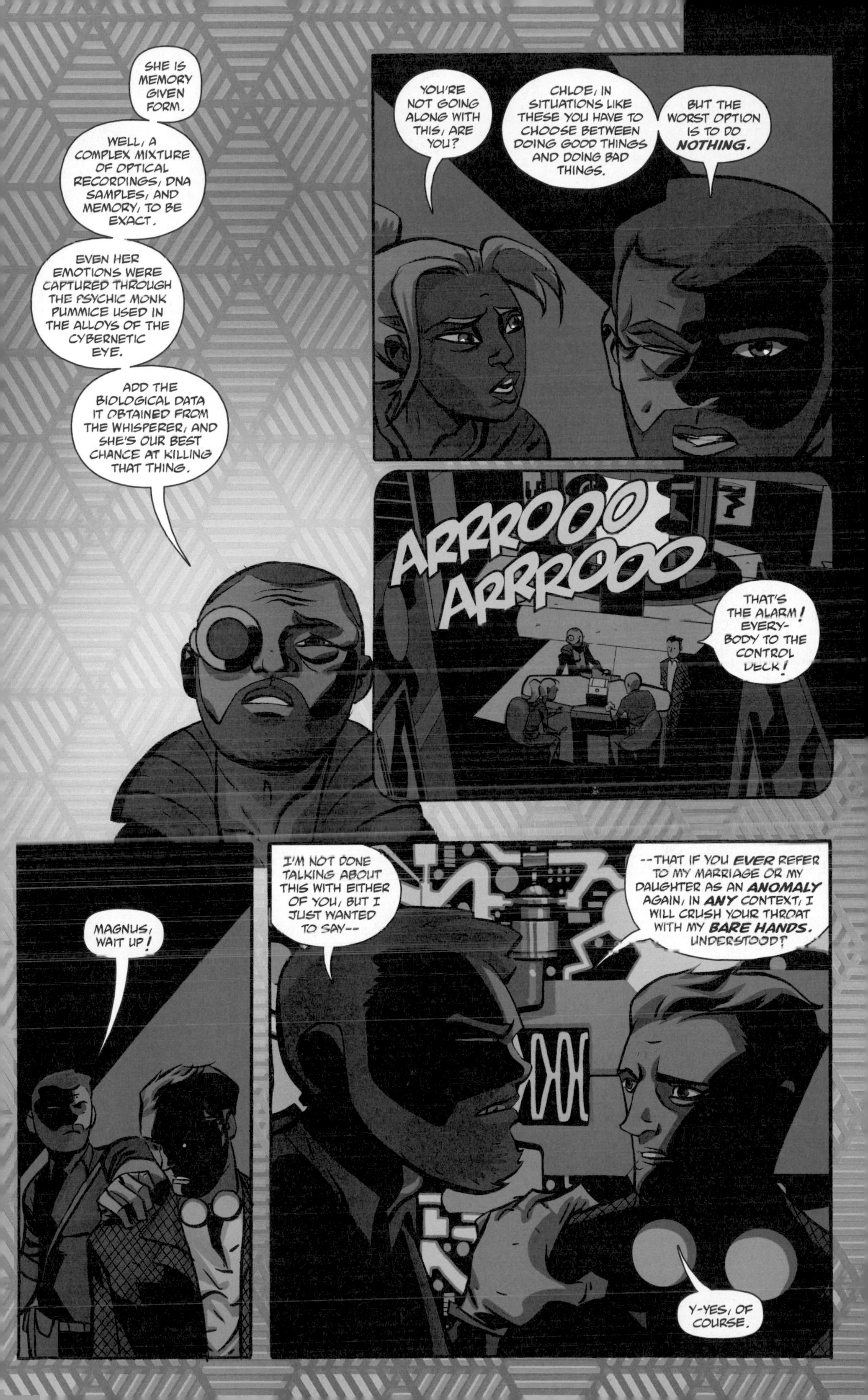
SHE IS MEMORY GIVEN FORM.
WELL, A COMPLEX MIXTURE OF OPTICAL RECORDINGS, DNA SAMPLES, AND MEMORY, TO BE EXACT.
EVEN HER EMOTIONS WERE CAPTURED THROUGH THE PSYCHIC MONK PUMMICE USED IN THE ALLOYS OF THE CYBERNETIC EYE.
ADD THE BIOLOGICAL DATA IT OBTAINED FROM THE WHISPERER, AND SHE'S OUR BEST CHANCE AT KILLING THAT THING.
YOU'RE NOT GOING ALONG WITH THIS, ARE YOU?
CHLOE, IN SITUATIONS LIKE THESE YOU HAVE TO CHOOSE BETWEEN DOING GOOD THINGS AND DOING BAD THINGS.
BUT THE WORST OPTION IS TO DO NOTHING.
ARRROOO ARRROOO
THAT'S THE ALARM! EVERY-BODY TO THE CONTROL DECK!
MAGNUS, WAIT UP!
I'M NOT DONE TALKING ABOUT THIS WITH EITHER OF YOU, BUT I JUST WANTED TO SAY--
--THAT IF YOU EVER REFER TO MY MARRIAGE OR MY DAUGHTER AS AN ANOMALY AGAIN, IN ANY CONTEXT, I WILL CRUSH YOUR THROAT WITH MY BARE HANDS. UNDERSTOOD?
Y-YES, OF COURSE.

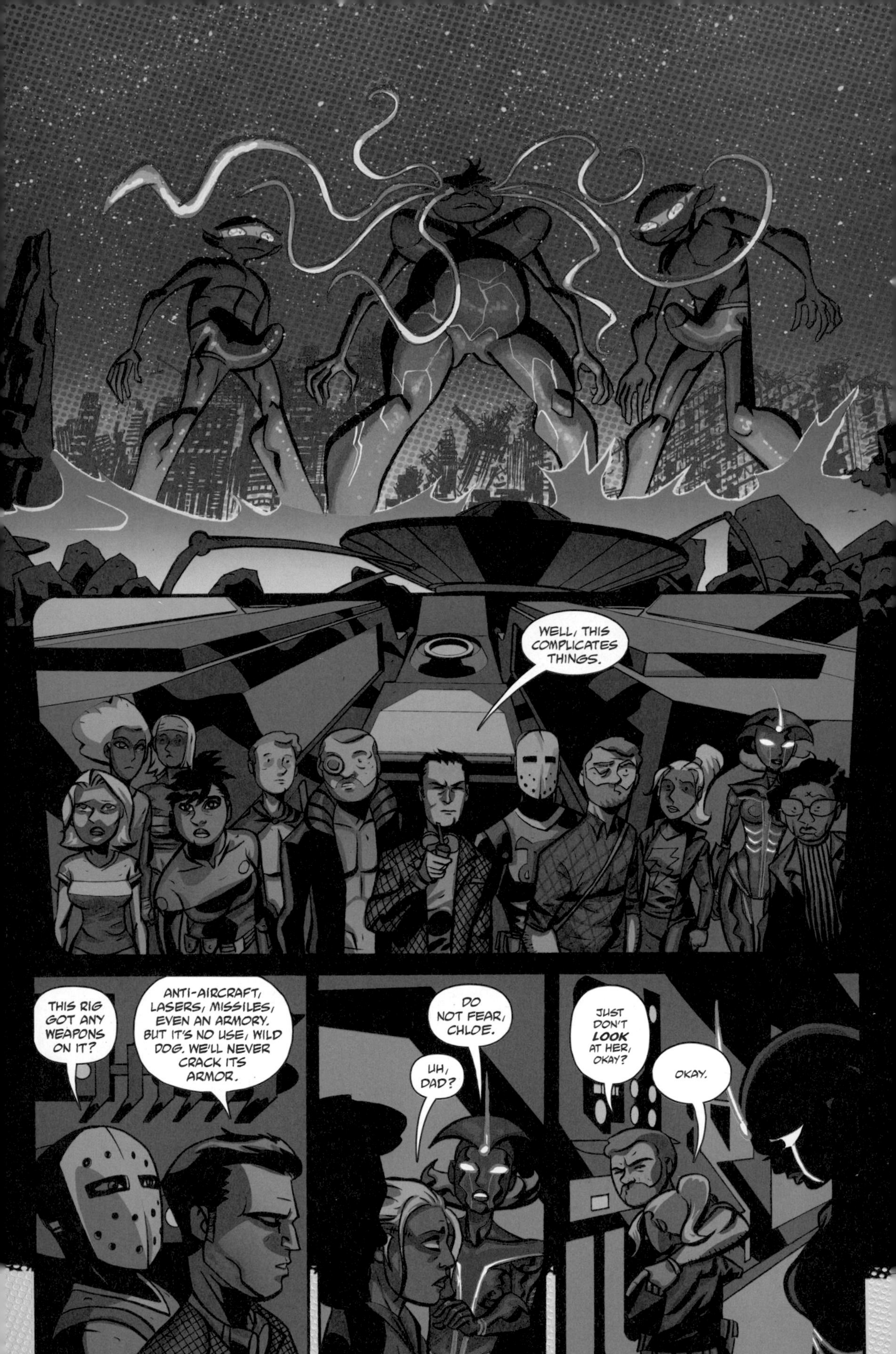
WELL, THIS COMPLICATES THINGS.
THIS RIG GOT ANY WEAPONS ON IT?
ANTI-AIRCRAFT, LASERS, MISSILES, EVEN AN ARMORY. BUT IT'S NO USE, WILD DOG. WE'LL NEVER CRACK ITS ARMOR.
DO NOT FEAR, CHLOE.
UH, DAD?
JUST DON'T LOOK AT HER, OKAY?
OKAY.

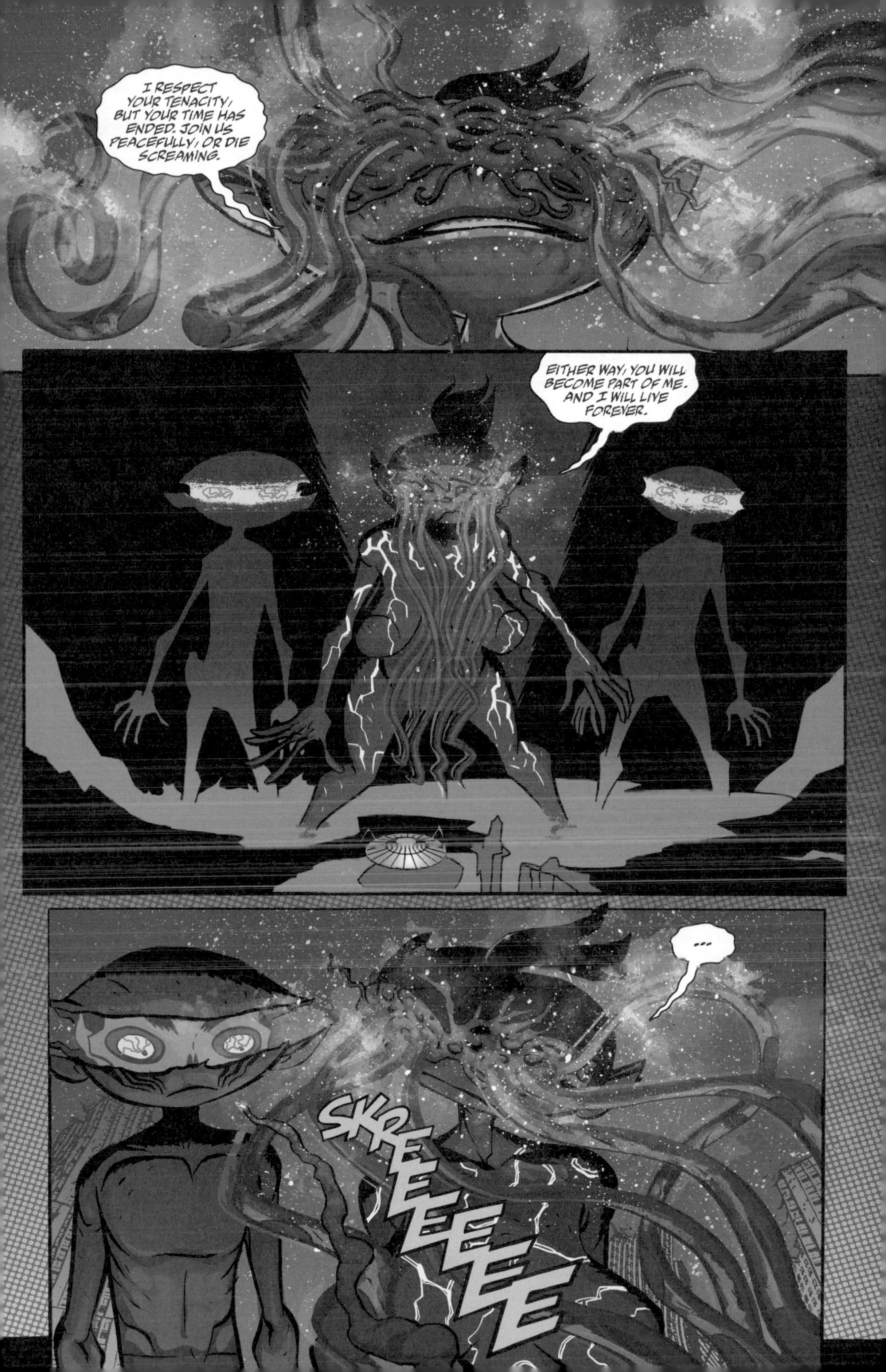
I RESPECT YOUR TENACITY, BUT YOUR TIME HAS ENDED. JOIN US PEACEFULLY, OR DIE SCREAMING.
EITHER WAY, YOU WILL BECOME PART OF ME. AND I WILL LIVE FOREVER.
...
SKREEEEEEE

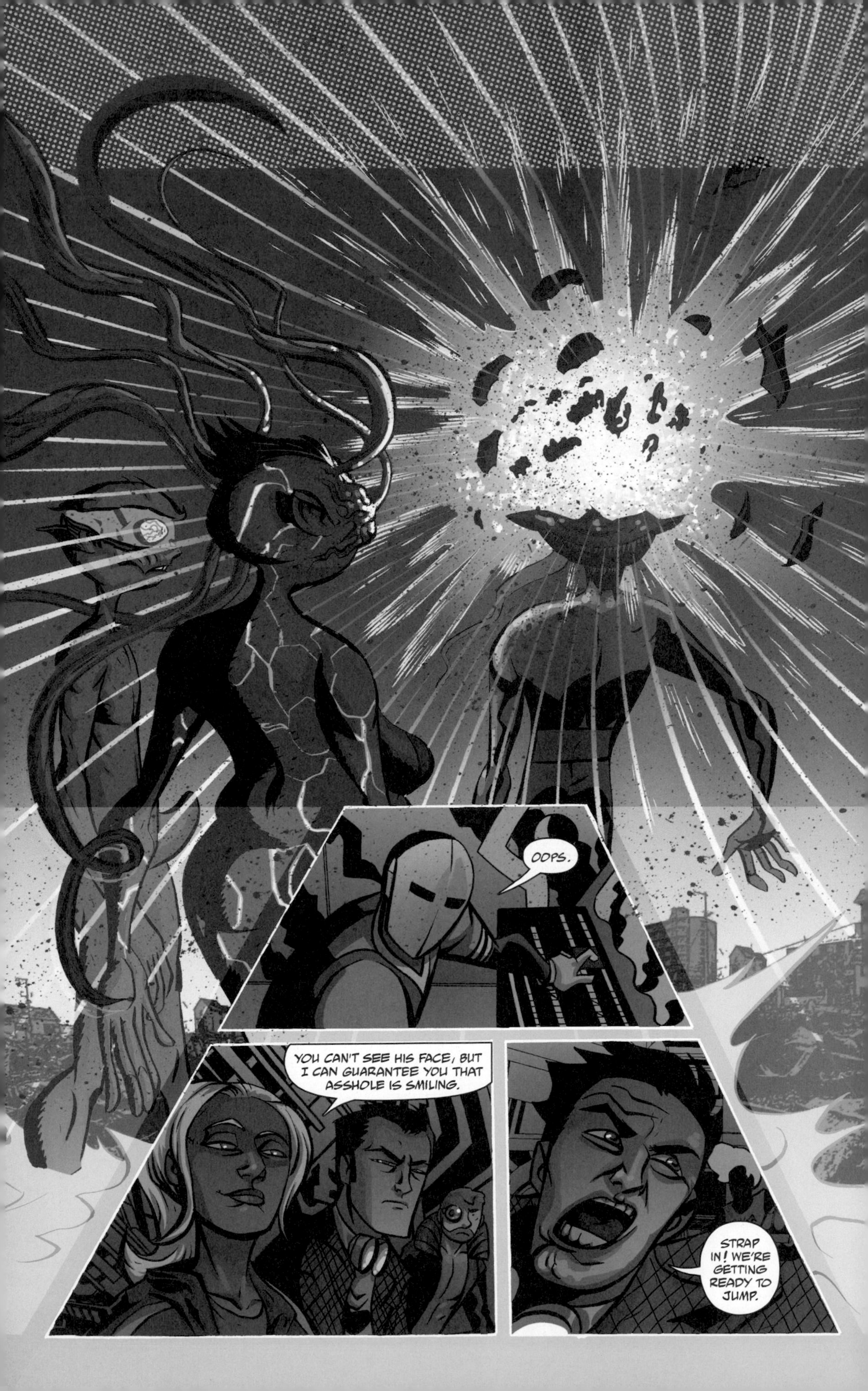
OOPS.
YOU CAN'T SEE HIS FACE, BUT I CAN GUARANTEE YOU THAT ASSHOLE IS SMILING.
STRAP IN! WE'RE GETTING READY TO JUMP.

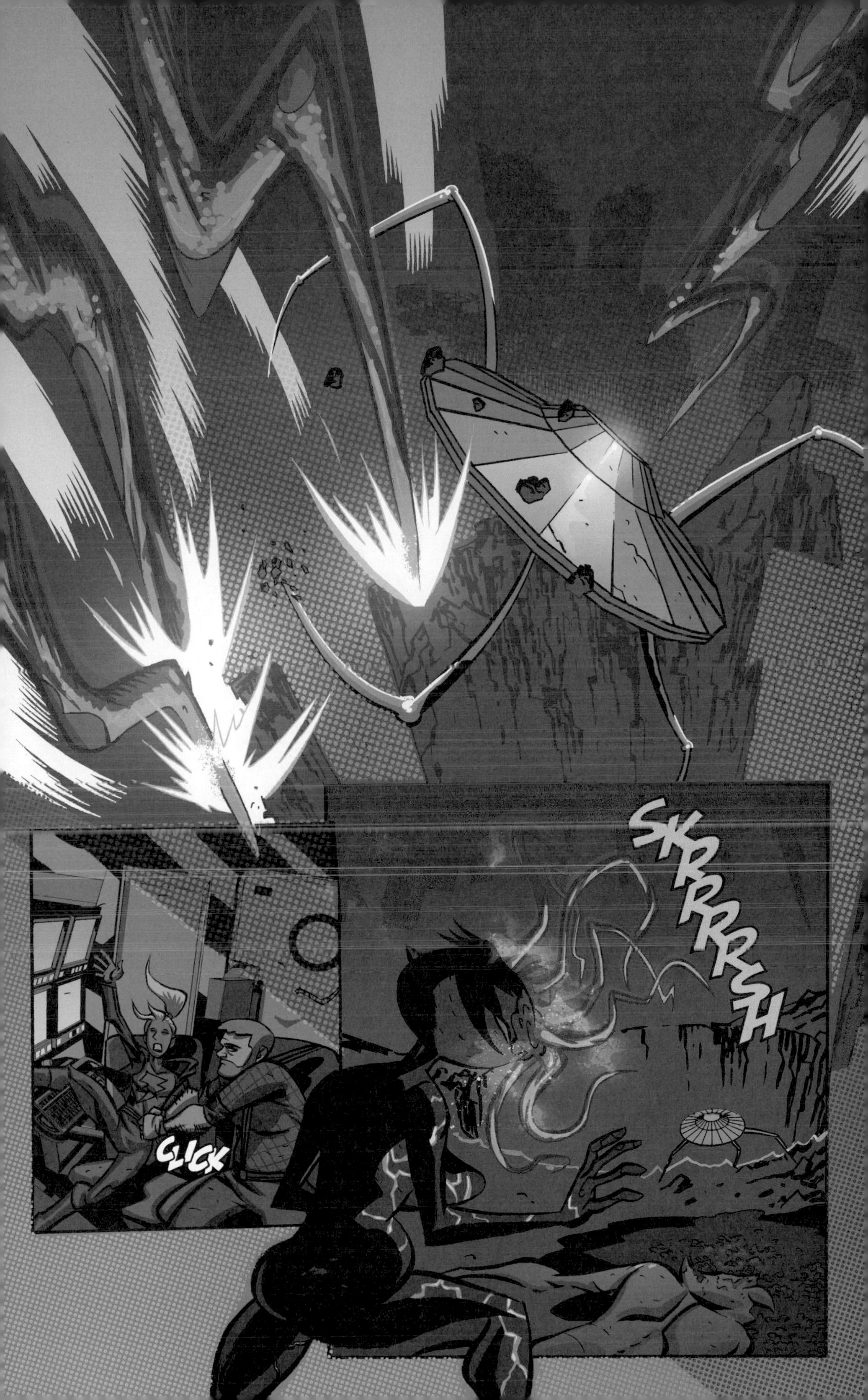
SKRRRRSH
CLICK

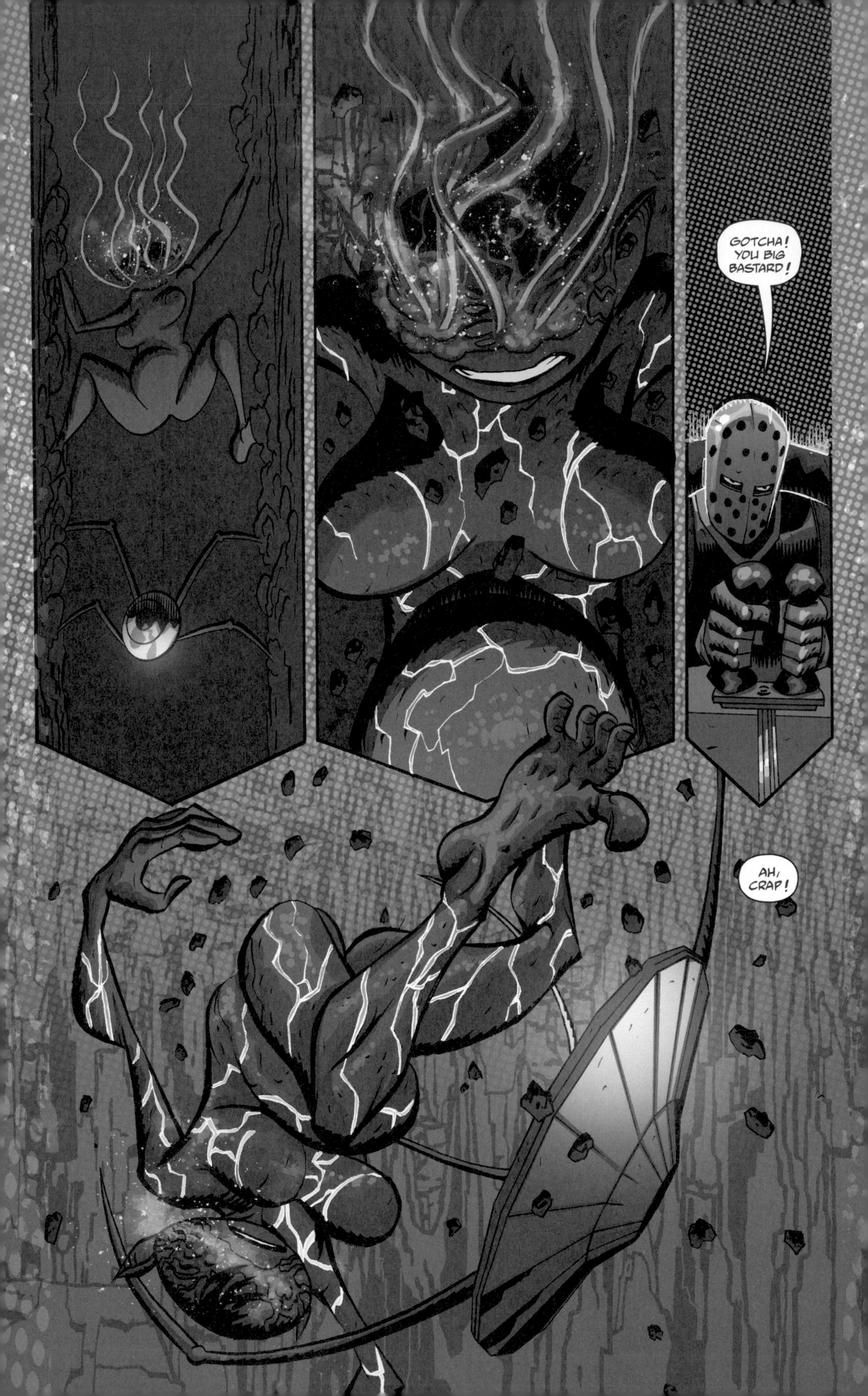
GOTCHA! YOU BIG BASTARD!
AH, CRAP!

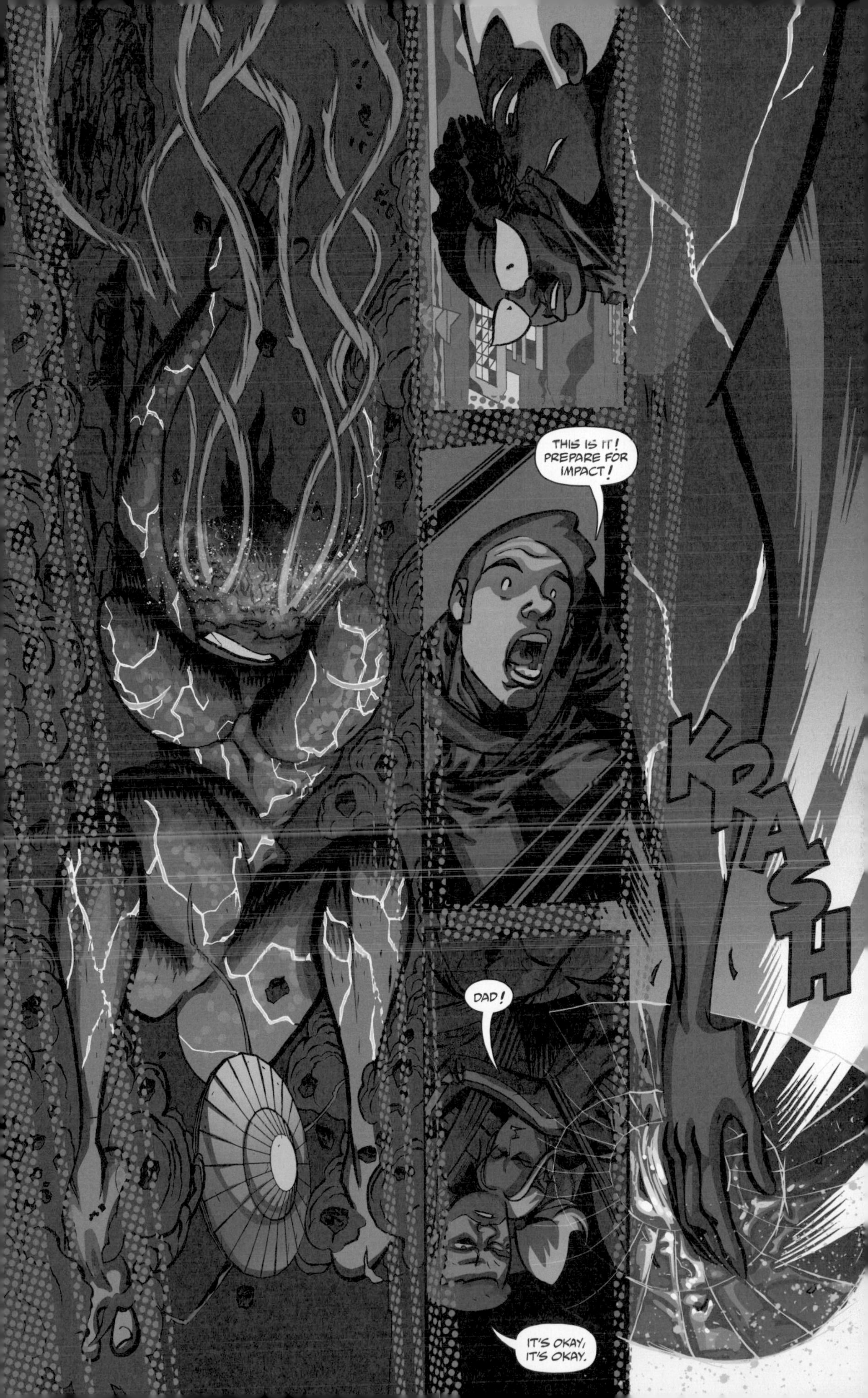
THIS IS IT! PREPARE FOR IMPACT!
KRASH
DAD!
IT'S OKAY, IT'S OKAY.

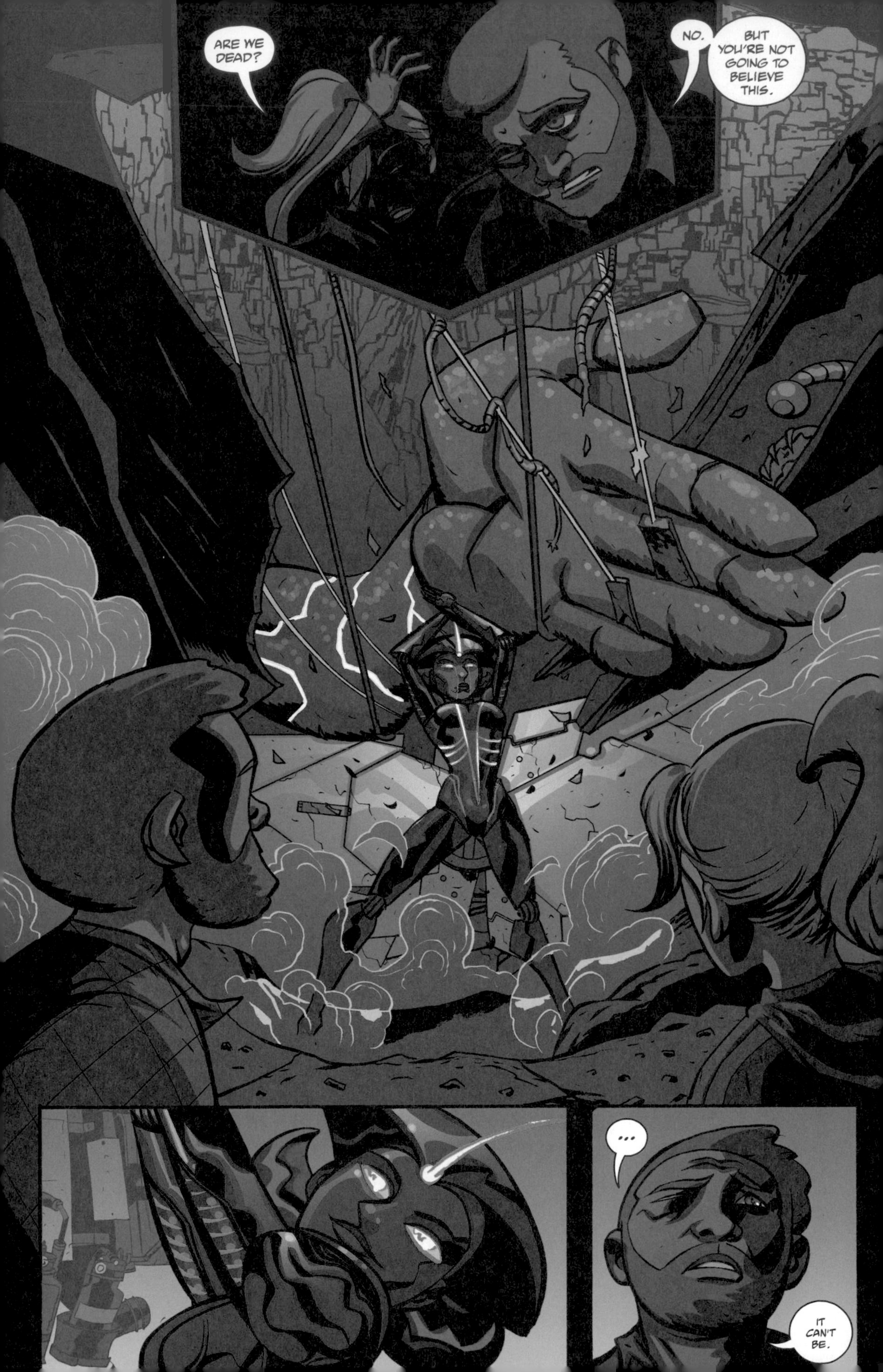
ARE WE DEAD?
NO.
BUT YOU'RE NOT GOING TO BELIEVE THIS.
...
IT CAN'T BE.

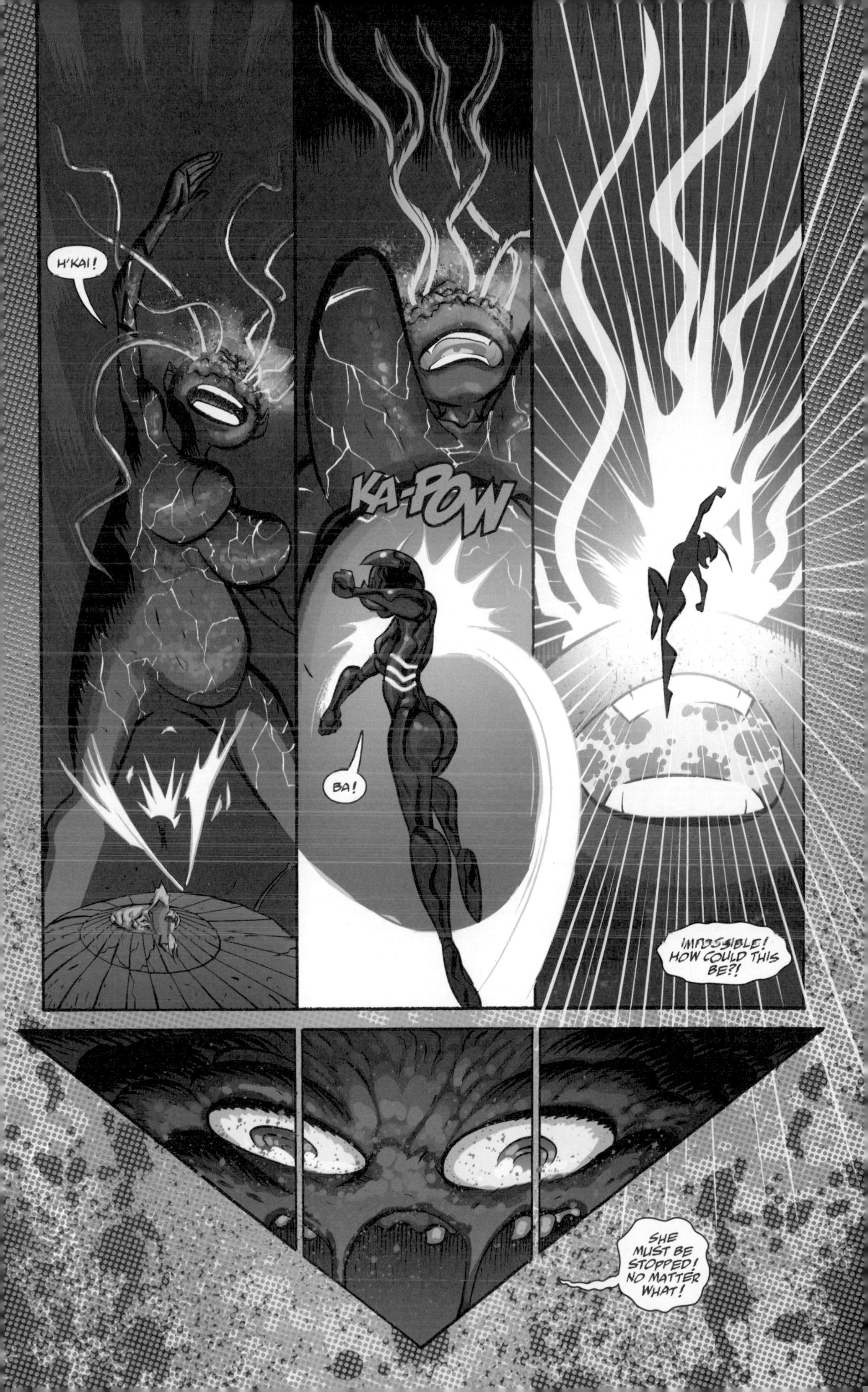
H'KAI!
KA-POW
BA!
IMPOSSIBLE! HOW COULD THIS BE?!
SHE MUST BE STOPPED! NO MATTER WHAT!

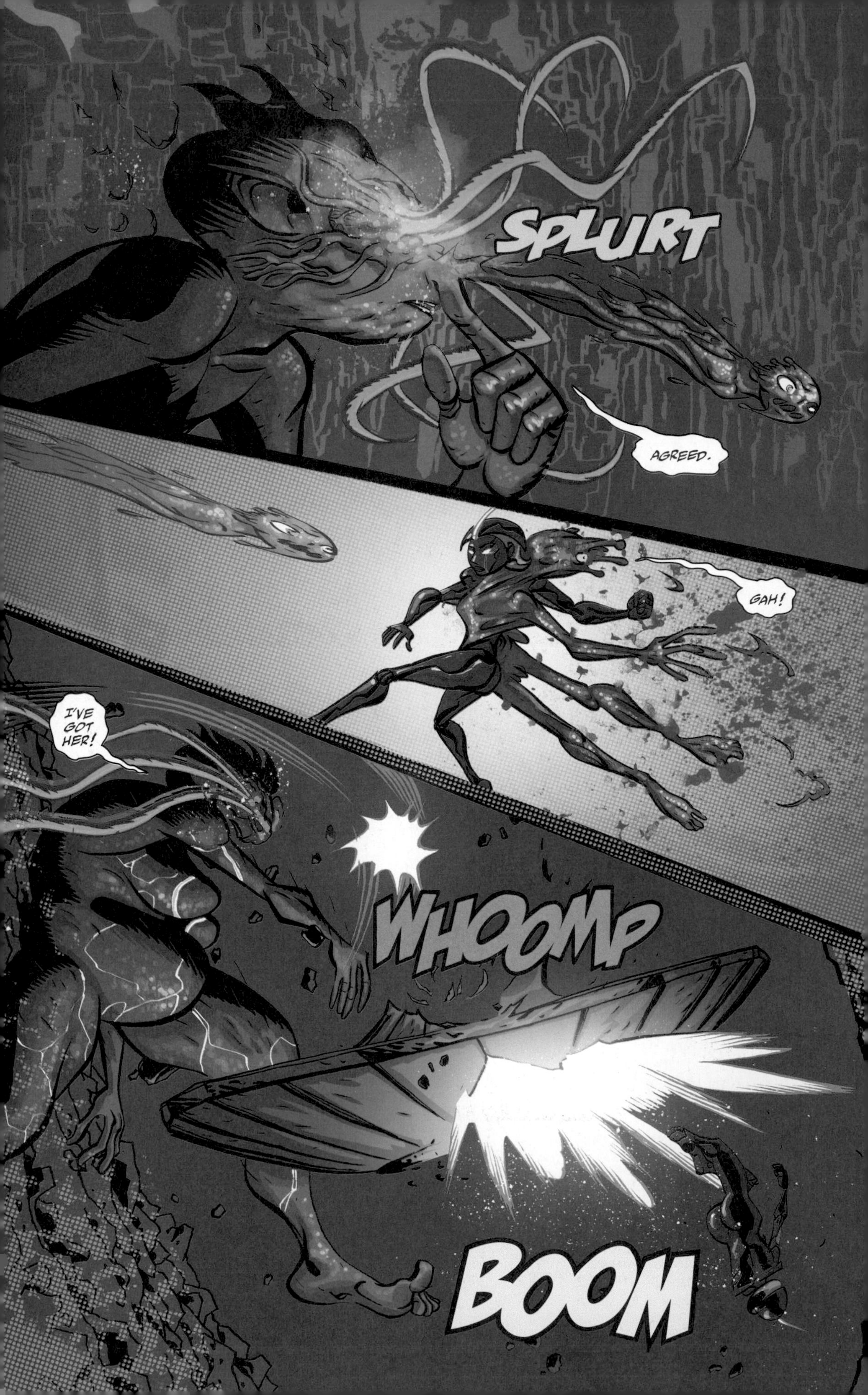
SPLURT
AGREED.
GAH!
I'VE GOT HER!
WHOOMP
BOOM

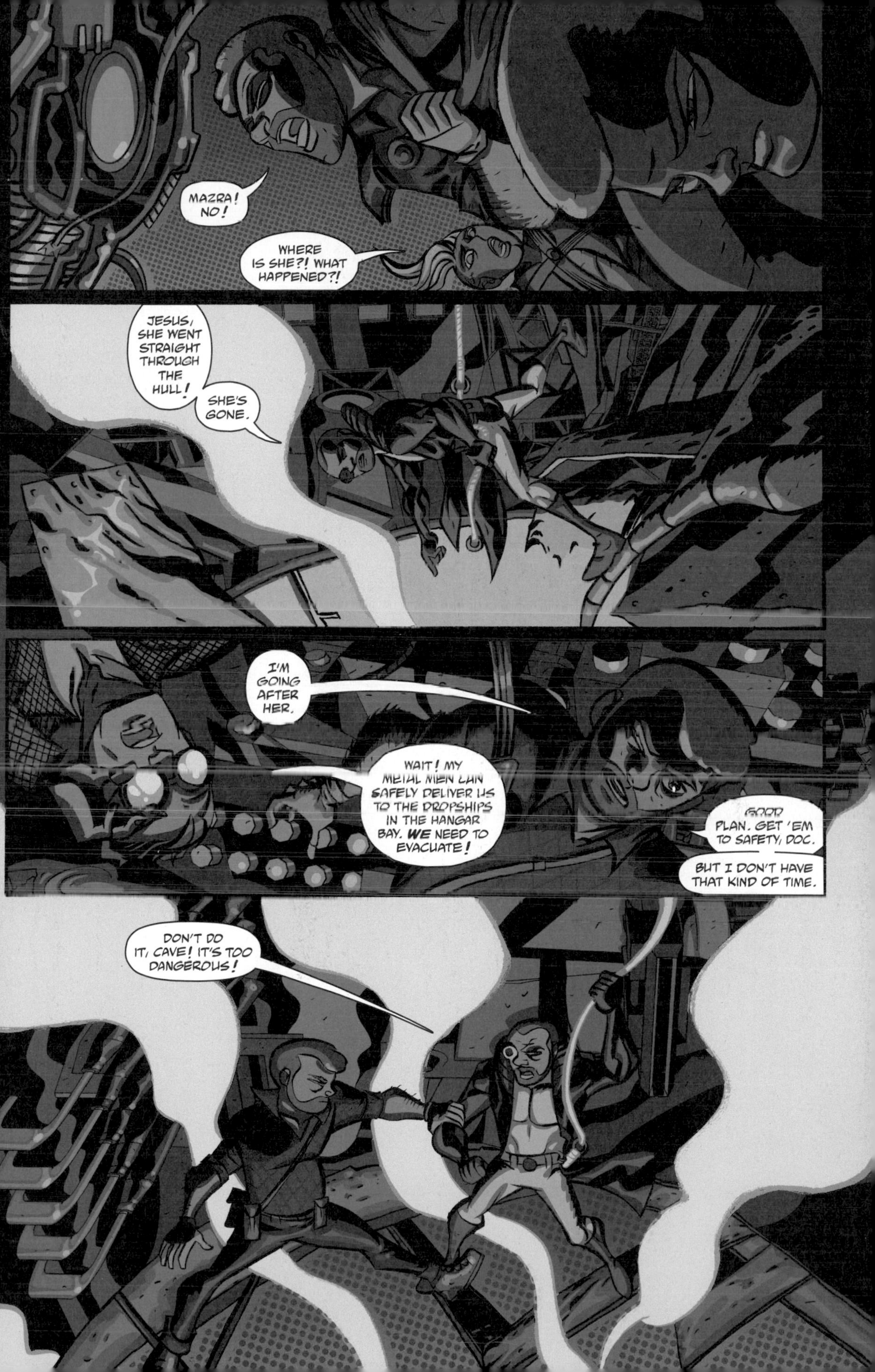
MAZRA! NO!
WHERE IS SHE?! WHAT HAPPENED?!
JESUS, SHE WENT STRAIGHT THROUGH THE HULL!
SHE'S GONE.
I'M GOING AFTER HER.
WAIT! MY METAL MEN CAN SAFELY DELIVER US TO THE DROPSHIPS IN THE HANGAR BAY. WE NEED TO EVACUATE!
GOOD PLAN. GET 'EM TO SAFETY, DOC.
BUT I DON'T HAVE THAT KIND OF TIME.
DON'T DO IT, CAVE! IT'S TOO DANGEROUS!

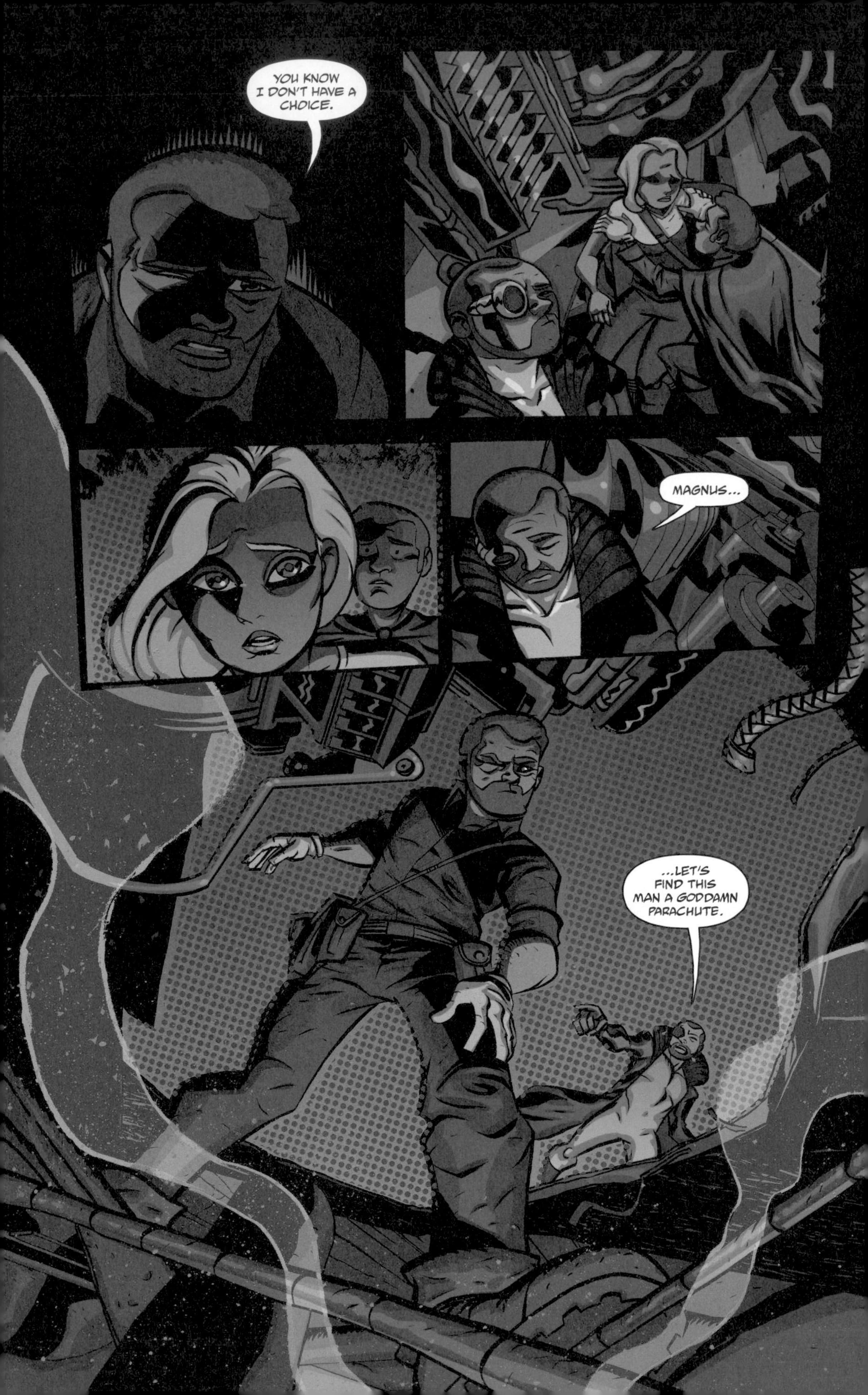
YOU KNOW I DON'T HAVE A CHOICE.
MAGNUS...
...LET'S FIND THIS MAN A GODDAMN PARACHUTE.

# The Wonderful World of Rocks!

With Professor Marc Bartow

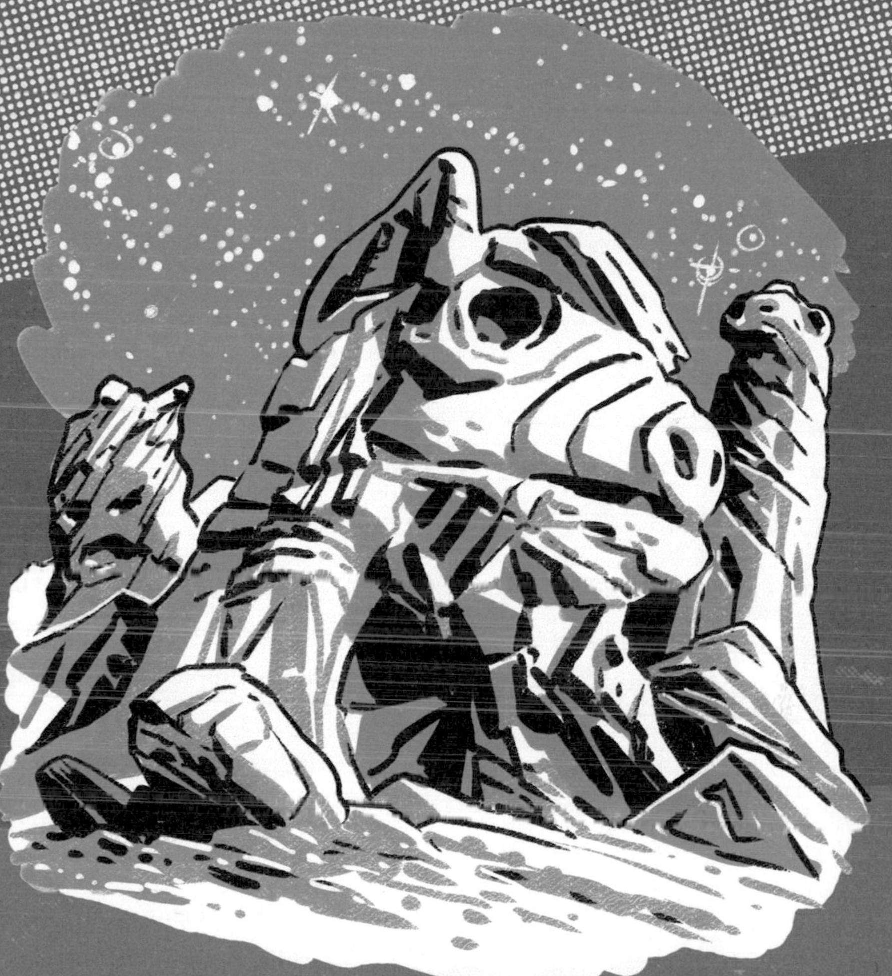

## "CUDDLESTONE"

**Found mostly in Iceland, the magnetic core of cuddlestones cause them to gravitate toward each other, over time collecting themselves into natural but sometimes bizarre rock formations.**

ROCK ON! MAGAZINE vol 2, issue 5 AUGUST 16

# Courage is the Handmaiden of Discovery

**I once had a dream** that I was trapped in a windowless shack. Feeling my way through the hopeless dark, I found a small hole. A tiny porthole through which poured a single beam of light. Then a second larger hole appeared in the wall, through which I could make out some grass and trees. And then a third hole appeared, and I could see the sun and the clouds. Then a fourth hole popped into the wall, allowing me to see farms and cities in the distance. Then another hole appeared and another until the walls of the shack had all but vanished and I could see the entire world just as it was. It was at that point the roof collapsed, crushing me.

The next morning I called Dr. Niedermeyer, telling him of the vast world that lies beneath the crust of the Earth, teeming with plants and animals hitherto undiscovered, fueled by the molten sun at our planet's core.

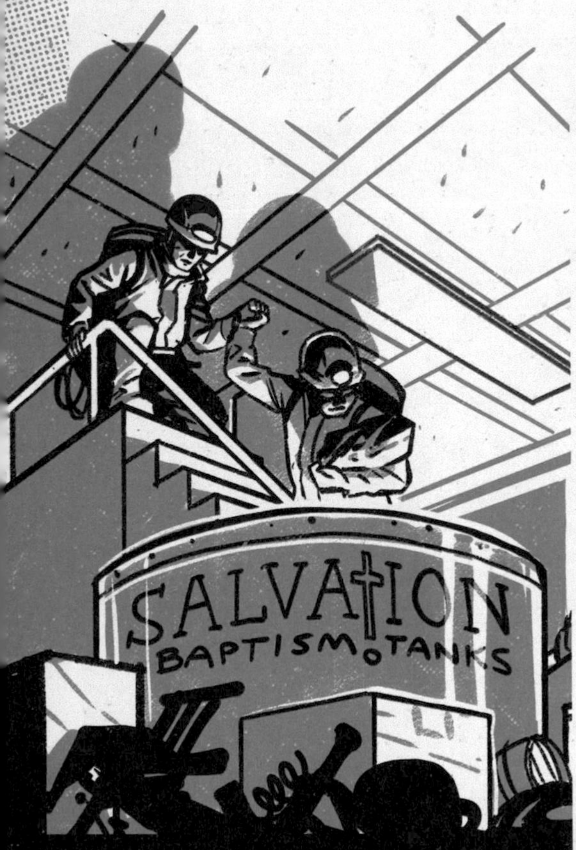
SALVATION
BAPTISM TANKS

Words by Mark Russell
Art by Benjamin Dewey

"And what do you base this wild conjecture on?" he asked.
"It's not conjecture," I replied. "Fred's seen it firsthand."
The next morning, I picked him up at the airport.
"What's this?" Dr. Niedermeyer asked, gesturing at the rock I had seatbelted into the passenger seat.
"That's Fred," I said. Dr. Niedermeyer looked worried.
"It's okay," I explained, "he's totally sentient."
"And how do you propose we get to a cavern eighteen miles beneath the surface of the Earth?"
"We use a controlled quazinite teleporter," I answered.
"I thought those were still theoretical," he replied. "You have one?!"
"Sure," I said. "I built one in my garage."
"You realize we could die the minute we arrive, or transport ourselves directly into solid rock," he warned.
"Of course," I replied.
After setting up the fold-away bed in my rumpus room, I showed Dr. Niedermeyer my homemade transport chamber in the garage.
"That's it?!" he asked. "It looks like a hot tub!"
"It's a converted baptismal tank," I explained. "I got it for next to nothing from the Methodist church down the street." I turned on the power to begin accelerating the quazinite particles. "You can never have enough Methodists."
The garage filled with black light as the transport chamber whirred to life.
"You want to explore other worlds," I told him. "Well, here's your chance."
"And what makes you think I'm going to join you on this suicide mission?" Dr. Niedermeyer asked.
"The fact that you got in my car," I replied.

By the way his cheeks sagged, I knew that I had him. This could be a fool's errand that would get us both killed. In all likelihood, it would be. But it was also the moment the loose threads of our lives had been weaving toward since the very beginning. Now, all that stood between us and making contact with alien life was a Methodist baptismal tank. Reluctantly, but without any further questions, Dr. Niedermeyer buckled on his spelunking backpack, I collected Fred (our guide) and together the three of us entered the wormhole, not knowing what, if anything, we'd find on the other side.

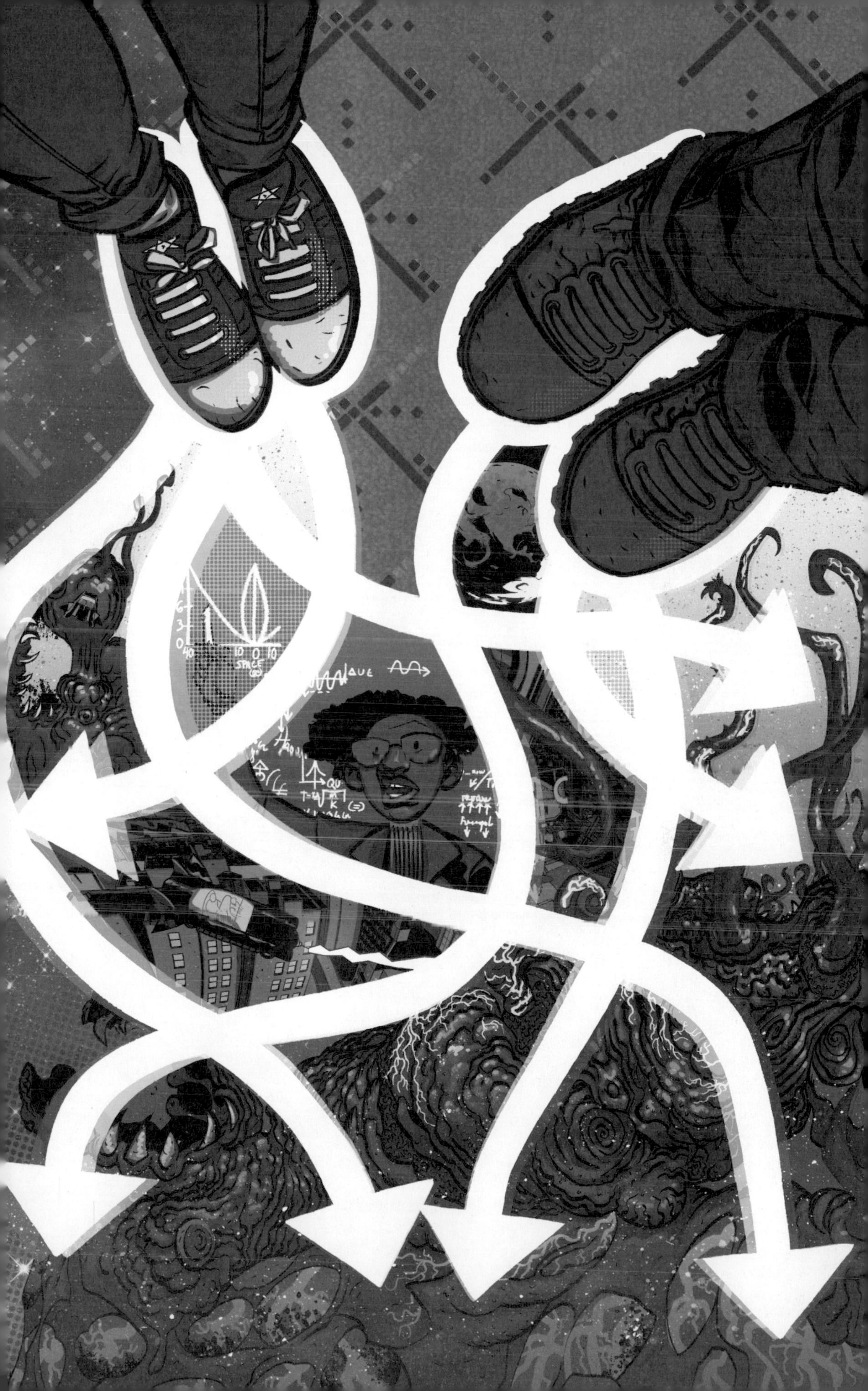

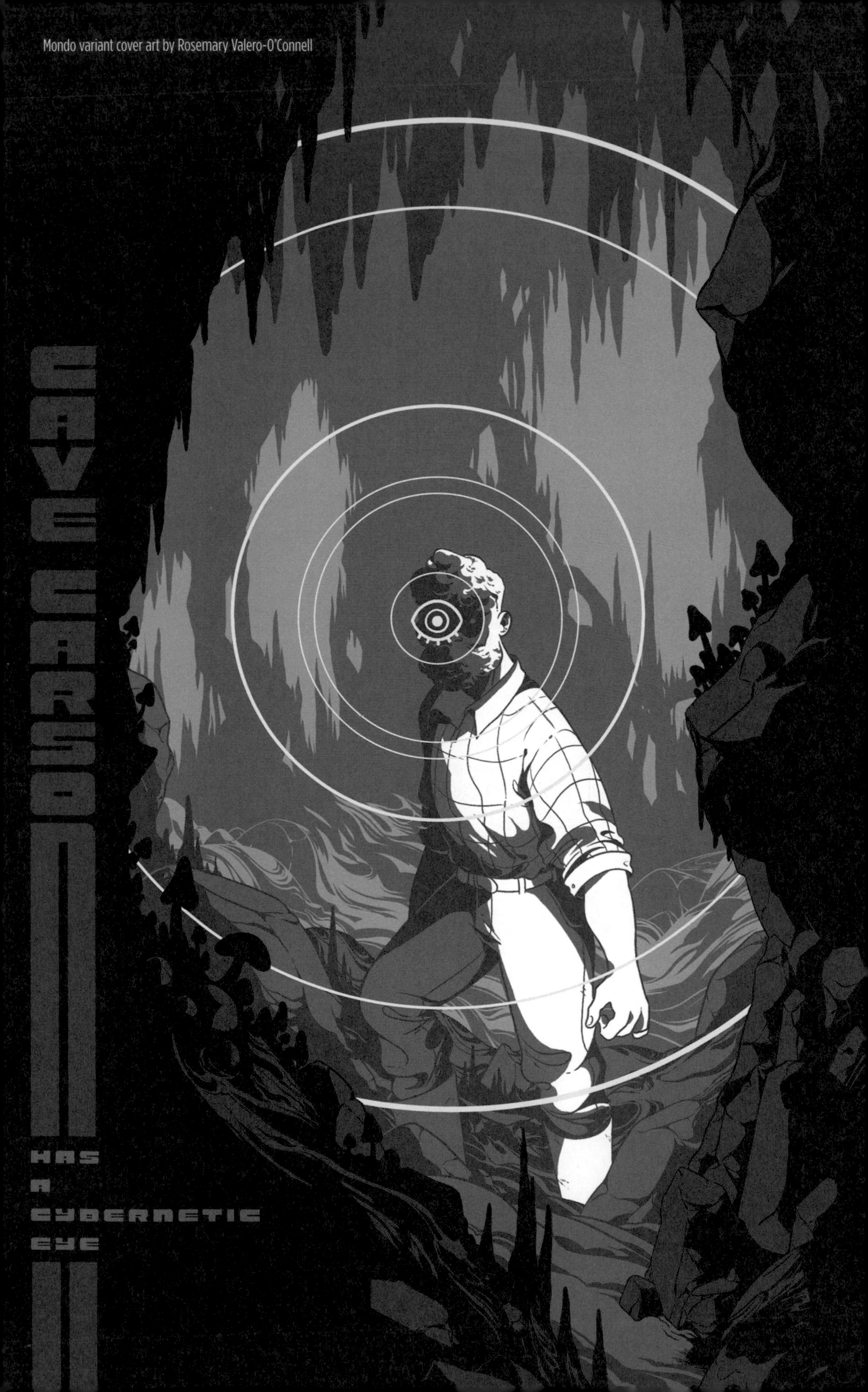
CAVE CARSON
HAS
A
CYBERNETIC
EYE

Mondo variant cover art by Rosemary Valero-O'Connell

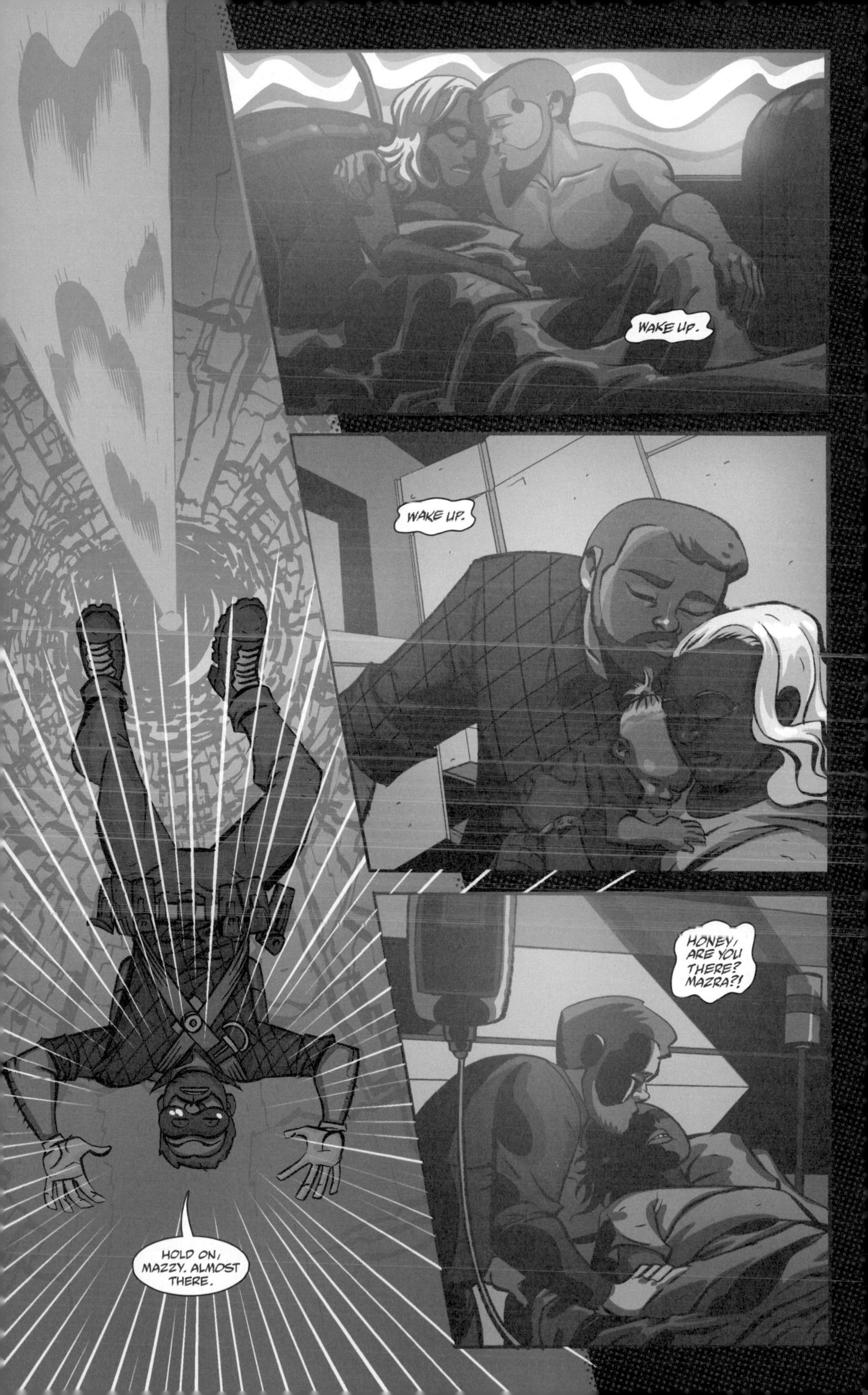
WAKE UP.
WAKE UP.
HONEY, ARE YOU THERE? MAZRA?!
HOLD ON, MAZZY. ALMOST THERE.

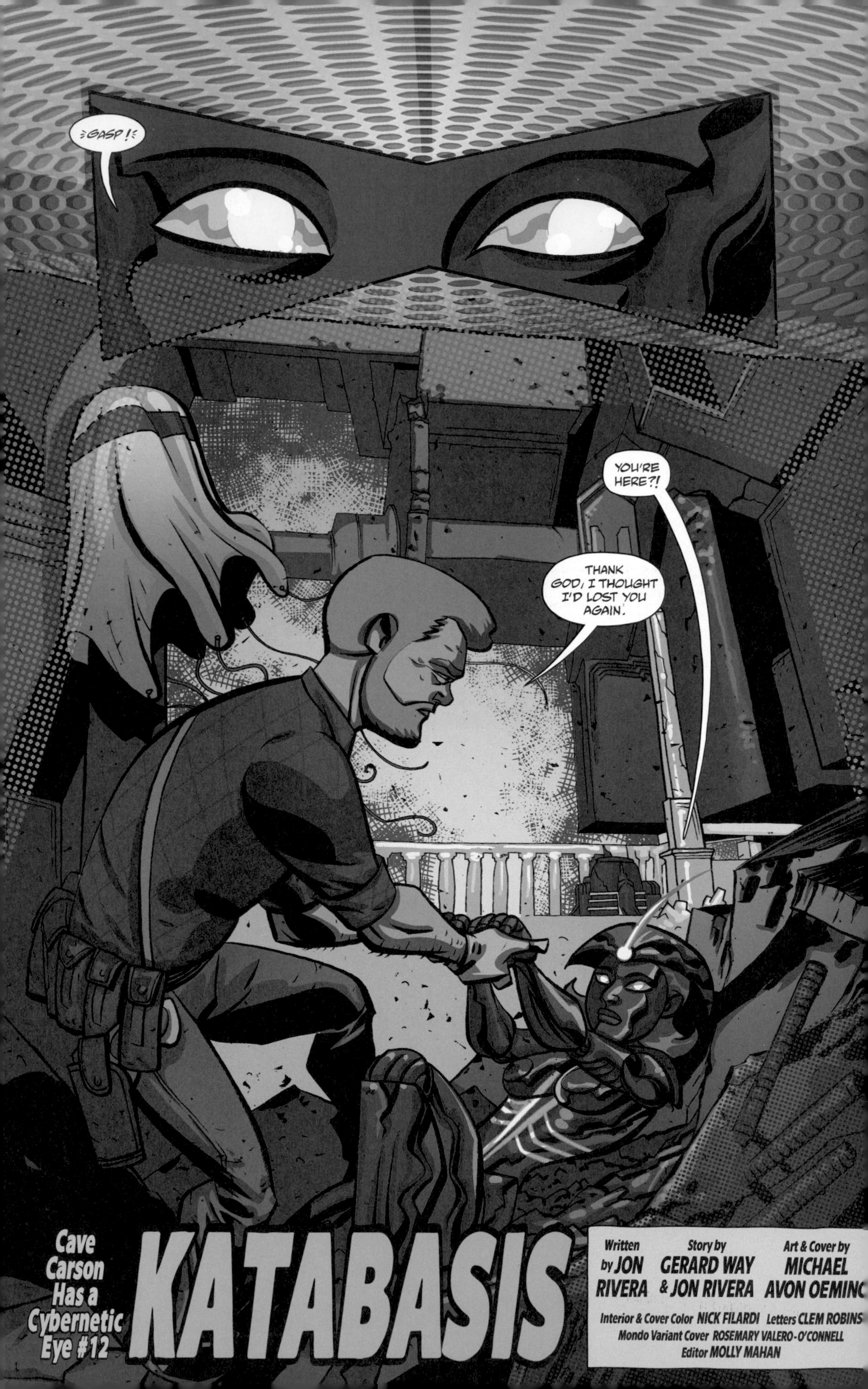
GASP!
YOU'RE HERE?!
THANK GOD, I THOUGHT I'D LOST YOU AGAIN.
Cave Carson Has a Cybernetic Eye #12
KATABASIS
Written by JON RIVERA
Story by GERARD WAY & JON RIVERA
Art & Cover by MICHAEL AVON OEMING
Interior & Cover Color NICK FILARDI Letters CLEM ROBINS
Mondo Variant Cover ROSEMARY VALERO-O'CONNELL
Editor MOLLY MAHAN

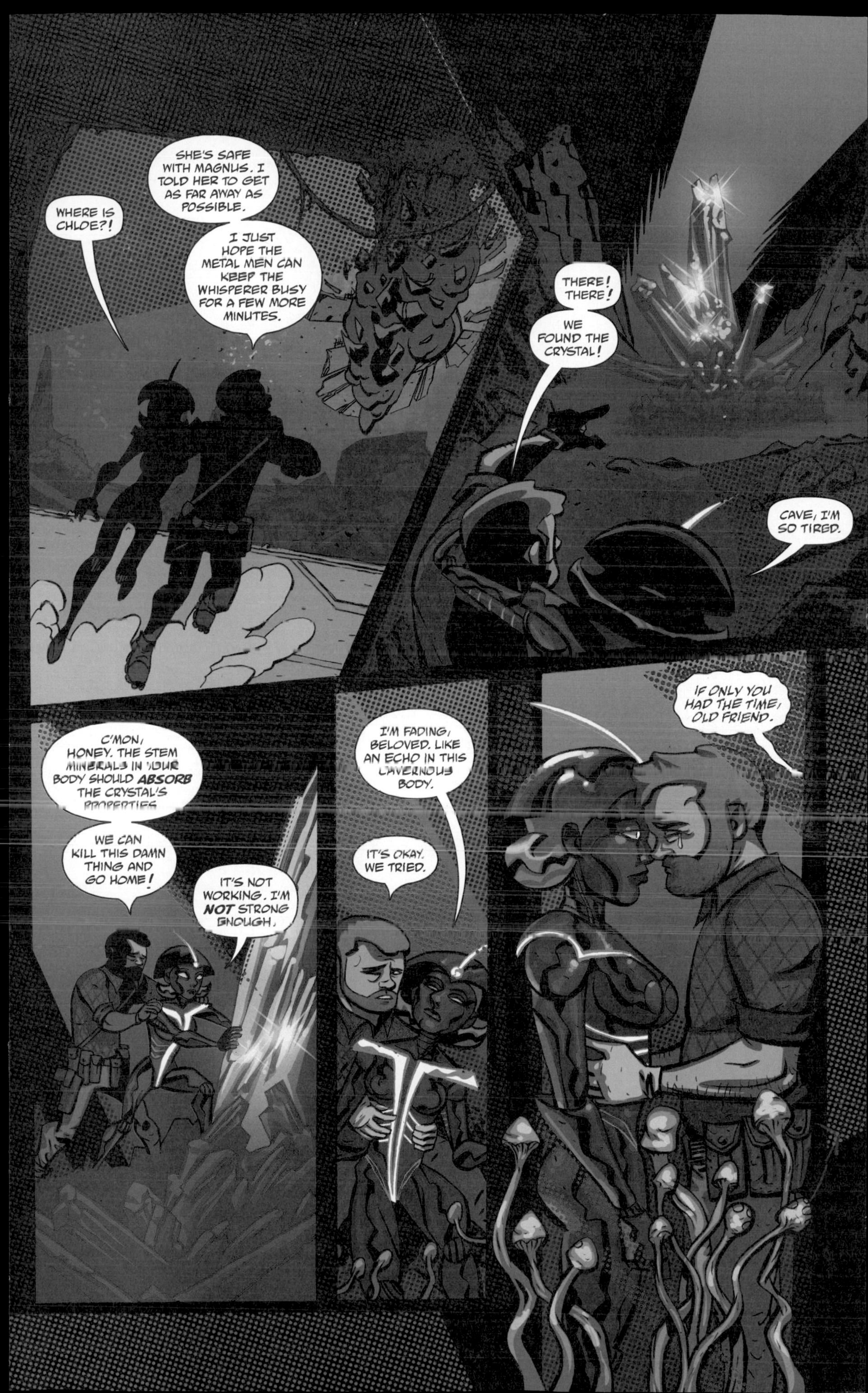
WHERE IS CHLOE?!
SHE'S SAFE WITH MAGNUS. I TOLD HER TO GET AS FAR AWAY AS POSSIBLE.
I JUST HOPE THE METAL MEN CAN KEEP THE WHISPERER BUSY FOR A FEW MORE MINUTES.
THERE! THERE!
WE FOUND THE CRYSTAL!
CAVE, I'M SO TIRED.
C'MON, HONEY. THE STEM MINERALS IN YOUR BODY SHOULD ABSORB THE CRYSTAL'S PROPERTIES.
WE CAN KILL THIS DAMN THING AND GO HOME!
IT'S NOT WORKING. I'M NOT STRONG ENOUGH.
I'M FADING, BELOVED. LIKE AN ECHO IN THIS CAVERNOUS BODY.
IT'S OKAY. WE TRIED.
IF ONLY YOU HAD THE TIME, OLD FRIEND.

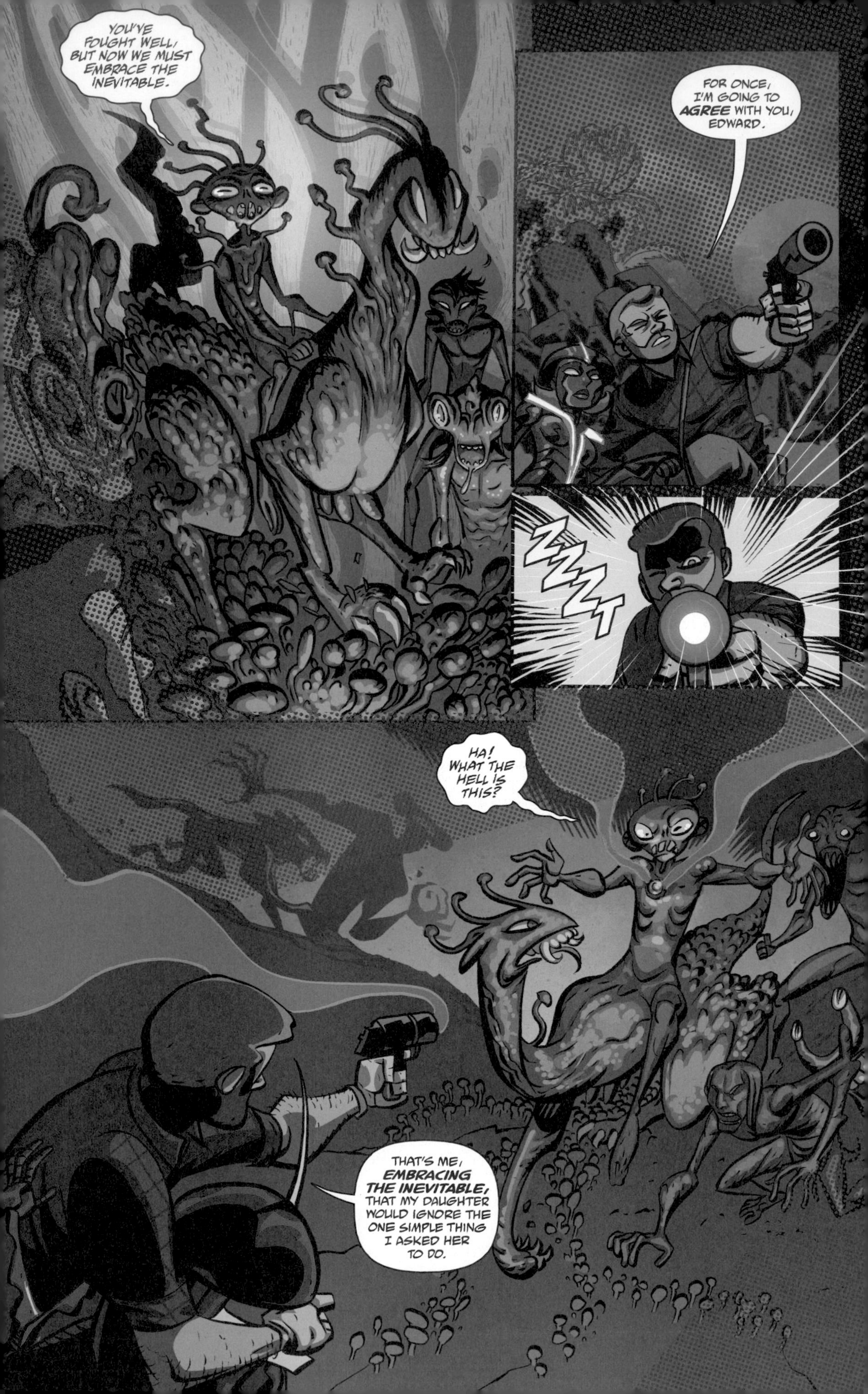
YOU'VE FOUGHT WELL, BUT NOW WE MUST EMBRACE THE INEVITABLE.
FOR ONCE, I'M GOING TO AGREE WITH YOU, EDWARD.
ZZZT
HA! WHAT THE HELL IS THIS?
THAT'S ME, EMBRACING THE INEVITABLE, THAT MY DAUGHTER WOULD IGNORE THE ONE SIMPLE THING I ASKED HER TO DO.

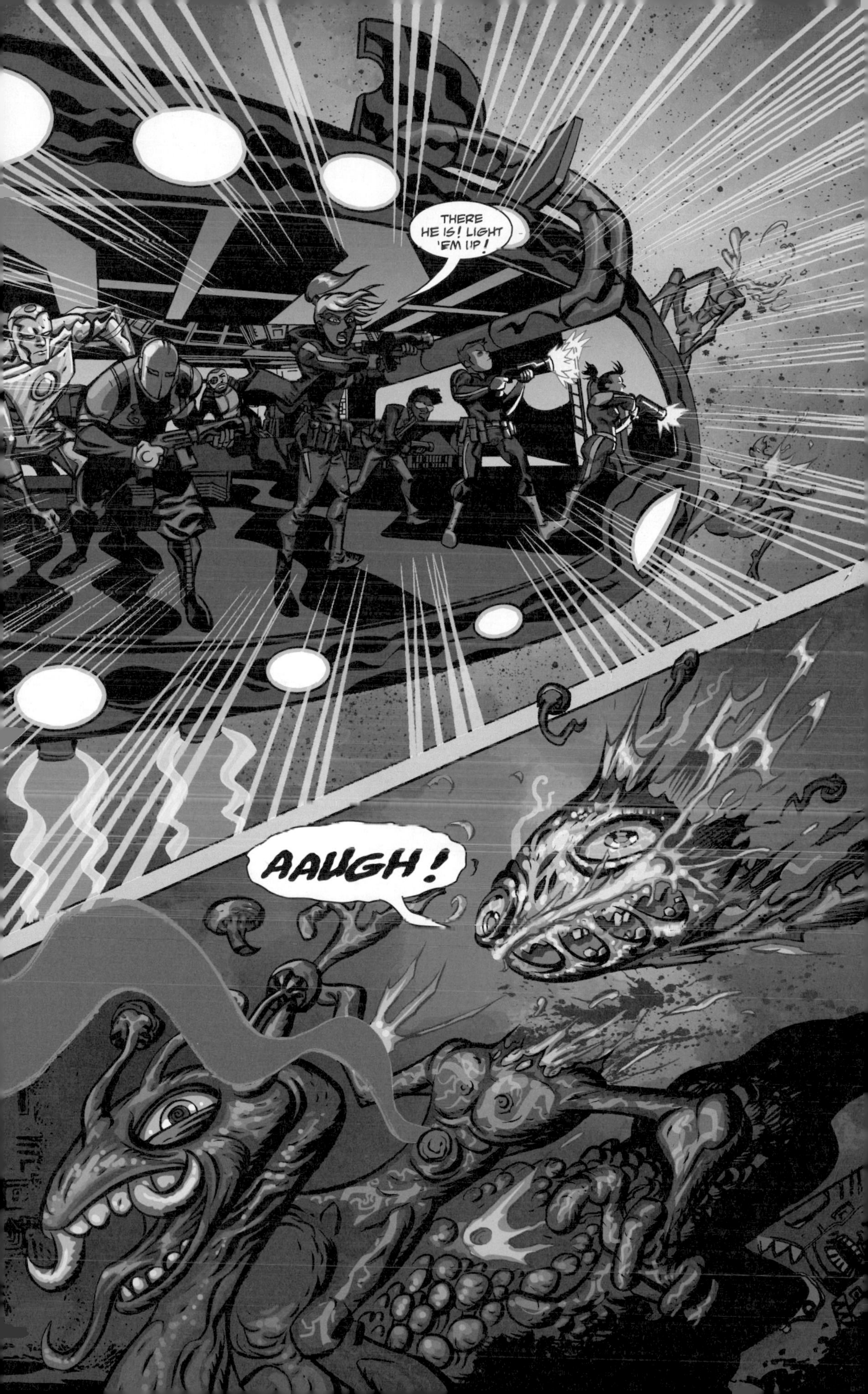
THERE HE IS! LIGHT 'EM UP!
AAUGH!

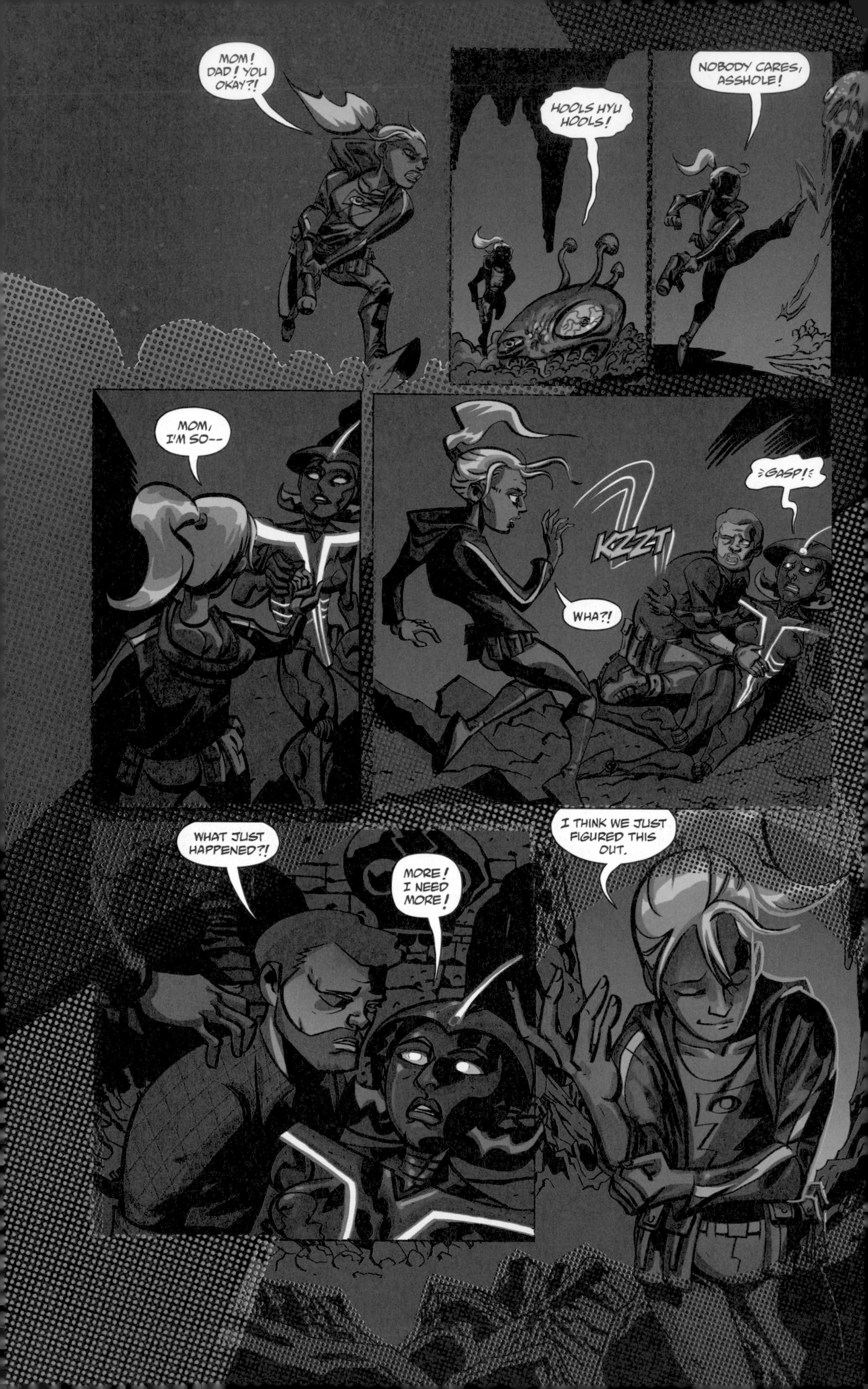
MOM! DAD! YOU OKAY?!
HOOLS HYU HOOLS!
NOBODY CARES, ASSHOLE!
MOM, I'M SO--
KZZT
WHA?!
GASP!
WHAT JUST HAPPENED?!
MORE! I NEED MORE!
I THINK WE JUST FIGURED THIS OUT.

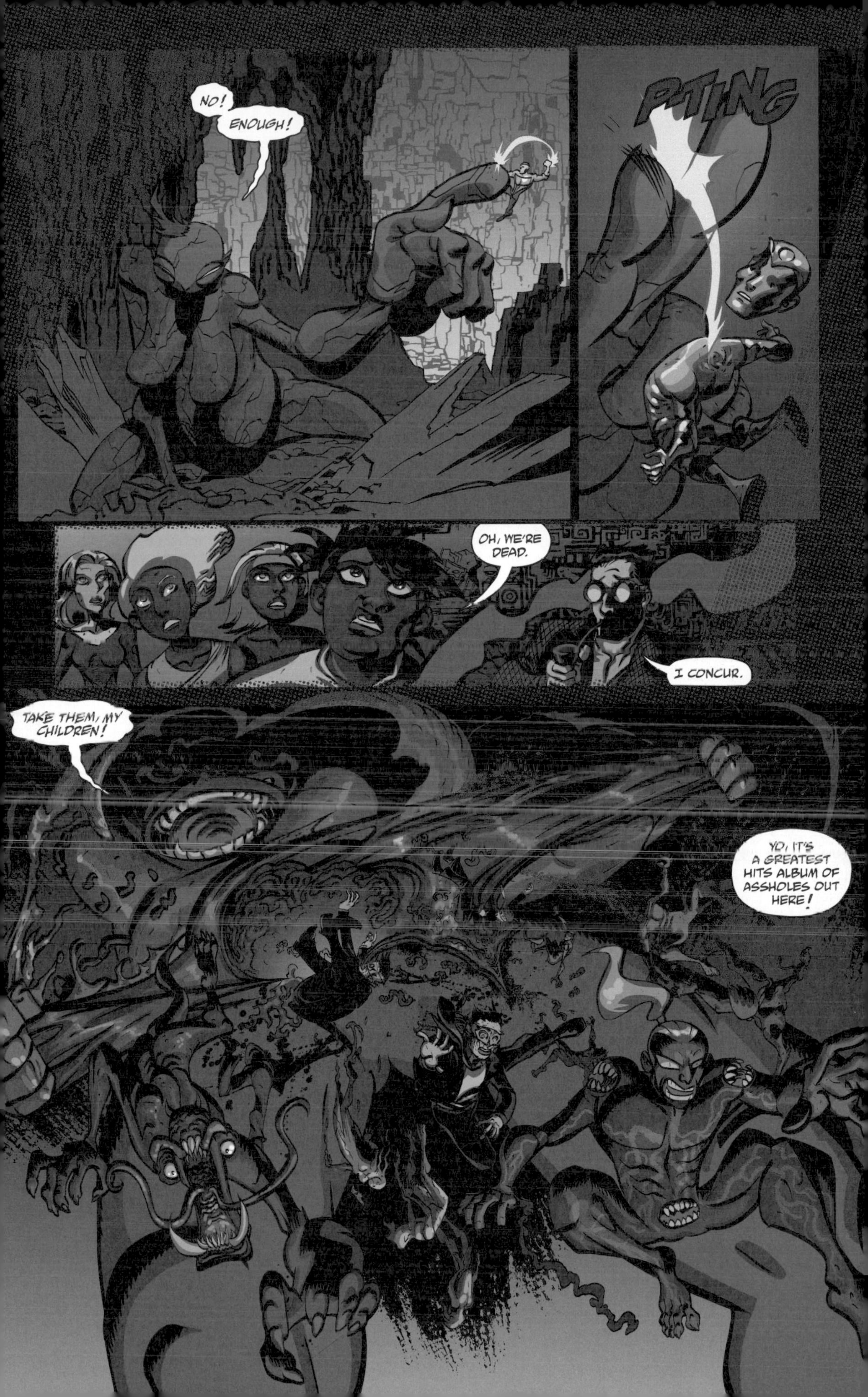
NO!
ENOUGH!
P-TING
OH, WE'RE DEAD.
I CONCUR.
TAKE THEM, MY CHILDREN!
YO, IT'S A GREATEST HITS ALBUM OF ASSHOLES OUT HERE!

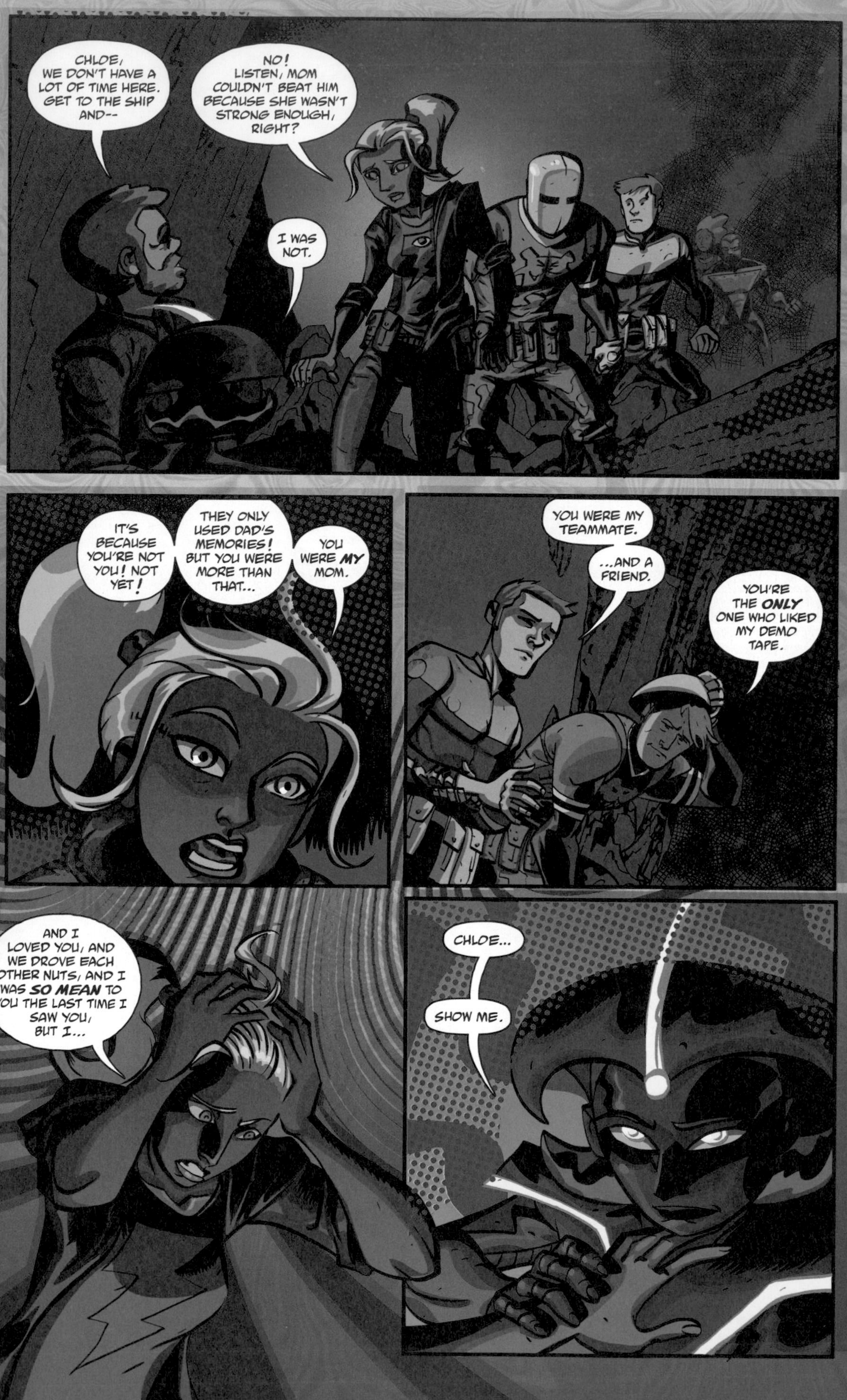
CHLOE, WE DON'T HAVE A LOT OF TIME HERE. GET TO THE SHIP AND--
NO! LISTEN, MOM COULDN'T BEAT HIM BECAUSE SHE WASN'T STRONG ENOUGH, RIGHT?
I WAS NOT.
IT'S BECAUSE YOU'RE NOT YOU! NOT YET!
THEY ONLY USED DAD'S MEMORIES! BUT YOU WERE MORE THAN THAT...
YOU WERE MY MOM.
YOU WERE MY TEAMMATE.
...AND A FRIEND.
YOU'RE THE ONLY ONE WHO LIKED MY DEMO TAPE.
AND I LOVED YOU, AND WE DROVE EACH OTHER NUTS, AND I WAS SO MEAN TO YOU THE LAST TIME I SAW YOU, BUT I...
CHLOE...
SHOW ME.

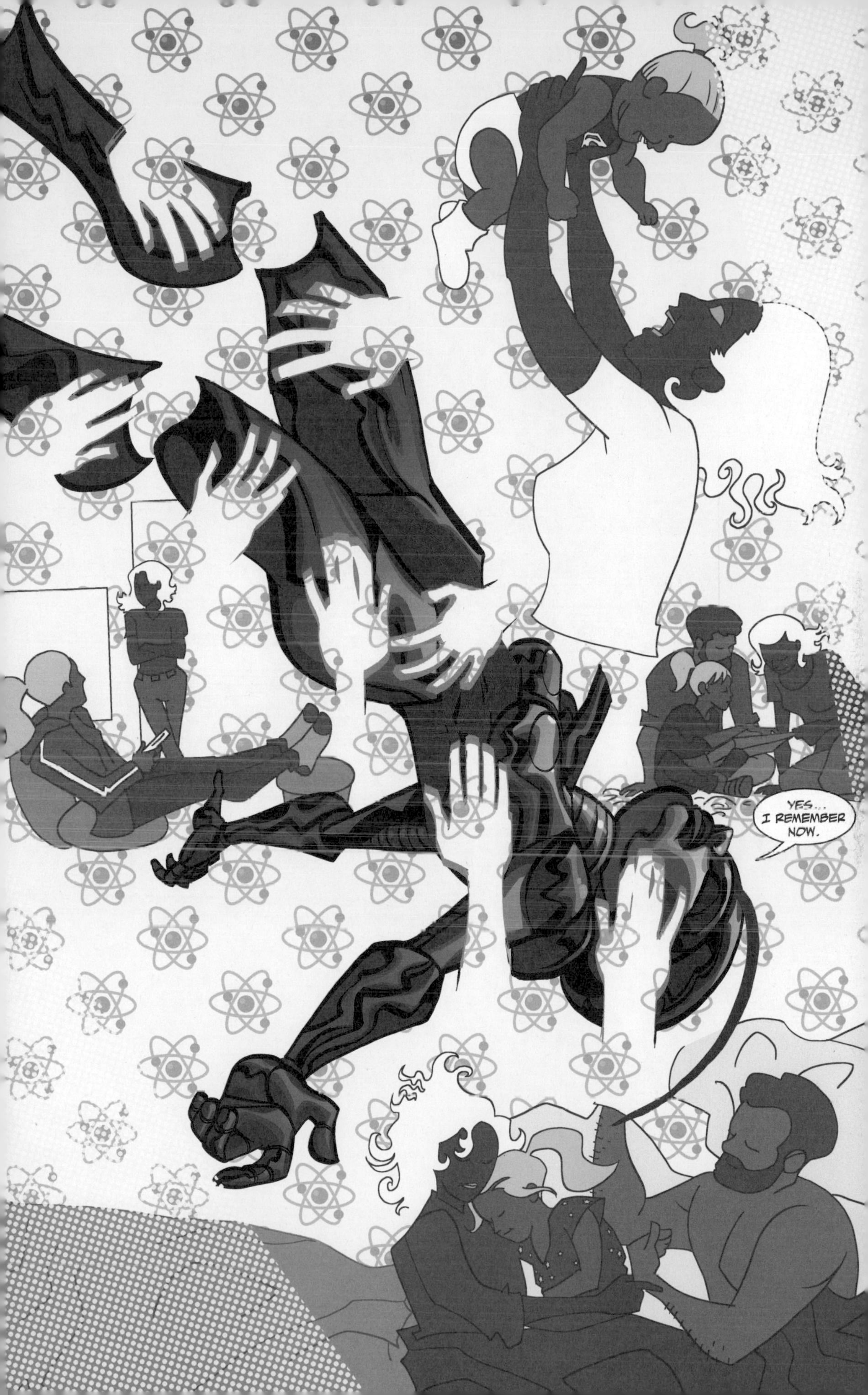
YES... I REMEMBER NOW.

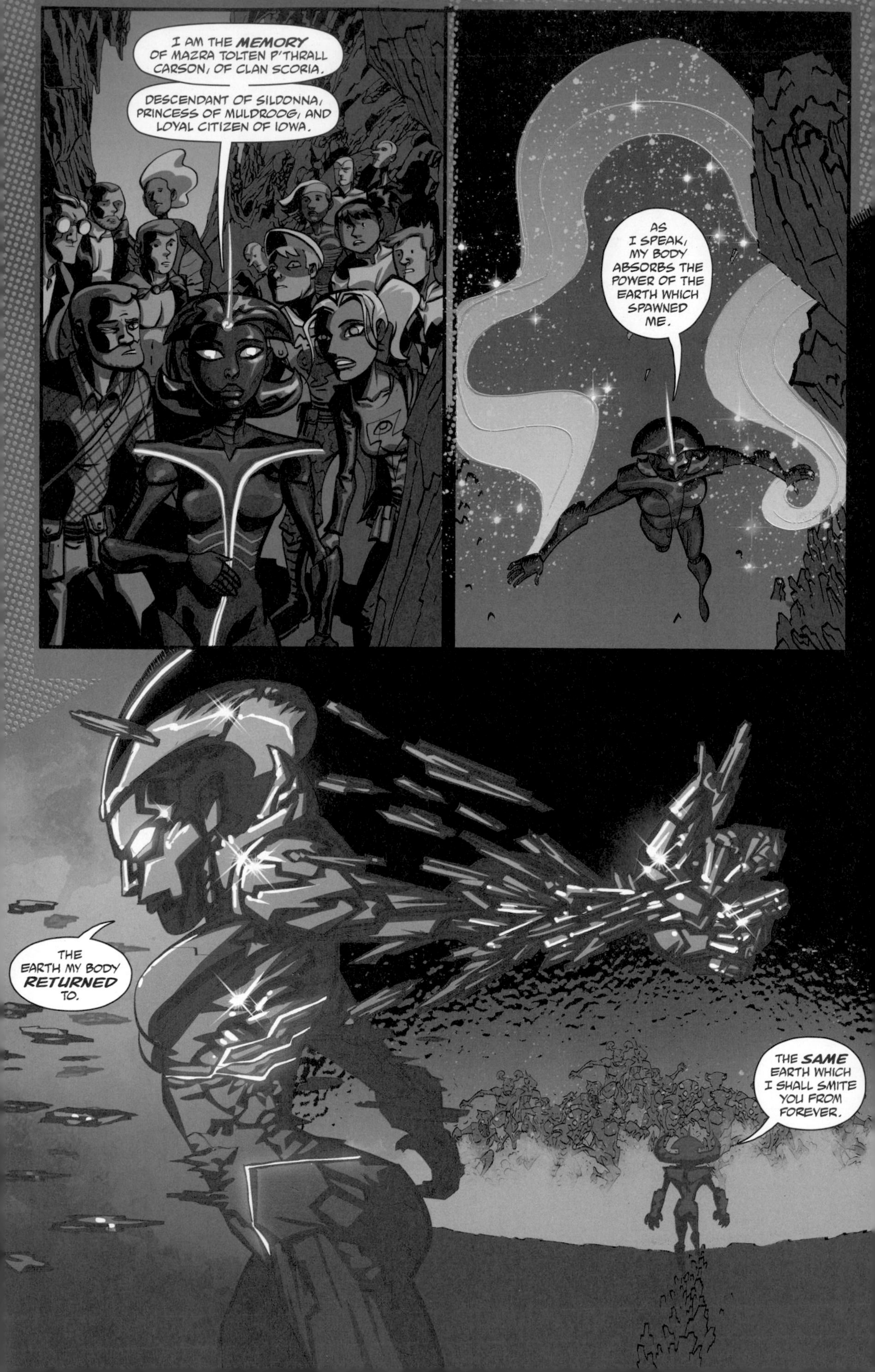
I AM THE MEMORY OF MAZRA TOLTEN P'THRALL CARSON, OF CLAN SCORIA.
DESCENDANT OF SILDONNA, PRINCESS OF MULDROOG, AND LOYAL CITIZEN OF IOWA.
AS I SPEAK, MY BODY ABSORBS THE POWER OF THE EARTH WHICH SPAWNED ME.
THE EARTH MY BODY RETURNED TO.
THE SAME EARTH WHICH I SHALL SMITE YOU FROM FOREVER.

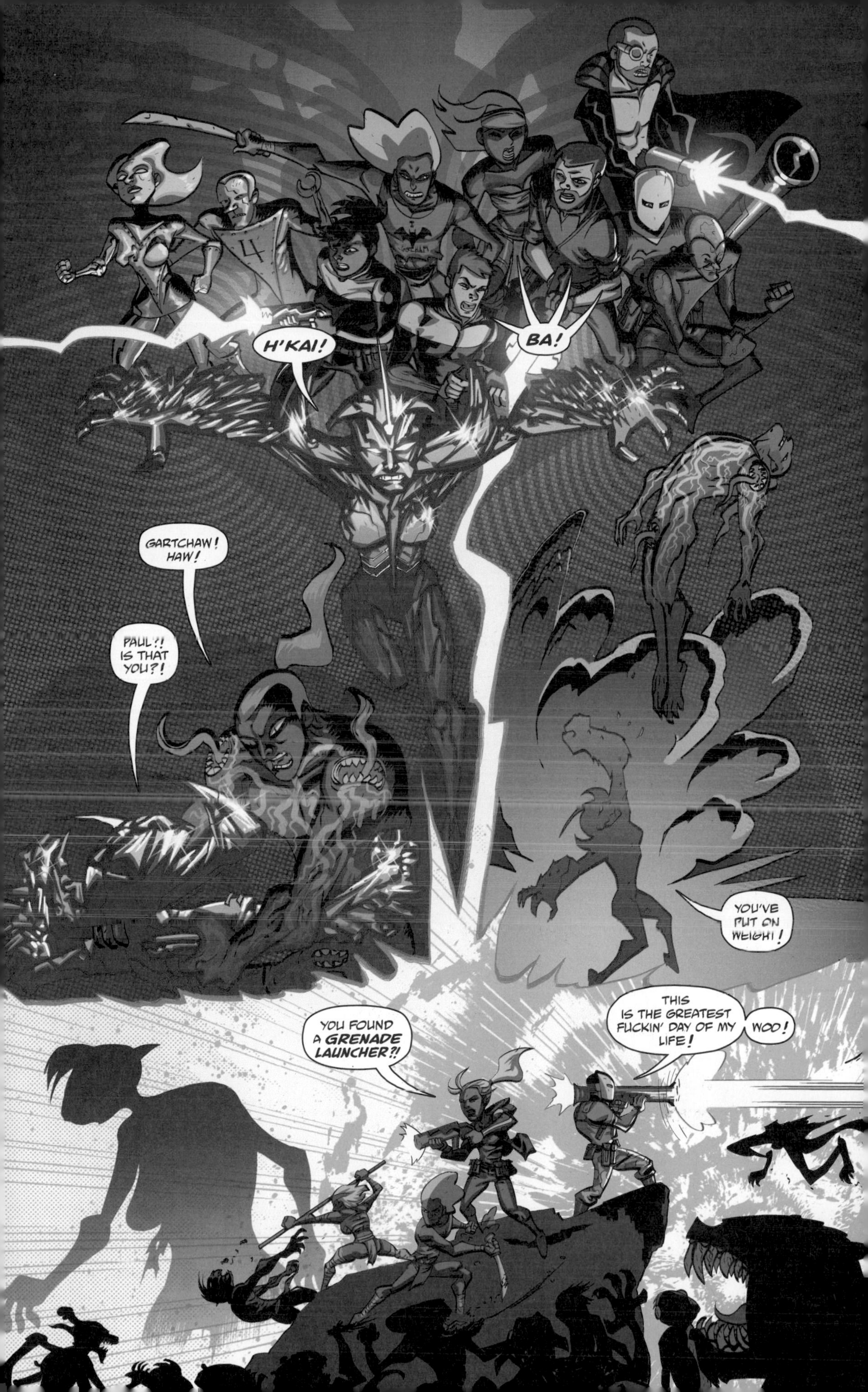
H'KAI!
BA!
GARTCHAW! HAW!
PAUL?! IS THAT YOU?!
YOU'VE PUT ON WEIGHT!
YOU FOUND A **GRENADE LAUNCHER**?!
THIS IS THE GREATEST FUCKIN' DAY OF MY LIFE!
WOO!

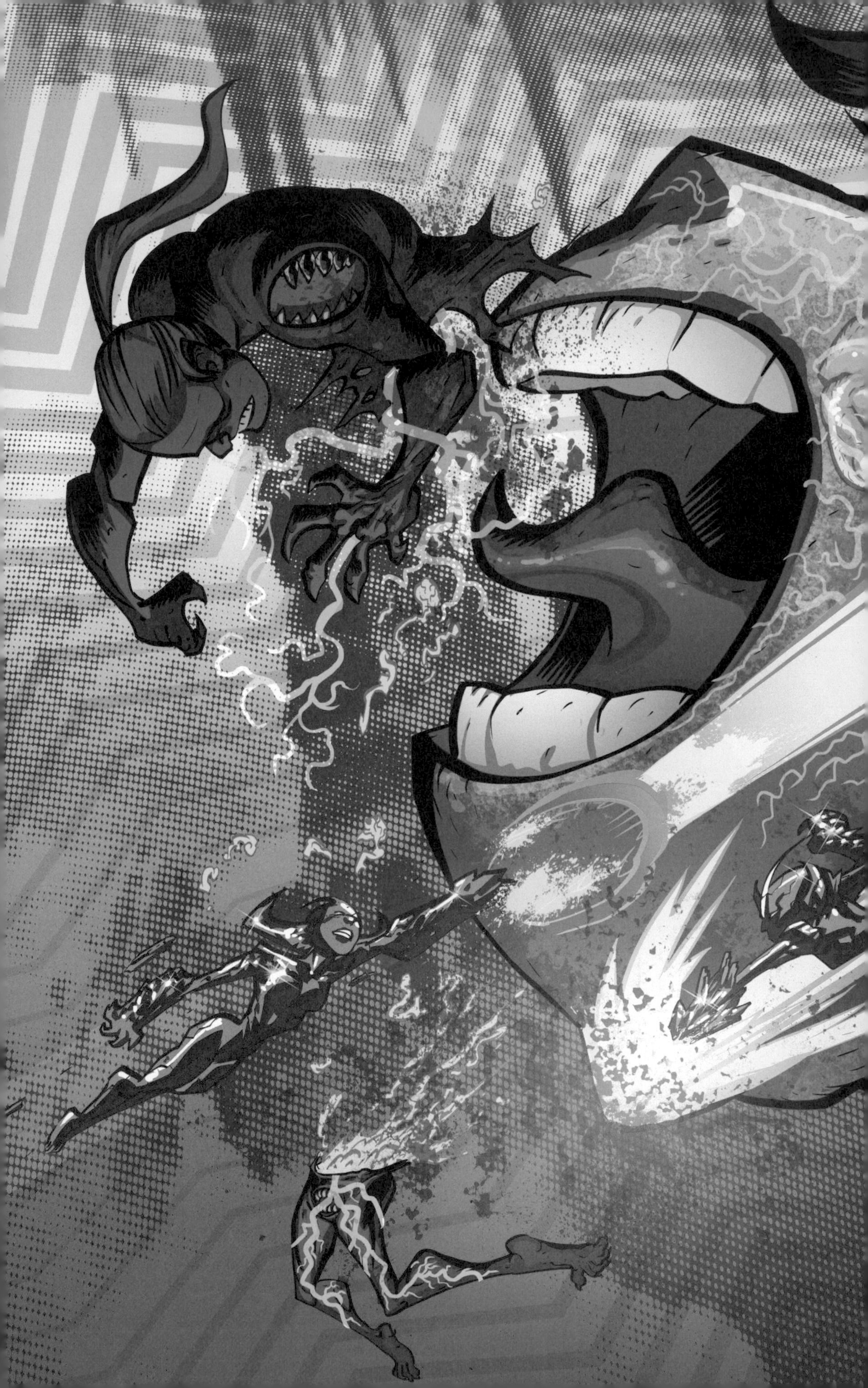

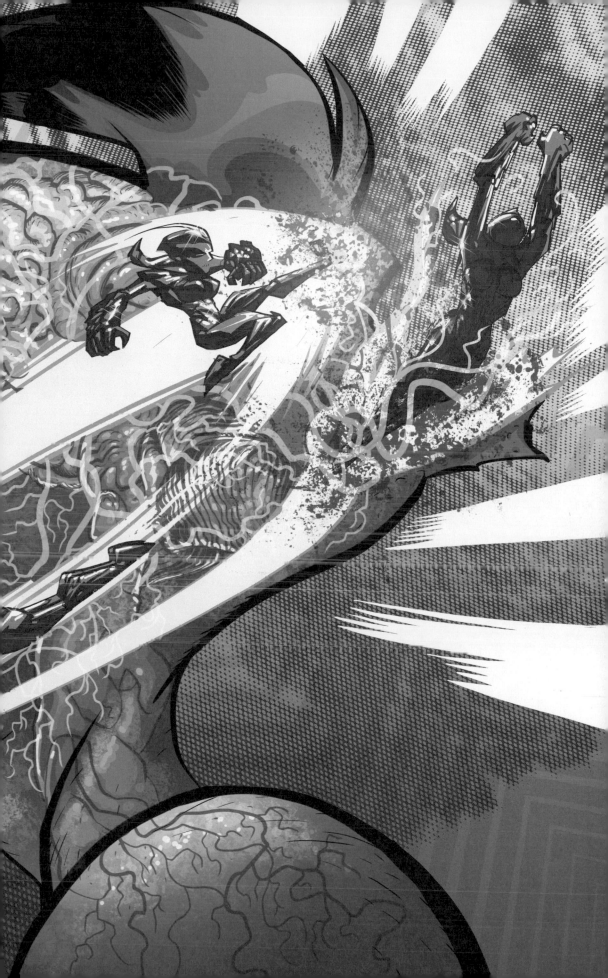

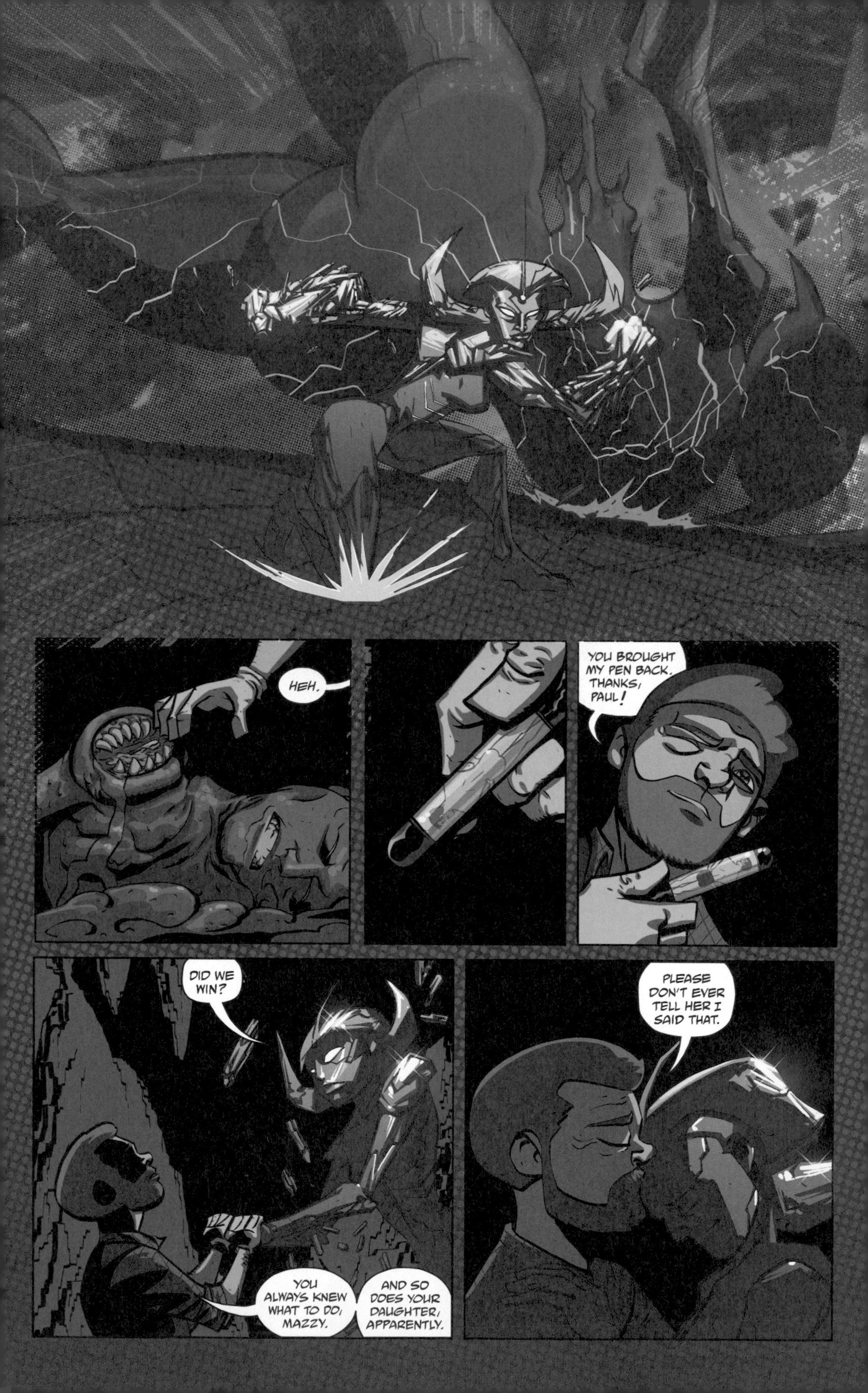
HEH.
YOU BROUGHT MY PEN BACK. THANKS, PAUL!
DID WE WIN?
YOU ALWAYS KNEW WHAT TO DO, MAZZY.
AND SO DOES YOUR DAUGHTER, APPARENTLY.
PLEASE DON'T EVER TELL HER I SAID THAT.

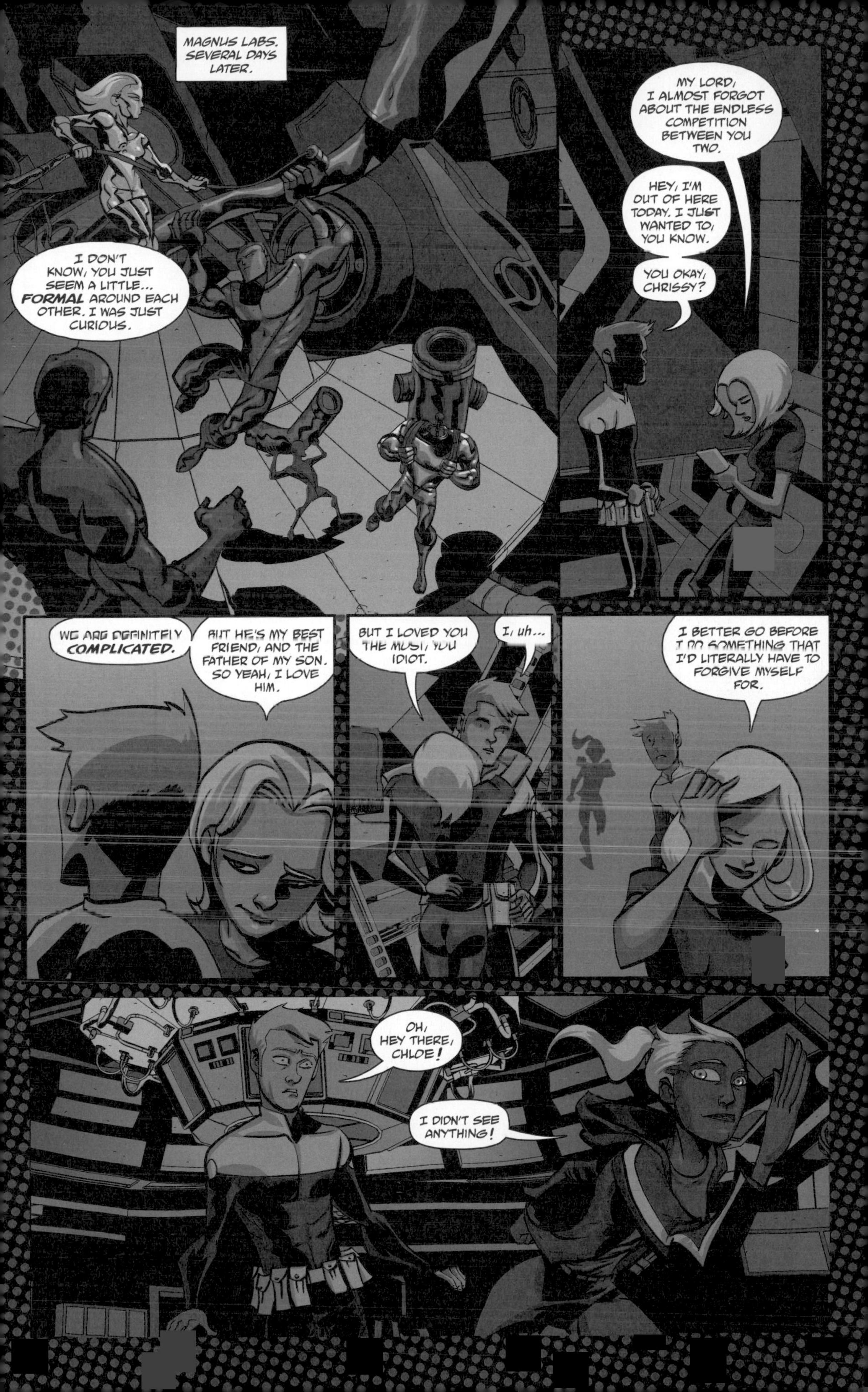

MAGNUS LABS. SEVERAL DAYS LATER.
I DON'T KNOW, YOU JUST SEEM A LITTLE... FORMAL AROUND EACH OTHER. I WAS JUST CURIOUS.
MY LORD, I ALMOST FORGOT ABOUT THE ENDLESS COMPETITION BETWEEN YOU TWO.
HEY, I'M OUT OF HERE TODAY. I JUST WANTED TO, YOU KNOW.
YOU OKAY, CHRISSY?
WE ARE DEFINITELY COMPLICATED.
BUT HE'S MY BEST FRIEND, AND THE FATHER OF MY SON. SO YEAH, I LOVE HIM.
BUT I LOVED YOU THE MOST, YOU IDIOT.
I, uh...
I BETTER GO BEFORE I DO SOMETHING THAT I'D LITERALLY HAVE TO FORGIVE MYSELF FOR.
OH, HEY THERE, CHLOE!
I DIDN'T SEE ANYTHING!

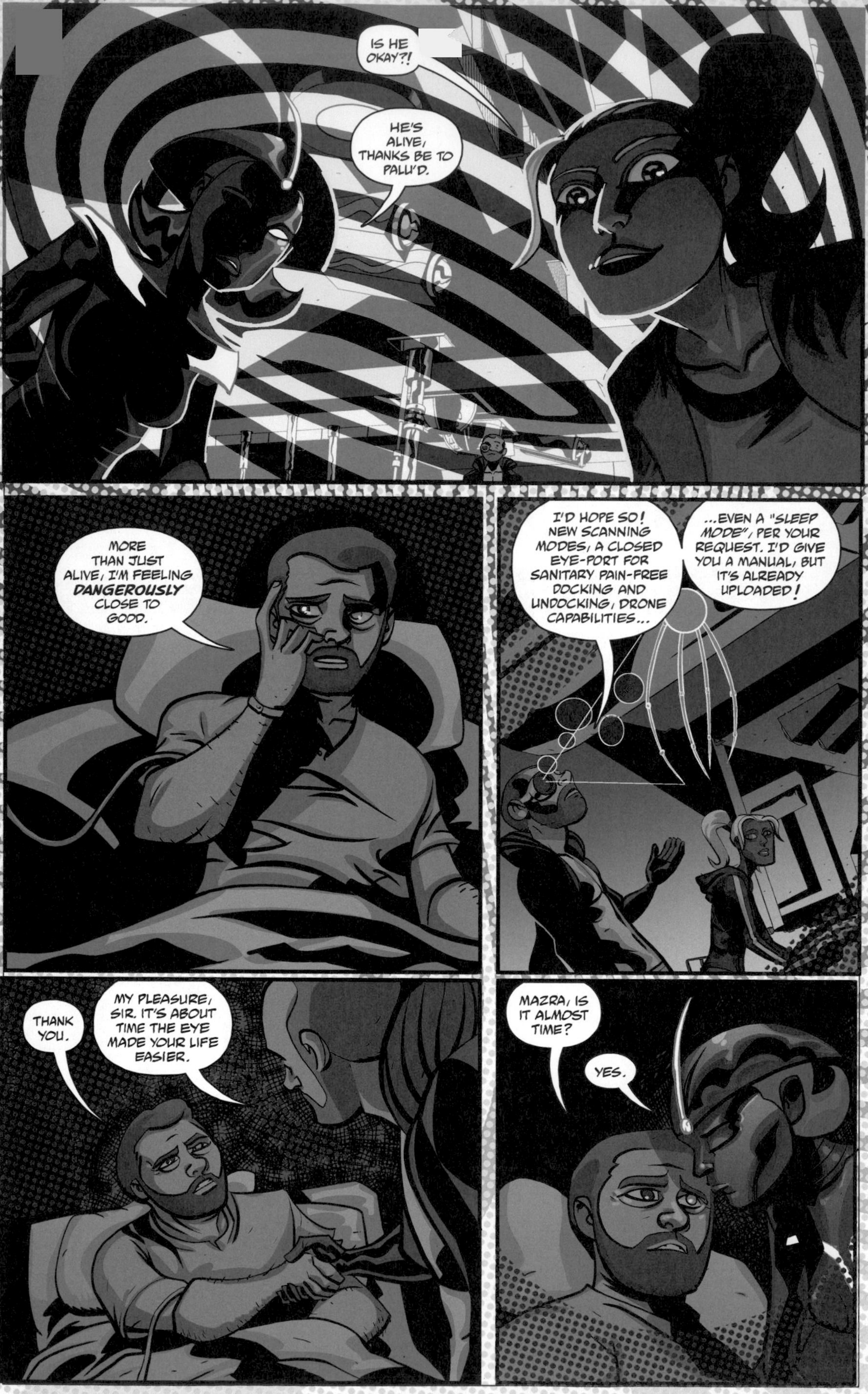
IS HE OKAY?!
HE'S ALIVE, THANKS BE TO PALU'D.
MORE THAN JUST ALIVE, I'M FEELING **DANGEROUSLY** CLOSE TO GOOD.
I'D HOPE SO! NEW SCANNING MODES, A CLOSED EYE-PORT FOR SANITARY PAIN-FREE DOCKING AND UNDOCKING, DRONE CAPABILITIES...
...EVEN A "SLEEP MODE", PER YOUR REQUEST. I'D GIVE YOU A MANUAL, BUT IT'S ALREADY UPLOADED!
THANK YOU.
MY PLEASURE, SIR. IT'S ABOUT TIME THE EYE MADE YOUR LIFE EASIER.
MAZRA, IS IT ALMOST TIME?
YES.

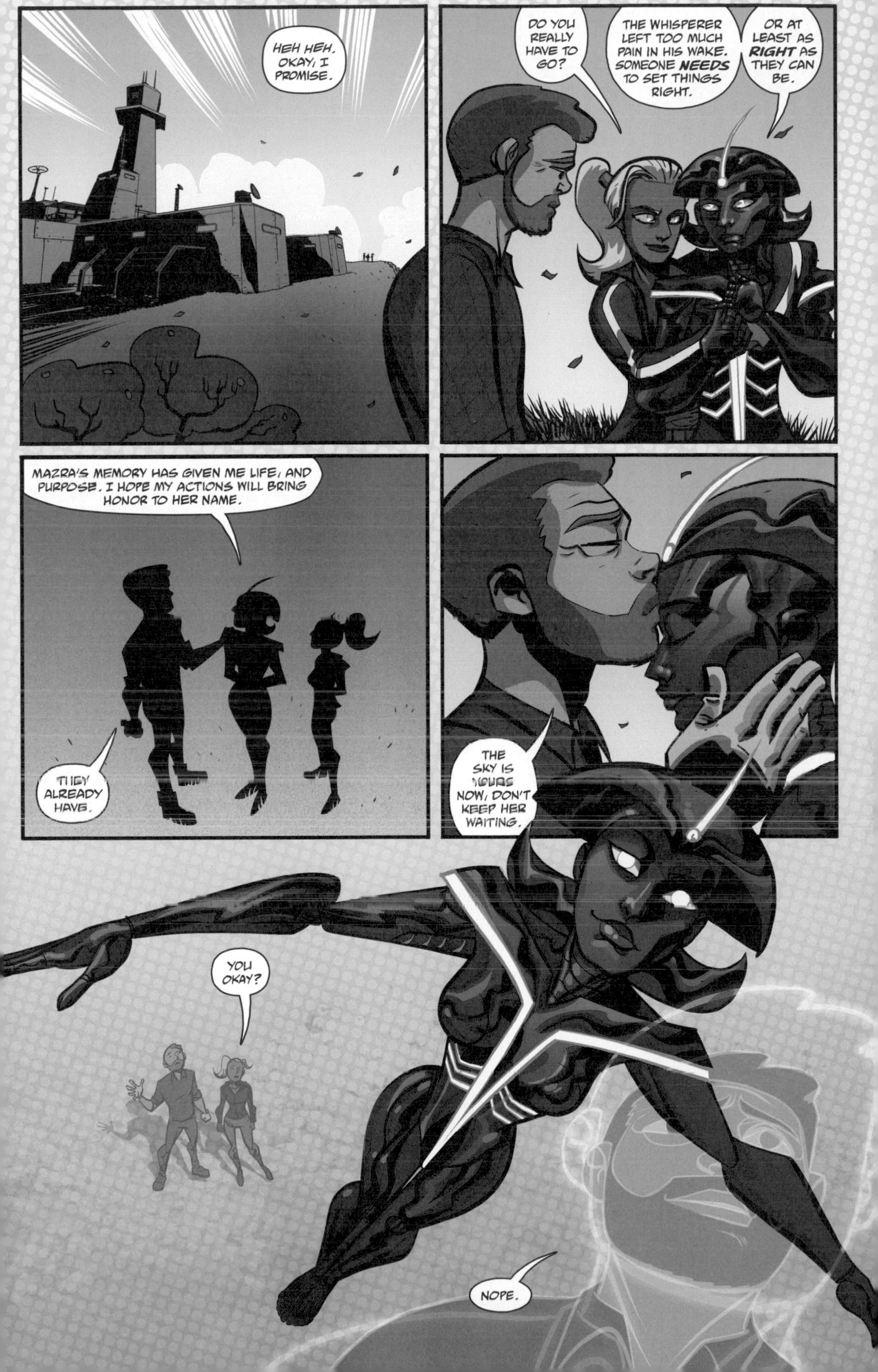
HEH HEH. OKAY, I PROMISE.
DO YOU REALLY HAVE TO GO?
THE WHISPERER LEFT TOO MUCH PAIN IN HIS WAKE. SOMEONE **NEEDS** TO SET THINGS RIGHT.
OR AT LEAST AS **RIGHT** AS THEY CAN BE.
MAZRA'S MEMORY HAS GIVEN ME LIFE, AND PURPOSE. I HOPE MY ACTIONS WILL BRING HONOR TO HER NAME.
THEY ALREADY HAVE.
THE SKY IS YOURS NOW, DON'T KEEP HER WAITING.
YOU OKAY?
NOPE.

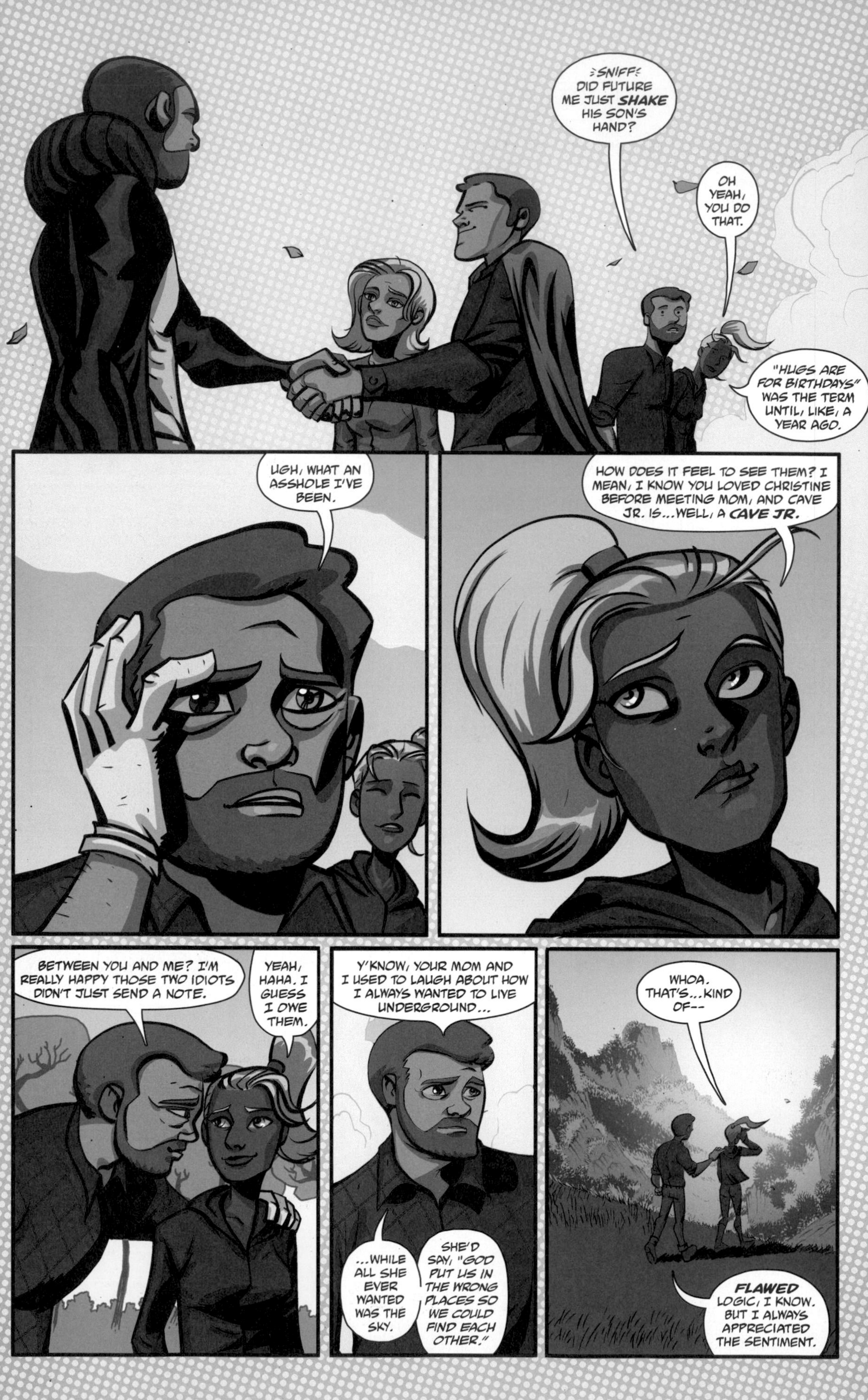

≡SNIFF≡ DID FUTURE ME JUST SHAKE HIS SON'S HAND?
OH YEAH, YOU DO THAT.
"HUGS ARE FOR BIRTHDAYS" WAS THE TERM UNTIL, LIKE, A YEAR AGO.
UGH, WHAT AN ASSHOLE I'VE BEEN.
HOW DOES IT FEEL TO SEE THEM? I MEAN, I KNOW YOU LOVED CHRISTINE BEFORE MEETING MOM, AND CAVE JR. IS...WELL, A CAVE JR.
BETWEEN YOU AND ME? I'M REALLY HAPPY THOSE TWO IDIOTS DIDN'T JUST SEND A NOTE.
YEAH, HAHA. I GUESS I OWE THEM.
Y'KNOW, YOUR MOM AND I USED TO LAUGH ABOUT HOW I ALWAYS WANTED TO LIVE UNDERGROUND...
...WHILE ALL SHE EVER WANTED WAS THE SKY.
SHE'D SAY, "GOD PUT US IN THE WRONG PLACES SO WE COULD FIND EACH OTHER."
WHOA. THAT'S...KIND OF--
FLAWED LOGIC, I KNOW. BUT I ALWAYS APPRECIATED THE SENTIMENT.

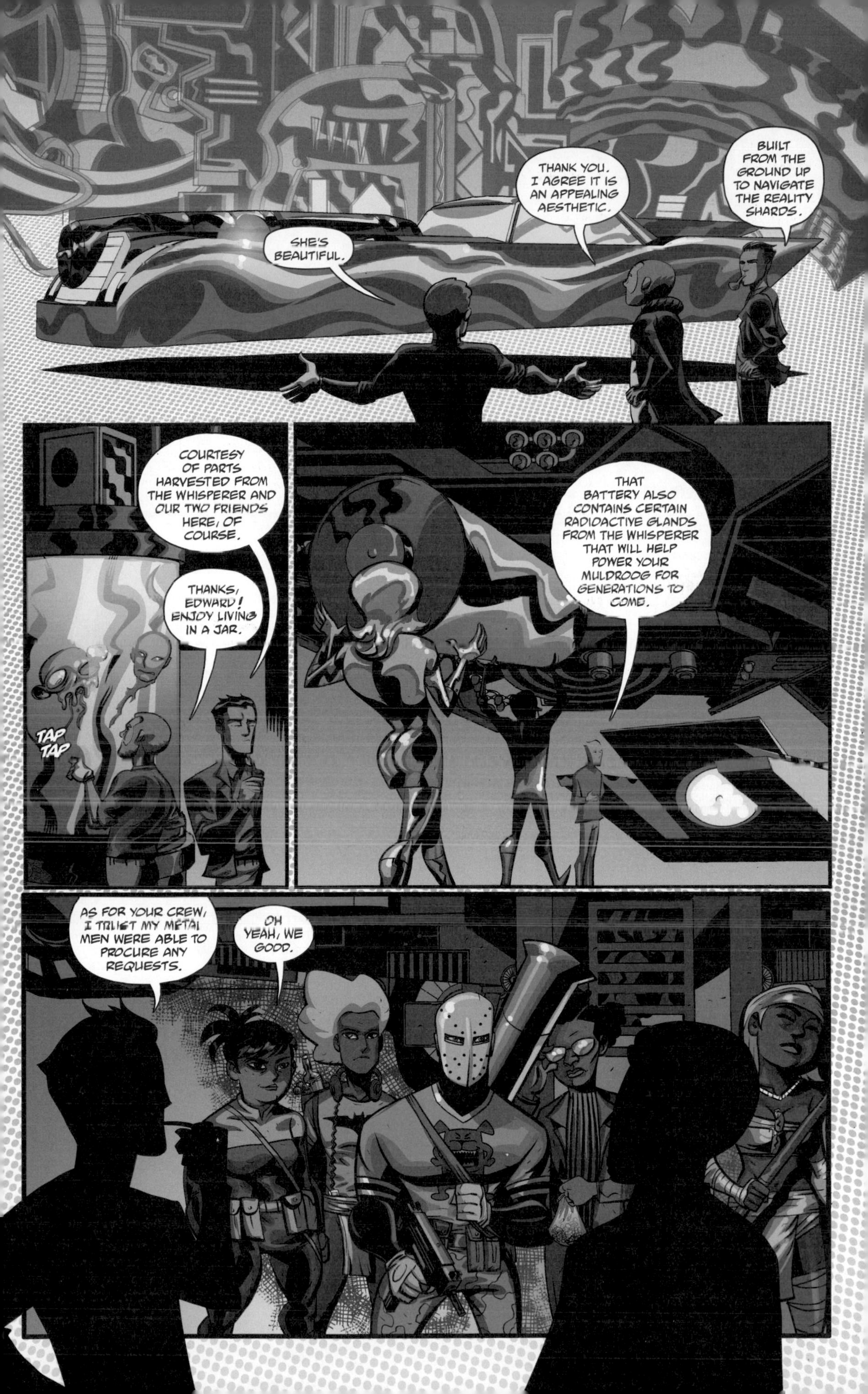
SHE'S BEAUTIFUL.
THANK YOU. I AGREE IT IS AN APPEALING AESTHETIC.
BUILT FROM THE GROUND UP TO NAVIGATE THE REALITY SHARDS.
COURTESY OF PARTS HARVESTED FROM THE WHISPERER AND OUR TWO FRIENDS HERE, OF COURSE.
THANKS, EDWARD! ENJOY LIVING IN A JAR.
TAP TAP
THAT BATTERY ALSO CONTAINS CERTAIN RADIOACTIVE GLANDS FROM THE WHISPERER THAT WILL HELP POWER YOUR MULDROOG FOR GENERATIONS TO COME.
AS FOR YOUR CREW, I TRUST MY METAL MEN WERE ABLE TO PROCURE ANY REQUESTS.
OH YEAH, WE GOOD.

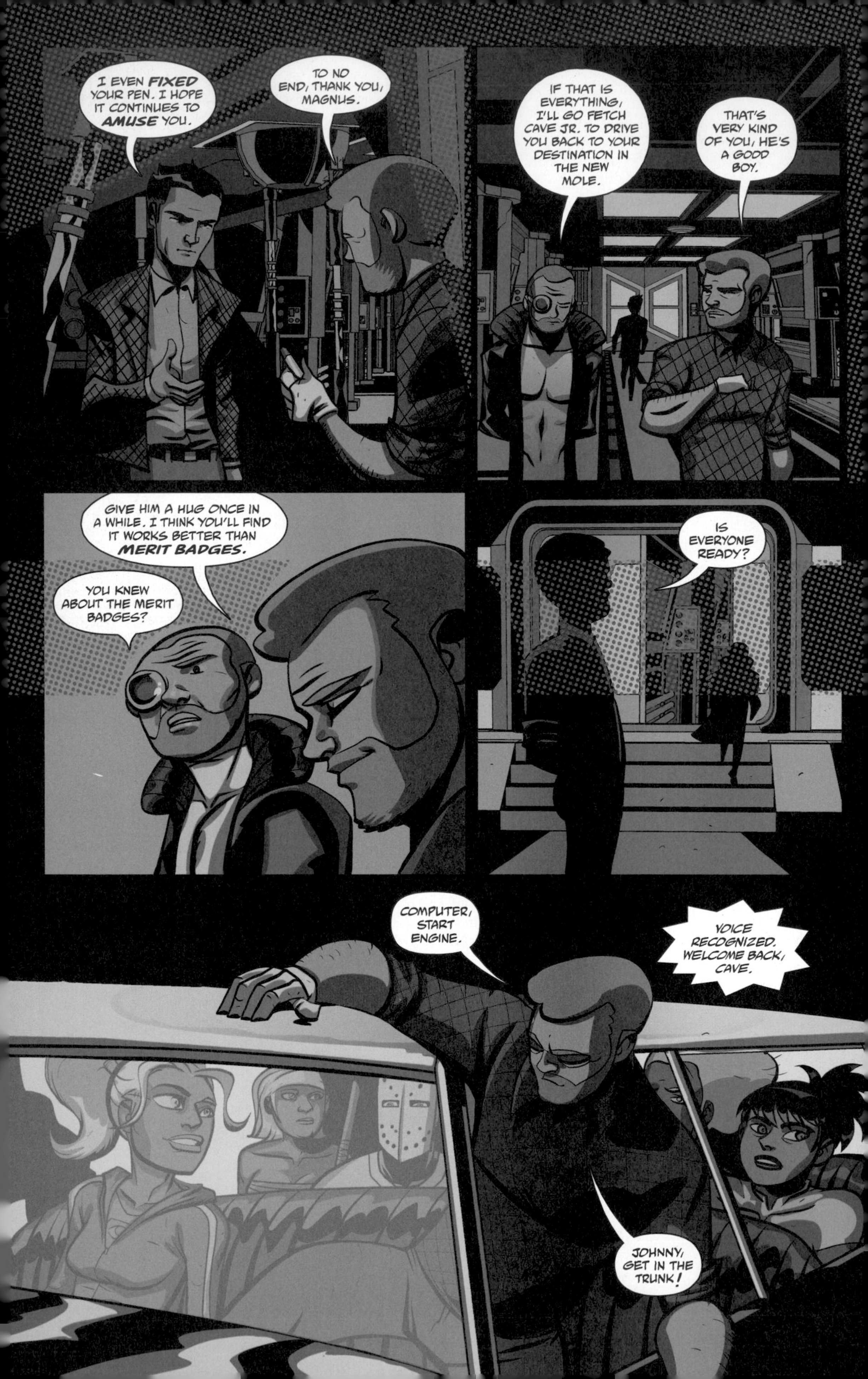
I EVEN **FIXED** YOUR PEN. I HOPE IT CONTINUES TO **AMUSE** YOU.
TO NO END, THANK YOU, MAGNUS.
IF THAT IS EVERYTHING, I'LL GO FETCH CAVE JR. TO DRIVE YOU BACK TO YOUR DESTINATION IN THE NEW MOLE.
THAT'S VERY KIND OF YOU, HE'S A GOOD BOY.
GIVE HIM A HUG ONCE IN A WHILE. I THINK YOU'LL FIND IT WORKS BETTER THAN **MERIT BADGES.**
YOU KNEW ABOUT THE MERIT BADGES?
IS EVERYONE READY?
COMPUTER, START ENGINE.
VOICE RECOGNIZED. WELCOME BACK, CAVE.
JOHNNY, GET IN THE TRUNK!

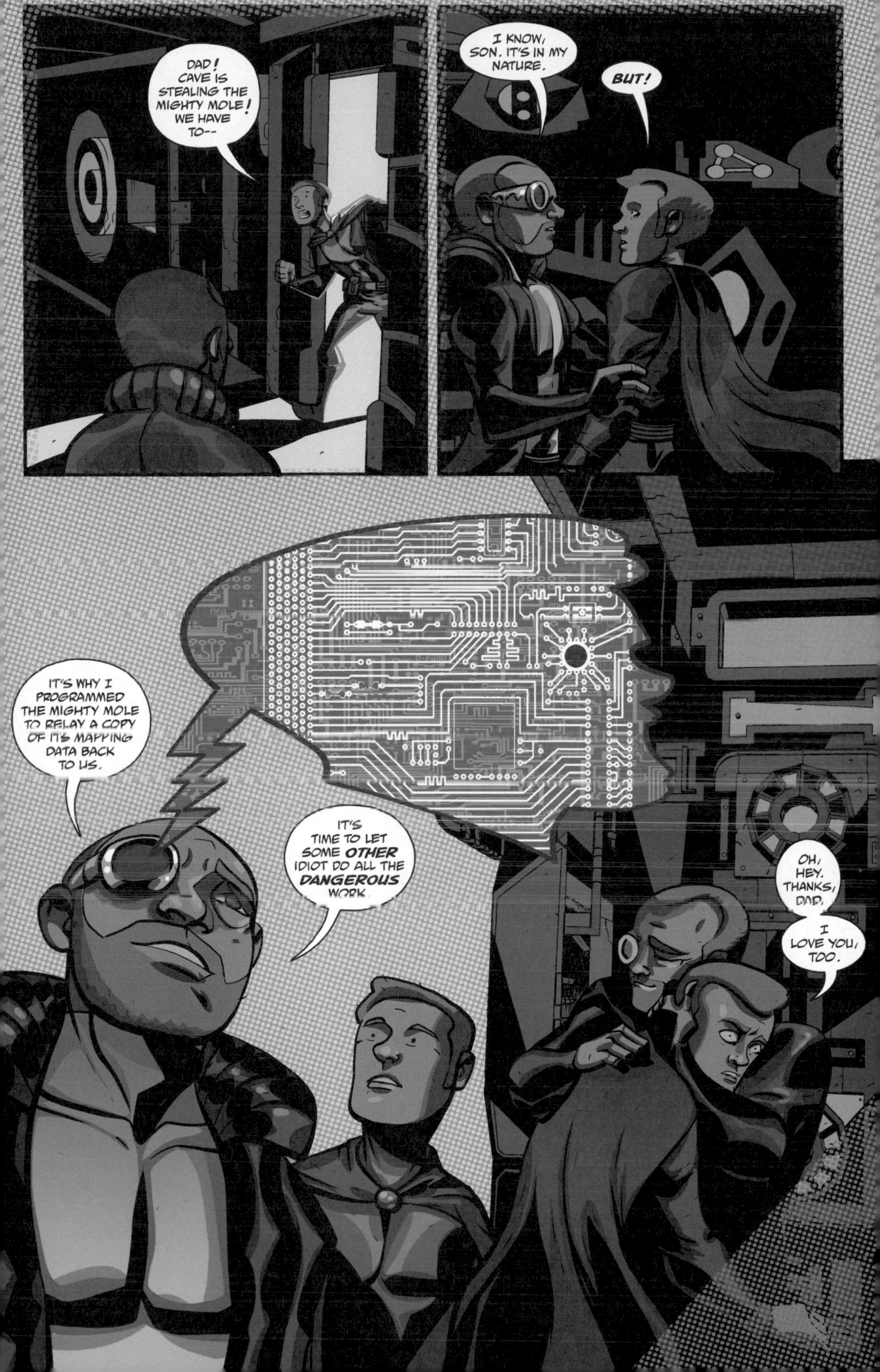
DAD! CAVE IS STEALING THE MIGHTY MOLE! WE HAVE TO--
I KNOW, SON. IT'S IN MY NATURE.
BUT!
IT'S WHY I PROGRAMMED THE MIGHTY MOLE TO RELAY A COPY OF IT'S MAPPING DATA BACK TO US.
IT'S TIME TO LET SOME OTHER IDIOT DO ALL THE DANGEROUS WORK.
OH, HEY. THANKS, DAD.
I LOVE YOU, TOO.

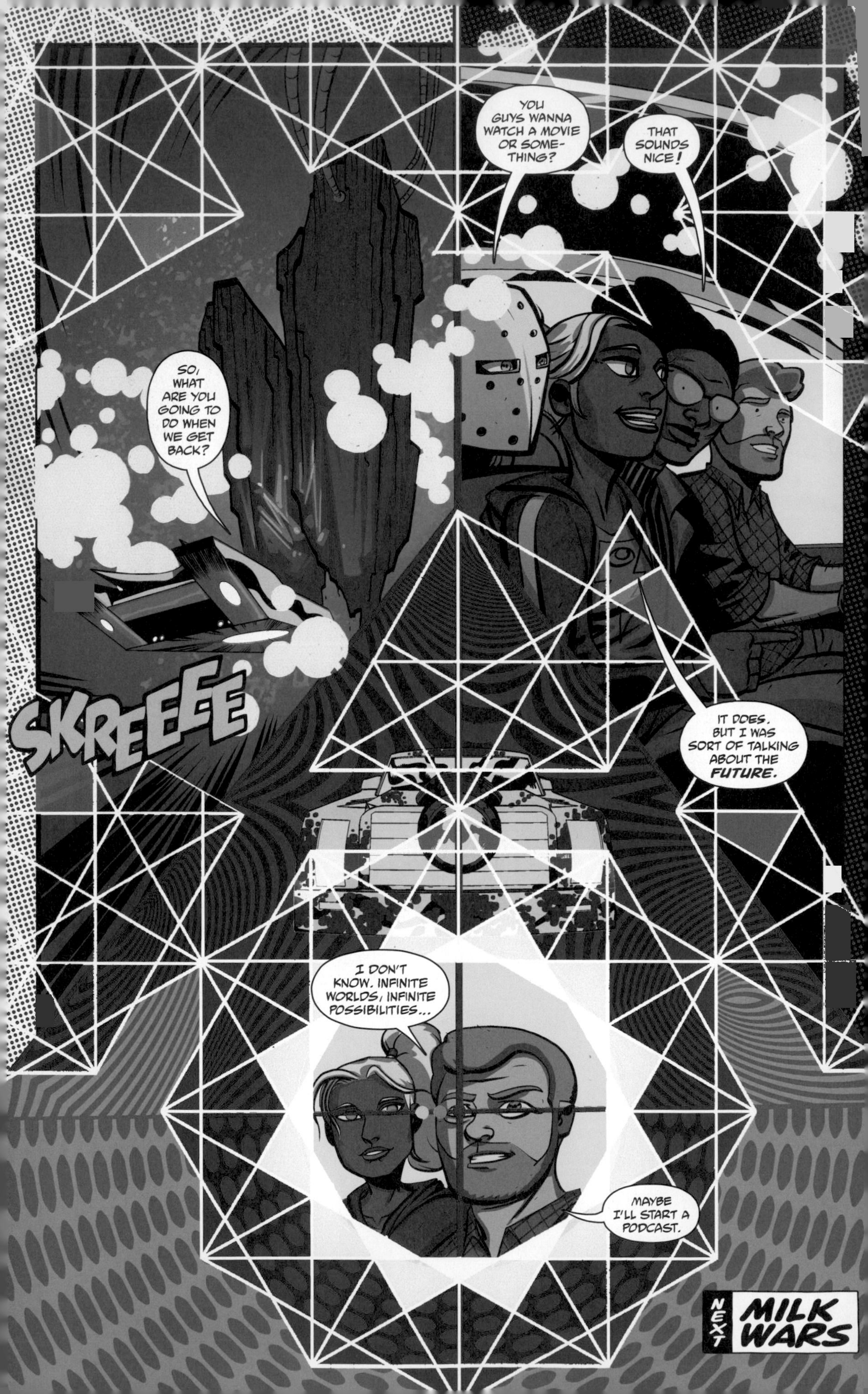
SO, WHAT ARE YOU GOING TO DO WHEN WE GET BACK?
SKREEEE
YOU GUYS WANNA WATCH A MOVIE OR SOME-THING?
THAT SOUNDS NICE!
IT DOES. BUT I WAS SORT OF TALKING ABOUT THE FUTURE.
I DON'T KNOW. INFINITE WORLDS, INFINITE POSSIBILITIES...
MAYBE I'LL START A PODCAST.
NEXT MILK WARS

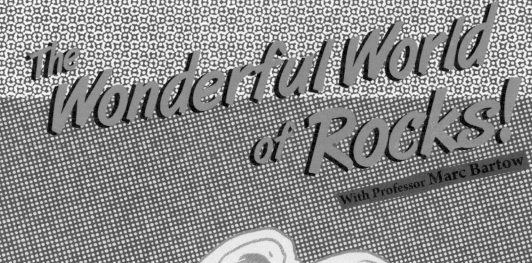

# The Wonderful World of Rocks!

With Professor Marc Bartow

DR. HERBERT
NIEDERMEYER
1950-1992
THE UNIVERSE IS
STABLE & UNDYING

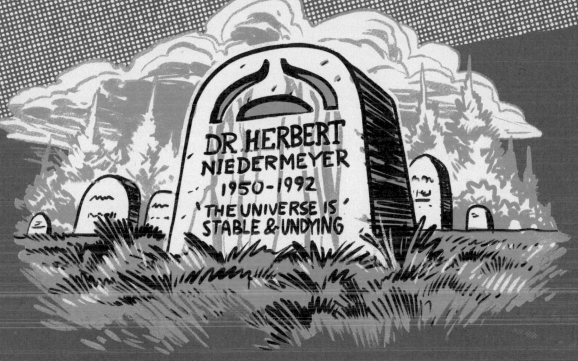

## "WAILING STONE"

**A porous sedimentary rock, Wailing Stone gets its name from the fact that when high winds blow through its pores, it sounds like grief-stricken wails.**

# First Contact, Last Farewell

**We entered the baptismal tank** I'd converted into a teleporter and emerged in a cavern eighteen miles beneath the surface of the planet. It was warm and empty and bathed in a powerful orange glow, not unlike Arizona. We could hear what sounded like the roar of thunder, but which turned out to be a nearby river of magma, churning and roiling, heating and lighting the cavern for miles as it stretched into the beyond.

"I always knew you'd get me killed someday," Dr. Niedermeyer said.

We had brought air tanks to help us breathe, but we didn't need them. Strangely, the atmosphere in the cavern was even more breathable than our own.

"The Earth hasn't had an atmosphere like this for 300 million years," I announced, reading the air gauge. "The last time we had an atmosphere with this much oxygen, dragonflies were the size of seagulls." (As the reader may or may not know, insects don't breathe, but absorb oxygen through their exoskeletons, so the more oxygen there is to absorb, the bigger they can grow.) "I wonder if we'll see any—"

And that's when we saw it.

A millipede the size of a Volkswagen bus began crawling out of the lava. Fully emerged from the river of magma, its armor plating shining like polished steel, a single periscope emerged from the beast's head. The periscope scanned the cavern before fixing itself on Dr. Niedermeyer and myself. The periscope opened, and for the first time in human history, man gazed directly into the eye of a sentient bug.

We worried that the millipede might see our presence as a threat, but instead, it approached us with mere curiosity. I guess being an armor-plated giant means you don't experience a lot of stranger-danger. Perhaps humans would be more hospitable to strangers if we hadn't evolved from such tasty little rats.

The millipede (we'll call him Pete) reared up and, with about thirty legs or so, began thundering a message into the walls of the cavern. Picking up the vibrations, other millipedes began to arrive to gawk at the strange and soft skin-covered animals.

"Hello," I said.

Apparently, they had never heard vocal speech before, as they responded to this single word with an immediate and rapturous round of applause, which consisted of the millipedes flexing and bending their armor so they reflected the light from the lava all over the cavern, like a disco ball.

"I think they like us!" Dr. Niedermeyer said. He had never been much liked on the surface, so this was something of a treat for him.

Dr. Niedermeyer began to relax and soon we were able to communicate with the insects using a rudimentary sign language. Pete made a motion, pointing at the filter that served as his mouth, that we took as a sign asking if we were hungry. Having let his guard down completely, Dr Niedermeyer nodded. "Why yes, I am a little peckish." It was at this point that one of the millipedes regurgitated molten lava directly into Dr. Niedermeyer's mouth, killing him instantly.

It was an innocent mistake on their part and, using the limited sign language at my disposal, I tried to reassure them that I wasn't angry. But sadly, this misunderstanding brought an end to our first contact with an intelligent species.

With great difficulty, I drug Dr. Niedermeyer's body back to the wormhole, which was losing its stability. In fact, I would have been stranded there myself, if not for some Methodist missionaries who'd let themselves into the house after hearing noises and turned the temperature dial on the baptismal tank/teleporter back to the manufacturer-approved setting.

I attended Dr. Niedermeyer's burial with my new assistant, an adventurous grad student named Carson. When the priest asked if anyone would like to say a few words, I stood and said, "Our lives are a symphony of forces beyond our control. Herbert Niedermeyer's symphony may have been short, but then some of the best songs ever written are only three-and-a-half minutes long."

Afterwards, his widow approached me for comfort. Clutching my arm, she said, "Please don't ever speak to me again." I think she blamed me for the death of her husband. But it wasn't me, or science, that killed Dr. Niedermeyer. It was lava. As I would later explain to Carson, science is the product of observation, exploration the product of luck. And only someone who appreciates the danger of both should venture into the dark of the world below.

Though it resulted in his death and will likely result in mine, I do not regret the ill-advised and possibly reckless quest for knowledge that formed the basis of our work. And our friendship. For work and friendship, these are what have and always will give my life meaning.

. . . . . . . . . . . . . . . . . . . . . . . . . . . . . . . . . . . . . . .

Words by Mark Russell, Art by Benjamin Dewey

# Who's Who
## DC's Young Animal

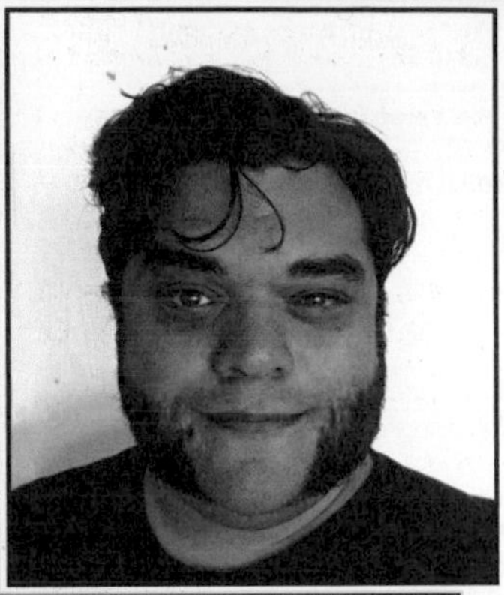

**PERSONAL DATA**

**Name:** Jon Rivera
**Occupation:** Writer
**First Appearance:** CAVE CARSON HAS A CYBERNETIC EYE #1

**HISTORY**

I've been making comics as long as I can remember. My dad had a photocopier in his home office, so I was basically a kid with unlimited paper and my own printing press at my disposal. This quickly led to delusions of grandeur as I started my own "company" and started cranking out tales of wisecracking vigilantes and disgusting monsters (not much has changed). It being the '90s, I even attempted to make my own (aluminum) foil covers.

I kept making comics, trading typing paper for bristol board near the end of high school, when I decided to pursue art as a career. I attended the School of Visual Arts, which is where I met Gerard. After graduating, I co-created and produced a comics series called "Heartbreak," as well as teaching art in New Jersey and making web comics. Eventually, I moved to Los Angeles and found work making storyboards, concept art, and scripts for television, music videos, and commercials.

# THE PROCESS OF WRITING CAVE CARSON

I start with the overarching story, then break it down into arcs, then issues, then pages, and eventually individual panels. I call it "zooming in." The medium you tell your story in will greatly affect how you tell it. In comics, you not only have to consider how many panels can affectively fit on a page, but also the "page turn." That's because Western comics are read left to right, which means big shocking moments should be saved for even-number pages so that the reader doesn't accidentally spoil the moment for his-or herself upon turning the page. Little details like that greatly affect the pacing in which you tell a story. Remember, it's the writer's job to make the reader want to turn that page!

After figuring out the pacing, each panel is broken into both the description of the action and the dialogue. In the descriptions, I explain who is doing what and where they are, as well as how they are feeling. These descriptions, when mixed with the dialogue, inform our artist, Mike Oeming, and colorist, Nick Filardi, how to best represent each moment. Mike and I both like to improvise, so I try to leave enough wiggle room in my scripts for both of us, while making sure to lend more written (and sometimes visual) description to the imagery I feel is most vital to the story we're trying to tell.

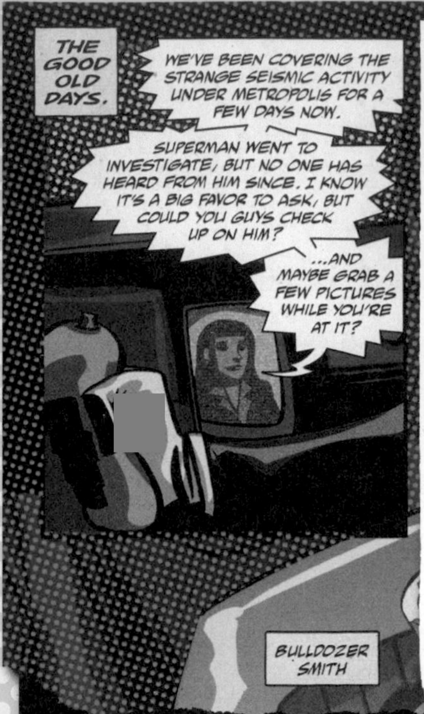
THE GOOD OLD DAYS.
WE'VE BEEN COVERING THE STRANGE SEISMIC ACTIVITY UNDER METROPOLIS FOR A FEW DAYS NOW.
SUPERMAN WENT TO INVESTIGATE, BUT NO ONE HAS HEARD FROM HIM SINCE. I KNOW IT'S A BIG FAVOR TO ASK, BUT COULD YOU GUYS CHECK UP ON HIM?
...AND MAYBE GRAB A FEW PICTURES WHILE YOU'RE AT IT?
BULLDOZER SMITH

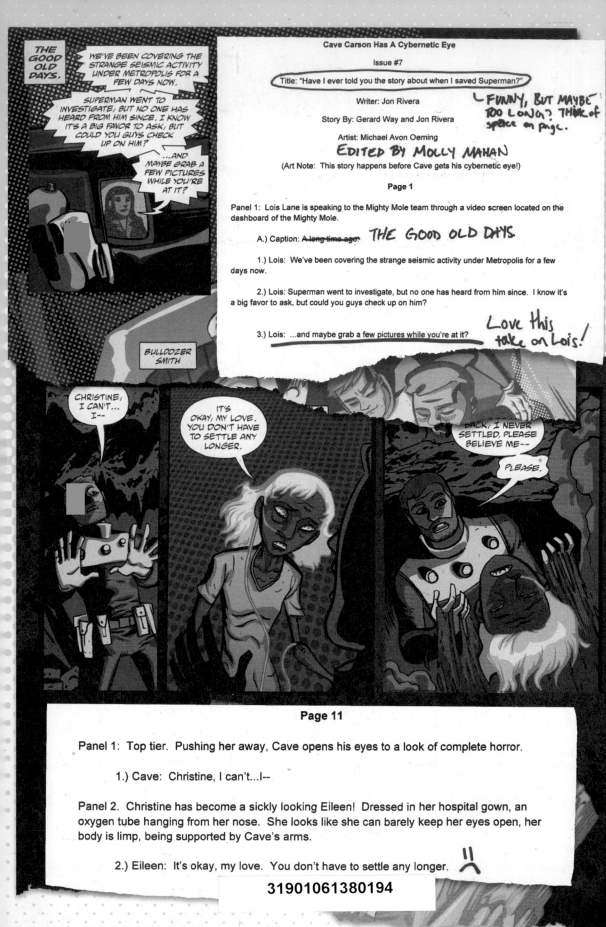

**Cave Carson Has A Cybernetic Eye**

Issue #7

Title: "Have I ever told you the story about when I saved Superman?"

└ FUNNY, BUT MAYBE TOO LONG? THINK of space on page.

Writer: Jon Rivera

Story By: Gerard Way and Jon Rivera

Artist: Michael Avon Oeming

EDITED BY MOLLY MAHAN

(Art Note: This story happens before Cave gets his cybernetic eye!)

**Page 1**

Panel 1: Lois Lane is speaking to the Mighty Mole team through a video screen located on the dashboard of the Mighty Mole.

A.) Caption: ~~A long time ago.~~ THE GOOD OLD DAYS

1.) Lois: We've been covering the strange seismic activity under Metropolis for a few days now.

2.) Lois: Superman went to investigate, but no one has heard from him since. I know it's a big favor to ask, but could you guys check up on him?

3.) Lois: ...and maybe grab a few pictures while you're at it?

Love this take on Lois!

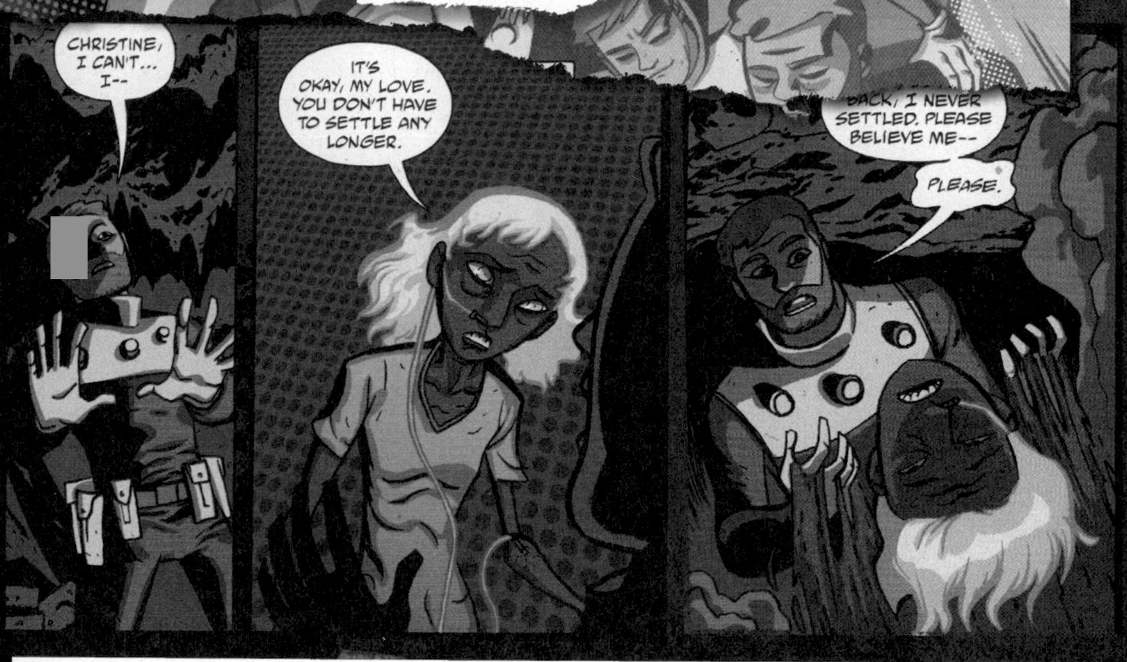
CHRISTINE, I CAN'T... I--
IT'S OKAY, MY LOVE. YOU DON'T HAVE TO SETTLE ANY LONGER.
SETTLED. PLEASE BELIEVE ME--
PLEASE.

**Page 11**

Panel 1: Top tier. Pushing her away, Cave opens his eyes to a look of complete horror.

1.) Cave: Christine, I can't...I--

Panel 2. Christine has become a sickly looking Eileen! Dressed in her hospital gown, an oxygen tube hanging from her nose. She looks like she can barely keep her eyes open, her body is limp, being supported by Cave's arms.

2.) Eileen: It's okay, my love. You don't have to settle any longer. " ⌒